HITLER'S DIPLOMAT

BOOKS BY JOHN WEITZ

Value of Nothing

Man in Charge

Friends in High Places

Hitler's Diplomat

HITLER'S DIPLOMAT

The Life and Times of
Joachim von Ribbentrop

JOHN WEITZ

New York 1992 TICKNOR & FIELDS

For information about permission to reproduce selections from
this book, write to Permissions, Ticknor & Fields, 215 Park
Avenue South, New York, New York 10003.

Library of Congress Cataloging-in-Publication Data

Weitz, John.
Hitler's diplomat : the life and times of Joachim von Ribbentrop /
  John Weitz.
     p.   cm.
  Includes bibliographical references and index.
  ISBN 0-395-62152-6
   1. Ribbentrop, Joachim von, 1893–1946.   2. Foreign
  ministers — Germany — Biography.   3. Germany — Foreign
  relations — 1933–1945.   I. Title.
DD247.R47W45   1992
943.086′092 — dc20
[B]   92-5918
            CIP

Printed in the United States of America

MP 10 9 8 7 6 5 4 3 2 1

For Susan and the "kids"

Acknowledgments

I AM DEEPLY INDEBTED to the following people:
Richard von Weizsäcker, President, Federal Republic of Germany,
for his generosity; Dr. Peter Sympher, Director, Institut des Auswäar-
tigen Amts, and Ambassador Leopold Bill von Bredow for their
friendship and help; Tom Wolfe for his insight; Eric Ambler for his
endorsement; Barbara Khoury for her capable help; and John
McLaughlin, Robert Lantz, and Joy Harris for courage under fire.

I also owe grateful thanks to Katja Aschke, Dr. Ludwig Biewer, the
Right Honourable Paul Channon, MP, David Clayson, Robert
Daley, Elizabeth Diefendorf, René Dreyfus, Jacques Français, John
Galliher, Gero Gandert, Dr. Vartan Gregorian, Christa and Wolf
Ulrich von Hassell, Dr. Dieter Heckmann, Dr. Hans-Jürgen Heim-
soeth, Dolly Haas Hirschfeld, Ruth Hollander, Peter Howes, Profes-
sor Dr. Werner Knopp, Herlinde Koelbl, Jonathan Kranz, Dietrich
Kraus, Siegrid Lüttich, Paul Makino, Henry Marx, Dr. Mario Count
von Matuschka, Dr. Michael Mertes, Dr. Franz Werner Michel,
Gebhardt von Moltke, Frederic Morton, Bernhard von der Plantiz,
Karl Max Count von Schaesberg, Lloyd S. Schaper (USAF, Ret.),
Arthur Schlesinger, Jr., Inge Sckirl, Joan Shorter, Peter M. F. Sichel,
Reinhard Spitzy, Margaret Spohn, Anja Stehmann, Anthony
Thompson, Lord Hugh Trevor-Roper, Prince George Vassiltchikov,
and Baroness Christina von Vietinghoff-Scheel.

CONTENTS

BOOK III

FOREWORD

by Tom Wolfe

IN 1922 the great German caricaturist Karl Arnold drew a cartoon for the magazine *Simplicissimus* depicting four toffs in white tie and tails, two of them wearing monocles, lifting their champagne glasses: "Between us, gentlemen: Long live His Majesty, the Kaiser — hurrah — psst — hurrah — softly — hurrah!" By then Kaiser Wilhelm was already exiled quietly and permanently in Huis Doorn, the castle in Holland where he spent the last twenty years of his life. But among the upper orders in Germany, despite Germany's defeat in the late Great War, national glory and antirepublicanism remained, *sotto voce*, very fashionable notions. They elevated one above the bourgeoisie, above "the ninnies," to use a term that had been borrowed, in the latest 1920s fashion, from the English. Foremost among the ninnies were the weak and incompetent middle-class ninnies who ran the Weimar Republic. On these three points — national glory, antirepublicanism, and antininnyism — the toffs wearing the evening clothes and monocles happened to agree with an obstreperous band of young radical socialists who called themselves the National Socialist German Workers Party, or Nazis, for short. This helps account for the presence among the leadership of the Third Reich of the unlikely figure of Joachim von Ribbentrop, the toff, the socialite, who became Hitler's foreign minister.

As we are about to see in John Weitz's portrait, von Ribbentrop, despite his *von*, was not an aristocrat. He was a wine importer, champagne being his long suit. The *von* he added himself. But the business once took him to Paris, London, and Rome, and he acquired a certain cosmopolitan polish. In the 1920s he and his wife became social climbers par excellence in Berlin at a time when the Berlin social

climb was a glamorously *louche* competition. It was the time of the
Cabaret, in Christopher Isherwood's memorable phrase, a time in
which *chic* took on a sharp, aggressively decadent, adventurously
amoral, bohemian edge. Smart women, most notably Marlene Dietrich, affected lesbian dress. Joachim von Ribbentrop affected the loud
young Nazis; he picked them up on the night terrain of the Cabaret
and presented them in his home as the antithesis of the ninnies, as "the
men who have a program for Germany." It was an example of what
would later be called (if one can forgive the term) radical chic.

I can't think of any writer in a better position than John Weitz to
bring the von Ribbentrop saga alive. Throughout the 1920s his father,
Robert Salomon Weitz, and Joachim von Ribbentrop were part of the
same world, and John Weitz himself grew up in its atmosphere. Bobby
Weitz — English nicknames were also fashionable in the Cabaret period — was Jewish, but he felt confidently, even supremely, German.
As a warrant officer in the Third Prussian Guards during the war, he
had been hit by shrapnel while advancing across an open field on the
Russian front and had been awarded the Iron Cross. His wounds were
so serious, he spent a year in the hospital. To a degree that is hard to
imagine today, wounded infantry veterans with the Iron Cross had a
romantic cachet in postwar Germany. On top of that, Bobby Weitz
had money, good looks, and great style. He and his wife, Hedy,
entered into the Cabaret every bit as swimmingly as the von Ribbentrops.

Bobby Weitz was a textile manufacturer, and Bobby and Hedy had
an apartment in Berlin's equivalent of Manhattan's East Sixties and a
country house in Kladow-Glienicke, southwest of Berlin. They spent
their winters in San Moritz, the Italian Riviera, the French Riviera,
San Remo, and Lake Como. Bobby's clothes were made by Germany's
most fashionable tailor, Knize; Hedy's, by France's most fashionable
couturière, Chanel. They were chums of Die Dietrich and all the other
swells of the nightclub and resort circuit. They had one child, John,
and packed him off to a boarding school in England, St. Paul's, which
had been founded during the reign of Henry VIII and had John Milton
and Samuel Pepys on its alumni roster. Even the Only Child was
comme il faut. Small families were the thing. A house full of children
made it hard to live the Cabaret life at top speed.

Bobby Weitz had done it all just right. Berlin was a city of 4.5
million souls, only 150,000 of whom were Jews. At the time, the
1920s, the social distance between Jews and non-Jews in Berlin was
far less than it was in New York. The firmament in which Bobby
Weitz starred was not Jewish Society but Berlin Society itself. He was

a distinguished German, not a distinguished German Jew. For precisely that reason he found it impossible to believe that Hitler was actually serious in his anti-Jewish campaign. By 1936 it was obvious that the campaign was serious — but it couldn't possibly be aimed at Jews like him. Finally he took to adorning the lapel of his suit, every day, with the rosette that showed he had won the Iron Cross in the Great War. He was not *that other kind of Jew.* Bobby Weitz did not leave Germany until August of 1938, two months before the door closed forever, and all remaining Jews were sent off to the extermination camps. By then he was a broken man, not because he had lost everything he possessed but because he had lost his very identity . . . as a proud German of the upper orders.

Joachim von Ribbentrop's journey from the Cabaret to the end of the night (to borrow Céline's phrase) was, if anything, more dreadful. At the outset the Nazis were his pet radicals. They lent his version of the Cabaret an exquisitely rowdy, louche, low-rent excitement. Before it was all over, however, he was the Nazis' pet toff. Hitler spoke of him with a teasing derision — to his face — as "my little champagne salesman." Like many others, von Ribbentrop did not seem to understand at first that the Nazis were precisely what they called themselves: socialists, members of the National Socialist German Workers Party. Their contempt for the business mentality, for bottom-line greed, was breathtaking. Hitler saw to it that in Germany the historic destiny of socialism was fulfilled: absolute tyranny with a self-righteous homicidal cruelty rivaling even that of the Soviet Communists and the Khmer Rouge. To make sure, he borrowed the extermination camp and the euphemism for it, *concentration camp,* from the man who invented both, Lenin. The little champagne salesman's own destiny was to be hanged as a war criminal in 1946.

John Weitz's personal history gives our story its final, fearsome symmetry. In 1944, now twenty-one years old and living in the United States, he took part in one of the OSS's most hazardous operations of the Second World War, to set up a liaison with the German Resistance.* The identity that had meant so much to Bobby Weitz — noble German warrior — had turned out to be a bitter sham. His son clothed himself in the sham . . . and had his vengeance.

But John Weitz was a warrior who was able to put vengeance behind him. In America today, of course, he is known as a fashion designer, author, and former racing car driver. In Germany he is also

---

*The Office of Strategic Services was the forerunner of the Central Intelligence Agency.

known as a man who for years has sought to bring about a reconciliation between the democratic Germany of today and the émigrés, Jewish and non-Jewish, who fled National Socialism in Germany two generations ago. His novel *Friends in High Places,* a portrait of an honorable and decent German who wound up as a Nazi brown shirt, became a cult book in West Germany, as a new generation of Germans began to look back at the National Socialist years. In 1986 he was awarded West Germany's highest honor for foreigners, the Order of Merit, and was offered renewed German citizenship, which, as a United States citizen, he declined.

The pages that follow are John Weitz's *Rückblick,* his look back, upon a brutal drama that lies at the heart of a century of socialist madness now drawing to a close.

PREFACE

I USED TO BELIEVE that my own fascination with the time of Adolf Hitler was due to my family's unhappy involvement with the Nazis and that the world had lost interest. I was wrong. Adolf Hitler has continued to rivet the attention of people worldwide. His name is in constant use. His deeds are unforgotten and unforgiven.

Joachim von Ribbentrop, a handsome young *arriviste,* was part of the jazzy, danger-filled Berlin of the late twenties. He had made and married a lot of money, was well connected internationally, spoke excellent English and French, played good tennis, and was socially ambitious. In many ways he resembled some of today's successful young big-city entrepreneurs, those familiar and beloved subjects of "life-style" profiles in financial publications and magazines about instant success.

Then, perhaps to address some irrational insecurity he felt for Germany's future, von Ribbentrop threw in his and his family's lot with a group of revolutionaries, the Nazis. He joined forces with men who were known brawlers and killers, who advocated the end of all personal liberties in return for a supposed "national cleansing and renewal." The Nazi creed was every bit as frightening as the worst of Bolshevism, but the Nazis touted themselves as "German," not "foreign" like the Communists. This may have made them more acceptable to nationalists like Joachim von Ribbentrop, but other upper-class nationalist Germans were more cautious. They may have had vague sympathy for the Nazis, but they were not yet ready to embrace them.

Von Ribbentrop's own attachment seems to have been more personal. He became suddenly and thoroughly besotted with the man

Adolf Hitler, and he made the quintessential deal with the devil. Perhaps he did so before he was fully aware of all its terms, but he was willing to continue once he knew the score. His Nazi time began as high adventure and the fulfillment of his daydreams. Later, if he had doubts, there remained neither the courage nor the chance to quit. All he could do was keep sufficient slack in the steel cable that tethered him to Hitler; else he would have fallen and been torn by the jagged road.

At first it must have been heady stuff for the young von Ribbentrops. Before 1933 Joachim and Annelies were hoping for acceptance by the "right" Berlin circles. Soon, as part of the Nazi entourage, they hosted prime ministers and kings and leading industrialists. The road from business executive to "His Excellency" was short and swift. Joachim achieved success in the game of international politics, where he negotiated treaties and obtained desirable terms for Germany. The world of striped-pants diplomacy was glamorous, filled with titles and protocol, infinitely more gratifying for him than the importing of liquors.

Von Ribbentrop provides a useful instrument for observing Hitler's times and events. He was like the man in the next Concorde seat, a tennis-playing, well-groomed fellow with city and country houses, a well-born, well-dressed wife, and several handsome kids.

With the exception of Hjalmar Schacht, Albert Speer, and Baldur von Schirach, most of the senior Nazis were malcontents and misfits, difficult to understand. Perhaps the professional therapist could read the motivations of a Goebbels, a Göring, a Hess, or a Himmler, but lay members of today's world would find them obscure. Somehow the revolutionary life of these top Nazis seemed predestined, but what of von Ribbentrop? He was no more primed for revolution than most of the members of an exclusive golf club or board room.

The von Ribbentrops began their Berlin lives as tireless aspirants to upper-class conventionality. They tried to arm themselves with all the machinery from aristo title to club memberships. Their fundamental and politically radical change of direction was baffling.

At first, writing about von Ribbentrop seemed a daunting task. Many knowledgeable people spoke of him as Hitler's parrot, a yes man, a supersecretary, a vain, arrogant, and stupid man of little character. Descriptions of his wife were equally pejorative. Several published biographical sketches echoed these views. Yet I knew enough about the time of the Nazis to question these judgments. The man who negotiated the 1935 Naval Agreement with Great Britain, formed the propagandistic Anti-Comintern Pact, and came up with the Soviet-German Nonaggression Pact could not be dismissed so lightly. Göring and Goebbels, two men who had Hitler's ear, despised von Ribbentrop but could never unseat him. Until the last day in the Hitler bunker, he was among the highest-ranking Nazis.

Of course, the real key to the von Ribbentrop story was Adolf Hitler and the sum of his semi-educated, pseudopolitical, and historical notions. Probably overriding all else in Hitler's life was his hysterical hatred of Communism and his fear of the supposed power of "world" Jewry. He was a vengeful man, a dilettante boiling with hatred.

Von Ribbentrop managed to help his final steps to power. Once in control, Hitler achieved an immediate string of perceived successes, all of which the experts had deemed impossible. These were then expanded into further daring acts that also succeeded until both Hitler and the majority of those who had doubted him were convinced that he was infallible, a man of destiny.

His ultimate gamble, however, proved that the experts who had doubted him were right. When Hitler stumbled, other Nazis tried to distance themselves from him, but von Ribbentrop kept his satanic bargain. His final payments involved infinite cruelty perpetrated without a thought for the consequences.

Much of the research for this book caused me deep pain. Reading about such cold-blooded and carefully reasoned murder often forced me temporarily to suspend further study. Not another word about bloodshed! Not another sum total of deaths!

The biography took me from the archives of Bonn's Foreign Ministry to archives all over Europe. I chased the ghost of von Ribbentrop from the mountains of Austria to London, Munich, Berlin, Nürnberg, Hamburg, and Washington, D.C.

I assembled my notes and wrote the last draft of this book against the background of the Gulf War. The nearby television screen provided a case study of dictatorship and its demands and what happens when the world says, "No. Not another inch!" I was mesmerized by the effectiveness of the post–Cold War United Nations while I was chronicling the failures of its predecessor, the League of Nations. I even heard a small country, Kuwait, described as an "artificial" patchwork to justify aggression. It was exactly what Hitler had called the small country called Czechoslovakia.

HITLER'S DIPLOMAT

BOOK I

1
THE END

MEN of the U.S. Army's Graves Registration Service are usually matter of fact. Theirs is not an enviable assignment, though it is a most necessary one; no one interferes much with the way they do their job. On the chill evening of October 16, 1945, a Graves Registration team waited snug in the pretty villa at Heilmann Strasse 25 in Munich-Solln.

They had been told to expect the ashes of eleven GIs who were cremated. The villa, which had once belonged to a rich Bavarian businessman, was a comfortable headquarters for their uncomfortable job, but the truck carrying the canisters with the remains, escorted by a guard car, arrived very late, and the men were peeved. It was long past their bedtime, so they stored the containers in the basement.

The next morning they followed instructions. The ashes were to be scattered into the small stream, the Conwentzbach, which ran immediately behind and below the villa. The men carried down the eleven shiny cylinders, lined them up in a row, and opened them with axes or kicked them open. The ashes were poured into the gurgling water by commissioned officers, according to regulations. What the Graves Registration enlisted men did not know was that one of the eleven shiny aluminum cans contained the ashes of His Excellency Joachim von Ribbentrop, Hitler's mighty foreign minister, and the rest held the remains of the senior war criminals. One, Hermann Göring, had committed suicide. The others had all been hanged.

2

WESEL TO LONDON
1893–1910

No Violin for Christmas

AS THE NINETEENTH CENTURY neared the twentieth, Wesel was still a small garrison town in the extreme northwest of Germany, a few miles from where the Rhine crossed the Dutch frontier. Today, Wesel is only a twenty-minute drive from the two Dutch towns of Nijmegen and Arnheim, where so many British and American paratroopers lost their lives in 1944 during the oddly named Operation Market Garden.

Ulrich Friedrich Willy Joachim Ribbentrop was born in Wesel on April 30, 1893, the second of three children. His brother, Lothar, was three years older; his sister, Ingeborg, was born in 1896. Their father, Richard Ribbentrop, was a professional soldier, a lieutenant in the Westphalian Field Artillery. His mother, Sophie, was a daughter of rich landowners in Saxony named Hertwig. Sophie was beautiful but doomed. She was tubercular, and at the turn of the century tuberculosis was almost always fatal.

The Ribbentrops were military people. Joachim's grandfather had won his Iron Cross First Class in the Brunswick Artillery. Richard won his in World War I, and so did Joachim. The Ribbentrops were typical Westphalians, usually considered tough and upright.

The Kaiser's Officer Corps was dominated by aristocrats, and an untitled commoner like Lieutenant Richard Ribbentrop had to be exceptionally good at his job. An officer had to be rich or had to marry a wealthy girl, because he had to show a personal fortune of 90,000 gold marks, or he did not get permission to marry.[1] In the nineteenth century, the officer's world was a titled world, based on the dubious premise of hereditary leadership. The assumption that squires and counts, "men on horseback," would inspire the dull burgher to do his military duty was widespread. Officers' messes in Britain, France, and Germany were filled with the sons and grandsons of the regiments. Viscount followed Earl. M. le Marquis followed M. le Marquis, and Herr Baron followed Herr Baron. Even the ugly matter of duels had to be resolved among equals. Only a Herr could offer satisfaction to a Herr. Fortunately, Britain was exempt from this barbarity, but the German officer thrived on it.

When Joachim was still a small boy, Lieutenant Ribbentrop was transferred to another beautiful garrison: Castle Wilhemshöhe, near the Hessian town of Kassel, where Wilhelm IX, Duke of Hesse, built his splendid *Schloss* and then, of course, named it for himself. Little Joachim's first recollections were of this castle and of the red brick house near the castle gate where the Ribbentrops lived. His father was commander of a battery of artillery. What a heroic view of one's father, dressed in splendid uniform, mounted on his charger. And then to hear the massive boom of artillery pieces firing at ceremonial occasions, which frightened a little boy or thrilled him.

Joachim's mother was bedridden. The children seldom saw her, because then as now tuberculosis was highly infectious, and she wanted to protect them. Despite her precautions, Lothar, the oldest, eventually died of the disease. It is very likely that Joachim also was tubercular.[2] When he was eighteen, one of his kidneys had to be removed, probably to prevent the disease's spread.[3] He was a handsome lad but was plagued by a drooping eyelid throughout his life, a sort of sad wink. Some doctors felt this may have been related to his infected kidney.

The Ribbentrop brothers were close and depended on each other. Their father was easier to respect than to love, and there was no compensation from their mother, who was unreachable and untouchable. But they were military children, who did not expect to be as pampered as civilian ones.

In 1901, Richard Ribbentrop was promoted to major and transferred from quiet, charming Kassel to Metz, the strict garrison city in Lorraine. Metz was the scene of Prussia's greatest triumph and France's great military disaster. In 1871, the entire French garrison of 100,000 troops had surrendered to the Prussians, and now Metz was very Prussian indeed. Metz was the army, and the army was Metz.

A young artillery major, especially one without a titled name, could easily become invisible. Fortunately, Major Ribbentrop came to the attention of General Haeseler, a much-feared eccentric, famous for his spartan ways and shabby, worn uniforms. He was the sort of general Richard Ribbentrop respected, because he was ahead of his time, almost in the mold of the American West Pointers.[4] To Richard Ribbentrop, being an officer was a beloved and honored profession. General Haeseler's successor also recognized Major Ribbentrop's talent and kept him as aide-de-camp.

How best to describe the brusque major? In his second son's conventional words, he had a heart of gold, was well versed in politics and the arts, and insisted that the hand was "for reaching out in friendship or grasping the sword. Nothing in-between."[5] Yet, given the time, the circumstances, and his profession, he seemed unusually caring. For the sake of his wife he avoided the crowded central section of Metz and rented a house in quiet, suburban Queuleu. The boys attended upper school in Metz, where Joachim was confident he would dazzle everyone. Yet of the fifty pupils in his class, at the end of the winter term he ranked only thirty-second. He earned a paternal thrashing and forfeited his long-expected Christmas gift: a violin. Major Ribbentrop had made his point.

Years later, the wife of Otto Meissner, President Paul von Hindenburg's state secretary, who had taught in Joachim's school in Metz, said he "was the most stupid in his class, full of vanity and very pushy."[6] Others said he got away with everything because of his great charm. Both views would obtain throughout his public life. Some of the old-time Nazis resented his closeness to Adolf Hitler and his worldly, international ways. Many of the professional diplomats, mostly of titled, aristocratic family, called him a parvenu, an *arriviste*, an amateur, a dilettante. Still, he remained unscathed in the volatile and dangerous world of Nazi politics. The success casts doubt on his reputation for stupidity, though his reputation for arrogance may have been justified.

Joachim's mother was sinking. To please her and to placate his father, he worked hard, and by Easter his school report was good. He was given his first violin. In his memoirs he wrote that music took a leading place in his heart. At thirteen, he played in several concerts and even thought of becoming a professional violinist.[7] "My violin went with me everywhere, throughout my life. It never let me down, as so many people did. Nürnberg proved that! My violin was always my comfort!" The would-be violinist was one day to join the would-be artist.

Later, much later, he was to own a Stradivarius, bought for a fortune in gold marks through Charles Evel, a famous Paris dealer in rare instruments, when the violin was put up for sale by its Jewish owner.[8] After von Ribbentrop's execution, it was stolen from his estate, probably by an Allied occupation soldier. It emerged for sale twenty years later, when the thief hoped the statute of limitations had expired. According to some experts, the Stradivarius turned out to be a fake, fabricated by Voller, a famed forger, in London.[9]

Sophie Ribbentrop died on February 28, 1902, when Joachim was nine. The children were devastated. She was buried on one of her father's Saxon estates in Groitsch, where the Ribbentrop children had often vacationed and had learned to ride ponies and to hunt.

Now the major and his children moved to Belle Isle Street in the center of Metz, and the boys returned to the upper school.[10]

Richard Ribbentrop, who had done all he could for his invalid wife, now felt free to marry again. His new wife, Olga Margarete von Prittwitz und Gaffron, was a charming and cheerful woman, but the children did not warm to her. It was understandable. Their mother had been a dream, a myth, a vague presence in an upstairs bedroom, unscolding, unpunishing.

Joachim managed to finish *Obersekunda,* the grade just below senior year.[11] He never sat for his *Abitur,* the final examinations, the equivalent of the French *baccalauréat* or the British A-level examination. This was not unusual. Many boys finished their schooling before the *Abitur,* particularly if they had no plans to enter the university. Joachim had plans that were far more adventurous.

Richard Ribbentrop's dream of seeing both boys enter a *Kadettenanstalt,* a military academy, which produced Prussia's corps of professional officers, soon foundered.[12] Lothar's health was too delicate for such rigorous schooling. Then Joachim cranked up his courage: he refused. He wanted to learn foreign languages and travel the world. Boys everywhere had caught the fever to go abroad, to explore. Each country had its new colonies; deserts were to be crossed, mountains to be climbed, jungles to be conquered. German boys were devoted to Karl May, the writer of adventure novels who gripped their imaginations. This was probably the first link between Hitler and Joachim although they didn't realize it. They were both Karl May enthusiasts. His closest ally was an elderly relative, his "aunt" Gertrud von Ribbentrop from the titled side of the family, who often stayed with them in Metz. Sometimes one branch of a family in a multiple-principality empire like Germany received a title but the other branch did not. Gertrud's father, Karl Barthold, had been quartermaster general to the King of Prussia. The Almanach de Gotha indicates that Karl Barthold von Ribbentrop, who lived from 1822 to 1893, was elevated to his title in 1884 in Berlin. So his daughter was indeed a von Ribbentrop; she was born in Berlin in 1863 and died in Naumburg in 1943.

Aunt Gertrud was the boys' friend. She understood their sense of adventure and, with her small income, was willing to help them.

Much later, on May 15, 1925, she was to be repaid for her early support.[13] At Joachim's suggestion, she adopted the thirty-two-year-old, by then a married man, and invested him with her *von*. In return, Joachim von Ribbentrop provided her with a lifelong monthly pension of 450 marks.[14]

With Gertrud's help, in 1907 Lothar and Joachim went to study at a boarding school in Grenoble; Joachim had won his first battle with his strict father. In his memoirs he would say, "I often wondered if this was the way to treat children and decided not to do the same to mine."[15] Indeed, Joachim and Annelies von Ribbentrop seem to have been caring and generous parents to their three boys and two girls.

The newlywed Richard Ribbentrops attracted many new friends and became favorite hosts and desirable guests in the tight military circle of Metz. Ribbentrop, now a lieutenant colonel, was a great admirer of Prince Otto von Bismarck, the Iron Chancellor, the man who forged the German Reich. At the same time, he admired the ambitious young Kaiser Wilhelm II, but when the Kaiser abruptly dismissed Bismarck over a difference in policy, Richard Ribbentrop was offended and there began many years of doubt about imperial policy. Despite his delicate assignment as senior aide to the commanding general of the garrison, he felt he could not keep quiet and openly criticized the Kaiser's military designs. In 1908, after an agonizing bout with his conscience, he resigned his commission.[16]

In an unusual show of concern, his commanding general asked him to reconsider, or at least to postpone his decision. The German Army could ill afford to lose a young staff officer of such talent. But Colonel Ribbentrop, the antithesis of the often-caricatured, tightly corseted, semiliterate Prussian officer-aristocrat, was adamant. He retired on a small pension and his late wife's money. Margarete also had some income.

His resignation and its rationale caused a sensation in a city totally wed to the Army.[17] Military officers usually kept their political opinions to themselves.

The Ribbentrops were sad to leave their friends in Alsace-Lorraine. Joachim von Ribbentrop always claimed a special affection for the French, their ways, and their language. Besides, Metz held splendid tennis tournaments, some of which Joachim had won. From Grenoble, the boys joined the family in Arosa, the glossy Swiss ski resort. Now came Joachim's first taste of *la vie internationale*. He steered his bobsled, *Meteor*, with a crew of an English girl and an English clergyman, and Richard Ribbentrop at the brake; they won several small races. The brothers also took private English lessons and practiced on the many British and Canadian vacationers. Their tutor, an eccentric expatriate Englishman, fascinated them with his Edwardian style and introduced them to some of the British classics.[18] During that winter in Arosa, the boys befriended a young Canadian girl and her family who would be important to them later, on the other side of the Atlantic. Meanwhile, they dreamed of seeking their fortunes in South or East Africa.[19]

For the first time, Joachim found a way to relate to his father. He listened carefully to Richard Ribbentrop's political views, probably his first introduction to the subject. Since his father was a Bismarckian, Joachim was certainly treated to a full measure of the Prussian-guided Pan-Europeanism of Prince Otto Eduard Leopold von Bismarck-Schönhausen. It is odd to think that the young Joachim, who was probably force-fed Bismarck's anti-Austrian views, would one day become the virtual slave of an Austrian.

In 1909, when Joachim was sixteen, the boys were invited to London by the family of Dr. Grandage, a famous surgeon and a friend of the senior Ribbentrops.[20] The Grandages lived in South Kensington, ringed by gardens and parks, and both boys were happily impressed by London and by the great kindness of their hosts. Before long, they became devoted to the "English way." As Joachim wrote in his memoirs: "The nonchalant ways of the British upper classes impressed my brother and me very much . . . Later, I found out that, despite their nonchalance, they were hard-working and committed, socially and politically." His liking for England was real, yet he never learned the ways of the British. He loved their style but failed to see their substance.

The rest of the Ribbentrops had remained in Arosa, enjoying their new freedom from the duties, constraints, and snobbery of Army life. Perhaps there were some remaining tensions between the boys and their stepmother. Whatever the cause, late in 1910 the boys announced that, instead of returning to Arosa, they wished to go on to Canada, and, surprisingly, there were no parental objections, even though the boys were only nineteen and seventeen. Richard Ribbentrop seemed reconciled to his sons' independence.

• • •

By now Joachim was a handsome, blond young man with a fashion-
ably bland face, blue eyes, and cleft chin. Years later, Sir Henry (Chips)
Channon, a well-known London wit, would say that the famed host-
ess Emerald Cunard "fell in love with Ribbentrop's dimple."[21] Lothar
was a charming, quiet boy who was beginning to show the first signs
of severe illness.

Why Canada? The answer is mysterious. Did the senior Ribbentrops accept Canada as a desirable option, a safer form of adventure
than Africa? Was it the lure of the New World with its Indians and
cowboys?

Was it because they knew that the young men would see their
Canadian friends from Arosa? Or perhaps it was because of the von
Alvensleben brothers, later known as the notorious Alvenslebens.[22]

The Alvenslebens from Berlin — Alvo and Eno — were land spec-
ulators and adventurers who began an investment business in western
Canada. In 1904, Alvo moved to Vancouver while Eno manned the
Berlin office. There he threw out the hooks for the "fish" that Alvo
reeled in, all the way across the Atlantic and the continent to British
Columbia. As the sons of a former imperial ambassador to the Court
of St. Petersburg, they were well-connected, and though they had little
cash, they had a lot of imagination and boatloads of charm. Alvo had
invested some of his family's money in the Vancouver area, and he
made a large profit, which he advertised. Soon he became the talk of
Berlin's financial circles. He married a wealthy Canadian girl and
became a fixture in Vancouver society.

Many prominent Germans, like the future Chancellor Bethmann-
Hollweg, the Prussian cavalry hero General von Mackensen, Emma
Mumm of the champagne Mumms, and eventually Kaiser Wilhelm,
soon invested with Alvo. Leading German families began to pour their
money and their youngest sons into western Canada. Finally, the
Alvenslebens got backing from German banks and collected an investment fund of ten million dollars, a huge sum of money at the time.

By 1911, German money, clubs, and societies dominated Vancouver. The Deutsche Club on Granville Street was one of the city's most
fashionable places and had members like the millionaire yachtsman
Hans von Grävenitz, romantic figures like one of von Mackensen's
grandsons, Lieutenant von Tumpling, a dashing, saber-scarred expatriate. There were also solid bankers like Johannes Wulfsohn.[23] Alvensleben then built an exclusive resort, a *Luftkurort*. Like many
young Germans who read about them, the Ribbentrop boys seem to
have been dazzled by the Alvenslebens. They had seen the Alvensleben

ads and read of the adventure they promised. Germans were talking about them and about making their fortunes in Canada.

Eventually, the Alvensleben enterprises would collapse, but it seems probable that Joachim met Alvo von Alvensleben in Canada. Certainly they had much contact later, and Alvo was friendly with Joachim for years.

One fall day in 1910 the Ribbentrop brothers set sail for Canada from England on a ship of the White Star Line.

3

CANADA
1910–1914

The Wild West

THE NEWLY ARRIVED Ribbentrop brothers were immediately treated to a boisterous dose of North Americanism. Their Canadian friends, as Joachim wrote, set out to "cure them of their pre–World War London airs." No more "how d'y' do?" or "don't y' know?" Several of their Montreal friends may have been vacationers they had met at Arosa, and probably some of them were Jewish. In his memoirs, Joachim von Ribbentrop protested that he was no anti-Semite and that his "Montreal friends could have given proof of that."[1] He loved Montreal "and its diversions — poker, tennis, rugby, and particularly ice hockey." He was a handsome boy, so it can be assumed that girls were among the "diversions."

His first job was clerking at Molson's Bank.[2] Then he became a timekeeper on a vast reconstruction project of the great Quebec Bridge, which had collapsed with a tragic loss of life and was being rebuilt. Documents about the project list the contractors M. P. and J. T. Davis, who were probably Joachim's employers.[3] Coincidentally, according to the boys, a prosperous Montreal family named Davis "adopted" them. If the Davises were Jewish, they may have been the friends who could prove he was not an anti-Semite.[4]

He seems to have spent little time in Montreal after he was hired by the Canadian Pacific Railroad as a clerk-timekeeper, the job that brought him to Vancouver and to his dream territory, the rugged and adventurous Canadian west. Lothar stayed in Montreal, and before leaving, Joachim arranged with the German consul in Montreal to waive his own obligation to serve as a one-year volunteer in the German Army.[5] Like most young men who had gone to upper schools, he had the right to volunteer for one year of duty and then become an officer candidate, rather than to serve the full three conscripted years. His dispensation was not unusual, since Germans studying abroad often received the waiver.

Finally Joachim was in "Alvensleben country." Nowhere else in North America was there such an overwhelming German influence. Joachim drank German beer in the Rathskeller in the Copp Building on Hastings Street in Vancouver, surrounded by German loggers, roustabouts, and vagabonds.[6] For a while, life was as he had dreamed of it in his boyhood. But then he had to return to Montreal to have his tubercular kidney removed.[7] As if to keep all blame from his late mother, he wrote later that he had contracted tuberculosis after "eating some infected eggs." He sailed back to Germany to recuperate with his family at their new house in Naumburg, while Lothar stayed in Canada, and in 1913 he recrossed the Atlantic to New York, where he stayed a few weeks. An acquaintance introduced him to some "prominent New Yorkers," and he did some free-lance newspaper reporting, which "taught him about the American mania for news, action, and sensations." His memoirs about this time are sketchy. However, all who knew him speak of his good looks and charm, and it is obvious he was what the French call a *débrouillard*. He soon joined his brother in Ottawa, where Lothar had moved in his absence, and together they began a small wine import-export business, financed by a modest inheritance from their mother. This was Joachim's first taste of business. It was good. Joachim also set about introducing himself to Ottawa society. Several things were in his favor: his good looks and precise "British" English, his love for dramatics and music, his tennis, and, strangely, the fact that he was a German.

Ottawa's social life revolved around Rideau Hall, the residence of His Majesty's governor general, His Royal Highness the Duke of Connaught, the younger brother of King Edward VII. His duchess was the former Princess Louise Marguerite of Prussia. The duke, like most of his generation of the royal family, spoke English with a strong German accent, in good part because of his German father. The entire Connaught household spoke German, including the servants. It was easy pickings for handsome young Joachim. He skated at the Minto Club, acted in amateur plays, attended costume parties, danced well, and was, according to Ottawa's ladies, "splendidly tailored." He was a success. He also paid his own way because the German mark was strong, and his little import-export business provided him with income. For him, the year 1913–1914 would have been paradise if only Lothar had been in better health. From all contemporary accounts, the Joachim Ribbentrop of those days was a thoroughly likable fellow. Canadian friends who saw him in London during the thirties could not believe the change in him; the "nice guy had turned into a stuffed shirt."[8] But in 1914, before the First World War, he was liked by both men and women, especially the latter. He even planned to marry a Canadian girl.

On August 4, 1914, Joachim had to face the choice of country or brother. War had broken out in Europe; Lothar was mortally sick. It was at his insistence that Joachim did set off for Germany. Lothar was interned as an enemy alien at St. Agathe Military Sanatorium in Montreal, where he was well treated. He died four years later in Lugano, Switzerland.[9]

Joachim, feeling duty-bound to join up — though with only one kidney he was "unfit" — took a train to New York and tried to book trans-Atlantic passage. Many shipping lines, however, refused to transport Germans because of the tight British blockade. When he discovered that Holland-America Line had decided to sell passage to a group of returning Germans on one of their steamships, the *Potsdam*, he immediately bought a ticket.[10]

Most of the voyage was boisterous. There were a hundred wine-swilling German passengers, many of them reserve officers on their way home to join their regiments.[11] There was much bragging, joke telling, gallows humor, and gambling, accompanied by a flood of radio reports of early German victories, which set off even more idiotic celebrations. Everyone was drunkenly happy, but Joachim was worried. According to his memoirs, before embarking in New York he heard that the Ottawa papers called him the sinister "spy" Ribbentrop.

There are several romanticized versions of his 1914 trip to Germany, some produced later by well-trained Nazi publicists. Actually, he began to chat with a British officer who came aboard when the ship entered British waters off Falmouth in order to check on the passengers. Joachim avoided suspicion by conveniently mentioning the Duke and Duchess of Connaught in flawless "Canadianized" English. By a happy coincidence, the very *pukha* British officer had once been the duke's aide. When the officer walked away, Joachim bribed a crew member to hide him in a coal locker below decks. It was dirty but safe, and he needed it only until the Dutch-flagged *Potsdam* cleared British waters. Several other German passengers were taken ashore to be interned for the duration.

From neutral Rotterdam Joachim made his way to his father's house in Naumburg, a small town on the Saale River, southwest of

Leipzig. Ever the patriot, Colonel Richard Ribbentrop had rejoined the Army, and now Joachim volunteered to join the 12th Hussars, his maternal grandfather's old regiment based in Torgau on the Elbe River, fifty miles south of Berlin. Using his family's connections with the regiment, and the account of his long trip across the Atlantic, he charmed his way past the medical examiners and was accepted. Among his new young regimental comrades was the eighteen-year-old Count Wolf Heinrich von Helldorf, who was to take a place of importance much later in Ribbentrop's life. Helldorf became one of the great crooks of the Hitler time and ended his life hanged, like von Ribbentrop, but by Hitler's SS.[12]

His Canadian years had reinforced Joachim Ribbentrop's immature views of the British, and oddly, he never seemed to outgrow them. His adoration of the British Empire seems to bear out the opinion of many of his contemporaries, that he may have paid allegiance to the revolutionary Nazi movement, but in truth was a royalist and an arch conservative. It explains why he favored nineteenth-century, power-bloc thinking while Adolf Hitler thought in twentieth-century ideological and racial terms. At times, Hitler reluctantly found himself impressed by the world of international aristocracy and trapped in his humble, Austro-Catholic roots. He would then point a disdainful finger at the so-called upper crust (Feine Leute), and since von Ribbentrop was often nearby, he became one of Hitler's favorite scapegoats. Whenever the Führer wanted to express his distrust or dislike of something worldly or upper class, it was "typically Ribbentrop."

The sum of certain early Ribbentrop delusions about the British after his years in Canada is startling. He wrote that he "often told Adolf Hitler about the artful system the British used to forge their future, the harmonious blending of continuing old nobility with ambitious, newly created aristocrats, all anchored by the crown." He obviously saw "Englishness" only in the top layer and had little understanding of the strength of Britain's working class. Had things gone differently, Hitler "might have adopted some of these ways." In Ribbentrop's words: "I cannot say whether the crown would ever have returned to Germany, but between 1933 and 1934 Adolf Hitler repeatedly told me, 'Everything for a German imperial house.'"[13]

Annelies, who edited the memoirs, noted: "In the summer of 1933 [a few months after Hitler became chancellor] we once breakfasted alone with Adolf Hitler in the [Hotel] Kaiserhof near the Presidential Palace. He spoke of restoring the Hohenzollern monarchy, and he did so with great emphasis and warmth. He indicated that he was thinking of Prince August Wilhelm ... At the celebration in the Potsdam Garrison Church, it was evident that in the section reserved for the imperial family, the empty central armchair was for the [absent] Kaiser."[14]

Prince August Wilhelm, familiarly and disrespectfully known in Berlin society as Auwi, was the fourth of the Kaiser's six sons and the only one who became a devoted Nazi. At first, Hitler paid court to him, then lost interest. But Auwi was devoted to the Führer, probably hoping for the day of an imperial restoration. Auwi was even made a Storm Troop (SA) general *(Obergruppenführer)*. After the Second World War, Auwi served thirty months in jail as a "co-conspirator," the technical term for those who helped the Nazis perform war crimes.

The Potsdam celebration mentioned by Annelies von Ribbentrop was staged by Hitler in an attempt to make his raucous movement acceptable to Germany's upper classes and the outside world. On March 21, 1933, forty-nine days after his appointment as chancellor, he used the Potsdam Garrison Church, Prussia's most sacred symbol of aristocracy and of the officer corps, to stage the opening of the first Reichstag of his regime. No one in the glittering diplomatic gallery of foreigners seemed convinced that Hitler's attempt to make the Nazis respectable had succeeded, but von Ribbentrop was willing to believe.[15]

4

WAR

The Hussar

IN 1914 THE 12TH Torgau Hussars were a typical elite cavalry unit of
the post-Bismarck era. German regiments were now numbered so that
they became part of the "new" German Imperial Army, but they often
retained local designations to celebrate pride and tradition. Other
regiments were named after their princes or their commanders. The
concept of a *German* Army was still new, and there was a residual
reluctance on the part of old regiments to de-Bavarianize, de-Hessian-
ize, or de-Saxonize themselves. The Prussian military spirit was dominant, but even Prussian regiments had their complaints. The Prussian
Guards, for instance, could not use the term "Royal," but certain
Bavarian regiments had this privilege.

Field-gray uniforms for combat and fatigue duties had been introduced as recently as 1910.[1] Old soldiers shuddered at the sameness of
gray. In 1914 all regiments adopted the color for general use, though
reluctantly. It unified the German Army, although, as Ribbentrop
pointed out, he became a "blue" Hussar, a reference to the cornflower-
blue tunics traditionally worn by the 12th Torgau.[2] The Hussars were
light cavalry, "raiding" cavalry, recalling Attila and his wild Mongol
horsemen. Their short braided dress jacket was still known as the
Attila. The Hussars afforded Ribbentrop a dashing way to be a soldier,
and his memoirs told the usual story of the young gentleman who
joins the cavalry and is told that he may think he can ride . . . but not
the Army way! Then follows the obligatory "meanest horse in the
squadron" and the *Schadenfreude* of the riding sergeant doubled over
with laughter at the tumbling recruit.

At the same time that Joachim was getting his equestrian comeup-
pance, hundreds of miles to the south, in Bavaria, a young Austrian
volunteer named Adolf Hitler was learning to be an infantry soldier in

the 16th Bavarian Reserve Regiment, known as the List Regiment after its commanding officer. Hitler was no officer candidate, and his regiment was by no means elite, but both recruits would later win the Iron Cross First Class. In the case of Adolf Hitler, according to the historian Joachim Fest, the Führer of the German Reich was never eager to show that he was recommended for the decoration by the Jewish regimental adjutant, Captain Hugo Gutmann.[3]

Ribbentrop simply reported that he served with the 12th Torgau Hussars on the eastern and western fronts as an officer and was wounded several times. His Iron Cross, according to him, was awarded in 1917 before he was found unfit for further combat duty and assigned to staff work.

There is an implication that he applied for the decoration long after he was assigned to staff duty back in Berlin.[4] Of course, this was forcefully denied by his widow. But that was by no means an unusual course. Many combat soldiers were decorated long after a specific act of courage. The rumor was probably circulated by Hitler's jealous "old fighters," the Führer's paladins since the "days of the struggle" in the early twenties. In their eyes Ribbentrop was a Joachim-come-lately, a man with a high number on his National Socialist Party membership card, betraying his late conversion, which took place in 1932. Hitler's own number was 7. Von Ribbentrop's was 1,119,927.

There were also rumors about the last year of the war, when First Lieutenant Ribbentrop did administrative work. Ernst (Putzi) Hanfstaengl, the Harvard-educated son of a Munich art dealer, a Hitler intimate who fell out with his Führer, claimed that Ribbentrop was absent without leave during his regiment's 1918 withdrawal to the east. A man named Douglas Glen published a book in London in 1941 which claimed that in 1915 Ribbentrop recrossed the Atlantic on a U-boat and became an espionage associate of Franz von Papen's, then an attaché at the German Embassy in Washington.[5] (Von Papen was expelled from the United States for his espionage activity.) Glen claimed that Ribbentrop later worked for von Papen as an espionage agent in Constantinople. While he was supposedly doing this secret work, he was being accused of desertion, and it was von Papen who convened a court of honor to "clear Ribbentrop of the charges." However, all this is a most unlikely scenario. Cut off by the war, Glen probably had few ways of getting legitimate facts, so he invented them. (Actually Ribbentrop *was* ordered to Constantinople.)

In October 1918, the Turks suddenly signed an armistice with the western Allies, and German officers had twenty-four hours to leave

Constantinople or be interned. They were given temporary shelter in the home of an acquaintance of Ribbentrop's, the Jewish manager of a German bank.[6] They then crossed to the Asiatic side of the Bosporus and tried to find their way home to Germany. Ribbentrop slipped back across the Bosporus again to destroy confidential papers in the deserted German Constantinople office.[7]

The Kaiser abdicated in November 1918. Ribbentrop and the others were interned in Turkey, but Swedish friends helped them get back to Berlin by way of Italy.

While in Constantinople, Ribbentrop met von Papen, who in 1932 was to play a major role in his political career. While Ribbentrop was working for von Falkenhayn in Constantinople, he was sent to Berlin to deliver his general's report about 1918 conditions in Turkey to the War Ministry.

The trip reinforced Ribbentrop's rightist views. He recalled that there were more than twenty thousand deserters hiding in Berlin but that the government "stuck its head in the sand [*Vogel Strauss Politik*] in order not to stir up a fuss."[8] He returned to Constantinople, dismayed by what he had seen and feeling betrayed. In the spring of 1919, he rented a small room in Berlin's Meineke Strasse, a small, fashionable street off the Kurfürstendamm. Berlin was in the midst of revolution. Mutinous troops roamed everywhere. Officers like Ribbentrop were instructed to remove their epaulets of rank. Lieutenant Ribbentrop, still in the Army, was employed at the War Ministry as a language specialist and was soon assigned to General Hans von Seeckt's German delegation to the Peace Conference at Versailles. There were 180 people in the delegation, but no one later recalled Lieutenant Ribbentrop.[9] Disgusted with the treatment of officers and Germany's meek acceptance of her fate, he resigned his commission before going off to Versailles, so he never witnessed the signing of the treaty he considered so shameful.

Today's political observer, accustomed to the self-interested generosity of the Marshall Plan or the benign regulations that followed the Gulf War, may find it hard to understand the harsh terms imposed on Germany on June 28, 1919, at Versailles. Most Germans of the time called it *das Diktat* (the dictate) rather than *der Vertrag* (the treaty) of Versailles.

The treaty was drawn unilaterally by France, Britain, the United States, Italy, and their allies. All the talking was done by Clemenceau of France, Lloyd George of Britain, Wilson of the United States, and Orlando of Italy. Any attempt by Foreign Minister Count Ulrich von

Brockdorff-Rantzau to plead the German case was met with threats of immediate military action.

Understandably, the Allies demilitarized their defeated enemy, but that was only the beginning.

Germany lost 73,845 square kilometers of land and control over seven million German nationals. German regions were handed to Poland, France, the newly formed Czechoslovakia, and, in 1923, to Lithuania. The major Baltic port of Danzig became a "free" port under Polish administration. The Saar territory was mandated to France for fifteen years, after which a plebiscite was to decide its future. Germany's main rivers, the Rhine, Oder, Memel, Danube, and Mosel, were internationalized. Austria was prohibited from any future union with Germany. Most of the Rhineland was occupied by Allied troops.

Massive amounts of raw materials, like coal, were requisitioned by the Allies. Heavy machinery and some entire factories had to be turned over. Livestock (including 140,000 dairy cows) was shipped out of Germany. Almost the entire merchant fleet was expropriated. All German holdings abroad, including those of private German citizens, were confiscated.

On top of these punishing terms, billions of marks were to be paid annually as reparations, and Germany's colonies were handed to the League of Nations and then individually mandated to the Allies.

Like the men who wrote it, the Treaty of Versailles was in the imperial tradition of the eighteenth and nineteenth centuries. It was the last of its kind, certainly in the twentieth. Victors to follow learned from the mistakes of Versailles.

Understandably, the driving force behind the occupation of the Rhineland, the Saar, and the transfer of Alsace was France. Twice in a half century, Germany had attacked France's eastern border from across the Rhine, and the French were desperately anxious to prevent a third such attack. History and their own lack of resolve would eventually prove their reasoning wrong. The other grinding terms of Versailles came about as the result of a "contest" to determine who could best humiliate the arrogant enemy.

Only the United States failed to ratify the treaty. A frustrated President Woodrow Wilson, one of the architects of the League of Nations, was forced to stay on the sidelines, and the United States never became a member.

On October 18, 1930, a cartoon in the *St. Louis Post Dispatch* showed a Hitler-like creature crawling from the cocoon of a rolled-up, seal-decorated Versailles Treaty.[10]

5

BERLIN
1919

The Champagne Salesman

JOACHIM RIBBENTROP found Berlin in 1919 a place where crooks flourished and young men tried to "wipe away the memory of their useless sacrifice."[1] Once more, he said, Germany was divided. Division was its inherited disease.

"Suddenly," he wrote, "everywhere there were Jews," who took a "less than pleasing" part in economic and cultural affairs. Still, according to Ribbentrop, there were "many Jewish families who felt just like my nationalist friends and suffered just as keenly about our loss."[2]

The defeated Germany of the First World War was not the defeated Germany of the Second World War. Nineteen eighteen had brought few obvious signs of defeat. Of course, there were those long lists of dead, wounded, and missing; the military hospitals were filled with crippled soldiers; and hardly a family had escaped some grim news about its men in uniform. But until the last day of the war, the newspapers told of victorious combat actions. The German combat soldier was still on foreign soil, and not a single enemy had crossed into the sacred *Vaterland*. It seemed a stalemate. To the average *Bürger* this was not a signal for disaster.

Compare this with the Second World War: in May 1945 Germany's cities lay in smoldering ruins; half of Germany's soldiers were dead, wounded, or captured in faraway places. What remained of Germany's battered troops had retreated from Russia, North Africa, France, Belgium, Holland, Norway, Denmark, the Baltics, and Italy. They were back inside Germany, too beaten to mount a final defense. The Russians were in the suburbs of Berlin, the Americans were entering Munich's Englischer Garten, and the British were nearing

Hamburg's Inner Alster. In 1945 Germans were homeless, shocked, and hungry, and all around them lay the bombed-out ruins of their great cities. The booming enemy artillery was within lethal reach.

Adolf Hitler's death did not come as a surprise (though he had promised to die fighting, and instead committed suicide). By contrast, the announcement on November 9, 1918, of the Kaiser's abdication came as a shock to many Germans. (Oddly, Wilhelm II vacated only the title of Kaiser. Perhaps he had the curious notion that he could eventually return as the King of Prussia.)

Revolution followed at once. Led by mutinous sailors from the north of Germany, Berlin's working classes mounted a red-colored revolt, named after Spartacus, the rebellious gladiator-prisoner of Rome. Compared with Moscow's, the German Communist revolution was mild. There were few deaths. The titled gentlemen members of the fashionable Union Club on Schadowstrasse were rousted from their red leather armchairs and harassed and insulted, but they were not physically harmed. The Imperial Guards at the various palaces and imperial residences surrendered without a fight. Their Kaiser had fled. Their oath was void. It must have been an extraordinary sight when a venerable Imperial Court chancellor signaled surrender from a balcony of Berlin's Imperial Palace by waving a small square of red cloth tied to an umbrella. That week, red hammer-and-sickle flags flew all over working-class Berlin, but the Spartacus revolution did not last more than a few days. A coalition for a democratic socialist republic under future President Friedrich Ebert was assembled as early as November 10, 1918. Then came various attempted coups of the left and the right, and some vicious political assassinations, like those of the Socialists Karl Liebknecht and Rosa Luxemburg, but somehow the new republic survived. It tried as best it could to deal with the pressing social and economic hardships of a beaten country that was further beset by the harsh demands of the victors. Many small businesses suffered, and unemployment grew. Germany's starchily inflexible middle class lacked the guts and the wit to help itself. It had always comprised professional underlings.

Meanwhile, entrepreneurs, new and old, who understood the international market made fortunes in real estate and war surplus goods. Companies that exported, like Siemens, the giant A.E.G., and Daimler Benz, did well, as did the international banking houses. But there were also profiteers. One man's loss becomes another man's profit when the seller is desperate and the buyer has "hard" currency.

Post–World War Berlin had not changed much. Its famous sense of humor and tolerance were strained but still in place. Joachim

Ribbentrop did not take long to find his way. Berlin was never a stuffy city, in part because of the early influence of the eccentric Frederick the Great, the Prussian soldier-king. Fredericus Rex preferred to speak French, loved flute concerts, encouraged French Huguenot immigration, and even made life easier for his Jewish subjects (generally if they made the beau geste of converting to Protestantism). At Sans Souci, his castle in Potsdam, he was host to radical thinkers like Voltaire and Rousseau. This liberal tradition introduced Berliners to a sense of freedom from the powers above. Besides, those who lived in the city on the Spree River were a mixture of Slavic, Celtic, Nordic, and Frankish. Berlin always welcomed the new, the exotic, the strange. The city's language — all through the time of Hitler — included Yiddish and French expressions as integral parts. Berlin's disrespectful big-city humor is legendary, and the Berlin of 1919 was raucous and dynamic. As Europe's youngest capital city, it lacked the traditions of London, Paris, and Rome, but it had elasticity and great recuperative power.

By 1920, though there were still riots in the streets, shots being exchanged between political demonstrators, the police, and hastily assigned troops, Berlin's West End had its cafés and cabarets, its *thés dansants* and dinner parties. Rich women went to their dressmakers and coiffeurs, and straying husbands visited their mistresses in cozy little Charlottenburg flats. Most upper-class Berliners were not suffering financially. Their main complaints were that Germany had lost the war ("How could it happen to *us*?") and that the government seemed a shambles compared with years of imperial security. Upper-middle-class Germans found it painful not to know exactly what to expect. Even Berliners longed for "order." As Stendhal had written: "For the Germans, truth is not what exists but what ought to be true according to their system." In this respect, Berliners were typical Germans. After all, the reassuring Imperial government had been right there in Berlin. This was the Berlin Ribbentrop found in 1919.

In July of that year, Dr. Paul Schwarz, a long-time member of Germany's elite Foreign Service, the Auswärtiges Amt, was lunching with Ottmar Strauss and some others. Strauss, a prominent industrialist and a Jew, introduced him to a recently demobilized young officer named Ribbentrop, who spoke German with a slight English accent. The young man explained that he had studied in London and had lived in Canada. He had been sent to meet Strauss by Mathias Erzberger, the minister of finance. Ribbentrop was pleasant company. He spoke several other languages and was descended from an old military family. And he was looking for a job. He was very courteous, very correct. He said he had heard Schwarz's name mentioned by German diplomats in Turkey who told him about Schwarz's Iron Cross First Class and how he had won it as a civilian. Schwarz played it down. Then someone ordered Henkell *Sekt* (champagne), and Ribbentrop said, "You must admit it doesn't compare with the real French stuff." He irritated some of the patriots at the table, but his host, Ottmar Strauss, agreed and said, "I just can't *get* the real stuff." Ribbentrop promised to get him a price list for French champagne. Schwarz thought him rather a bore.

Schwarz met the well-mannered young Ribbentrop at several dinners given by Strauss at the Hotel Esplanade. One evening, Strauss said he told Ribbentrop's patron, Erzberger, not to worry about his protégé. "He won't need a job.[3] He'll be marrying Otto Henkell's daughter, Annelies."

As it happened, the Henkells were friends of Schwarz, who had spent much time at the family's home in Wiesbaden. Otto Henkell asked him about Joachim Ribbentrop, and Schwarz said that Ribbentrop was well dressed and well brought up, and that he kept his word. (He had provided both Strauss and Schwarz with the promised wine price list.)[4]

Joachim Ribbentrop's first postwar business deal, in August 1919, was the sale of six cases of Moët & Chandon champagne, vintage 1911, to Ottmar Strauss. The cases came from a British officers' mess whose mess sergeant was bribed. Ribbentrop made a small profit.[5]

Years later, in October 1933, eight months after Hitler became chancellor and von Ribbentrop was still a nonentity among the Nazis, Ottmar Strauss needed a favor from von Ribbentrop. He said that von Ribbentrop treated him warmly, opening his letters with "My dear friend" and still using the familiar *du*. But in 1937, when Strauss was in Zürich and needed some help, things had changed. Von Ribbentrop by then was ambassador to the Court of St. James's and "special, personal adviser to the Führer." When Ottmar Strauss tried to contact him, "Joachim behaved like a swine. After all, hadn't I done everything for him in the old days when *he* needed help? I never expected this. A secretary of the consulate general in Zürich just called me up and informed me that Herr von Ribbentrop is unable to answer your letter."[6]

This treatment of his old friend is one of many examples of Joachim von Ribbentrop's fluctuating attitude toward Jews, an attitude that persisted throughout his life. It was not unlike the sort of anti-Semitism one finds in socially ambitious and insecure people in

London, Paris, or New York. When one fears being snubbed, one often finds someone to snub.

Even demonstrably anti-Nazi officials of the time often failed to recognize Jews as fellow German citizens. On April 22, 1933, three months after the Nazi takeover, Ernst von Weizsäcker,* who was later von Ribbentrop's state secretary, clearly and stubbornly anti-Hitler, wrote, "It is extremely difficult for foreigners to understand anti-Jewish acts because they themselves do not get swamped by Jews [*hat diese Judenüberschwemmung nicht am eigenen Leib verspürt*]."[7]

In many ways, von Ribbentrop's life had none of the normal stages of most men's lives: no before-and-after school, before-and-after the Army, before-and-after marriage. The drama of Joachim von Ribbentrop had only two acts: before Hitler and after Hitler. The longer he took part in the second act, the more he lost those things which he had felt and learned during the first act. Most men build on the foundation of their youth. Von Ribbentrop dismantled his. Most men's careers follow a certain logical progression. A few film stars or athletes achieve sudden international prominence when they are still young, but few businessmen, having gained the sort of mature success, wealth, and local position they consider their goal in life, are then suddenly launched onto the world's center stage. The von Ribbentrops were highly successful big-city people, but they had few of the skills for dealing with world fame. Before Hitler, comparatively few people knew them. They had many friends in international business circles and had even made brief forays into international society or to the edge of politics, but on the scale of international renown they ranked near zero. Then, with the sudden and irreversible power of an avalanche, the whole world began to see them, read about them, gossip about them, and fear them. Kings and prime ministers flattered them and catered to them, while unseen others berated, ridiculed, and condemned them.

For this reason, little has been reported about the pre-Hitler von Ribbentrops, while there is a mountain of opinions and information about them during the Hitler era.

The von Ribbentrops — and they must be judged as a couple — did much to deserve condemnation because of the bestiality they helped to sustain with their own deep-seated fears and ambitions. How this banal business couple marketed grief, their own and that of millions, lies at the core of their story.

---

*Ernst von Weizsäcker was the father of Richard von Weizsäcker, the present president of Germany.

6

BERLIN

*He Could Walk Over
Dead Bodies*

ALTHOUGH EX-LIEUTENANT Ribbentrop had made some money
selling champagne to his friends, it was time to get a job, and he found
one in the Berlin office of a Bremen cotton importer. He liked his
kindly, understanding, "typically Hanseatic" employers* but did not
enjoy the textile field.[1] He stuck with it only because he needed the
money. Many of his brother's hospital bills in Lugano remained un-
paid. His father tried unsuccessfully to tackle them and had even
mortgaged his house in Naumburg.[2] Joachim soon settled them in full
and also paid off his father's mortgage.

He wanted to start a business of his own, much like his little wine-
importing firm in Canada, and he did so with a loan from a Jewish
banker named Herbert Guttmann of Dresdner Bank, who was a friend
of Ottmar Strauss's.[3]

There are several versions of how Joachim met Annelies Henkell,
of the wealthy champagne family. The year was 1919. Some say he
got in touch with the Henkells through his new wine business and was
invited to their splendid home in Wiesbaden. As Ribbentrop remem-
bers it, he was vacationing at Bad Homburg, the smart spa, and he
and Annelies met during a tennis tournament. After a short engage-
ment they were married, on July 5, 1920, at the Henkell villa.

Twenty-six years later, shortly before his execution, Joachim von
Ribbentrop wrote of his warm love for his wife: "My wife gave me
over twenty-five years of immeasurable happiness and gave me 'our
five,' our three sons and two daughters. It is more than a mere mortal

---

*Cities of the medieval Hanseatic trading league, like Bremen, Hamburg, and
Lübeck, were famed for their relaxed, unhurried ways.

may ask of the Fates." Indeed, theirs was a close marriage. Many of his contemporaries agree that it may have been the cause of his downfall. The ambitious Annelies Henkell has even been described as his Lady Macbeth, but there were never any complaints from her husband.[4]

She was a rebellious young woman, keenly aware of her parents' poor opinion of her handsome new husband. She was also often pain-ridden and depressed.[5] Many called her difficult. Throughout her life she suffered from severe sinus infections, and the headaches made her moody and irritable even when she was young. Later, several operations scarred her forehead with a permanent frown. As a young woman she was attractive, though not as beautiful as her sister Fänn Artzen. People called Annelies chic; no one thought her a great beauty.

Shortly after their wedding, Joachim Ribbentrop was offered a partnership in the Berlin sales agency that represented Henkell. He was never offered a partnership in the Henkell firm, nor was he ever associated with the management of Henkell.[6] Joachim was content with Otto Henkell's offer and the chance to live in Berlin, which was at center stage for his plans. In Berlin he and Annelies could lead the life they chose and keep their independence from the powerful senior Henkells.

There was never much love between the Henkells and Joachim. Otto Henkell once told a friend how sorry he was that Annelies ever met him.[7] Even Annelies's sister Fänn detested her brother-in-law. It was reported that later Ribbentrop sued Otto Henkell for being in arrears on payments promised to Annelies.[8]

Annelies's brother Stefan Karl, who was killed in the war, had married a rich Dutch girl, Lilli Fentner van Vlissingen, a Shell Oil heiress who was outspokenly anti-Nazi. After her husband's death in combat, she was jailed for making remarks against Hitler. Neither her sister-in-law Annelies nor Joachim von Ribbentrop, then a major Nazi official, came to her aid.[9]

Joachim Ribbentrop's new parents-in-law were an extraordinary couple. Otto Henkell was worldly and witty. His wife, Käthe, was born a Michel, a member of Mainz's oldest wine-growing families. She was an eccentric, fearless, monocle-wearing dowager who either loved or hated, with no shadings in between. At the family mansion on Beethoven Strasse in Wiesbaden she held a powerful salon of politicians, artists, academics, and men of industry. She said, "Anne-lies is willful and capricious. I tried to prevent her marriage to that adventurer. I detest him. He terrifies me. He could walk over dead bodies. He does not fit into our family. And that trick of getting

himself adopted!" She was referring to the *von* he added to his name
in 1925. "He is a laughingstock! His so-called society friends are
laughing!" She thundered on, "I am a Michel of Mainz, the daughter
of Geheimrat (Privy Councillor) Michel. Our family pokes fun at our
'titled' son-in-law. He is a nasty fool, a dangerous fool."[10]

But Annelies and Joachim von Ribbentrop clung together in rebellious union. Between his new job and her Henkell dowry they had
plenty of money. They bought a superb home and property in garden-
filled Dahlem and added a tennis court and swimming pool. In the
twenties, these were rare luxuries, even in a prosperous suburb. The
mansions of Berlin's old, aristocratic families were in the Tiergarten
district or near the Imperial Palace along Unter den Linden, but much
of its new society, its successful industrialists and professionals, lived
in Dahlem, where streets were quiet and tree-lined, and houses were
called villas. Each villa had its butlers, chauffeurs, and upstairs and
downstairs maids. Dahlem's Protestant church was one of Berlin's
"smart" churches, and its pastor, Martin Niemöller, a former U-boat
captain, was the "society" pastor. Today's Dahlem is virtually unchanged, although the von Ribbentrop villa at 7–9 Lentzeallee is no
more.

Joachim and Annelies seemed to have a sound marriage. Handsome Joachim was a bit of a *boulevardier,* and there are reports of his
early philanderings in Berlin's heated round of tea dances, parties, and
cabarets. He was often seen alone, and he was a serious dancer. He
treated dancing almost as an art form, and he wore white tie and tails
with great flair. One of his constant comrades on the dance circuit
was a young Russian-Jewish immigrant named Hoffelmann, and they
were known as Ribb and Hoff, or Hoff and Ribb.[11] One of the reasons
for Joachim Ribbentrop's lonely forays was that Annelies was mostly
pregnant. She bore two children in quick succession: Rudolf in Wiesbaden on May 11, 1921, and Bettina in Berlin on July 20, 1922.

When the young Ribbentrops were out as a couple, they were
usually with the nouveaux riches. Despite their villa and their wealth,
they had not yet found their place in upper-crust Berlin.

The mood of Berlin between 1920 and 1930 was strangely light-
hearted and full of humor, considering the political turmoil. After the
failed left-wing Spartacus revolt, there followed some right-wing attempts. In March 1920 came the Kapp putsch, named after its perpe-
trator, a prominent East Prussian reactionary. It was supported by
small units of mutinous Reichswehr called the Ehrhardt Brigade, led
by Captain Hermann Ehrhardt. The brigade moved into Berlin and

installed itself near the Brandenburg Gate; an armored train arrived at Anhalter Station. But several of the senior Reichswehr generals cautioned that "Reichswehr will not shoot at Reichswehr," so the government moved from Berlin to Stuttgart. Despite the reluctance of the legal government's generals to defend the new constitution, the Kapp putsch failed. It simply was not supported by the majority of Berliners, who protested by mounting a massive general strike.

Most Berliners maintained their composure during this Berlin brand of insurrection. One Socialist cabinet member switched the doorplates from the offices of the Socialist deputies to the reactionary German Nationalist offices. "The hell with them," he said about the expected invaders; "let them wreck the other party's typewriters!"[12] Minister of the Interior Wolfgang Heine would not leave Berlin. He refused to run (Zu türmen). When the cabinet returned to the capital after the putsch, he greeted them with a booming "Oh, it's you again?" and soon resigned.

Another right-wing blow was struck by the group of reactionary nationalist former officers who murdered Walter Rathenau, the foreign minister, on June 24, 1922. They shot him as he was being driven to his office in an open car. Rathenau had ignored several threats and refused to take precautions. The assassins objected to Rathenau's reasonable policy of trying to prove to the Allies by logic that Germany could not pay the Versailles reparations. The nationalists also hated him for signing the Rapallo Treaty of April 16, 1922, according to which Germany and the young Soviet Union agreed to waive all mutual war claims, to unfreeze each other's holdings, and to cooperate in the future. And they hated Rathenau, who had given up a leading post in German industry to join the government, for being a Jew.

In 1925, stolid President Ebert died, and old Field Marshal Paul von Hindenburg, the darling of the conservatives and royalists, was elected president. He was a towering figure, physically and metaphorically, who remained unalterably the Junker, the quintessential Prussian officer. On his first visit to the newly renovated State Opera in 1928, he arrived a few minutes early. The head porter rushed to the curb and bowed deeply. The old marshal, looking right through the man, asked, "No one here to report properly?" At that, the head porter crashed to stiff, military attention, cracked his heels together, and yelled, "Head Porter Wilhelm Schulze reporting, sir!"

Now von Hindenburg seemed to see him. "Ex-service man?" he asked.

"Cavalry sergeant, sir, Iron Cross First and Second!"

Von Hindenburg shook his hand, and they had a leisurely chat about the war while the director of the opera and the other dignitaries stood waiting.[13]

Berlin was reviving as an international diplomatic center. After the war, the decisions were made in London, Paris, and Washington. The first of many heads of state to visit the newly republican city was the exotic potentate King Aman-Ullah of Afghanistan. At one state ceremony, the Muslim King drank the republic's health in water. He then wanted to present a decoration to the head of Parliament, who, regretfully and apologetically, turned it down. "We are a republic, sire. You, sire, do not drink alcohol, and we cannot accept titles or decorations." However, the magnificent red Afghan coat that accompanied the decoration was accepted and passed on to State Secretary Weissmann, a bon vivant who sported it a few nights later. The Berlin street wits promptly dubbed him Weissmannulla.

Next came the pragmatic King Fuad of Egypt, who in French-accented German said, "During the mornings I work at the King business. During the afternoons I work for myself, the banks, *les maisons*, the estates."

King Faisal of Iraq appeared in civilian clothes. He was a modern monarch and wished no fuss.

The first postwar U.S. ambassador to Berlin was the wealthy and much-liked Fredrick Sackett, a great party-giver with a beautiful wife. They invited many young Berliners and even received acceptances from some Prussian aristocrats, who, as a matter of principle, snubbed most invitations to the embassies of their former enemies, particularly the French.

The spirit of Berlin was reviving in other ways. In 1919, for the first and only time, the German Derby, usually run in anglophile Hamburg, was moved to Berlin's Grunewald Racetrack. The winner was German-bred Gibraltar; ironically, his jockey was named Kaiser.*

Many people found irresistible the comparison with their runaway monarch. Most of Berlin's horse-breeding families, several of whom were Jewish, belonged to the Grunewald Jockey Club. Joachim and Annelies were always happy to be invited to the club. Jockey Club Jews were not too Jewish.[14]

Postwar Berlin was as bewitched with theater, film, and music as were the other capitals of the world, but nowhere else was there such

---

*Kaiser Bill, as he was dubbed in Britain and America, was living in comfortable exile in a half-million-guilder mansion named House Doorn. It had been purchased from the van Heemstra–de Beauforts, the family of film star Audrey Hepburn.

a mania for sports. The Sportpalast, a large indoor arena, Berlin's equivalent of New York's Madison Square Garden or London's Olympia, was always filled to overflowing with spectators. Everyone was there, from society people in evening clothes to workmen out for the night in their sweaters and knickerbockers. Six-day bike races, boxing, horse shows were invariably sold out. If Berlin's great singing stars, like the monocled Richard Tauber or Hungary's blond diva Gitta Alpar, were in the audience, they could always be persuaded by the crowd to sing their most famous melodies during intermission. It was all in the family. Small wonder that later Hitler often requisitioned the Sportpalast for his most important speeches.

Berlin's sports heroes of the twenties were Paavo Nurmi, the Finnish runner; Arne Borg, the Swedish swimmer; America's Bill Tilden of tennis; Norway's Sonja Henie of skating; foreigners all, but immediately and affectionately adopted by Berlin. Everyone knew that Tilden's racquets were strung with purple gut. Tiny Sonja Henie became Häseken, the baby hare. Nurmi's name was part of the Berliner's language. Any thief who was chased by the cops "ran like Nurmi."

Nowhere else was there such a love affair between a big metropolitan city and its film people. The premiers of *Blue Angel, The Cabinet of Dr. Caligari, All Quiet on the Western Front, Mädchen in Uniform,* and *The Congress Dances* became events of tremendous importance, and, in the case of *All Quiet,* of political rioting. The Nazis considered the war novel by Remarque and the film that followed it to be "pacifist treason to the brave men who fought and died" and an "unpatriotic slander to their sacred memory." The theater had to cancel some performances to avoid riots. Peter Lorre, Luise Rainer, Elisabeth Bergner, Marlene Dietrich, Conrad Veidt, Pola Negri, Emil Jannings, and even the Swedish Greta Garbo were all launched in Berlin, as were the directors Ernst Lubitsch, George William Pabst, and Billy Wilder.

Theater? The names Max Reinhardt, Erwin Piscator, Bertolt Brecht, Kurt Weill, evoke new, sometimes jarring ways to present famous pieces. Bert Brecht's *Threepenny Opera* and *Mahagonny,* once called monstrous and repetitious, have become classics. The Bauhaus and its multinational stars stunned the world of architecture. Ludwig Mies van der Rohe, Walter Gropius, Erich Mendelsohn, shaped new offices and dwellings from concrete and glass. The world still is influenced by Bauhaus architects, although Hitler, an architectural dilettante, damned flat roofs as "oriental" and the use of glass and concrete as "foreign." Berlin's painters of that time were usually political. George Grosz, Käthe Kollwitz, Otto Dix, Christian Schad, were all pacifists and bitter critics of Germany's upper strata. Their exhibitions were usually political events. (In the long run, the nonpolitical artists' names of the time became more famous: Oskar Kokoschka, Paul Klee, Emil Nolde.) The conductors Wilhelm Furtwängler, Werner Klemperer, and Bruno Walter, the composer Arnold Schönberg, and the Berlin Philharmonic brought music lovers of the world to Berlin. There was also a mediocre violinist named Albert Einstein.

In the Berlin of the twenties and thirties the automobile was king, just as it was in New York, London, and Paris. But Berlin was also married to motor sports. Great race drivers became the spoiled, much-invited darlings of Berlin society. Every schoolboy knew the German champion "Karatsch" (Caracciola, a German despite his Italian name) and his personal white two-seater supercharged SSKL Mercedes, license number 1A—4444. Twice each year the AVUS road, normally a wide highway to the wealthy suburbs, became an automobile race-track, and over 100,000 Berliners flocked to watch Karatsch and the other German aces race against the French, the Italians (Signor Ferrari was the team manager for Alfa Romeo), and the English.

Mercedes-Benz was the "prestige" car, preferably the big Kompressor (supercharged) one with its tubular outside exhausts; that is, unless one was rich enough to own an American Packard, which was considered *prima*. In fact, most American and English fads or stars were *prima*, from Josephine Baker to "Yes, we have no bananas" *(Ausgerechnet Bananen)*. The Charleston was danced, cocktails were offered, and the very worldly, the very rich, and the very dissolute sniffed cocaine. The Berlin versions of New York's vaudeville or London's revues were Berlin's Varieté, complete with long-legged English chorus girls. Berlin loved the English. To excuse anything lopsided, Berliners said, "Lopsided is English, and English is modern" *(Schief ist englisch und englisch ist modern)*. Many Berliners bought cheap cars, Opels and DKWs, and they got them *auf Stottern* (literally, "stuttering") or in installments. No matter how precarious the economy, Berlin's roads were always jammed on weekends as people streamed out of the city to *das Grüne,* the beloved outdoors. Working-class families made day excursions to the nearby lakes and woods. The rich owned villas on the beautiful lake called Wannsee, where they played tennis, danced, sailed, played golf, and partied.

Later, Berlin's mania for automobile racing became one of Adolf Hitler's favorite propaganda tools. Hitler himself was a second-to-none enthusiast of the automobile, with a superstitious preference for Mercedes; once when he was a passenger in a Mercedes that was involved in an accident, the other car was demolished, but the Mercedes survived easily.

His regime gave massive subsidies to Germany's two all-conquering Grand Prix teams, Mercedes-Benz and Auto Union. (The old Auto Union four-ring symbol is used today by one of its former brands, Audi.) Foreigners were impressed by German might and efficiency, and millions of Europeans got their first view of blitzkrieg-style action by watching Germany's 600-horsepower Mercedes or Auto Union's race cars thunder past their cowed opponents.

Later, in 1938, a blue French Delahaye driven by the French champion driver René Dreyfus (the symbolic Jewish name) beat a Mercedes in a race at Pau in front of a delirious French crowd. But no one around Hitler took the sportsmanlike view. It was one of the few times German race cars lost.

Hitler was involved even with car design. The original drawings for the Volkswagen were Hitler's own sketches. He asked that the engineering be done by Professor Ferdinand Porsche, his favorite automotive designer.

But all of Berlin's playful revival of the twenties could not hide its economic ills. A 1923 edition of *Berliner Illustrirte,* a weekly news magazine, carried this "medical" essay on the illnesses of Europe:

> Britain: two million unemployed. France: excessive military costs and a decrease in the birth rate. Spain: troubles in Morocco and a vast deficit. Italy: border disputes and weak currency. Switzerland: recession. Austria: negative trade balance. Czechoslovakia: economic crisis. Hungary: constitutional crisis. The Balkans: political confusion. Greece: near civil war. Turkey: depression from 10 years of war. Poland: currency problems and internal conflicts. Russia: economic collapse, epidemic, and hunger. Lithuania, Latvia, and Estonia: baby countries with severe teething problems. Norway, Sweden, and Denmark: recession. And Germany? in the middle of it all lies the carrier of the infection, Germany, which has been inoculated with the pestilential bacillus of Versailles. *
>
> No one wishes to administer the necessary antidote, yet everyone wonders why they can hear a death rattle all over Europe.

Berlin newspaper photos from the same year show long queues for even the most staple of foods. The elderly waited in the snow in front of Salvation Army soup kitchens, and crippled veterans marched for their rights.

Even angry American war veterans were massing in front of the White House. Perhaps to these hopelessly hungry and unemployed citizens of Europe and the United States, the Soviet option was ap-

*The Treaty of Versailles.

pealing, but the democratic standpoint was not ignored. On November 7, 1927, this was *Berliner Illustrirte*'s commentary on the tenth anniversary of the Soviet Union: "The Soviet Union started with the bloody torso of the Russian colossus. Finland was lost. Poland was lost, also Estonia, Latvia, and Lithuania, which had depended economically on Russia while providing her with access to the sea. Another blow was the repossession of Bessarabia by Romania. Lost also was the concept of 'Russia.'"

The article then expressed its admiration for Soviet achievement against these odds, but pointed out the obvious penalties of the Leninist system: loss of personal freedoms without proportional increases in the standard of living, and the economic and intellectual penalties of ideological isolation.

The specter of a Soviet-sponsored revolt continued to haunt middle- and upper-class Germans. Other nations soon would be confronted with depression, unemployment, hunger strikes, and demonstrations, but the western nations had developed certain democratic skills and had few delusions about their system of government. They knew that the democratic system was often harsh and disappointing and that it tested the patience of even its most enthusiastic advocates.

Most Germans knew little about the discipline and patience required by a democracy under economic attack. Unlike their grandchildren, the Germans of the twenties had never tasted the rewards of a successful capitalist republic, nor did Germany's conquerors have twentieth-century minds. The Treaty of Versailles was written with a nineteenth-century pen.

In the late twenties, Joachim von Ribbentrop was a successful young entrepreneur who had built a wide circle of business friends abroad. He never missed the opportunity during these trips to "convince foreign friends of the senselessness and dangers of the Versailles Treaty." He complained that "only a few foreigners understood. They hid behind those concepts which felt comfortable for the victors."

He also met some foreign diplomats through business friends and invited them to Dahlem, where he could "speak unencumbered by official position."[15]

In 1924, Weinhandlungsgesellschaft, his Berlin firm, had a practical monopoly on the sale of Henkell champagne. He had persuaded Baron de Mum of Pommery French Champagne and Sir Alexander Walker of Johnny Walker Scotch Whisky to appoint his firm as their exclusive agent. Von Ribbentrop's senior partners were two men named Muther and Schönberg. Muther died in 1924, and Schönberg, a gambler, soon got into trouble. Otto Henkell paid off Schönberg's debts, with the proviso that Joachim von Ribbentrop would become a senior partner, so the name of the firm was changed to Schönberg und Ribbentrop, IMPEGROMA (acronym for Importers of Great Brands, in German).

After January 1, 1924, when Germany lifted all import restrictions, the firm prospered.[16] Eventually, on October 17, 1931, the partnership was dissolved, and von Ribbentrop became the sole owner. Even in the midst of diplomacy, he stayed the businessman and believed in old business friendships. When France fell in 1940, de Mum of Pommery became head of the French Champagne Group. IMPEGROMA, run for him by a Henkell family member, lasted well into the Nazi time, securing the von Ribbentrop fortune even while von Ribbentrop held major government positions. (In 1940, after the conquest of France, the Berlin telephone listing for IMPEGROMA was still Pallas 3747.)

In the Berlin of the late twenties, the von Ribbentrops continued to battle for their place in society. Annelies von Ribbentrop was the driving force. She was determined that the von Ribbentrops and their children would be accepted as full members of Berlin's top group. It is astonishing how many people who knew them or were part of their circle insist that Annelies von Ribbentrop was the "evil influence behind" Joachim von Ribbentrop's final desperate journey through life.

Trying to create contacts among Berlin's foreign diplomats, they met the much-liked American ambassador Jacob Gould Schurman, who introduced them to Lord D'Abernon, the British ambassador. An invitation to the British Embassy was considered a social achievement, and they badgered the British envoy by "leaving their card."

D'Abernon finally had them assigned to the rather inclusive R list (Receptions only).[17]

Von Ribbentrop's explanation of his new *von* met with varying degrees of success. To a French business friend, Count Polignac, he hinted that it had been given retroactively as a reward for bravery in the war, an unlikely action by a republican Germany, which accepted his *von* merely as an addition to his name, with no implication of nobility.[18]

Von Ribbentrop's first attempt to join Berlin's exclusive Union Club on Schadowstrasse failed when he was blackballed. The Union Club's membership ranged from royalty to untitled bankers, and the members were Protestant, Catholic, and Jewish. But it observed its taboos, such as adding a *von* for social advancement. Von Papen, his old acquaintance from Turkey, persuaded the admissions committee to reverse its decision.[19] Ever the businessman, von Ribbentrop made it a point to cultivate some of the distinguished Jewish bankers who were members, men like the Weinbergs, Oppenheims, Goldschmidt-Rothschilds, von Friedlander-Fulds, and the Herzfelds. Among the other members, he already knew Herbert Guttmann through business, and Ottmar Strauss had been one of his early patrons after the war. At one point, the von Ribbentrops had so many Jewish friends that Count Oskar von Platen-Hallermund, a former chamberlain to the Kaiser, said to the amusement of a dinner party, "Ribbentrop, it seems I'm the only Christian friend you have!"[20]

At the Union Club von Ribbentrop also met some of the young titled members of the Foreign Service, the attachés.

The matter of von Ribbentrop's anti-Semitism in his pre-Hitler days is moot. It seems improbable that he was an anti-Semite early in his Berlin career days or early in his marriage.[21] The Henkells, like most international business families, had close Jewish connections. A surviving member of the family reports that Otto Henkell's sister was married into a Rhineland Jewish family named Opfermann. Her husband was on the board of directors of Henkell. Opfermann, a World War I veteran with an Iron Cross, was a great German patriot. The Henkell family lawyer, Dr. Oppenheim, was also a Jew, as was von Ribbentrop's personal family secretary, Susie Fried. She remained his secretary all through the Nazi period. After the war, she worked for the Michel branch of the family, and she died in Freiburg about 1960. "I have no idea," said a relative, a man now in his fifties, "whether Annelies was ever aware that Susie Fried was Jewish." In the Berlin of the twenties and early thirties it was almost impossible for a socially ambitious couple not to develop some Jewish contacts, although there were only 150,000 Jews among Berlin's four million citizens.

Among the city's most charming couples, the arbiters of a certain level of civilized Berlin society, were Freddy and Lali Horstmann. Freddy, a professional diplomat and a long-time member of the Auswärtiges Amt, the Foreign Ministry, had held many key posts abroad. He was independently wealthy and an avid collector of objéts d'art and attractive people. Lali, *née* von Schwabach, was the daughter of a banker friend of the Kaiser's who was an honorary British consul and one of the few foreigners to wear the British Order of the Garter. The von Schwabachs were Jewish. In his foreword to Lali Horstmann's memoirs, Harold Nicolson wrote that during a time when Prussia's pouting aristocrats and military people refrained from entertaining foreigners, the Horstmanns' Berlin home was an international haven of civilized dining and conversation.[22] Their mansion on the Tiergartenstrasse was the scene of memorable parties. Horstmann, a former minister to Belgium and Portugal, headed the British desk at the ministry, and many foreign diplomats were devoted to him and to Lali. The Horstmanns also owned an exquisite country estate.

They entertained the most beautiful women, the most charming men, the greatest wits, the most creative writers and artists. Members of the younger set were invited after dinner to dance to the latest American tunes, and a white-gloved footman serviced the wind-up record player. Somehow, the young von Ribbentrops got invited to the Horstmanns' and finally met some of those elusive Berliners they had longed to know. The young Russian Princess "Missie" Vassiltchikov, who lived in Berlin during the Nazi time, wrote of evenings of "subtle defiance" of the "Brown Regime" after Freddy Horstmann resigned his ministry post in silent protest.[23]

A former Berlin society débutante, *née* von Richthofen, who now lives in California, used to attend these soirées. She said that after the Horstmanns were bombed out of their large home in Berlin, they moved into a tiny apartment and remained the city's favorite hosts.

Freddy Horstmann's life ended in tragedy. Bombed out of Berlin and their country estate, Kerzendorf, the Horstmanns hid in the nearby woods while the Red Army approached. At Freddy's insistence, Lali escaped toward Berlin, but he refused to leave his treasures. He was captured by the Russians and starved to death in captivity. Lali escaped to England with the help of her many western friends.

Bubi von Schwabach, Lali's brother, once wrote to Ambassador Joachim von Ribbentrop in London, begging for help. He wanted to leave Germany. He received no reply. Von Ribbentrop told his secretary, Reinhard Spitzy, "You know how the Führer feels about such things! I can't speak to him about Jews."[24] Von Schwabach was one of many old friends who were let down by von Ribbentrop.

At the very beginning of the Nazi period, von Ribbentrop often seemed to misjudge Hitler's purpose and aims. He told worried Jewish acquaintances and business friends, "Don't take Hitler's anti-Semitic talk too seriously. It's only a political gesture. It's aimed at the eastern Jews, not at German Jews. Everyone knows that German Jews lost a higher percentage of men during the war than Germany's aristocrats."[25] The day after the first anti-Jewish boycott, April 1, 1933, when Storm Troopers stood in front of Jewish stores bullying "Ar-

yans" not to buy from Jews, Ribbentrop, still essentially a businessman with tenuous Nazi connections, invited several Jewish social and
business friends to a "reassurance" lunch at the Hotel Adlon. He was
immediately denounced by Nazis who saw him there, and Hitler
summoned him and reprimanded him for his "offense." Von Ribbentrop came out of that meeting in shock.

In 1930, three years before Hitler seized power, von Ribbentrop
was still much involved with Jews both socially and professionally, so
when Count Helldorf, his old regimental friend and now a Nazi
bigshot, suggested he join the Nazi Party, he could not do so without
business risk. He did not join then, but he had discovered the thrilling
and dangerous world of radical politics. Here, in his own words, was
his reasoning:

> Since 1929 the German economy had been approaching a crisis. The
> screws of the Versailles reparations were too tight. Gold reserves
> shrank, and our balance of payments slid. There were millions of
> unemployed, and investment capital fled abroad. By 1930 it looked as
> if Germany would fall to the Communists. I was convinced that only
> National Socialism could save us. I watched the collapse of the mod-
> erate political parties. I suspected that you got nowhere without force.
> Only when catastrophe brewed did we get concessions. I did not wish
> to involve myself in politics but was forced to help in forming a
> coalition between my party, the DNVP [the right-wing National Party
> he had joined in the late twenties] and the NSDAP [the Nazi Party,
> which he joined on May 1, 1932].

It is difficult, though, to guess the truth about the von Ribbentrops'
attraction to right-wing politics. No doubt in part it was a matter of
conviction. After all, Joachim was a former officer, the son of an
Imperial officer and the grandson of an Imperial officer, and he resented the lost war and Germany's vanished international prestige.
But there was also opportunism and self-promotion. By touting anti-
Communism, one could be guaranteed the attention of the "best"
people. The von Ribbentrops began what one of their former neighbors described as a "political salon." Many prominent Berliners, some
friendly with the von Ribbentrops, others only casual acquaintances,
were invited to their villa on Lentzeallee in Dahlem, where they met
and listened to various right-wing politicians of all shadings who
offered their plans for a "cleansed and pure" Germany, a strong and
rearmed Germany, a Germany with its "prewar honor" restored. Their
simplistic theories promised an end to the years of submission, compromise, and empty debate, an end to the stringent penalties. The war
would have been won but for a "stab in the back," or *Dolchstoss,* a

favorite nationalist explanation for Germany's seemingly inexplicable collapse in 1918, although it is generally acknowledged that Germany was near bankruptcy and unable to continue more than two weeks when it agreed to the Armistice. This new Germany would regain its rightful place among Europe's great powers. Most of all: beware of the Bolshevist plague!

The von Ribbentrops became important hosts. They offered their guests, along with a serving of right-wing politics, an attractive evening in a civilized household.

Meanwhile, the wine business prospered, the two von Ribbentrop children were a joy, the house was filled with interesting guests, and if the family in Wiesbaden was still aloof, that could not be helped. Annelies had proved her point. Joachim and she had made their life a success. It was not the first nor the last time that insecure *arrivistes* had used political radicalism to further their social ambitions.

On the twenty-ninth of October 1929, the *New York Times*'s front page read: EUROPE IS DISTURBED BY AMERICAN ACTION ON OCCUPATION DEBT; immediately to the right of that headline:

STOCK PRICES SLUMP 14,000,000,000 IN
NATION-WIDE STAMPEDE TO UNLOAD.
BANKERS TO SUPPORT MARKET TODAY.

Other stories that day: "French troops withdraw from the Rhineland after a settlement in the Hague."

"Arabs attack Jews in Palestine after an argument over use of the Wailing Wall."

"Hitler appoints Heinrich Himmler to head the SS."

"Russia, Poland, Romania, Estonia, and Latvia sign a pact condemning war . . ."

A few months later, in 1930, Germany suffered the consequences of the disaster on New York's Wall Street. The American bill would have to be paid, and all the world's countries rowed on the same monetary lake. The wave set off by the New York stock market crash upset the precarious financial balance of war-battered Europe. That included the struggling, vulnerable new Republic of Germany.

In the 1930 parliamentary elections, Hitler's NSDAP won 107 seats, the largest single bloc, though not a majority. To control them, President von Hindenburg chose the conservative Heinrich Brüning as chancellor, in the hope that he could form a coalition government of the right.

German patience was wearing thin. After years of upheaval, everyone wanted stability. Both the Nazis and the Communists promised political and economic solutions, but the Nazis looked for support from Germany's powerful middle and upper class by playing on their fear of Bolshevism. Many Germans, unskilled in self-determination, were fearful of a democratic system that gave the ultimate responsibility to the individual citizen. Britain and France were long accustomed to the laborious movement of the wheels of representative government, and the United States had never known any other system. But in twentieth-century Germany, an immature, forty-three-year-old Bismarckian empire had been replaced by an even less mature republic. Germans who felt betrayed by the Kaiser did not yet trust their new government. They were accustomed to leaders who were strong and decisive, who embodied the "soldierly qualities." As it said in the old cavalry song: "On the field of battle man still has worth" *(Im Felde, da ist ja der Mann noch was wert)*.

Can one generalize about the Germans of those decades? And yet many a German university graduate proudly wore his dueling *Schmiss,* the facial scar attesting to supposed "courage when faced with cold steel," a barbarous anachronism of German university life. University dueling *(Schlagen)* was conducted in an almost token manner so that only the cheeks could get scarred. Fighting stopped at first blood, and cuts were specially treated to produce scars. The dueling societies were *Brüderschaften,* fraternities. This form of Teutonism also appealed to certain German Jews. Many Jewish university graduates had scarred cheeks.

In its most extreme form, it even produced bitter anti-Semitism among Jews. A Berliner named Max Naumann, a decorated World War officer and a Jew, was a member of the DNVP (the same nationalist organization as von Ribbentrop).[26] He agitated for the total assimilation of Jews into the body of Germany — if they were pure German Jews. He formed an organization called the League of Jews of German Nationality, which advocated the expulsion of "eastern" Jews from Germany as "harmful bacteria in the body of the nation." In 1935, the Gestapo eliminated his organization as "enemies of the state." Naumann died in Berlin in 1939.

The Berlin of 1931 in which the von Ribbentrops were advancing to prominence was now the seat of the Brüning government. Heinrich Brüning was a controlled, introverted man who headed the Catholic Center Party. Von Hindenburg unrealistically expected that Brüning could block the Nazis while holding off the Communists. Abroad, Brüning was supposed to arrange an end of the heavy Versailles reparations. Economically, Brüning was expected to stem the shock wave of the 1929 earthquake that began on Wall Street. Few men would have been equal to the task. Brüning was cool and judicious, unemotional and rational, eliciting neither popular support nor enthusiasm. To stem the economic downturn, he took all the right emergency steps, but the medicine tasted too bitter. To deflate the heated economy, he reduced wages and pensions, infuriating the workers and the fixed-income, lower-middle-class pensioners. Price control angered the farmers. Controls over banking upset the financial people. He wanted to break up the subsidized and debt-ridden Junker land holdings into smaller, individually farmed parcels, and angered the landed gentry who were part of von Hindenburg's own set. Brüning could not last, and he did not last.

For the 1932 presidential election Hitler, who had finally become a German citizen, on February 25, decided to challenge von Hindenburg for the presidency: the Austrian corporal against the Prussian field marshal.* Von Hindenburg was narrowly re-elected on March 13. The slim margin was a shock. Worse, Hitler was supported by many of the same right-wingers who had originally installed von Hindenburg. The marshal could not have won without cooperation between the liberals and the hated Communists. What uncomfortable allies these were for von Hindenburg! Nevertheless, Brüning, ever the unemotional intellectual, was pleased. He had preserved his patron. The Nazis won majorities in the next regional elections, and the president would no longer support Brüning. On May 30, 1932, Brüning resigned.

The great French statesman and wit André François-Poncet, who was then the French ambassador in Berlin, wrote:

> Brüning's errors were typically German. He did not realize that the praise he got abroad rendered him suspect at home. He never realized to what pitch of blind fanaticism nationalist passion might rise, a frenzy too fierce to be assuaged by any victories he might have won. He tried the velvet glove. The Germans preferred the mailed fist. He was repelled by the drastic and brutal methods which would have saved him. He had two excellent opportunities to smash the Nazis: they were twice discovered planning treason and insurrection. Arms were found and plans for a coup d'état. Everything could be proved. But Brüning would not smash his opponents.[27]

General Wilhelm Gröner, the minister of war, had no such scruples. He persuaded the president to let him ban the SA, the Storm

---

*The province of Brunswick appointed Hitler state counsellor, thereby granting him citizenship.

Troopers, and he did so on April 13. His troops also raided their barracks. But Gröner found no support from his own colleagues, and von Hindenburg soon reversed himself. On June 14 the Storm Troopers were back on the streets in all their brown-uniformed strength. While Brüning had tried to govern Germany, the right-wingers had consolidated. On a raw autumn day in October 1931, in the old Harz Mountain spa of Bad Harzburg, a fierce assembly of nationalists came together for the first time. Leading the factions were Hitler and his SA. Then came the nationalist Stahlhelm (Steel Helmet) group and their chief, the fat Alfred Hugenberg. There was also flotsam: the Pan-German League with their boss, Heinrich Class, a lawyer, and the right-wing General Count Kolmar von der Goltz with the obscure Vaterländischer Bund patriotic party.

But there were also individuals of great prestige: the banker Hjalmar Schacht, the steel industrialist Ernst Poensgen, white-mustached General Hans von Seeckt, the founder of the Reichswehr, and a group of Nazi-prone royals: the Duke of Saxe-Coburg, Prince William of Lippe, and Prince Eitel Friedrich, a son of the Kaiser. This was the first time that men of such seeming substance had endorsed Adolf Hitler's plans for Germany by their presence.

The months between this Congress of Harzburg in 1931 and Brüning's resignation in 1932 had set the stage: Adolf Hitler's coming was now imminent. The end of democracy was at hand. In his Nürnberg memoirs von Ribbentrop wrote, "To my foreign friends I said: give Brüning a chance and he may succeed. Scuttle him and we will be Nazi or Communist."

Like millions of their countrymen, the von Ribbentrops were about to face drastic changes. Their pre-Hitler days were over.

BOOK **II**

7

HITLER TO 1934

Hidden Fantasies

BRÜNING WAS GONE, and the new chancellor was von Ribbentrop's old friend von Papen, whom he had known since the days in Turkey and who had sponsored him for the Union Club.

Von Papen was a member of the Catholic gentry, a man whose style pleased von Hindenburg. The President was sure von Papen could do it all: block Hitler, get the support of industry, repulse the Bolshevists, deal with the French and the English. Von Papen had formed a cabinet, snidely known as the Barons' Cabinet because the members were almost all titled. They were taken seriously by no one and ignored by friend and foe.[1] These were not the men to grapple with the monstrous problems facing Germany. Von Hindenburg had misjudged, badly.

There was one man in the cabinet whose firm hand could have saved the day, Defense Minister Kurt von Schleicher, an able man, a soldier-politician, and the natural choice to follow von Hindenburg. Von Papen was aware of the challenge, and, being vain and ambitious, was about to make a compromise with the devil to keep his chancellorship. He asked his old protégé von Ribbentrop to "go down to Bavaria to see if this fellow Hitler could be talked into some sort of coalition." In his memoirs, von Ribbentrop wrote about his own political situation and views. He was then a member of DVP (Deutsche Volks Partei), (formerly the DNVP). Because of the economic turmoil, "I did not want to involve myself in politics but found myself wishing that I could help to form a coalition between DVP and the National Socialists."

It all sounded understandable, rational, even laudable. He owed von Papen favors. Besides, he was probably flattered that the chancellor of the German Republic would ask him, a business executive, to undertake this delicate mission. Like most Germans, he knew a good deal about the external Hitler, the man with the Austro-Bavarian accent who expressed in severe terms the simplistic solutions everyone wanted. Many Germans of the working class and lower middle class found in him a "German" option to Communism, which seemed somehow foreign because its red heart beat in Moscow. Among the higher German social echelons, Hitler caused the chills people feel when they secretly admire brutal solutions. He appealed to the hidden thug that can be found behind many civilized faces.

In all probability, von Ribbentrop set out for Berchtesgaden with some snobbish disdain for the semi-educated former lance corporal he was to meet. After all, von Ribbentrop was more eager than most to guard his own social status, and he was going there to speak for a lordly chancellor.

He traveled to Munich and then up into the mountains to a chalet called Haus Wachenfeld, which Hitler had bought with the help of his admirers. Wachenfeld was a pretty place, formerly a vacation villa in the Bavarian farm style, near Berchtesgaden, with stunning views of the mountains and the valleys below. It was soon to become the center of the compound known as the Berghof, which can be seen in many photographs of the Hitler era.

Von Ribbentrop's mission for von Papen was to convince Hitler to join the chancellor's cabinet as vice chancellor. This would block Defense Minister von Schleicher. Also, von Papen would have formed the conservative coalition he had promised von Hindenburg and would be able to control Hitler by having him close at hand.

Von Ribbentrop had never met Hitler; no one knows exactly what happened to change the life of a man as seemingly assured as von Ribbentrop. After all, from boyhood to Canadian entrepreneurship, from life as a young Prussian officer to wealthy Berlin internationalist, Joachim von Ribbentrop had taken good care of his own fate and fortune. According to his account, he was "convinced" by Hitler.

And it was an angry Hitler who greeted him. Von Ribbentrop was immediately told that Hitler wanted no part of a deal with von Papen. Instead, he believed in von Schleicher, because "one can trust a German general."[2] Politics or the truth? Was he threatening von Papen with von Schleicher, or did he really believe in the general? Any doubts in von Ribbentrop's mind were removed by a classic Hitlerian technique. Somehow, Adolf Hitler frequently found the energy to explain himself to listeners by pouring out his views, his dreams, his arguments, in an hours-long, drama-filled barrage of words. These "lectures," dissertations, verbal assaults, were aimed, instinctively, at the vulnerable core of the audience, which might range in size from ten thousand to the one person sitting in front of him. No matter how often people have tried to describe their personal impressions of Hitler, they invariably speak of his powers to convince through this combination of seeming logic and brute force.

Von Ribbentrop had never dealt with anyone who so touched the best and the worst in him. Hitler must have reached the hidden fantasies, both brutal and vainglorious, that Joachim von Ribbentrop had harbored but was too embarrassed, too "mannerly," and too conservative to express. After two hours of Adolf Hitler's verbal pounding, he was convinced, converted, and devoted.

Hitler finally said he might be willing to join a coalition and become vice chancellor.

When von Ribbentrop brought this answer back to von Papen, the chancellor rushed to sell President von Hindenburg on the idea. He failed abysmally. The old man snorted, "That Bohemian corporal?" and refused even to consider it. Von Papen's cabinet soon fell, and on December 3, 1932, von Schleicher became chancellor. Despite von Ribbentrop's failure in Berchtesgaden, Hitler had convinced him he was the right man for the future of Germany.[3]

Von Ribbentrop, "drunk" with Hitler's ideas, donated six thousand marks to the NSDAP, which he had joined in May at the urging of his old regimental comrade Count von Helldorf.[4] The handsome von Helldorf was a crook, one of several black-sheep aristocrats who had become part of the Nazi coterie following his service in the 12th Torgau Hussars, where he was one of the regiment's youngest officers. After the Armistice, like many other unemployed ex-officers, he joined one of the roving Freikorps, the semimilitary groups that attached themselves to right-wing political parties. Naturally, he took part in the Kapp putsch. When that failed, he joined the Storm Troopers, where he quickly reached high rank. The proletarian SA and its brawling captain, Ernst Röhm, always tried to recruit ex-officers and aristocrats, which helped to mask their reputation as thugs. After the Nazi takeover, von Helldorf blackmailed several Jews and then gambled away the money on horses at the Jockey Club in Berlin.[5] Göring, who appreciated scoundrels, helped von Helldorf to become chief of the Berlin police in 1935. It is even possible that von Helldorf, at Göring's instructions, took part in the planning of the infamous 1933 Reichstag fire.[6] In May of 1932 he was delighted to help the new Hitler convert, von Ribbentrop, become a party member. It was von Ribbentrop's first public commitment to the Nazi movement.

To von Ribbentrop's disappointment, his new hero, Hitler, now ignored him, despite their lengthy meeting in Berchtesgaden. After all, Joachim and Annelies von Ribbentrop were people to be reckoned with in better Berlin circles, and his having joined the Nazi Party constituted something of an endorsement. Nevertheless, there was nothing but silence from the man in Bavaria.

Annelies, who was pregnant, hated von Helldorf — he had often borrowed money from them — and she wished that they had better contacts with the party.[7] The breakthrough came after a small stag dinner, a *Herrendiner* at the home of Prince Wied, where von Helldorf introduced von Ribbentrop to Count Vico von Bülow-Schwante, another titled reprobate and Hitler satellite.[*]

One day Hitler complained to von Bülow-Schwante that he wanted to read the London and Paris papers. If only someone could translate! Von Bülow-Schwante, probably with the hope of receiving the grateful thanks of the rich von Ribbentrops, suggested to Hitler that the right man was von Ribbentrop. Not only did Joachim speak foreign languages, but the von Ribbentrops were a wealthy, worldly couple with many connections abroad. They were part of Berlin's upper crust, to which they could introduce the party and its Führer. Even more important, they could make the Führer known to influential Londoners and Parisians. He showed Hitler some of the circular letters about the new Germany that von Ribbentrop had been distributing to his friends and acquaintances abroad. Hitler was impressed. In 1946, at the War Crimes Trials in Nürnberg, von Bülow-Schwante claimed that he introduced von Ribbentrop to Hitler at a Prince Wied dinner in 1930, two years earlier. He is said to have complained, "I introduced Joachim to the Führer, and now he's foreign minister, and I'm out of a job!"[8] However, the 1932 date in Berchtesgaden seems more likely.

Von Bülow-Schwante's idea worked. Hitler finally showed some interest in von Ribbentrop. He accepted several of his invitations to small dinners *en famille* in Dahlem. While Joachim held forth on the ways of influential London and Paris, Annelies gently coached the gauche Austrian in the art of table manners. She usually avoided having other guests because Hitler "was not someone you could invite anyone with."[9] For Hitler, it was a glimpse into a new world. He

[*]Von Bülow-Schwante was dismissed from the Foreign Ministry for being caught *in flagrante delicto* in a train compartment with a well-known lady. Prince Wied was head of a small principality and eager to gain influence. His family once held the Albanian crown for less than a year. He was one of Hitler's aristocrat followers.

relished the well-run household, the tasteful furnishings, the carefully trained servants and beautiful grounds. He was delighted with the *kultivierte* atmosphere. He agreed with von Bülow-Schwante that the von Ribbentrops would be important to the future of the movement.

Occasionally, Annelies did invite a few carefully selected guests to meet Hitler: the von Bülow-Schwantes came, as did Joachim's father, Colonel Richard Ribbentrop, who was not impressed with Hitler's pomposities. The Henkells were never invited.[9] Joachim and Annelies probably feared that the imperious monocled Käthe Henkell would turn the evening into a shambles. One of the few genuine society couples they asked were Count and Countess Alexander Dörnberg. She was a school friend of Annelies's, and red-haired Alexander von Dörnberg, known as *der lange Sandro* or the Red Tower, was related to many royals, including the Battenbergs, who later changed the name to Mountbatten. The von Dörnbergs stayed close to the von Ribbentrops for years and became part of the embassy staff in London.

Whenever he visited Lentzeallee 7–9, Hitler probably felt that he deserved better from life than the crude, beer-brawling world of his old Nazi cronies. Besides, Annelies spoiled him with special fruit from Rollenhagen, the Fortnum & Mason of Berlin, and the kind of flower arrangements Hitler loved.[10]

What Hitler "magic" had bewitched Joachim von Ribbentrop? Some men never found it, among them Sir Nevile Henderson, Britain's ambassador to the Reich during the fateful late thirties. He wrote: "Many Germans, women in particular, used to descant to me upon the radiance of his expression and his remarkable eyes. I must confess he never gave me any impression of greatness. He was a spellbinder for his own people. To the last, I continued to ask myself how he had risen to what he was and how he maintained his ascendance over the German people."[11]

Others were completely enthralled, but in truth there was hardly a secure, intelligent person who fell completely under Adolf Hitler's spell. His closest associates, almost without exception, seemed flawed. Some others, like Schacht, the banker, stayed rational in his presence and used him opportunistically. Still others were less charmed than plain frightened. This is how André François-Poncet described the Führer:

A pale face, globular eyes, the faraway look of a medium or a somnambulist. At other times, animated, colorful, swept away with passion and violence. Impatient of control, bold, cynical, energetic. Sometimes a 'Storm and Assault' face, the face of lunatic! At other times naïve, rustic, dull, vulgar, easily amused, a thigh-slapper, a face like a thousand other faces.

Sometimes he was all three in one conversation. He ranted on for ten minutes, a half hour, three quarters of an hour. Then he was exhausted. At that time one could speak, and he would even smile. He was no normal human being, a morbid, quasi-mad Dostoyevsky figure, a man possessed. He was an Austrian with a passionate love for Germany, wildly romantic, full of half-baked theories of Houston Stewart Chamberlain, Nietzsche, Spengler. He wanted a new Germany to replace the Holy Roman Empire, a purified race, an elite. He lived Wagner!

A dreamer but a cold-blooded realist and schemer. He was *lazy* and hated regular work. He wanted oral information, not written reports. He allowed great freedom but knew every move his collaborators made. He willed or tolerated every excess, all crimes. He used intuition for the sudden power of decision. He was tied to the masses and had contempt for them. He lulled opponents by signing treaties while planning to wriggle out of them.[12]

François-Poncet believed Hitler eventually failed because of "pride, swollen out of proportion by success and flattery. His success since the beginning convinced him that Providence protected him. He was antireligious but the elect of the Almighty. The stars had told him that he would have success and then suffer disaster. He counted on only ten years."

This was the man Joachim von Ribbentrop had first met in Berchtesgaden. Now, he thought, he and Annelies had "tamed" him. They were not the last people who mistakenly thought they had secured Adolf Hitler's admiration, his thanks, and good will. At the end, of all the dozens of these men who were closest to their Führer, only Goebbels would be there in the bunker under the Chancellery to share his fate. The others all made the error of thinking that Adolf Hitler cared for them, and they learned at last that he cared for no one, not even the German people. He wanted to consign them all to death for not choosing to follow him to a fiery, Wagnerian end. His last orders were to destroy everything and to flood the Berlin subways, where tens of thousands had taken shelter.

After Brüning's resignation in May 1932, it is unlikely that von Ribbentrop saw more than the surface ripples on the ocean of intrigue, politics, and short-lived alliances of the second half of the year. The choice of Franz von Papen, with his conservative views, his promise to control the Nazis and Communists, and his assurance that he would deal with the insufferable reparations of the Versailles Treaty, protected the staunchly Protestant von Hindenburg from any accusations of anti-Catholicism. But von Papen failed to keep the President's confidence. The Storm Troops, banned under Brüning, were legitimated once more by von Hindenburg at the suggestion of von Papen. He negotiated with the French and came up with a treaty to pay French reparations in a few discounted lump sums, which raised unending protests. His promised battle against Nazi influence seemed unnecessary, because the Nazis suddenly lost votes in the November 1932 elections. Von Papen's own cabinet soon disowned him, and von Hindenburg reluctantly dismissed him. Part of the farewell was a signed, framed photograph of the marshal inscribed with the first words of the old German soldier's lament: *"Ich hatt einen Kameraden"* (I once had a comrade).

His successor, General Schleicher, was half soldier, half politician. Since 1920, when the General Staff assigned him to be a political expert, he had developed his own plans for the future of Germany. After the Nazis lost votes in late 1932, von Schleicher approached one of Hitler's more moderate rivals in the Nazi Party, Gregor Strasser, in an attempt to split the Nazis. He also tried to attract the cooperation of the labor unions. On December 3, 1932, he took charge, but he too did not last. Hitler regained a firm hold over his Nazis, and the labor unions defected from a coalition with the general. Like most European republics, the Weimar Republic was ruled by prime ministers (chancellors) who depended on coalition governments that could be challenged for "no confidence" and often had to resign.

Early in 1933, von Schleicher admitted defeat and retired to private life. Once more the path seemed clear for von Papen and his new ally, Adolf Hitler. All the machinations ended on January 30, 1933, when Hitler was legally appointed chancellor. Democracy had failed a people without the patience, the skill, or the will to fight for individual freedom. The German people chose a dictator; like most nations, they probably got the government they deserved.

During those final, fitful days of the Weimar Republic and almost without knowing how, the von Ribbentrops suddenly became useful commodities to Hitler. Their new friendship with him, their old relationship with von Papen, and the discreet and convenient location of their villa all helped set the stage for the historic meetings of January 1933.

The sequence of events that led to Hitler's appointment was launched by a speech given on December 16, 1932, by von Papen at the Herrenklub, the right-wing political Gentlemen's Club in Berlin. Still ambitious for power, he hinted at a coalition with Hitler, for which he had dispatched his friend von Ribbentrop to Berchtesgaden. One of the members, the banker Kurt von Schröder, took the hint and translated it into a meeting on January 4, 1933, between von Papen and Hitler at his home in Cologne.

Before going to Cologne, Adolf Hitler invited Hanussen, the stage clairvoyant, to Berchtesgaden, and Hanussen prophesied that the coming meeting would bring the long-awaited chancellorship. He even predicted the date: January 30, 1933. He did so in rhyme, a vague poem in the manner of Nostradamus, which could be interpreted to accommodate the occasion:

> *In three days the bank will change all things.*
> [Von Schröder was a banker.]
> *The day before the month doth end, your goal is reached, your road will bend* [January 30].

Hitler, deeply superstitious, ever one to believe in destiny, was apparently reassured.[13] The participants in the Cologne meeting were Hitler, Rudolf Hess, Heinrich Himmler, von Papen, and von Schröder, the host. From the outset, the sly von Papen did not speak of Hitler as chancellor. Instead, he offered to negotiate between Hitler and von Schleicher for an NSDAP role in von Schleicher's cabinet. Like a Cantonese menu, he offered many combinations. Perhaps a chancellorship shared by von Schleicher and Hitler? Or eventually a von Papen–Hitler combination? There was also the hope that Germany's major industrialists would subsidize a coalition of conservatives and Nazis. But it was not to be. The meeting was inconclusive.

Many industrialists had been invited, but they stayed away just as they had from the meeting at Harzburg in October 1931. Germany's capitalists, though they have often been accused of being Hitler's earliest financial "angels," were actually reluctant to participate. In 1932, according to Heinz Höhne, a leading German historian, Friedrich Flick, a coal and steel magnate, donated a token 50,000 marks to the Nazi Party. In contrast, that same year he donated 1.8 million marks to conservative political causes, most of it to help re-elect von Hindenburg. In fact, von Papen had met with the leading industrialists, including Gustav Krupp, on January 7, 1933, in Düsseldorf but found little enthusiasm. The businessmen were not inclined to contribute funds toward a collaboration between von Papen and the Nazis. Instead, they had suggested that von Papen ally himself with some of the less radical nationalist parties. Carl Duisberg and Carl Bosch, I. G. Farben, and Carl Friedrich von Siemens, of the Siemens concern, had actually resisted Hitler.

On January 5, the newspaper *Tägliche Rundschau* reported the supposedly secret Cologne meeting. Von Papen returned to Berlin on January 9. Of course Chancellor von Schleicher was furious. He had seen photos of the conference, taken by a former army officer. (Von Schleicher's dentist had arranged for these photographs after hearing about the conference. He had warned von Schleicher and had received a lecture about "the honor of men toward each other" for his pains.[14])

When von Schleicher confronted him, von Papen strenuously denied any idea of self-promotion, and blamed the "unbridled press." Von Schleicher's suspicions were well founded. Actually, von Papen still lived in the old chancellor's apartment in the Wilhelmstrasse, from which it was easy to meet secretly with the President, whose office was but a few steps away, across a garden. Von Papen, according to Alexander Stahlberg, one of his young assistants, still preferred to be addressed as "Herr Reichskanzler," though he was ex officio.

Stahlberg's memoirs show him to be resistant to the Hitler hypnosis: "I was not unprepared for my first meeting with him [Hitler]. I had been told that his eyes were 'incredibly fascinating.' Hitler stopped in front of me and fixed me with his blue eyes, but I felt at once that this 'look' was fake, nothing but a pose, studied in front of the mirror."[15] Stahlberg was then asked to hang up Hitler's trenchcoat, which was unusually heavy. He found two large pistols (manufactured by Walther, finished in chrome) that Hitler carried in his pockets.

Then on January 10, 1933, history chose the home of Joachim and Annelies von Ribbentrop as the site of the crucial meeting that preceded the *Machtergreifung* — the seizing of power — on January 30.

At 9 P.M. on January 10, the Ribbentrops' chauffeur, Fritz Bohnhaus, collected Franz von Papen from his apartment on the Wilhelmstrasse.[16] Bohnhaus was dressed in civvies, not in livery, to avoid "looking official." With the exception of Landgraf, the butler, all the von Ribbentrop servants were sent to the villa's upstairs servants' quarters. Hitler and his group arrived at 10 P.M. Landgraf served refreshments while Bohnhaus patrolled the grounds.

This meeting also went badly. Hitler demanded the post of chancellor. Von Papen, who had assured von Hindenburg that Hitler would not try to be chancellor, was in a dilemma and told Hitler that von Hindenburg would never consent. They began to argue angrily, and Hitler threatened to leave. He did agree to another meeting on

January 12, but he canceled later "in order to await the outcome of the regional elections in the state of Lippe." The previous November, the Nazis had lost many votes in the larger states, and Hitler now saw a chance to reverse the slide. Heinz Höhne wrote: "It was grotesque. Lippe was a midget state. The fate of seventy million Germans was to be decided by 100,000 voters!"

The Nazis made gigantic efforts to win the voters of tiny Lippe, village by village, town by town. They presented this election as a weathervane. Indeed, they finally won 39.5 percent of the vote after using a sledgehammer to kill a fly, and they trumpeted their "fantastic change of fortune." Hitler called a meeting of his party's leaders on January 16 in Weimar to rid himself of his critics, including Gregor Strasser, whom he never forgave for his "treachery" with von Schleicher.

Now von Ribbentrop persuaded a more confident Hitler to return to Dahlem. On January 18, when von Papen, Hitler, Röhm, and Himmler met again, von Papen was convinced that there was no way around Hitler's demands. The propaganda value of his victory in tiny Lippe was bound to evoke popular enthusiasm. Von Papen would have to reassure the President that he could load the cabinet with conservatives who would control Hitler. The next meeting was scheduled for January 22. The two men von Papen invited specifically to help to persuade the old marshal were his son, Colonel Oskar von Hindenburg, and his state secretary, Otto Meissner. François-Poncet wrote acid portraits of these two men: von Hindenburg's son was "tall, brutal, semi-educated, with none of his father's nobility." Meissner was "a strange creature too tightly encased in his clothes, who would serve any regime."

Von Papen arrived, again in the von Ribbentrop car, and an hour later, at 10 P.M., came Hitler, Wilhelm Frick, Göring, and Oskar Körner, a friend of Göring's. Frick, an early Hitler supporter, was a rabid ideologue.

Oskar von Hindenburg and Meissner had begun the evening at the opera. They left unnoticed in the dark, and took a taxi to Dahlem, where they used the back entrance through the garden. When they entered the villa at 10:30, Hitler paid no attention to Meissner but took Oskar von Hindenburg to a neighboring room, where they spent two straight hours behind locked doors. After they emerged, long after midnight, von Hindenburg seemed convinced. In a taxi back to the city he told Meissner that Hitler had to be taken seriously as future chancellor.

What was said during those two hours? Hitler obviously had made promises and used persuasion and charm, but it is also possible that there was a much harder edge. On two matters the von Hindenburg family was vulnerable: the tax status of their magnificent estate, Neudeck, in East Prussia, and the Osthilfe scandal. The von Hindenburgs were an old Prussian family, but they owned no land. To tie the old marshal to his fellow Junkers, a group of landowning aristocrats had persuaded some industrialists to underwrite the purchase of the vast Neudeck estate in West Prussia, which was presented to Paul von Hindenburg in 1927, on his eightieth birthday, "by a grateful nation." However, the estate was registered in the name of Oskar von Hindenburg, his son, in order to cheat the government out of eventual death taxes. The fact was of course not widely publicized.

The other matter, Osthilfe (Eastern Help), was potentially a much greater scandal. In 1930, Germany's heavy industry had approved subsidies to the agricultural east of Germany. The ostensible purpose was to strengthen this area as a consumer market. Billions of marks flowed into what soon turned into a bottomless pit. Much of the money went into the coffers of the richest landowners in Germany, who bought luxury cars, yachts, and horses, and gambled away fortunes in Monte Carlo. The figures speak for themselves: in 1932, 12,000 small farms received a total of sixty-nine million marks, and 722 large landowners received a total of sixty million marks. Hermine, the wife of the former Kaiser, one of the richest landowners, claimed and got Osthilfe while she was living in faraway Berchtesgaden. Von Oldenburg-Januschau, the man who had arranged the gift of the Neudeck estate to the von Hindenburgs, collected 621,000 marks, with which he added a fourth estate to the three he already owned.[17] Heavy industry finally canceled Osthilfe and put the money into exports.

No matter what he mentioned in those two hours, Hitler must also have made some promises: Oskar von Hindenburg was promoted from colonel to general shortly after Hitler came to power, and thousands of acres were added to the Neudeck estate.

The day after this meeting brought more twists and turns in alliances and proposals. Von Schleicher realized his ruling days were over. He had received a flat *no* from von Hindenburg when he asked for emergency powers, and he knew that he was being undermined by von Papen and by his own chief, the old marshal. Von Hindenburg had no further trust in a Prussian general who wanted to reach out across all strata of German society even to the Socialists and who had failed to favor his Junker brethren in the Osthilfe scandal. Suddenly von Schleicher saw everything clearly: General Field Marshal Paul von Hindenburg, the President and symbol of upright manliness, his idol, was faithless and disloyal. And this was not the first time. He had scuttled Brüning and von Papen, and now he was scuttling von Schleicher. Outraged, von Schleicher accused the old man to his face of disloyalty. Von Hindenburg made only a mild response: "My dear young friend, soon I shall be up there, looking down. Then I'll see whether I was right or wrong."[18]

His Nazi associates as well as von Papen tried to convince the insecure Hitler to accept a government of National Unity, a coalition cabinet incorporating Nazis and more moderate Nationalist Conservatives. Meanwhile, von Papen explored his own options, which included the possibility of an alliance with von Schleicher. Or could he form a cabinet with Alfred Hugenberg, the Nationalist Conservative Hitler hated? Hugenberg and his nationalist movement were not to be denied. They insisted on a place in the cabinet. Von Schleicher thought he might return to the cabinet as Reichswehr minister, but von Hindenburg had already selected a new man: General von Blomberg, a rival of von Schleicher's.

Von Schleicher called together the senior generals and convinced them to arrest von Hindenburg before the old man handed over absolute power to Hitler. On the afternoon of January 29 they sent out Werner von Alvensleben, one of the same von Alvenslebens who had once lured young von Ribbentrop to Canada, to issue a stern warning to Hitler that the Army was ready to launch a putsch from its lair in Potsdam to "clean out the whole mess in government." They wanted to scare Hitler into withdrawing, but they had miscalculated. Von Alvensleben found Hitler's group having afternoon coffee and cake at Joseph Goebbels's apartment on Reichskanzlerplatz (later Adolf Hitler Platz, now Theodor Heuss Platz). The alarmed Hitler ordered von Helldorf, now the head of the Berlin Storm Troops, to mobilize his thugs from every *Kneipe* (pub) and beerhall. Hitler warned Meissner, and an immediate date was set for the swearing-in of the coalition government Hitler had wanted to avoid. Hitler and two Nazis would join the cabinet. The others would be conservatives.[19] The talk of a putsch also reached the President, and the wavering von Hindenburg finally made up his mind to accept Hitler.

The time for the swearing-in was fixed at 11 A.M. on January 30. Rumors of a military revolt multiplied: the presidential Reichswehr guards were alerted; escape plans were made; a plane was ordered to stand by. Oskar von Hindenburg himself went to the railroad station to intercept the new Reichswehr minister, von Blomberg, who was arriving from the Geneva Disarmament Conference. Von Blomberg was told to avoid his new offices at Army headquarters in the Bendler-strasse lest he be arrested. Instead, von Blomberg walked to the Presidential Palace. Hitler, Göring, Goebbels, Ernst, and Röhm were at the Kaiserhof Hotel across the street from the Chancellery. Superstitious Hitler was driven the few yards in his large black Mercedes. He wanted to make an impressive entrance. Waiting in Meissner's office for the time to be sworn in, the other candidates for office argued and haggled until Meissner told them it was time. In fact, they had already kept the old President waiting fifteen minutes. Shortly after 11:15 A.M. they walked through a dusting of snow to the presidential reception hall.[20] Von Hindenburg was in a foul mood, so the ceremony was brief.

Hitler's anxious group peered through field glasses from the Kaiserhof and searched for Hitler's face. When he came out of the Chancellery, he looked somber. A few minutes later he was among them, tears in his eyes. He was chancellor!

The group of enthusiastic Nazis in front of the hotel yelled, *"Heil! Heil Hitler!"*

Only a half hour earlier, von Papen's wife had looked across her wintry garden at the line of men following one another toward the ceremony. She turned to young Alexander Stahlberg and in a shaking voice said, "Oh, my God! Oh, my God, I am afraid!"

That night, there was to be a huge torchlight parade through the Brandenburg Gate to celebrate the appointment of Adolf Hitler. Von Papen had rented a balcony suite at the Hotel Adlon, overlooking the square in front of the Brandenburg Gate. His family and friends were there to view the Storm Troopers parade through the gate's immense arches and in front of "jubilant crowds." The torchlight parade did indeed take place, but the crowd was slim and apathetic. The suite underneath the von Papen suite was rented by Hans Albers, Germany's dashing blond film hero, who appeared in full evening dress on his balcony, flanked by two beautiful girls in low-cut gowns despite the chill. They were all drinking champagne, toasting the sparse crowd, and waving. Now the people on the sidewalks below had something to cheer about. The Albers party tossed packs of expensive cigarettes from a silver tray to their "audience." Albers was no Nazi sympathizer, and this was probably his way of making fun of them and distracting them from the parade.

The world has often seen photos and films of that torchlight parade, but the marchers they saw did not parade on the night of January 30, 1933. It was much too dark that night, the marchers were ragged, and no searchlights had been placed. The whole parade was restaged a day later by Hitler's propaganda genius, Goebbels, with floodlights and cameras in place and film directors to channel the brown-shirted, torch-carrying marchers. It was the first typical Third Reich fabrication.[21]

And what about the von Ribbentrops, now that Joachim's new idol and pupil would decide the future of Germany? Joachim had waited at the Kaiserhof Hotel with Göring, Röhm, and Goebbels, but no one had paid attention to him. Feeling snubbed, he returned home to Dahlem.

At first, Joachim and Annelies hoped that, once the first rush of events had died down, they would be asked into the new chancellor's circle to be thanked for their friendship and help and then given some tokens of respect and distinction. They waited in vain. Others had previous claims, mainly Hitler's "old fighters," who were sure they would now be rewarded with important posts. These old Nazis, the real revolutionaries, had their own vision of a Nazified Germany. The last thing they would permit was a bunch of arrogant aristocrats to continue to run the Army and the government. There were millions who wore SA and SS uniforms and who now considered themselves Germany's true soldiers. As the "Horst Wessel," the party's anthem, proclaimed: "Hold high the flag, close your ranks! SA is marching!" The second verse began, "Clear the street for the brown grenadiers!"*

The SA's chief, Ernst Röhm, would see that his men got their due.

The next claims were made to Hitler by the Military Ministry and the Foreign Ministry and heavy industry precisely because of these street brawlers. The General Staff of the Reichswehr wanted to be reassured, and the titled gentlemen of the Foreign Ministry wanted to be reassured, and the heads of heavy industry wanted to be reassured. Ambassadors had to report these German events to their governments. Some were openly cynical. Some were warily optimistic. The French, British, American, and Italian ambassadors, all signers of the Versailles Treaty, now had to deal with a man who had sworn to do away with the treaty and its reparations. Fascist Italy was still on reasonable terms with Great Britain. Benito Mussolini viewed Hitler with the tolerance of a master for the pupil, but he was soon taken

---

*Horst Wessel was a Berlin pimp who joined the SA, was killed in a brawl, and was raised to Nazi sainthood by party propagandists.

aback by the brutal anti-Semitism and fierce methods of the Nazis. He was waiting for moderation and hoping for the best.

The von Ribbentrops had only secondary claims for attention; they would have to wait their turn. Joachim von Ribbentrop was unable to make contact with his former dinner guest, and he pouted. According to von Papen, von Ribbentrop approached him, asking that he be proposed for the job of state secretary of the Foreign Ministry. He suggested that von Papen could discuss the matter with Konstantin von Neurath, the foreign minister. At von Hindenburg's insistence, von Neurath had remained in the cabinet, and his state secretary, Bernhard von Bülow, was a respected professional.

If, indeed, von Ribbentrop had proposed himself for this post, it was an absurd notion. In the structure of German ministries, a state secretary had to possess great administrative, legal, and diplomatic skills. He had to be a professional. However, von Papen had the habit of bending the facts, and his version is suspect. It is unlikely that Joachim von Ribbentrop, even if goaded by Annelies, would have had the temerity to confront the professionals of the Wilhelmstrasse.

Baron Konstantin von Neurath, the foreign minister, tall, corpulent, well tailored, was the former ambassador in London under Brüning. He then became a member of von Papen's "Barons' Cabinet" as foreign minister. His contemporary, André François-Poncet, offered a full catalogue of adjectives for von Neurath: "good-humored, simple, dignified, polite, south German." Also "not frank and a liar, no moral courage and . . . lazy." Nevertheless, von Hindenburg trusted and admired him. Von Neurath, a diplomat of the old school, cheered the old man's Junker heart even though "he was from the south."

Prussians usually considered south Germans jolly but slack and undependable. Von Neurath had met von Ribbentrop briefly, and from the very beginning no love was lost between the mature diplomat and the ambitious young wine merchant. The staff of the Foreign Ministry was aware that Adolf Hitler had been listening for months before his appointment to von Ribbentrop's notions of foreign policy during the private dinners in Dahlem. Hitler, never reluctant to play off one adviser against the other, probably quoted the opinions "of Herr von Ribbentrop" to von Neurath, raising his hackles. But the professionals in the Auswärtiges Amt were not the only ones to show disdain for Joachim von Ribbentrop. Old Nazi Party cronies had watched with alarm while "their" Adolf became a constant visitor at Lentzeallee. They feared that Hitler would be diverted from his revolutionary course and led into the ways of the *haute bourgeoisie*. Champagne, tennis courts, swimming pools, and butlers went counter to the true National Socialist ideal. The Horst Wessel song warned against those who had become the victims of "Communism *and the reactionaries.*" Besides, von Ribbentrop's fairly recent entry into the party made him suspect, an opportunist, a fake Nazi. In the years to come, the old party members never lost their disdain for Joachim von Ribbentrop. It drove him to ever greater efforts to prove that he was a true National Socialist and would cause him to make some of his greatest errors in judgment.

To short-cut any criticism, he soon joined the SS (Schutz Staffel, or protection squads) and stayed a member for the rest of his life. At the time of his death, he held the honorary rank of SS general. Through-out his career in the service of Adolf Hitler, there were only two "party" portraits on his desk: one of the Führer and one of Heinrich Himmler, the head of the SS and one of the few old party men with whom von Ribbentrop exchanged the familiar appellation *du,* the mark of close friendship among Germans. But in 1933 at the head of the Hitler hierarchy stood Göring, Hess, Frick, Goebbels, Röhm, Himmler, and, just below them, the *Zweite Garnitur,* the second level. Von Ribbentrop did not rate.

The real party troops were the brown-shirted men of the SA (Sturm Abteilungen) under their brutal leader, Ernst Röhm. Röhm, a World War I captain, was the classic mercenary, a scar-faced, thick-bellied, snub-nosed man who stood on stubby legs. He looked more like a drill sergeant than an officer, and the aristocrats who commanded the Reichswehr shuddered at the sight of him. They were also alarmed by his brawling, knee-booted army, recruited from the millions of unem-ployed workers. The brown shirts were really tan shirts; the uniforms were cheap copies of British Colonial khaki shirts and riding breeches, including the Sam Browne belt and shoulder strap. The whole outfit was completed with store-bought riding boots. They also wore a vague version of the French Army képi, usually with chinstrap down. The whole effect was supposed to be tough. In party propaganda illustrations, the SA man always had a boxer's broken nose and a thick neck.

The Reichswehr's commanders were quite aware that Röhm pic-tured himself as the commander of Germany's real Army. Plain, old-fashioned snobbery aside, the vulgar Röhm represented a real danger and much more than a mere embarrassment in the officers' mess.

Only two months after Hitler's becoming chancellor, the SA mounted a brawling boycott of Jewish stores. Armed with nightsticks, they planted themselves in front of shop entrances, daring anyone to walk past them. Their placards read: "Germans, defend yourselves!

Do not buy from Jews!" Stars of David were smeared on display windows, and posters with threats were plastered everywhere. It was the first such public outrage. The police stood by because the SA had just been legalized as "auxiliary" police by decree of Hermann Göring. It was on the day of the boycott that an embarrassed von Ribbentrop, known for his Nazi sympathies, but considered "civilized," invited several Jewish business associates to that lunch at the Hotel Adlon,[22] with the unpleasant result mentioned earlier.

News of the boycott soon reached the United States, but Americans were more concerned with the Depression and hoped the newly elected Franklin D. Roosevelt could bring back the "Happy Days" his campaign song had promised. The United States of 1933 was still racially segregated, *de jure* below the Mason-Dixon Line and *de facto* everywhere else, and Americans freely used terms like wop, mick, polack, kike, and nigger. The country was widely anti-Semitic. Many clubs, apartment houses, resorts, hotels, and entire townships were "restricted," a euphemism for "Jews not wanted," and they were often advertised as such. America's Jewish population had a steep division between the descendants of German Jews who had landed in the early and mid nineteenth century and the more recent arrivals from the ghettoes of Russia, Poland, and the Balkans.

The German Jews had brought their Germanisms with them. They loved order, decorum, *Kultur*. They were bankers and merchants who founded their own clubs, built their own apartment houses. Their rigidly structured world was dominated by families like the Kuhns, Loebs, Lehmans, and Schiffs. They snubbed eastern European Jews, whom they considered uncouth, vulgar. Their attitude was not unlike that of the old Jewish families in pre-Hitler Germany.

The bad news from Nazi Germany left many of America's German Jews strangely apologetic. Cyrus Adler, president of the German-dominated American Jewish Committee, said, "There is too much public discussion [about the Nazi acts]. Our Christian fellow citizens will get tired of us."

When a large number of American "eastern" Jews demanded an immediate trade boycott of Germany, the American Jewish Committee objected. Despite them, Rabbi Stephen S. Wise, a powerful American Jewish leader with direct access to President Roosevelt, called an anti-Germany protest meeting. Twenty thousand people jammed Madison Square Garden; another thirty-five thousand stood outside.

Many newspapers headlined Berlin's brown-shirted barbarities. Both the tiny *Poughkeepsie News* and the influential *Chicago Tribune* reported the beatings of Jews and Reichstag deputies, the existence of concentration camps and the newly coined term "protective arrest." On April 15, 1933, the *New York Evening Post* carried an article about the atrocities, as did the *Toledo Times* and *Augusta* (Maine) *Journal*. Other papers, like the *Columbus Journal* and the *St. Louis Post Dispatch,* were still unconvinced. The *Washington Post* was incredulous.[23] During the first months of 1933, American reporters in Berlin were often urged by U.S. diplomats to moderate their stories.[24]

On March 27, 1933, Hitler issued a statement through his new foreign press aide, Ernst (Putzi) Hanfstaengl, that "all allegations of brutalities are base lies." Foreign Minister von Neurath and Hitler's banker, Hjalmar Schacht, issued similar denials.

The first tenuous moment of American anger at Nazi Germany had quickly come and would soon have gone, but American journalists like Louis Lochner, William Shirer, and H. R. Knickerbocker kept reporting the ugly facts from Berlin.

By now von Ribbentrop's old friend Count Wolf von Helldorf was the head of Berlin's SA, but von Ribbentrop was "safely" in the SS, like so many doctors, lawyers, and businessmen who shuddered at the proletarian SA. In 1933 the SS was a small, elite section of the SA. It had a distinctive uniform (black breeches, tunic, and cap), and most of its members were upper school or university-educated. At first, the SS functioned as a politicized "weekend soldier" organization, a vicious form of London's cheerful Honourable Artillery Company or New York's snobby National Guard Squadron A. Full of fancied mythical Teutonic lore and ideas, the SS was a haven for upper-class National Socialists and their way of distancing themselves from the rabble in the SA. (For unknown reasons, the SS had special appeal for physicians. "Aryan" medical doctors were seven times more likely to become SS members than other professionals.[25])

The SS had three "faces":

1. There was the "weekend" *(Allgemeine)* SS, which von Ribbentrop had joined.

2. There were the SS units under Reinhard Heydrich that included the Party Police (SD, or Sicherheitsdienst) and, eventually, the Einsatzkommandos (Action Squads) of the SD, which pillaged and murdered in the wake of the Army's Polish, Baltic, Balkan, and Russian campaigns. General Walter Schellenberg, who headed foreign espionage for the SS, was also under Heydrich. Equally frightening were the Death's Head (Totenkopf) units, which ran the concentration camps under the command of Oswald Pohl, who matched Heydrich in rank.

3. Finally, beginning with the war came the Waffen SS (SS at arms), virtually a combat-ready army spawned from Hitler's Guard Battal-

ion, the Leibstandarte. Waffen SS had its own infantry, artillery, armor, cavalry, signals. It also recruited from the police, the Death's Head concentration camp units, and from foreign countries. There were Waffen SS Divisions of Latvian, Estonian, Lithuanian, Norwegian, Ukrainian, Danish, Dutch, Belgian, and even Indian troopers. Young Rudolf von Ribbentrop, Joachim's son, served in the division that grew from the Leibstandarte.

The sense of horror that all SS uniforms usually conveyed often sprang from the second category of police, Gestapo and Death's Head units and Einsatzkommandos. With the beginning of the war, the "weekend" SS lost importance, although for the Foreign Office there remained a certain opportunistic symbiosis. At the end, the ministry entered a time of self-protective and sycophantic cooperation with Heydrich's SD, although Heydrich despised von Ribbentrop.

In 1933 the first concentration camp was opened at Oranienburg, near Berlin, for "political re-education." It was run by the SA in the most brutal way. The original concentration camps were used for political revenge, not for racial "cleansing." The inmates were mostly the Nazis' old political enemies, Communists and Social Democrats. Gangs of Storm Troopers raided the Communist Party offices and also arrested Socialists, labor unionists, and anyone who had ever shown open opposition to the Nazis, written an article about them, or ridiculed them from a cabaret stage. A large number of innocent citizens were in constant danger of getting beaten up and locked up because Storm Troopers usually settled their personal scores and fancied insults without warning. Any SA man who was ever fired, dispossessed, or dunned now took his revenge. Any supposed insult was "righted" with rubber truncheons and steel knuckles. The streets of Berlin became dangerous for anyone who had dark hair and eyes and who would not give an immediate Hitler salute to a roving squad of shouting and singing SA, either on foot or in one of their open swastika-flagged trucks. Incident followed incident. A British Embassy member who did not salute was beaten up despite his diplomatic papers.[26] A few months later, the Portuguese consul general in Hamburg was set upon by an SA squad and had to be hospitalized, mainly because of his "Jewish appearance."

A black-humor Berlin story of the time tells of a famous anti-Nazi cabaret comic, a homosexual who was badly beaten up by Storm Troopers. The following night from the stage, limping and swathed in bandages, he blurted out his story. Two SA thugs had followed him on a dark street. They caught him, pulled down his trousers, and began beating him with their steel-buckled belts. The cabaret comic rolled his two blackened eyes to heaven and, smiling through mangled teeth, lisped, "And it turned out to be a wonderful evening, after all!"

Those who were sympathetic to the new regime insisted that "these brutal things were done without the knowledge of Adolf Hitler." Later, when Nazi terror was more widespread and organized, many people in Germany still said, *"Wenn der Führer das nur wüsste!"* (If the Führer only knew!). Eventually everyone would learn that Adolf Hitler knew all. He approved of every horror, every debauch. He was the very force that powered the monstrosities.

There is no way that von Ribbentrop could have failed to see what was happening on the streets of Berlin. All Berliners were aware of the SA thugs and avoided confrontations. To pre-empt any negative reports abroad through Berlin's foreign embassies, State Secretary Bernhard von Bülow immediately instructed all German heads of missions in capitals all over the world to "exert a calming influence."

The Nazis had always accused Jews of "dominating" the scene. For instance, "everyone" had a Jewish doctor. The fact is that in 1933, when Hitler came to power, Jewish citizens were less than 1 percent of the total population, 550,000 out of sixty-two million. In Berlin, the Jews numbered 150,000 out of four million, or less than 4 percent. In all of Germany, there were nine thousand Jewish or part-Jewish doctors out of Germany's fifty-two thousand doctors, or about 17 percent.[27]

While the SA rampaged through the city of Berlin, Adolf Hitler quickly demonstrated to von Papen and the other Conservatives in the cabinet that he would not be harnessed by them. On February 1, 1933, he dissolved the Reichstag. On February 4 he dissolved the provincial and municipal assemblies. With the aid of his fellow Nazi Wilhelm Frick, now the minister of the interior, and Göring, now the Prussian minister-president, he fired the top police officials and installed three Nazis: Rudolf Diels, Admiral Magnus von Levetzov, and Kurt Daluege. The SA had already been sworn in as auxiliary police.

On February 27, the Reichstag building burned. Of all the possible explanations throughout the years, the most likely is that the fire was set by a mentally retarded Dutch Communist named Marinus van der Lubbe and then was spread by a group of Storm Troopers, who used the old underground passageway between Göring's new official residence and the Reichstag building. Count von Helldorf was again at the center of trouble. Later, he claimed to have been involved. An SA officer named Kruse, an aide of Röhm's, said that he and twenty-three troopers were the actual arsonists.[28] In retrospect, one wonders how the burning of any building, no matter how important, could so disrupt the political process. The burning of the Houses of Parliament or the Capitol would not shatter Britain or the United States. Two notes of murderous finality trailed after the Reichstag fire. Berlin's fire chief, Walter Gempp, was arrested and "found shot" in his cell. It is assumed he knew too much. Then Hanussen, the nightclub clairvoyant, who had advised Hitler before the Cologne meeting and was said to have "recruited" van der Lubbe for his friend von Helldorf, was found shot to death in the woods near Berlin.[29]

On March 7, using an emergency decree for the second time since his appointment on January 30, Hitler ordered five thousand people in Prussia and two thousand in the Rhineland arrested "for the defense of the state." On March 16, Hitler convinced the old marshal that the country needed a minister for "enlightenment and propaganda" and Dr. Joseph Goebbels joined the cabinet. Then came Goebbels's invention, the hypocritical Potsdam Act of State. To attest to the cleverness of the man, it was he who insisted that the old Junkers and the military appear at Potsdam's Garrison Church in full parade uniforms, with decorations and swords and sashes, while Hitler wore a modest black civilian cutaway coat and striped trousers. It was time to lull the conservatives and the world by making a calming, obedient "statement." It was short-lived.[30]

After a downpour on that March 20, the sun shone on Potsdam. Hitler made a subdued speech, dwelling on his deep respect for Prussian tradition. At the end of the sham Hitler pledged peace and shook hands, respectfully, with the old marshal. The Reichswehr gave an outstanding display in the parade that followed.

On March 23, the Reichstag reconvened at the lavish Kroll Opera House and heard Hitler address the assembly, which was packed with SA and SS uniforms and presided over by Göring. Hitler promised to:

1. Respect property and individual initiative.
2. Grant a debt moratorium to farmers.
3. Aid the middle class.
4. Increase the number of jobs.
5. Give special attention to the Reichswehr.
6. Work for peace.

Then he demanded absolute power to carry out his program without presidential endorsements. Courageously, the senior Social Democratic delegate, Otto Wels, refused to vote for the full powers Hitler demanded. The chancellor launched a vicious attack on him. The political party that was supposed to provide some equilibrium, the Catholic Center Party, under Monsignor Kaas, was unwilling to fight Hitler, who was now voted full powers, by 441 to 94. He no longer needed President von Hindenburg's signature to enact laws.

The fake humility of Potsdam had been a solemn swindle.[31] Almost instantly all unions were disbanded, the Socialists were outlawed, and, ironically, the right-wing Stahlhelm organization, which had backed Hitler since the Congress of Harzburg in 1931, was abolished. Three Nationalist Conservative cabinet members, Foreign Minister von Neurath, Minister of Finance Count Lutz Schwerin von Krosigk, and Vice Chancellor Franz von Papen, quickly abandoned fellow cabinet minister Alfred Hugenberg, head of the Stahlhelm. He was out.

Meanwhile, Hitler's round of domestic brutalities continued. Following on the heels of the anti-Jewish riots of April 1, instigated by the Nazis' vulgarian anti-Semite, Julius Streicher, the legislators enacted severe anti-Jewish laws. Streicher, a former schoolteacher, was one of Hitler's old comrades. On July 14 came new laws for the sterilization of those with hereditary illnesses and incurable diseases. As François-Poncet wrote, "Nazism is debasing Germany and isolating her from civilized societies."[32] At villages and small towns all over Germany the local SA commanders hoisted banners over the roads leading into each municipality: JEWS NOT DESIRED. Restaurants and hotels posted similar signs.

This was the Hitler the von Ribbentrops finally managed to entice back to Dahlem for dinner. They needed not have counted it a victory. Adolf Hitler always did exactly what was right for himself. He now faced decisions about foreign policy, and he refused to rely only on the guidance of von Neurath and his Foreign Ministry experts. As usual, Hitler wanted several sources and opinions, all from rivals for his favor, and it was von Ribbentrop's turn. Between bites of his specially prepared vegetarian meal, Hitler declared that he wanted peace, but Germany had to become "an equal among nations." He wanted revisions of the Versailles Treaty. Most urgently, he wished to establish connections with England. He declared his friendship for Italy and his disdain for France, and he was fanatical in his hatred of Soviet Russia. To Annelies, as an aside, he confessed he was sorry he had ever "signaled" any of these views on foreign policy in *Mein Kampf*. During that whole evening, he made no mention of the Jews, and von Ribbentrop did not bring up the subject for good reason. He was not willing to face another argument, another rebuff, another possible breach, as had occurred after the "Jewish lunch" in Berlin.

In the library after dinner, Hitler proclaimed his fascination with Great Britain. He asked von Ribbentrop to tell him how Britain's leading circles viewed National Socialism. Von Ribbentrop "could not report much that was favorable." Yet he "sensed Hitler's admiration for Britain" and felt that "our mutual feelings about the English became the basis for our mutual trust." Von Ribbentrop's memoirs (written shortly before his execution in Nürnberg) continued:

Hitler stated facts others simply had to accept. He was very self-possessed, a man without compromise. He could be courteous and warm, but there was a certain distance he could not help. I am sure it troubled him at times. He could speak freely and amusingly about his Army days or his own beginnings, and when he spoke of architecture, one could sense the artistic side of his nature. He could be enormously charming and supremely convincing when he tried to persuade someone. Many men went to "tell him the real truth" and reappeared totally convinced of *his* view. I also fell under his spell although he called me his "most difficult" subordinate because I would calmly defend my ideas after he thought he had convinced me. He could be incredibly loyal, but he could also be unreasonably suspicious. He could hurt people deeply. I never understood this split in him. "Divide and Conquer" was used by him so frequently that there was constant conflict among his collaborators. Particularly in the matter of foreign policy, everyone thought he could participate . . .

Adolf Hitler had a quick temper, often out of control. At Godesberg [1938] he wanted to break off the Chamberlain talks when the Czechs mobilized. He jumped up with his face telltale red. The same at Hendaye with Franco, when Suner [Franco's foreign minister] said some clumsy things. Same with Henderson [British ambassador, 1937–39] in the Poland crisis, when Henderson slammed his hand on the table. Every time it happened I managed to calm things down. He said to me much later, "You know I just can't control myself!" . . .

No one got close to him except, possibly, Göring. When Göring was in a meeting, I barely seemed to exist . . . Perhaps he was even a bit frightened of Göring! When I once offered to speak to Göring about giving up command of the Luftwaffe in 1944, when it had failed, Hitler said, "God help us, no, Ribbentrop! You should have seen how angry Göring just got when I spoke to him!"[33]

Clearly, Joachim von Ribbentrop wanted to be involved in forming Germany's foreign policy. He felt qualified by virtue of his years of travel, his knowledge of the international world, his service in the war, his inherited obligation of political participation. After all, his father had sacrificed his career for political principle. Why would the

Foreign Ministry's aristocrats and clubmen be better able to advise Adolf Hitler than he?

Von Ribbentrop was not the only one. There were three other men who were sure they could help to guide their Führer to formulate Germany's future *Aussenpolitik,* its foreign policy: one was an international businessman named Kurt Lüdecke; another was Putzi Hanfstaengl; and then there was Hitler's long-time associate Alfred Rosenberg.

Kurt Lüdecke, a right-wing exile, had led an adventurous life as a dealer in aircraft and tires, mostly in Latin America. He held a Mexican passport but was renaturalized when Rosenberg asked him to return to the "new" Germany. For a short time, he was press attaché at the embassy in Washington, but he returned to Berlin to help Rosenberg advise Hitler. Somehow he ran afoul of Göring and was sent to a concentration camp. He escaped, but by the end of 1933 he was no longer in contention.

Putzi Hanfstaengl, towering over the other senior Nazis at six-foot-three, was a rich young man from Munich, whose family owned a famous art gallery and whose mother was a Sedgwick from Boston. He had graduated from Harvard. An early backer and follower of Hitler since 1930, he was the Nazi Party's foreign press "expert." Adolf Hitler often solicited his views, particularly about America and Berlin. Rich Putzi became the favorite target of the old party guard. They subjected him to unending pranks and practical jokes. He was a born raconteur, an amateur bar pianist, and court jester, and he never seemed to object to his tormentors.

Eventually, the pranks became more serious. When he was sent out on a plane and "warned that he might be ejected without a parachute," supposedly a joke, he began to fear for his life. He fled to England and remained there comfortably. It is possible he was in a position to blackmail certain senior Nazis. His son was at London's St. Paul's School while Ambassador von Ribbentrop's son, Rudolf, attended the rival Westminster School, but for obvious reasons, the boys' parents avoided contact. Obviously, Hanfstaengl was no longer a rival to von Ribbentrop.

The third and most serious contender for the unofficial post of foreign policy adviser was the strange Alfred Rosenberg. Born in Latvia of German parents, Rosenberg, an architect, was a man with a fervor for racism and the "purity" of the National Socialist creed. His book, *The Myth of the Twentieth Century,* a jumble of racist philosophy and political theories, became the second bible of National Socialism. (The first, of course, was Hitler's *Mein Kampf.*) To Rosenberg,

National Socialism became an embracing religion. He was the only senior Nazi who objected to the 1939 Soviet pact on ideological grounds ("a betrayal of the National Socialist Revolution"). He had studied in Riga and Moscow, was an expert on Russia, and had witnessed the Russian revolution. His contacts among White Russian émigrés were worldwide. It was he who "unearthed" once more the oft-discredited and poisonous *Protocols of the Elders of Zion,* the slanderous anti-Jewish fraud that "exposes" Jewish "plans for world domination." He brought them to the attention of his idol, Adolf Hitler. Although even Hitler was inclined to dismiss Rosenberg's theories about the world of superior Aryans and inferior non-Aryans, he agreed with certain of Rosenberg's basic contentions about the "inferiority" of certain "bloods."

Rosenberg had his chance at foreign policy. In 1933 he was sent to England by the party, at his own suggestion. He promised he could "forge certain links" for his Führer and convince leading British circles that Germany's fight against Communism would benefit all Western civilization.

He was invited by F. W. Winterbotham, who was actually a British Intelligence agent,[34] and met Prime Minister Ramsay MacDonald's secretary, as well as Lord Hailsham, the secretary of war, and some senior RAF people. Toward the end of his trip, Rosenberg placed a wreath at the foot of the Cenotaph, London's main war memorial. Unfortunately, the wreath was bedecked with swastika pennants. It was soon snatched from the memorial by a British officer and thrown into the Thames. The officer was fined forty shillings and was delighted to pay the fine.

Rosenberg's mission to London had turned into a debacle. He neither made friends nor influenced anyone, and he caused much laughter because of the anti-Nazi incident. Of course, he had no idea that he was being used by British Intelligence.

A reluctant von Ribbentrop, at Hitler's request, had helped Rosenberg formulate ideas for the London trip. With Rosenberg's failure, von Ribbentrop at last seemed to have the field to himself. He was given rooms in the offices of the Führer's party deputy, Rudolf Hess, across the street from the Chancellery. So began the Ribbentrop Büro (office), on April 24, 1934. It was financed by the party and was responsible only to the Führer. For the next four years it would plague Foreign Minister von Neurath and his ministry.

8

BÜRO TO EMBASSY
1934–1936

The German People's
Supreme Judge

AS LATE AS DECEMBER 1933, at a dinner given by François-Poncet, von Ribbentrop complained that he still had no job in government.[1] He even expressed some doubts about the Nazi Party's future.

But the Büro's small beginnings changed all that. The new "adviser to the Fuhrer" had to take into account that Adolf Hitler was a man of action, often precipitous action. Since February 1933, Hitler had shown his anger at the lack of progress made at the Geneva Disarmament Conference since the departure of the German delegate, General von Blomberg, now Reichswehr minister. General von Blomberg's former aide in Geneva told friends that his general was not a great Hitler enthusiast and had accepted the ministry only because of von Hindenburg.[2]

Two party bigwigs had come to Geneva to attend the conference as part of the German "team." One of them, Reinhard Heydrich, appeared with the "simulated" SS rank of major general. At first he kept quiet, but he grew more presumptuous as the days passed. He even insisted that a swastika flag be raised over the hotel where the delegation was housed. Rudolf Nadolny, the Foreign Ministry official who headed the German mission, put Heydrich in his place, and the SS "general" soon left Geneva. Nadolny reported the contretemps to Berlin and was told that Hitler approved of his actions. Then Nazi leader Robert Ley and Danzig Gauleiter Albert Forster appeared in Geneva. Ley was often drunk and behaved badly. When the South Americans would not accept his credentials, he called them monkeys.

But this time Hitler stuck with his man. He insisted that Ley's credentials be accepted, and Ley returned to Berlin in triumph. Next, Goebbels came to Geneva. The delegation came to call him the "tricky dwarf." He faked a Berlin press dispatch of his supposed statements in Geneva and then yelled at a Berlin reporter for having published them. Then he screamed with laughter at the man's discomfort before telling him it was a hoax.

One of Goebbels's aides was fired when he got drunk, and someone faked a police telegram to collect the aide's body at the morgue.

Obviously the party did not intend to take the Geneva Disarmament Conference seriously. Nevertheless, Hitler stated publicly on May 17 that he did "not aim to change the face of Europe by force." The French proposed a probationary period during which an international team would inspect German arms facilities, and the next meeting of the conference was scheduled for October 18, 1933. Four days earlier, Germany withdrew from the conference and, on the nineteenth, from the League of Nations. Hitler declared that the conference's proposal for international inspection was "against Germany's national honor." The sudden withdrawals sent shock waves throughout Europe. Nor were they greeted with joy by von Neurath at the Foreign Ministry or General von Blomberg at the Reichswehr Ministry.[3] As if to advertise his disdain for the League of Nations, Hitler urged von Neurath to initiate and conclude a German-Polish treaty of nonaggression on his own. Ambassador François-Poncet told this story: During 1934, a group of ambassadors, led by François-Poncet, held monthly dinners at Horcher's, Berlin's leading restaurant. The diplomats were shocked when Josef Lipski, the new Polish ambassador, told everyone on January 25 that some rumored Polish-German discussions were "only of an economic nature"; the following morning, the Polish-German nonaggression pact was announced. Lipski was never again invited to the ambassadorial dinners. The ten-year nonaggression treaty, concluded secretly, outside the League of Nations and behind the back of Poland's ally, France, brought western distrust for Colonel Josef Beck, the Polish foreign minister. It is even more ironic in the light of events in 1939, when Beck's actions were a factor that prevented the Russians from closing a treaty with the French and British. The Poles refused to allow the Russians into their country in case of a German attack on Poland, and it was this which opened the door for the German-Soviet Pact, which soon destroyed Poland.

Hitler decided the time had now come for von Ribbentrop to "go on patrol" for his Führer. On February 2, 1934, von Neurath advised the German ambassadors in Paris and London ("in strictest confidence") to receive a gentleman named Joachim von Ribbentrop, at the suggestion of Chancellor Hitler.[4] A few days after, the British ambassador in Berlin, Sir Eric Phipps, wrote to his foreign minister, Sir John Simon, about von Ribbentrop. "No doubt the man is a friend of Hitler's. However, I doubt if he has the influence he claims. Ribbentrop and his wife are self-promoting people, nationalists who deserted the sinking ship of the Republic and in 1933 [sic] joined the party just in the nick of time." Phipps's view was no doubt colored by von Neurath's telling him, on February 5, that von Ribbentrop was "insufficiently acquainted with our policy to speak with authority."[5]

During that month, however, von Ribbentrop met with Ambassador Phipps to propose various plans for armaments and troop parity. There was to be an army of three hundred thousand men but a limit of fifty thousand Storm Troopers. The German Air Force was to be gauged against the size of the combined French and British air forces. A naval agreement was to allow thirty-five tons of displacement to each hundred British tons.

Von Ribbentrop continued to dabble. On March 7 the German ambassador in Paris reported that the puzzled French foreign minister, Jean Louis Barthou, had met on Sunday, March 4, with "a Herr von Ribbentrop," introduced by a mutual friend. Von Ribbentrop was charming, knowledgeable about music, and had tried to initiate matters of diplomacy.[6] Barthou, who wanted clarification of von Ribbentrop's role, had suggested that these questions be handled through normal diplomatic channels. The German ambassador asked for instructions from his chiefs at the Foreign Ministry. State Secretary von Bülow said in reply that von Ribbentrop was "an old party member, a special intimate of the chancellor with wide international connections who was traveling with the knowledge of the ministry to clarify the position of the German government." He explained that, "historically, such agents had been used in the past," although he admitted that President von Hindenburg "had not found it advisable."[7] Von Ribbentrop got an equally tenuous reception in London. Through Ernest W. Tennant, a Berlin-based British businessman and friend of von Ribbentrop's, he met with the influential Stanley Baldwin. Meanwhile, Barthou, who had been sarcastic to von Ribbentrop, nevertheless sent him a book on Richard Wagner, inscribed, *En mémoire d'une conversation dans laquelle Wagner a joué le rôle de rapprochement.* (To remind us of a conversation in which Wagner played the role of peacemaker). But von Ribbentrop considered Barthou a bitter foe of Germany.

Only a few weeks later, von Bülow advised the German Embassy in Paris that von Ribbentrop had been instructed by the chancellor to invite Barthou to Germany. Von Ribbentrop was sure that his British and French missions had failed because of reports then circulating in London and Paris that an anti-Hitler putsch was about to take place.

(Before assuming his 1934 semiofficial status, von Ribbentrop made some preparatory private trips. One was to London late in 1933. He had breakfasted with the Conservative Stanley Baldwin and met with him again in the afternoon at 10 Downing Street, where Prime Minister Ramsay MacDonald joined them. Von Ribbentrop had emphasized Adolf Hitler's wishes for friendship and arms parity. He believed that Baldwin's speech in Parliament on the following day showed he had been favorably impressed. Von Ribbentrop also took credit for having persuaded Hitler to give a conciliatory interview to the Paris paper *L'Information* and its foreign editor, Fernand de Brinon. Finally, von Ribbentrop was sure he had influenced Adolf Hitler to consider giving up German claims to Alsace-Lorraine, where von Ribbentrop had spent so much of his francophile boyhood.)

On April 20, 1934, at the urging of Adolf Hitler, President von Hindenburg appointed von Ribbentrop "Plenipotentiary for Disarmament"; he was supposed to report officially to von Neurath. Actually, von Ribbentrop's reports went directly to Hitler. Von Ribbentrop now had his first governmental title. At last he was a man with official status.

By getting him the appointment, Adolf Hitler had completed one of his typical maneuvers. He had rattled the aristocrats at the Foreign Ministry, startled foreign governments, and also propped up the vanities of the ambitious von Ribbentrops. At the same time, he signaled his special regard for von Ribbentrop to his overbearing old Nazi cronies.

Adolf Hitler's powers of persuasion with the marshal must have been unique. The old man had asked, "What, that wine merchant?" But Otto von Meissner assured him von Ribbentrop was from "an old military family."[8] That was good enough for the marshal.

The diplomats who ran the Foreign Office now made a protective chess move of their own. They appointed one of their brightest young men, the thirty-one-year-old Erich Kordt, an expert on disarmament, to act as their liaison man at the new emissary. Strangely, the normally suspicious von Ribbentrop was pleased with the appointment. Perhaps he realized he would need expert guidance. At the same time, von Ribbentrop widened his fledgling Büro by recruiting a staff of advisers. He requested and was assigned his own suite of offices opposite the Foreign Ministry at Wilhelmstrasse 74–76, one floor above street level in the old Bismarck Palace. The Büro was small and so dark that the conference room was called the Blue Grotto.

Erich Kordt described his new chief, the forty-year-old Plenipotentiary for Disarmament.

"Elegantly dressed, graying hair, watery eyes with one half-closed, a tic in the cheek muscles. Trying to look energetic. Nothing natural about him. He walks up and down, keys in pocket clinking. Then lunch at the Dahlem house: elegant, in the English style, much good art. Frau von Ribbentrop seemed ill. I hear she has many operations, constant headaches."[9]

The first four associates to join the Büro ranged from a shipbuilder to a prince. Soon there were thirteen on the staff. The following year there were thirty-three, and at its peak, in 1936, the enlarged Büro, now called Dienststelle (Agency), had a staff of 150 and a budget of ten million marks, paid by the Nazi Party, not by the government.[10] To assist the party, heavy industry was "induced" to produce some of the money. Roland Brauweiler, the head of the union of industrial companies, complained of the party's "endless shnorring" *(uferlose Schnorrerei)* using the Yiddish term for "begging."

In May, von Ribbentrop returned to London. Bypassing the German ambassador, von Ribbentrop and Kordt found rooms in the Savoy through one of von Ribbentrop's business friends. The evening papers headline was: MYSTERY EMISSARY FROM HITLER HAS ARRIVED. On May 10 he met with Sir John Simon, Lord Privy Seal Anthony Eden, Lord Stanhope, the First Lord of the Admiralty, and Sir Robert Vansittart, under secretary for foreign affairs. Once more he assured them of Hitler's warm feelings for Britain and asked them to postpone the German disarmament conference. They told him, courteously, that it was impossible. To Kordt's dismay, Ribbentrop's report to Berlin nevertheless implied that he had achieved the postponement, and on his return on May 15 he was greeted at the door of the chancellor's anteroom by a happy Adolf Hitler. Kordt was sure von Ribbentrop had ruined himself. He was wrong. Von Ribbentrop had a believing patron in Berlin.

On May 18, von Ribbentrop went to Rome, where he stayed with the German ambassador, Ulrich von Hassell. He called on Mussolini on the nineteenth, trying to get help for postponement of the disarmament conference.

Despite all his efforts, the conference began on May 20. What were the feelings at the Foreign Ministry among the professionals who were being bypassed by this new "shadow" ministry backed by the Nazi chancellor and his Nazi cabinet ministers? Kordt wrote, "They are highly critical of the Nazis, but mostly they are loyal officials." Also, a few real Nazis had recently joined the ministry, and one needed to be careful of them. That most descriptive of attitudes, "inner emigration," now began. For the next thirteen years people would speak of the way people hid within themselves, withdrew, and became silent.

The first true Nazi in the ministry was Prince Josias zu Waldeck und Prymont. He was assigned to the personnel department. This gave him dangerous control over those to be hired, fired, or jailed. There was also an old department called Referat Deutschland, originally the liaison between ministry and the political parties, so innocuous it was manned by one official. It was now expected to monitor the ministry's political activities and to spy on it. Its new head, protesting this unsavory mission, was denounced by Prince Waldeck und Prymont and was arrested by the Gestapo on June 30, 1934. When he was freed, he was "cured" of any further urge to criticize.

Von Ribbentrop, not an old party comrade or part of the establishment, made sure to stay close to the Reichs Chancellery and to Adolf Hitler. By 1934, a bizarre court had developed around the person of Adolf Hitler. Kordt, who visited the Chancellery frequently, wrote these impressions:

> To enter the Chancellery, one had to pass police, Army guards, then SS guards. One finally entered a big anteroom, which was constantly filled with twenty or thirty hangers-on and permanent private emissaries from the various top Nazis like Göring. [Otto] Dietrich, the press chief of the Chancellery, was always there. Some people were waiting for special audiences. Everyone mumbled in subdued, respectful tones or read the blue Auswärtiges Amt reports, which contained the foreign news not published in the press. These reports were known as the Blue Plague. Then a voice boomed, *"The Führer is coming!"* and silence would fall and certain gentlemen who had been loitering would disappear in a hurry.[11]

Hitler loved to keep people waiting in order to humiliate them. Some people waited for days in that anteroom, gradually losing prestige in the eyes of the others.

Von Ribbentrop developed into a skilled anteroom "waiter." He listened to Hitler's statements, repeated by people who had just seen the Führer, and then reported arrogantly, or resignedly, what Hitler had said about this or that. If people agreed with Hitler and things went wrong, said Kordt, Hitler never got angry. He assumed there was no solution except his own. Professional "yes-men" were usually happy. If you disagreed or failed to agree with him and things went wrong, then he slashed at you.

On June 5 a sudden rumor made the rounds that Ernst Röhm, head of the Storm Troops, tired of the Reichswehr's conciliatory attitude toward the Geneva arms talks, wanted to take over the Army with his SA and install himself as Reichswehr minister. General von Blomberg, who held that post, and the top Army and Navy people were "ready to shoot." Erich Kordt and his brother, Theo, met two of von Blomberg's aides at a friend's house. One of them, the naval aide, voiced his hope that there would soon be a test of strength.

In mid-June 1934, von Ribbentrop made his own attempt to convince the French to change their stance on the harsh disarmament terms of the Versailles Treaty. Several important French, Belgian, and Luxemburg industrialists and bankers were in Berlin for a conference. He invited them all to a dinner, using the connections of Reichsbank president Hjalmar Schacht and the prestige of Count Schwerin von Krosigk, the minister of finance, both of whom were asked to attend. The guests were senior people from Arbed, the French-Belgian-Luxemburg steel company, and from the Banque d'Industrie et du Commerce. Using these contacts and additional ones, including Lazard Frères, he went to Paris on June 16 and was introduced to the influential French politician Edouard Daladier, under the sponsorship of the pro-Nazi Fernand de Brinon. Daladier said that French-German relations were *"dans un état lamentable."* After all, on June 6 Hitler had ordered the tripling of the Reichswehr from 100,000 to 300,000 men. Von Ribbentrop also met again with Barthou, the foreign minister, at the Quai d'Orsay. However, a meeting with the prime minister, former President Gaston Doumergue, was not as simple. Protocol demanded a formal diplomatic introduction, and von Ribbentrop was below ambassadorial rank. Embarrassingly, he had to turn to the German ambassador, who gleefully prepared the audience and sent along an embassy official as chaperone. In Doumergue's anteroom, the rumor was that the "mystery visitor" was Kurt von Schuschnigg, the Austrian politician, since von Ribbentrop left his Austrian-made Habig hat in the cloakroom during the meeting.[12]

A cascade of events would soon make it difficult to explain Germany to foreign observers. It began on June 16, when Franz von Papen, the vice chancellor, raised some eyebrows.

In an uncharacteristically open speech at Marburg University in Hesse, he lamented the suppression of German Christianity and called the single-party system only a temporary necessity. He asked how Germany expected to fulfill its mission in Europe by removing itself from the realm of Christian nations. He hinted at the lack of character, the self-seeking arrogance, the vulgarity, and the untruthfulness that were behind this German revolution.[13]

At the time, Edgar Jung, one of von Papen's associates and the man who had written the speech, had only thirteen days left to live. He was murdered by the SS. Von Papen's office in the Voss Strasse was raided by the SS and the Gestapo, and his press aide, Herbert von Bose, was shot at his desk. This was only the beginning.

Rumors that shook the Nazi regime and sent shock waves abroad focused on Röhm, one of Adolf Hitler's closest friends and long-term comrades. Röhm had made his complaints and ambitions known openly. He despised the "decay" of the National Socialist revolution and its compromises with "reactionary elements" in the Army and the aristocracy. He visualized a new, aggressive Germany led by a revolutionary people's army, under the command of men who had emerged from the National Socialist "gut" of Germany. He despised the Army's theoreticians and "old fogies."[14] He commanded 500,000 SA men, and he had even made an appeal to a small group of opportunistic young Reichswehr officers. In February 1934 Röhm confronted General von Blomberg, demanding that all national defense be turned over to him and his Storm Troops. Von Blomberg appealed to Hitler, and on February 28 Hitler negotiated a compromise. The Reichswehr would be the nation's only Army, but the SA would train men before and after they served in the Reichswehr. After leaving the room, Röhm shouted that he would never "stick to this ridiculous agreement," and that "the corporal would now have to go on leave. If we can't get there with him, we'll get there without him."[15]

One of his top aides, SA General Viktor Lutze, denounced Röhm to Himmler, head of the SS and one of Röhm's oldest Nazi comrades. Himmler turned to Heydrich, one of the new young SS leaders, who eventually carried out the brutal plan for removing Röhm and his group. Heydrich, cashiered by the Navy for offenses against its code of honor, had enrolled in the SS. He had already shown his style at the Geneva Disarmament Conference and would soon become the coldest, most brutal man in the cold and brutal SS. Himmler also convinced Röhm's rival, Göring, to cooperate.

Röhm and Hitler had further stormy meetings. On June 8 the party newspaper, *Völkischer Beobachter,* suddenly announced that Röhm had to take several weeks' sick leave at a Bavarian spa, Bad Wiessee, and the entire SA would go on one month's furlough, beginning July 1. Röhm seemed beaten. This squelched Heydrich's plan to accuse Röhm and his SA leaders of insurrection and then to slaughter them.

Until the Röhm trouble, Hitler had been playing his usual hand. He wanted the SA to act as a counterbalance to the Army, and he wanted the Army to keep Röhm in check. This was no longer possible. The Army was fed up, and Hitler could wait no longer. The SS Leibstandarte's chief, Sepp Dietrich, a street brawler turned SS general, drew weapons from the acquiescent Army for his SS men. Hitler ordered all SA chiefs to meet him on June 30 for a special conference at Bad Wiessee.

After he was fed two false rumors that an SA insurrection was scheduled for that very day, a nervous, shaking Hitler flew to Munich. Munich's SA chiefs were immediately arrested. Hitler drove on to Bad Wiessee through the early morning mountain mist. At 6:30 A.M. he entered the inn where Röhm and his men were staying, pushed his way past a startled, awestruck innkeeper, and burst into Ernst Röhm's room, gun in hand, backed by SS and police. He ordered Röhm arrested.

Other SA chiefs, one with his male lover, were dragged out of their beds, ordered to get dressed, and were sent to Stadelheim jail in Munich. The SS now embarked on a bloody campaign of terror all over Germany. Six senior SA leaders were immediately shot in the Munich prison yard. Several senior civilian officials in Munich were also murdered. Anyone who had ever been an enemy or a seeming enemy, anywhere in Germany, was shot. This included the former chancellor General von Schleicher and his wife, dozens of senior SA leaders, Gregor Strasser, Hitler's old comrade and rival, and even Captain Ehrhardt of the Kapp putsch.

Afraid that Göring and Himmler would become too powerful without Röhm, Hitler almost spared the SA chief, but Göring and Himmler both insisted on Röhm's death. (On June 29 in Dahlem, during dinner, Annelies von Ribbentrop had asked Heinrich Himmler what ever happened to Röhm; she had not seen him around Berlin. Himmler told her that Röhm was "as good as dead."[16])

The half-naked, sweating Röhm was finally shot in his Munich cell by three minor SS officers after scorning the chance to kill himself. In all, eighty-three people were murdered.[17] Hitler told the Reichstag, "In this hour I was the German people's supreme judge."

Later, besides accusations of treason and sedition, there was a flood of Hitler's "righteous disgust" about Röhm's homosexuality.

Hitler had known since the early Nazi days that Röhm was a homosexual. In 1925 Röhm had sued a Berlin gigolo for theft. The man claimed he had refused Röhm when the Nazi chief wanted to perform homosexual acts. He did "steal" a suitcase from Röhm that contained compromising love letters.[18] In 1932 a Munich newspaper, the *Münchener Post*, published a story stating that Röhm was a homosexual. The Nazis did not sue. They knew they had no chance.[19] In 1934, the Cardinal of Cologne confronted Hitler with an account of Röhm's homosexuality. Hitler denied it and called it a malicious lie.[20] Until June 30, 1934, Hitler said that Röhm's preference was a "private matter," but it was not, because the SA chiefs supplied their commander with young men. Among SA headquarters troops, Röhm's sexual appetites were a very public matter.

Foreign newspapers headlined these events in Nazi Germany. The cruelty of the bloodbath, the display of Hitler's callousness toward his former comrades, the murder of the von Schleichers and of Gregor Strasser, who were all known among influential foreigners, caused waves of revulsion abroad. German diplomats in London, Paris, Rome, and Washington suddenly confronted a frigid world. Those foreigners who had shown sympathy for the "new" Germany now kept an embarrassed silence.

For the second time since the 1933 anti-Jewish boycott, Joachim von Ribbentrop was face to face with events that went against his nature. He was a rational, conventional man of conservative background, an international businessman who cared about his own and his family's place in German and foreign society. He had always worried about the reputation of his country among other nations; Annelies was a lady of good family and careful upbringing.

The mass murders of Hitler's former Nazi associates and friends and of the von Schleichers could not have been part of the normal world of the von Ribbentrops, and one can imagine how these things were seen by the Henkells in Wiesbaden, or for that matter by the von Ribbentrops' friends in Paris and London.

Then, as if to shake off any doubts he may have had, Joachim von Ribbentrop made a potent symbolic gesture: Erich Kordt reported that June 30, the day of the Röhm affair, was the first time he had seen von Ribbentrop dressed in full SS uniform. The die was cast. It is inconceivable that Annelies von Ribbentrop had failed to approve.

Germans were presented with several *faits accomplis*. The *Völkischer Beobachter*, dateline Munich, July 1, 1934, ran these front-page headlines:

RÖHM ARRESTED AND DEPOSED
THOROUGH CLEANSING OF THE SA.
THE SA SPIRIT IS VICTORIOUS.
RÖHM EXCLUDED FROM PARTY.
THE FÜHRER ORDERS LUTZE TO BECOME THE SA'S NEW
   CHIEF OF STAFF.

There was no explanation for Röhm's fall, but one of the newspaper articles implied that Röhm's "unfortunate tendencies" had brought about the Führer's "crisis of conscience."

Elsewhere in the paper were articles about the "harsh treatment of Austria's workers by their government," a report of "deep right- and left-wing conflicts" inside France, and, ominously, a piece about the "cruelty of Austrian Chancellor Dollfuss's police." These were typical Goebbels signals of things to come.*

Should the Goebbels message of July 1 have failed to penetrate, the July 14 edition, dateline Berlin, carried the following headline:

DEATH IS CERTAIN FOR ANYONE WHO RAISES HIS HAND
AGAINST THE STATE

(Es soll jeder wissen dass wenn er die Hand zum schlage gegen den Staat erhebt der sichere Tod sein Los ist).

Subheadlines said:

THE GERMAN REICH IS NO LONGER A GEOGRAPHIC TERM BUT
   A POLITICAL UNIT.
A WAR WE HAVE BEEN FIGHTING FOR ONE AND A HALF YEARS.
THE WHOLE PEOPLE STANDS BEHIND THE FÜHRER.
THE ONLY ONES TO CARRY ARMS IN THE REICH ARE THE
   ARMED FORCES, AND THERE IS ONLY ONE CARRIER OF
   POLITICAL IDEAS: THE PARTY.
HE BROKE HIS FAITH WITH ME, AND I HAD TO MAKE HIM PAY
   THE CONSEQUENCES.

In effect, the entire newspaper was filled with these statements from Hitler's speech to the Reichstag of Friday, July 13, 1934. There was no mention of the murders of the von Schleichers, Gregor Strasser, or von Papen's assistant, Jung, although men in von Ribbentrop's position could not but know all these facts and Berlin gossip was

---

*Among the advertisements was a half page from Horn's, a Munich men's clothing store, offering SA uniform shirts in "first-class poplin with two spare collars, color SA brown, fadeproof, for 5.25 Reichsmarks" and breeches "in the new SA olive brown or in black, 9.00 Reichsmarks."

rampant. As François-Poncet pointed out: "Germans are talkative. Danger excites them. Despite censorship, police, and denunciations, they love to gossip."

The *Völkischer Beobachter* of July 14, 1934, listed the senior Nazis in attendance at the Reichstag, but von Ribbentrop was still not among them. In 1934, he was nowhere near the party's top echelon. The other top Nazis were unimpressed by him, with the exception of Heinrich Himmler of the SS; he wanted to enlist the cooperation of the Berlin "society businessman" who appealed to Hitler. In May 1934 he created von Ribbentrop a colonel in the "weekend" SS. Von Ribbentrop, taking advantage of Himmler's friendship, declared himself part of the victorious and newly powerful fraternity by frequently wearing his black uniform. To reward the SS for its actions in Bad Wiessee, Hitler had elevated it to independent status.

On July 24, William Dodd, the new American ambassador, was a guest in Dahlem. The von Ribbentrops tried to reassure him, but what followed would have given serious pause to any foreign diplomat who had to deal with the German government.

Engelbert Dollfuss, chancellor of Austria, the country of Hitler's birth, was so tiny that he was known among Vienna wags as the Millimetternich. To counteract the Nazis and still satisfy conservative Austrian appetites, he banned the Communist Party, virtually abolished representative government, and introduced a pseudofascist regime based on close friendship with Austria's big neighbor, Mussolini's Italy. Dollfuss had begun to heal Austria's ailing economy by arranging major loans from France and Britain, but the money was tied to Franco-British understanding that Austria would remain independent of Germany. Dollfuss's party, the Vaterländische Front, seemed to militate against a takeover by Austrian Nazis, which could lead to unification with Germany.

But on July 25, 1934, Dollfuss was murdered by Austrian Nazis. Despite instant denials from Berlin and the immediate recall and firing of the German ambassador to Vienna, Dr. Kurt Rieth, the western world blamed Adolf Hitler for Dollfuss's murder.

An astonishing commentary on the way Adolf Hitler had changed Germany is a story told by Franz von Papen, then still vice chancellor in name, but totally estranged from Hitler after his controversial Marburg speech and the murder of his speechwriter, Jung.[21] He and his son, at their country estate, were summoned by a sharp knock on the front door. Expecting to be arrested, they drew their pistols, opened the door — and were not surprised to find three SS men.

"Herr von Papen, the Führer wishes to speak to you on the phone at once. He is in Bayreuth." Von Papen thought he might get shot while he was on the phone, but, instead, was given an immediate phone connection with Hitler, who came straight to the point: "I want you to go to Vienna as ambassador." Von Papen, who knew nothing about the Dollfuss murder, asked why Hitler had called him after all that had happened between them. A nervous Adolf Hitler told him about Dollfuss and said, "You must go to Vienna. Rieth has behaved in an impossible manner and should actually be put before a military tribunal. You are the only man for the job." Von Papen asked how he could be expected to accept the assignment after the events of June 30, but, typically, did not say no to the Führer. Von Papen always landed like a cat.

Most western diplomats and journalists were sure that the Dollfuss murder had been engineered in Berlin. Although the June 30 SA purge might have been considered "an internal matter," a Berlin-directed murder of Dollfuss could not be so construed. Reports in the French and British press ranged from dismay to condemnation, and there was anger in Rome. Mussolini had been repelled by the June 30 massacre.[22] He called Hitler a "cruel and ferocious character, an Attila." The Dollfuss murder brought a much harsher reaction, because Austria was Mussolini's ward. He wanted to preserve an independent Austria.[23] On July 28, Rome's newspaper *Il Messaggero* wrote, "Only fools fall into the same trap twice," referring to Mussolini's earlier show of trust for Hitler. Italian troops were rushed to the Austrian border. Mussolini guaranteed Austrian independence to the right-wing Prince Starhemberg, Austria's vice chancellor. Mussolini was bitterly disappointed when France and Britain failed to do the same.[24] Nevertheless, Hitler seemed in retreat. He even fired Theo Habicht, the Nazi Party's chief in Austria.

Although von Ribbentrop assumed that German embassies everywhere were bound to report negative reactions to the Foreign Ministry, he made it his business to calm the Führer; that was exactly what Adolf Hitler wanted and needed. Even though the disarmament plenipotentiary's voice was not a major one, at least it was positive. Adolf Hitler often grasped at the straws of pleasant fiction in an ocean of unpleasant truth.

On August 3, Hitler closed the Austrian branch of the Nazi Party. Two days later he gave an interview to George Ward Price, senior correspondent of London's *Daily Mail*, in which he tried to calm the troubled waters: "No colonies . . . no thought of Austrian Anschluss . . . possible return to the League of Nations . . . end of war psychosis."[25]

The last brake on his arbitrary ways was about to be released. On August 1, unwilling to wait for the actual event, the cabinet decided that the offices of President and Chancellor would be combined after von Hindenburg's death. In the future, Hitler would not need presidential approval for any of his acts. The law was to take effect a day after the old President's death.

And on the following day, von Hindenburg died. Always prepared to clothe the unconstitutional in respectability, the government "put to the popular vote" the unification of President and Chancellor two weeks later. On August 19 the German people approved the measure, predictably, by 89.9 percent.

For two weeks, no last will of von Hindenburg's could be located. On August 15, Oskar von Hindenburg "found" an envelope with five red seals and gave it to von Papen. He, in turn, brought it to Hitler at the Berghof. It contained a "will," in which the old Junker praised Hitler and put the fate of Germany into the hands of the man he had often disdainfully called the "Austrian corporal." It was generally considered bogus, a fabrication of von Papen, Oskar von Hindenburg, and State Secretary Meissner.[26] A grateful Hitler rehabilitated von Papen and promoted Oskar von Hindenburg to general. Meissner remained state secretary to the Führer and chancellor.

Another act of obedient surrender took place when Reichswehr Minister von Blomberg ordered that the Reichswehr take the oath of allegiance not to the German Reich, but to the person of Adolf Hitler. Unlikely though it may seem today, in later years many disgusted and disillusioned German officers shied away from assassinating Hitler precisely because of this personal oath.

Later in August, von Ribbentrop was invited to England by Lord Rothermere, the publisher of the *Daily Mail*. The invitation impressed Hitler, and von Ribbentrop's stock rose still higher. He now became Adolf Hitler's advance man in the battle for an alliance with Britain. Other clever men in Hitler's circle might have been assigned more strategic work, but von Ribbentrop was given a very specific task to go with his title. He was to begin by signing some form of arms agreement with Great Britain and was to continue to enlist sympathetic British men of influence. The arms agreement could be focused on land, sea, and air.

It was unusual for Hitler to assign one task to one man. Often several competitors were assigned the same job. Each thought he had the most important responsibility and his Führer's total trust and attention. No doubt Joachim von Ribbentrop felt that he was Hitler's most trusted adviser.

In November von Ribbentrop, accompanied by Erich Kordt, set out to London for another meeting with Sir John Simon and Anthony Eden. This time the subject was an Anglo-German naval agreement. He launched an effort to establish "close and warm relationships" in Britain. Von Ribbentrop's informal arrival at Brown's Hotel signaled an unexpected display of British amity. All the evil of the bloody purge of June 30 and the murder of Dollfuss now seemed to have been forgotten in Britain as "not our business." Von Ribbentrop was entertained by Lord Londonderry, the Earl of Athlone, the Archbishop of Canterbury, and Arthur Henderson, the former foreign secretary.[27] In turn, he invited to breakfast the Lords Lloyd and Stonehaven, Mr. Norman Davis of the U.S. Embassy, Major Astor, and Mrs. Greville, a major Cunard shareholder. There were invitations to London's best clubs and to various hunts. The press was also eager to have his attention.

Von Ribbentrop was not quite so well received at a dinner party of Lord Cecil's, where Sir Austen Chamberlain expressed his anti-German feelings and George Bernard Shaw vented his spleen by telling von Ribbentrop to "stop talking peace! Talk attack, mayhem, and bloody battle, and these English will give you anything you want!"

Also somewhat reluctant was Lord Lothian, one of the architects of the Versailles Treaty.[28] Lothian, now regretting some of the harsh Versailles terms, said he had no objection to German rearmament if "they could convince the world of their peaceful intentions." Kordt thought that Lothian looked at von Ribbentrop as more of a courier than a diplomat.

E. W. Tennant, who had prepared von Ribbentrop's first unofficial meeting with Stanley Baldwin in 1933, claimed that Baldwin said he "liked von Ribbentrop's face" after their first breakfast conference, although Tennant's friend, J. C. C. Davidson, at whose home that meeting took place, denied this.[29] Von Ribbentrop also managed to intrigue the press lord Esmond Harmsworth, son of Lord Rothermere. He arranged for a dinner on December 19, 1934, with Hitler in Berlin for both Rothermere and Harmsworth, along with George Ward Price and Ernest Tennant.

British journalists were also invited to the party rallies at Nürnberg. These annual events were vast productions, which the Nazis organized beginning in September 1933. Hundreds of thousands of men and boys in uniforms from the Hitler Youth to Storm Troopers and SS filled an immense field that had once been the landing base for dirigibles. The party transformed it into the world's largest parade ground. From a platform high above the massed formations of ardent followers, the Führer preached his fierce sermons, sending his message to his people and to the whole world. At night, hundreds of antiaircraft floodlights surrounding the field were beamed straight up toward the sky, a "temple surrounded by pillars of ice," as it was described by its designer, Albert Speer, Hitler's favorite young architect. On one end of the field, facing the participants, stood a Greek revival structure a quarter-mile long, fronted by a speaker's platform twenty yards high and backed by a ten-yard concrete swastika straddled by its hovering eagle. These party rallies were part Wagnerian opera, part pagan ritual. Uniformed Nazi legions swore allegiance to the thunder of massed kettledrums, shouting their oaths with deep-throated synchronized roars.

Reichs Propaganda Minister Goebbels made strenuous efforts to assure good reports in the foreign press. Certain British free-lance journalists were paid to write enthusiastic articles; among them were the alcoholic Clifford Sharp of the *New Statesman,* Graham Seton Hutchinson, and James Murphy, who translated *Mein Kampf* into English.[30] Murphy eventually became an employee of Goebbels's Propaganda Ministry in Berlin. Schoolmasters were also approached. Dr. Robert Birley, headmaster of Charterhouse, told Harold Nicolson that Dr. Goebbels had arranged a trip to the rally for some of the pupils.

At first von Ribbentrop could count on some sympathy. The historian Richard Griffiths has pointed out that ever since the 1929 economic crisis, leading British Conservatives had begun to express doubt about the moral value of representative capitalist democracy and to regret its materialism and greed. The idea of corporate government, in which a country was run by a board of capable appointees, as demonstrated by Mussolini's fascism, had great appeal in some surprising quarters. Fascism seemed to show true concern for the working man without brutalizing the bourgeoisie and upper classes as Communism did. Ramsay MacDonald, Austen Chamberlain, and even Winston Churchill had all expressed praise for Mussolini. Writing from Rome for the *Times* of London on January 21, 1927, Churchill said about Mussolini, "If I were an Italian, I'd follow you against Lenin. But we in England have not had to fight this danger and have other ways of doing things."[31] In 1927, George Bernard Shaw wrote in a letter, "Mussolini is more Socialist than the British Labour Party." Many voices from unlikely quarters expressed doubt about democracy. In 1932, H. G. Wells wrote the pessimistic *After Democracy;* in 1933, the Socialist Harold Laski wrote *Democracy in Crisis;* J. R. B. Muir in 1934 wrote *Is Democracy a Failure?*

As Griffiths noted, many new nondemocratic governments had emerged:

Mussolini in Italy in 1922.
Mustafa Kemal Ataturk in Turkey in 1923.
Admiral Horthy in Hungary in 1920.
Pilsudski in Poland in 1926.
In Spain, between 1920 and 1930 Primo de Rivera.
Japan was run by decree.
Salazar's Portugal was a dictatorship.

These were all non-Communist countries, friendly with the western democracies. At first the emergence of Hitler's Nazi government following Germany's "incompetent republic" seemed natural. But after Nazi brutalities like the 1933 anti-Jewish boycott, the 1934 blood purge of Röhm, and the 1934 murder of Dollfuss, many profascist British conservatives began to draw a distinction between "constructive" fascism and the "animal brutality" of the Nazis. The fascists were "moral and upright"; the Nazis were "brutal and barbarian."

In 1934, von Ribbentrop could nonetheless count on the pacifism and isolationism of a Britain that had shed so much blood in the trenches of the Great War. The well-meaning seekers after some new form of "moral" government, and those who believed in "peace at any cost," were joined by the many who shrugged off reports of Nazi cruelties with "What concern is it of ours?"

Von Ribbentrop's efforts and even his early blunders were treated generously by many of Britain's upper class, even though they were not Nazi sympathizers. British hunger for peace misled both von Ribbentrop and his master until five minutes before midnight.

The list of those Britons whose sympathies were available to von Ribbentrop in 1934 was immensely varied. At one end stood the lunatic fringe, the racists, the chauvinists, the haters. Most successful of these was Sir Oswald Mosley, originally a man of great charm and imagination, who began his political life as a Conservative MP, but on October 1, 1932, founded the British Union of Fascists, with all the black-shirted, arm-raising, "thunder and lightning" trappings. Mosley's attitude was that the "drama was necessary and efficient" and the working classes had no sense of the ridiculous.

By 1934, the BUF had lost many of its intellectuals but attracted some upper-middle-class conservatives and some working-class members. By 1934, when von Ribbentrop made his first real efforts in Britain, the BUF still tended to separate itself from Nazism, which was "too barbaric and pagan."[32]

On June 7 the BUF held a major rally in Olympia, using it as a London *Sportpalast*. Violence broke out between BUF and its opponents in the hall, and the BUF goon squads duplicated the worst of the SA's brutality. This finished the union for many, who now saw it as nothing but a British Nazi Party.[33] It also brought an end to any support from Lord Rothermere's papers, and many earlier Mosley supporters defected, in part because of Mosley's ranting attacks on Jews. To conservative fascists, however, these were more a matter of style than of content.

In 1934 some right-wingers formed the January Club, led by Sir John Squire, an editor and writer and an admirer of Mussolini. It began as a study group of "men interested in modern systems of government." It gave a largely upper-class platform to the fascist and corporate-state points of view and also gave fascists the chance to listen to those who were not fascist. Among the speakers were contributors to the *English Review,* known for fascist views.

The BUF still attempted to seem "respectable," but it decided not to accept Jews as members and claimed it was "under attack from an international conspiracy."[34] On July 14, 1934, Lord Rothermere finally declared himself in the *Daily Mail*. In an open letter to Mosley he said he was against fascism, dictatorship, the corporate state, and anti-Semitism. Other conservatives agreed.

British anti-Semites ranged from those who believed in a "conspiracy theory" to those who practiced the banal sort of social ostracism and stereotyping. Typical expressions were T. S. Eliot's poem *"Bleistein with a Cigar,"* whose subject was a "Chicago Semite Viennese," and the popular Bulldog Drummond books by Sapper (Cyril McNeile), in which a particular villain's "hooked nose proclaimed his race."[35] The "international Jewish conspiracy" group was headed by Mrs. Nesta Webster, an amateur historian, whose name was prominent in British fascist circles until the war. She maintained that Bolshevism was the creation of German Jews. The main publication that gave a platform to anti-Semites like Nesta Webster was the small newspaper *The Patriot*.

A much stranger publication was *The Aeroplane,* basically a magazine for amateur pilots. Its editor, C. G. Grey, used it to deliver himself of astonishing theories about "good" and "bad" Jewish tribes, even trying to point at the "bad" Japhetic Jewish Communist influence on Welsh miners.[36] The anti-Semitic writer Gordon Bolitho said in 1934 that the "reason we hear Jews first is that they wail more loudly," and Percy Wyndham Lewis, a warm Nazi sympathizer, wrote in 1931 that anti-Semitism is a "mere bagatelle," which must stand in no one's way. These were only a few of the many Nazi apologists. Rolf Gardiner wrote in his book, published in Berlin in 1933, that the "smell of Asia was in Ghetto beards" and that every country "had the Jews it deserved."

At the absolute extreme end of the British Nazi scale stood the Imperial Fascist League, headed by a surgeon, Arnold Leese, a war veteran. He turned down an invitation to join with Mosley's BUF because he claimed Mosley's first wife, Cynthia Curzon, was the granddaughter of Levi Leiter, a Jewish grain dealer from Chicago. Leese even proposed a gas chamber solution to end the Jewish problem.

At that time the British royal family was still firmly under the command of its paternal monarch, King George V, who would soon chastise his heir Edward, the Prince of Wales, for delivering a speech friendly to the German war veterans in June 1935. The speech contained the sort of ideas von Ribbentrop still held in 1936, when he became ambassador to Great Britain. He was never able to shake his schoolboy view of Britain, almost unchanged since his boyhood visit to London, or his Ottawa-born theories about the British Empire and the political power of its aristocracy. Among the influential members of "society" was the eccentric, American-born Emerald Lady Cunard, who conducted a potent society salon. It was she who introduced Wallis Simpson to the Prince of Wales. The witty, flirtatious Emerald Cunard saw Joachim von Ribbentrop as a delicious "real, live Nazi" to be served on a platter to her friends, ironically not unlike the von Ribbentrops' own Nazi presentations in Dahlem in 1932.

For many British society people, Nazi Germany was the latest tourist attraction, where "one was invited and escorted everywhere by uniformed Nazis." They told exciting tales of being received by von Ribbentrop and then meeting Hitler. A thrilling safari into deepest Naziland.

Harold Nicolson described the syndrome, and the salons at which it flourished. "The harm which these silly, selfish hostesses give is immense. They convey to foreign envoys the impression that foreign policy is decided in their own drawing rooms. They convey an atmosphere of authority and grandeur when it is only flatulence of the spirit!"

As 1935 came, so did the next Hitler "shock." On January 13, the Saar region, which had been under French mandate, voted by 90.67

percent to return to Germany. On January 17, the Saar's citizens decided that the reunion would take place on March 1, 1935. France's new foreign minister, following Barthou's assassination, was Pierre Laval, who considered the Saar's defection legal. He had just signed an agreement with Mussolini clearing Italy's "economic way" into Ethiopia, though this would eventually not be enough for Mussolini. George Ward Price of the *Daily Mail* wrote an interview in which Hitler threatened that anyone who tackled Germany "would reach into thorns and thistles." To put some force behind his words, he decided to lift the cover of secrecy from his new Luftwaffe. Germany admitted to owning twenty-five hundred planes.

The British government soon published a White Paper accusing Germany of secret rearmament. Probably as a result of this official blast, Foreign Minister von Neurath informed the British government early in March that a planned visit to Berlin by Sir John Simon, the foreign secretary, and Anthony Eden, Lord Privy Seal, would have to be postponed. More pressure, although the official explanation was that the Führer "had a cold" and had to "recuperate in Bavaria."

France lengthened its time for compulsory military service from one to two years to bolster the size of its military. The very next day, Hitler reintroduced compulsory military service to Germany, which until then had only the professional 100,000-man Reichswehr.* The plan was to raise an army of 580,000 men. On March 18 the British protested this new breach of the Versailles Treaty; on March 21 the French and Italians made their own protest. But there was no doubt: Hitler was raising the stakes.

On March 25, despite the postponement by Hitler, Sir John Simon and Anthony Eden arrived in Berlin to discuss the state of armament with Hitler, von Neurath, and von Ribbentrop. Hitler told them that Germany now had air parity. His *faits accomplis* taught von Ribbentrop lessons in modern statesmanship, conducted the Nazi way.

On April 11 in Stresa, Britain, France, and even *Italy* condemned German rearmament, conscription, and other treaty breaches.† And then the League of Nations issued a similar protest. Von Ribbentrop could well gloat over his Führer's string of successes, despite the Stresa condemnation. It seemed that Germany's best diplomacy was indeed the mailed fist.

The time had come to modify the Nazi "blood" laws for diplomatic convenience. Probably with Japan in mind, the German Minis-

---

*Officially. It was actually larger.
†Italy was trying to protect its godchild Austria.

try of the Interior, which administered the racial laws, issued a decree on April 18 that, provided they were not Jews, those who were of foreign blood could be treated as "Aryans" and exempted from the racial laws if it was found "in the interest of foreign policy."

Two economic agreements were signed by Germany in April 1935, one with Soviet Russia, giving the Russians long-term credit, and one with Italy, relating to foreign currency. Von Ribbentrop was learning further lessons, though the ones relating to Britain must have been almost painful for so devoted an anglophile. A man does not like to discover the clay of his heroes' feet. It also must have cost him some embarrassment, after his tales of admiration, to admit to Adolf Hitler that the British were "just another weak democracy."

Doubts must surely have assailed the conventional von Ribbentrops from time to time; no matter how often he wore his black SS uniform, Joachim von Ribbentrop must have been aware of the contradiction of his upbringing. During these early Nazi times his untitled father was a silent and probably disapproving spectator. Colonel Richard Ribbentrop's natural loyalties were to the senior Army officers whose few dissenting voices were among the first of any consequence to be heard. As for the Henkells of Wiesbaden, they kept a deep silence. Otto Henkell's respected brother-in-law Opfermann, a Jew, had recently committed suicide in sorrow over the Nazis.[37]

But whatever doubts von Ribbentrop may have had quickly seemed to vanish when he was named Extraordinary Ambassador of the German Reich on Special Mission. The pompous title was bestowed for several reasons. Von Ribbentrop had often complained that his lack of ambassadorial rank impeded his dealings with foreign ministers. Also, he was frequently snubbed by Germany's ambassadors in London and Paris. He could no longer tolerate these humiliations and bitterly complained to his Führer, who then consented to award the rank of ambassador. Von Ribbentrop had also won the right to bypass the conventional Foreign Office channels. Usually, ambassadors reported to the foreign minister, von Neurath. Von Ribbentrop could now report directly to Hitler while submitting a parallel "courtesy" report to von Neurath. Von Ribbentrop retained this status and arrangement until 1938, when he himself became foreign minister. But until that time, all of his dispatches were addressed to "Führer and Foreign Minister." It was part of Hitler's system to duplicate missions and foster rivalries.

The main purpose of the appointment was to arm von Ribbentrop with rank for his London negotiations of the Naval Agreement of 1935. The British signaled that the treaty was acceptable. Only the actual numbers were still open, although German demands could have come as no surprise to the British. The ratio of 35 to 100 tons had been openly mentioned on several occasions both by Hitler and by von Ribbentrop. According to Dr. Paul Schwarz, a former ministry official, both von Neurath in Berlin and Ambassador Leopold von Hösch in London had called the terms impossible and declared that they would never be accepted by the British. Hitler insisted that von Ribbentrop could close the agreement, and he was right. Three days before the actual signing, Ambassador von Hösch, while attending a ball in London, heard his own naval attaché, Captain Wassner, confirm that the deal was as good as made.

At this time two nations changed leaders. Stanley Baldwin became the British prime minister, and Pierre Laval became France's. The two men were of entirely different character. Baldwin was extremely steadfast; Laval was forever the opportunist.

On May 2, 1935, the Franco-Russian Mutual Assistance Pact was signed, giving Hitler both offense and excuse. He relished such pretexts for sudden acts of policy and now called an emergency meeting in Munich on June 8 to discuss Danzig, the free port on the Baltic, once German and Hanseatic and then mandated to the Poles after the war. The participants: Hitler, Göring, von Blomberg, Hjalmar Schacht, and the two Nazi Party heads in Danzig, Albert Forster and Arthur Greiser. With things churning in Germany, von Ribbentrop was once more on his way to London, this time for the naval negotiations. He climbed into a big Junkers plane with the letters D-AMY; it was to be his private plane for years to come. Traveling with him, but in other planes, were Kordt and Ambassador Paul Otto Schmidt, the Foreign Ministry's brilliant chief interpreter.* The thirty-six-year-old Schmidt was a ministry professional, who predated the Nazis. He was the man whose face appears in nearly every photo taken of Hitler with foreign dignitaries. Schmidt was fluent in English, French, and Italian. In the case of Turkish or Japanese, he would use the common alternative language, French with the Turks and English with the Japanese.

However, he was even more valuable because of his photographic memory. He had total recall. Both German and foreign negotiators knew they could rely on Schmidt to give an accurate account of the oral record. Schmidt did not become a party member until 1943. Also in von Ribbentrop's group were Admiral Karl Georg Schuster, a Cap-

---

*He was actually *Gesandter*, just below senior ambassador. It was an unusually high rank for an interpreter.

tain Kiderlen, and Dr. Ernst Woermann, the "British" expert in the ministry.

Others came several planeloads later, forty in all. They took two floors of the Carlton House Hotel, and five Mercedes cars were shipped over for them. Von Ribbentrop insisted that the swastika flag be hoisted over the Haymarket entrance of the hotel, causing no small sensation. The treaty had already been prepared down to the smallest detail by Captain Wassner, the naval attaché, whom some considered the real architect of the agreement.

First, however, came the celebrations for the Silver Jubilee of King George V and Queen Mary. Each man in the delegation had been issued white tie and tails for the many London Silver Jubilee balls, including one at Londonderry House.

Dr. Paul Schwarz described a party to watch the Jubilee Parade given by Ambassador von Hösch on the terrace of the German Embassy, which had the best view in London, overlooking Pall Mall. There was also the magnificent parade for Trooping the Colours. Three distinct groups had formed: British society guests, then von Hösch, his staff, and Diplomatic Corps friends, and finally the von Ribbentrop delegation. The German visitors around von Ribbentrop raised their arms in the Hitler salute for the passing of the royal family. Although there was obvious dislike between von Hösch and von Ribbentrop, the latter carefully made some friendly gestures, which paid dividends. The mollified von Hösch later arranged that von Ribbentrop be invited to a dinner of Emerald Cunard's, where he was introduced to the Prince of Wales and Mrs. Simpson. Leopold von Hösch was a wealthy, witty, and charming bachelor who was much liked by London society.[38] He and the prince both loved jazz, and the two had good rapport. Von Ribbentrop, after having met Wallis Simpson, made it a custom to send her seventeen roses. No one ever knew why. Diplomats gossiped and even Hitler asked but got no explanation. The recipient seemed equally perplexed. It certainly was not a matter of romance.

Immediately following the great parade on June 3, treaty discussions began at the London Foreign Office. Von Ribbentrop was blunt. He began by saying that the Führer had instructed him to insist on the 35–100 formula without any further negotiations. According to the interpreter, Schmidt, these were the actual words: After stating that Germany wished 35 tons to Britain's hundred, von Ribbentrop continued, in Schmidt's translation, "If the British government does not accept this at once, we see no purpose in continuing these discussions.

We must ask for an immediate decision." Sir John Simon was clearly taken aback by this undiplomatic opening. Red-faced and uncharacteristically angry, he excused himself before the end of the meeting. After returning to the hotel, the ever-suspicious von Ribbentrop insisted that all Carlton House conversations be held in a whisper and at the center of each room to avoid any microphones supposedly planted in paintings or mirrors by the wily British Secret Service.

The next day Sir Robert Craigie of the Foreign Office came to the Carlton House and invited the delegation to meet at the Admiralty at ten the next morning, June 5, for "a pleasant surprise." There would then be a luncheon at 10 Downing Street. The next morning the Germans were conducted into the legendary Board Room of the Admiralty, where for hundreds of years the First Lords of the Admiralty and their associates had made their most important decisions.[39] Next to the First Sea Lord's high-backed chair was an ancient map with a sort of needle that told the direction of the wind in the Channel. Once upon a time this was the deciding factor for the island nation in time of crisis. The First Sea Lord, Sir Bolton Eyres Monsell, informed von Ribbentrop that the proportional strength of 35 to 100 tons was deemed acceptable.*

The British cabinet had agreed after a short discussion, thereby scuttling part of their Stresa protest of six weeks earlier. Privately, Erich Kordt, who predated the Nazis in the Foreign Ministry, was furious. He believed that if Brüning, the old Weimar chancellor, had been given such quick acceptance of any breaches of the Versailles Treaty, Germany would have remained a democratic republic. The crude new Nazi tactics were confirmed by a luncheon in von Ribbentrop's honor at 10 Downing Street, attended by the cabinet members Baldwin, Neville Chamberlain, Sir John Simon, Sir Samuel Hoare, Eyres Monsell, Eden, and others. Kordt, Schmidt, and the other professional German diplomats must have been shaken by the discarding of everything they deemed acceptable international custom and by the success of the Hitler style of diplomacy.

Von Ribbentrop soon got into the habit of putting his cards on the table, "take it or leave it." He was now convinced Hitler was right. Schmidt wrote, "Perhaps von Ribbentrop's rough methods worked. I often remembered that later whenever I had to translate certain dis-

---

*The 35–100 proportion of tonnage (rather than ships) led Hitler to order the immediate building of two "pocket" battleships with maximum armament on minimum tonnage.

tasteful statements made by Hitler or von Ribbentrop that would once have been considered a slap in the face by our pre–1933 diplomats."

D-AMY flew von Ribbentrop directly to Munich to report his triumph to his Führer at Berchtesgaden's Haus Wachenfeld, as the Berghof was still called. This was where he had first met Hitler. The chalet's front door became one of the most famous photographic "sets" of the Hitler era. Neville Chamberlain, the Duke of Windsor, and David Lloyd George were all photographed stepping out of a 7.7 litre *Grossen* Mercedes and climbing up these stairs with their SS guard. The step on which Hitler stood to greet them denoted his respect for the visitor. If he descended the entire flight and stood at the bottom, the visitor was of great importance to him. After waiting for a day in Munich, von Ribbentrop and his group were invited to proceed to Berchtesgaden and were greeted as returning heroes. The delegation then returned to London to complete the Naval Agreement, which was signed on June 18. From London, von Ribbentrop flew to meet Hitler in Hamburg, where he assured his delighted Führer that a wider Anglo-German treaty was now feasible. Twenty million marks were allotted as a reward to the Ribbentrop Büro, which then officially became the Dienststelle Ribbentrop, the Ribbentrop Agency, although everyone still called it the Büro.

There were instant protests from France about the Naval Agreement. Laval complained that the Versailles Treaty seemed to have become a private matter between Germany and England. Eden had to go to Paris to soothe ruffled feelings. Meanwhile, Mussolini had his own surprises for the world. He decided to expand Italy's influence in Africa and threatened war in Ethiopia.

July 1935 was a glorious month for von Ribbentrop. He basked in his success and became Hitler's star adviser in all matters of international diplomacy. Annelies was six months pregnant, and Adolf Hitler had promised to be godfather. The next child, born on September 2, 1935, was named Adolf.

At a July 3 meeting in Berlin with Colonel Josef Beck, Poland's foreign minister, officially listed in order of attendance were Ribbentrop, Göring, von Neurath, and Josef Lipski, the Polish ambassador. Also on July 3, von Ribbentrop stated that from then on he would be responsible for the conduct of colonial policy. On July 11, von Ribbentrop met with U.S. Ambassador Dodd about German-Japanese relations. Von Ribbentrop's star was on the rise. He was involved in meetings that were once reserved for von Neurath. The rumor that he had Hitler's ear caused many foreign statesmen to bypass normal channels.

That July a group of Veterans of the British Legion was received by Adolf Hitler. It was von Ribbentrop who had, through unofficial contacts, arranged this visit. And it was Eden who suspected that the men would be used for Nazi propaganda, as, of course, they were. Following a visit to the "sanitized" camp at Dachau, Heinrich Himmler was host at a "small family dinner for them all."

The Dachau concentration camp of 1934 and 1935 was not the crematorium-equipped hell of the forties. The Nazis used it as a demonstration facility for distinguished foreign visitors: "This is how we re-educate our criminals."

Sometimes that backfired. After Sir Arnold Wilson, MP, a man known as sympathetic to appeasement, was proudly shown through Dachau, he wrote, "There was in the atmosphere of the camp something against which my soul revolted." Admiral Sir Barry Domville, who was apologetic about most of Nazi Germany's offenses, said only that he "admired Dachau's administration."[40] Startling in its eccentric notion is the statement by T. E. Lawrence (of Arabia) that Hitler, like him, was ascetic, poor, lived in a small house, and was misunderstood by the press. Lawrence died later that year in a motorcycle crash.[41]

The tenth of September marked the opening of the 1935 party rally in Nürnberg. Looming over Europe was Mussolini's threat of war in Ethiopia; the League of Nations planned sanctions against Italy. But for Adolf Hitler's Germany, the world's attention focused on Nürnberg and that vast parade ground. The rally's theme in 1935 was Freedom. In ironic contrast, Hitler simultaneously proclaimed the new racial laws, technically known as the Reichscitizenship Law and the Law for the Defense of German Blood and German Honor *(Reichsbürgergesetz und das Gesetz sum Schutze des deutschen Blutes and der deutschen Ehre)*. The laws were later known throughout the world as the Nürnberg Laws, although they were signed in Berlin by Minister of the Interior Dr. Frick on September 15, 1935.

The original version was comparatively mild. It replaced the notion of race with that of *blood* in the following words (the convoluted Nazi style sounds equally clumsy in translation):

German blood does not of itself form a race. Instead, the German people is composed of the members of differing races. However, what all of these races have in common is that their blood is mutually compatible, and that a mixture of these bloods, in contrast to bloods that are not of a related sort, will not cause any inhibitions or tensions.*

This avoided the untenable notion of a "pure" German race and, instead, spoke of compatible "German bloodedness" *(Deutschblutigkeit)*. The laws could specifically be pointed at Jews, Gypsies, Slavs, Semites (Arabs), Africans, Orientals, Mongolians, and anyone whose blood was "not akin *(artverwandt)* to German bloods."[42]

The original laws claimed they were so structured that they excluded Jews without "causing hardship." But, of course, the lawyer, architect, government official, or businessman who could not be accredited or licensed by the state was facing extreme hardship.

Here is the original explanation of the laws given in 1935 by Reichsminister Frick:

> The Reichscitizenship Law and the Law for the Protection of the Blood as well as the attached regulations shall not have the purpose of lowering the standing of members of the Jewish people because of their [exclusion from] membership in the national community. Instead, the exclusion of Jews from official German life and the prevention of racial mixing are imperatively necessary to secure the continuation of the German people's existence. Jews in Germany shall not be prevented from pursuing a livelihood. However, the fate of Germany shall in the future be solely in the hands of the German people.[43]

These original regulations were endlessly changed, modified, and brutalized during the coming years. They became unspeakably cruel in major matters, and were also seeded with endless chicanery in minor matters. For instance, three years later, on September 30, 1938: "In conformity with Paragraph 3 of the Reichscitizenship laws of 1938, certification of all Jewish physicians shall be canceled as of September 30, 1938." This eliminated the nine thousand Jewish doctors, of whom 3152 still practiced in Germany in 1938. Seven hundred and nine of them, all decorated for gallantry in the World War, retained a form of temporary certification as "medical practitioners," with permission to treat Jews and certain non-Jews. These racial laws, which ruined so many lives and cost so many more, seeped into the most unlikely quarters and even in their least virulent form destroyed human decencies.

As an example, a young Foreign Ministry official, an honorary SS officer named Eberhard von Thadden, wished to marry. He came from a distinguished, titled military family and had been assigned his SS

*Translation by the author.

rank by decree. In the routine prenuptial "racial purity" investigation, the SS found that he had a Jewish great-great-grandfather on his maternal side. They refused permission for his marriage and began proceedings to throw him out of the SS, which would have ruined his career in the foreign service. Von Thadden set out to prove that he was really the illegitimate great-great-grandson of a Russian prince and was therefore Aryan.[44] The SS accepted his illegitimacy. Von Thadden could now marry and continue his career in the ministry, ironically, in the Jewish affairs department.

In the Third Reich it was better to be an illegitimate Aryan than to be of distinguished family and have a Jewish great-great-grandfather. Actually, von Thadden's Jewish great-great-grandfather, Ludwig Epenstein, was great-uncle of Ritter (Knight) Dr. Hermann von Epenstein, who was Hermann Göring's godfather and who was of Jewish descent. It was Göring who had interceded for young von Thadden. These were the first small tragicomic manifestations of the vast evil that was to follow and the bloodbath that would soak German honor.

Meanwhile, Joachim von Ribbentrop enjoyed his new role. On September 27, 1935, accompanied by Kordt, he paid a visit to Belgium. He met with the prime minister, Paul van Zeeland, and informed him that Germany was dropping its claims to Malmédy and Eupen, two towns that had been discussed by Germany as a claim. He also assured the Belgians that Germany was "their last bulwark against Communism," his usual sales pitch. He received an unexpected answer. Van Zeeland said, "If one improves living standards, there is a decreased danger of Communism, and we have managed to do that." They also talked inconclusively about some former German colonies then under Belgian mandate.

Next, the "strange blood but still compatible" theory was brought into play.[45] Von Ribbentrop began the first move in one of his favorite plans; he made friends with Japan's military attaché in Berlin, Lieutenant Colonel Hiroshi Oshima, son of the German-trained war minister of Japan. The first flickerings of the Anti-Comintern Pact now showed on the horizon.

Von Ribbentrop had been a busy diplomat since the signing of the Naval Agreement, and Konstantin von Neurath had not failed to notice. He was aware, too, that the Führer had great distrust and even disdain for the slow, meticulous, judicious, titled diplomats at the Foreign Ministry in its traditional home at Wilhelmstrasse 74–76. To Hitler they seemed inflexible, unimaginative, snobbish, and overbearing. On the twenty-fifth of October, the month the Nazis also called by the ancient Teuton name of Gilbhardt, the very *ancien régime* von

Neurath offered his resignation to Adolf Hitler. It was refused. Hitler was not yet ready to depend on his own duo of Ribbentrop to the west and Rosenberg to the east.

Nor did he want Göring or Goebbels to attempt to elbow his way into the field of foreign policy. He liked things the way they were, with everybody around him hating and distrusting everybody else while he enjoyed their contest. Von Neurath's resignation would have cost him the apparatus of professional German diplomats and their relationship with foreign professional diplomats. He need not have worried; von Neurath did not resign. Konstantin von Neurath liked to present himself as the classic aristocrat, diplomat, and *grand seigneur,* but often he showed his true opportunist colors, as in the contents of a letter of October 30, 1934, Ref. 83-63 17/10 to Hess, Frick, and Goebbels. It concerned a directive he had sent to the German ambassador in London about a Jewish group that had asked for help. Ambassador von Hösch probably sympathized with the Jews.

> About negotiating or dealing with any Jewish organizations, such a gesture should be an expression of our strength and not of our weakness. The Jewish question must be addressed only from a position of strength and not as a result of any economic or political pressure. To give in on the Jewish question would not lead to a satisfactory resolution of any political situation, nor would it satisfy our Jewish enemies. Instead, it would undermine the ideological position of National Socialist Germany. The worse their economic position, the less should we compromise on the Jewish question.
>
> [signed] Frhr. von Neurath

It is assumed that the Messrs. Hess, Frick, and Goebbels were properly impressed by the man's Nazi fervor. There is no report of the reaction of the highly respected Ambassador von Hösch in London.

In 1935 von Ribbentrop was not the only one who would hoist the swastika flag like the one he had ordered flown over the Carlton House Hotel during June of that year. An event in faraway New York Harbor assured that every German mission, agency, or ship anywhere in the world would fly the Hakenkreuz (Hooked Cross) flag. One night a group of men came aboard the German liner *Bremen* when she was docked in New York, tore down the swastika flag, which she flew instead of the German merchant flag, and threw it into the Hudson River. The following day an angry Hitler decreed in a typical show of temper that the swastika flag would henceforth be the only national flag of the German Reich.[46]

● ● ●

For Joachim and Annelies von Ribbentrop the beginning of 1936 was filled with triumphs, to be followed by setbacks. The year started with groups of German war veterans visiting London on January 4 and 19. The visits were completely overshadowed by the illness of old King George V, who died on January 21. No doubt von Ribbentrop, after a ceremonial moment of mourning for the crusty old anti-German King, was gladdened by the presence of a new king, Edward VIII. Edward was by then in love with Wallis Simpson and friendly with some German sympathizers, like Emerald Cunard.

Von Ribbentrop's February in 1936 was to be focused on Hitler's anger about the Franco-Soviet Pact, which was ratified by the French Chamber of Deputies on the twenty-seventh by 353 to 164. It had expected consequences. On February 14, von Neurath, von Ribbentrop, Göring, and von Blomberg met with Hitler, who told them of his plan to send German troops into the demilitarized Rhineland in revenge. This would be the first military move. Hitler also briefed General von Fritsch, chief of staff of the Wehrmacht. The reactions of his advisers was halfhearted. Von Neurath and Göring urged caution, as did von Blomberg. It is probable that von Ribbentrop sat on the fence until he could gauge Hitler's true intentions. Eventually, the discussion narrowed to the Führer and the Army's chief of staff. General von Fritsch said, "Don't!" But Hitler insisted, "It's my responsibility."

On March 7, using the "breach of the Locarno Pact (the Franco-Soviet treaty) by France" as an excuse and trumpeting that Germany's borders were "threatened by France, indirectly through its new ally Russia and directly by Russia's ally, Czechoslovakia," German troops moved into the demilitarized Rhineland.

There are few eyewitnesses, but rumor has it that on the night of March 6–7, while his troops were on their way west, Hitler had fits of nervous hysteria. The troops had orders to withdraw if there was any sign of French resistance. It would have been an international embarrassment if Hitler's nineteen battalions of infantry and thirteen artillery sections, about thirty-five thousand men, had had to turn tail. In the Rhineland, jubilant people greeted the German soldiers.

The Franco-Soviet treaty was only one item on a list of international developments that primed Hitler's Rhineland move. In January, Soviet Russia doubled its military budget. In February, the Socialists were voted into power in Spain. In March, Léon Blum, a Socialist and a Jew, became the French prime minister. To Hitler, the whole left-wing world was conspiring against Germany.[47] Following a Hitler Reichstag speech justifying the Rhineland move, Bolshevism became the next *leitmotif* of every conversation held by von Ribbentrop in France or Britain as justification for the new Luftwaffe and the introduction of conscription. Did the Führer not warn the French in his February 21 interview with Bertrand de Jouvenal of *Paris Midi* to consider the consequences of their Soviet pact? There was "no arch enmity between Germany and France." The journalist had asked, "What about your anti-French statements in *Mein Kampf?*" and Hitler replied, "I'll correct those in the great book of history."

On April 10 D-AMY and von Ribbentrop bounced their way back across the Channel to London. This time the Extraordinary Plenipontiary was carrying a full peace plan to be handed to Anthony Eden. This was Hitler's way: hit them and then propose peace. The proposal contained nineteen points, among them a twenty-five-year nonaggression pact with France and Belgium, reinforcement of the troops now in the Rhineland, no gas warfare, no bombing of open cities, the scrapping of tanks. The proposals went on and on. Eden promised to "study them carefully."[48]

Nevertheless, the General Staffs of Britain, France, and Belgium held a joint conference, which von Ribbentrop had hoped to see postponed because of Hitler's peace offer, and there was no immediate response to the proposals. Furious, von Ribbentrop climbed into D-AMY and returned to Berlin.

One month later, on May 7, Sir Eric Phipps, His Majesty's ambassador in Berlin, handed the Foreign Ministry a lengthy questionnaire asking for clarification of many details of the Hitler proposals. Hitler probably deemed it a typical exercise in British sarcasm. He called it "an insult" and ignored it. The British questionnaire was indeed ironic and terse; the easily affronted Hitler was not amused.

But Adolf Hitler had occupied the Rhineland, and explanations, such as they were, had to be tendered to the League of Nations and the signers of the Locarno Pact. A conference was convened in London to demand clarification from Germany. Von Ribbentrop was chosen to represent his country.

In London, there already existed a degree of understanding. After all, some people said, the Rhineland *is* German, and Baldwin and Eden calmed the House of Commons. This, they explained, was no hostile move. While the French shared a common frontier with Germany, Britain did not.

The French saw things differently. The Rhineland had been demilitarized so that no surprise attack could ever again be launched into France. The Locarno Pact signatories of the League of Nations had convened their meeting in London, where Germany was now asked to come to explain its side.

Von Ribbentrop appeared before the committee accompanied by Kordt and Hans Dieckhoff, by Dr. Woermann, the ministry legal expert, and by a team of fifty from the Büro. Hitler had expressed the desire to go to London himself to present his view, but, knowing the Führer's mercurial temper, von Neurath and von Ribbentrop, unusual allies, had dissuaded him. Now Hitler wished von Ribbentrop to help smooth the way in front of the committee by hinting at an offer from Germany to re-enter the League.

The venue for the conference was beautiful old St. James's Palace. Using the same arguments he had called on in defense of the Rhineland move — namely, accusations against France, Russia, Czechoslovakia, and their supposed plans of aggression — von Ribbentrop stood up and made his statement. The council then retired to consider its verdict.

During the time the council deliberated, von Ribbentrop was invited to Sir Robert Vansittart's country house, probably at the suggestion of the well-liked Ambassador von Hösch, who was also a guest. Von Hösch knew that Under Secretary for Foreign Affairs Vansittart and his American wife were no admirers of von Ribbentrop's, but he thought he could ease the way for him. After all, he was a foreign service officer, and von Ribbentrop was Hitler's protégé.

The council of the League of Nations delivered its verdict: to condemn Germany. The vote was eleven of twelve. Only Chile abstained. The Versailles article deemed as breached was number 43. Von Ribbentrop, after some meetings with sympathizers in London, returned to Berlin to reassure his Führer that, despite the League's verdict, he need expect no further repercussions from the Rhineland move.[49] Then to doubly reassure himself, Hitler asked the German people for a vote of confidence. On March 29 the vote was cast: 98.8 percent in favor of the Führer. Germany and the League were still going their separate ways.

On April 10, Ambassador Leopold von Hösch died in London. In his memoirs, von Ribbentrop says he mourned him deeply, but according to the former diplomat Paul Schwarz, von Ribbentrop did not even attend von Hösch's funeral in Berlin. His dislike seems petty to the point that he even had the grave of von Hösch's little pet dachshund in the London Embassy garden leveled.

April 1936 also marked the beginning of the sad and often misunderstood career of Charles Lindbergh as a political figure and an unwilling ally of Nazi Germany. It started at the American Embassy in Berlin, on the Tiergartenstrasse, a few miles from the Foreign Ministry.

The American embassies in Berlin and London were run by men of different views. William E. Dodd in Berlin was decidedly and militantly anti-Nazi. Joseph Kennedy in London, after 1937, was worried about the Nazis but inclined toward accommodating them while urging the United States to "stay away" from trouble. Kennedy was an American isolationist; he believed Germany had become more powerful than England and France, and he did not want the United States to go to war in Europe on the losing side. He had arrived in London with his large family and with some of his inborn Irish Catholic suspicions of the English.

The Dodds lived in Berlin with their son and daughter, the latter a beautiful, vivacious, and intelligent girl who seemed at first to be much taken with all the handsome young men in Berlin. In fact, to her father's dismay, she began an affair with a young Nazi named Rudolf Diels, who was the first head of the Gestapo. It did not last.

In 1936 both Kennedy and Dodd had contact with Charles Lindbergh. Von Ribbentrop got involved because later the seemingly warm Lindbergh-Kennedy relations gave him false hope. He thought they would have a strong influence on Roosevelt.

Lindbergh's involvement with Nazi Germany began with Major Truman Smith, the military attaché at the U.S. Embassy in Berlin. Smith, one of America's brightest young General Staff officers, was troubled by Germany's growing airpower. He wanted to learn more about the new Luftwaffe, but obviously his access was limited. He had heard that the Lindberghs were living in England, still avoiding the publicity created by the murder of their kidnaped baby. At breakfast one morning, Smith read in *Paris Herald* that Lindbergh had visited a French airplane factory.[50] Smith had an idea. Why not persuade Lindbergh to look into the rumors about the new Luftwaffe? Lindbergh was a colonel in the U.S. Army Reserves, so he could be approached on the basis of soldierly patriotism. Smith broached the idea to Ferdinand Mayer, the U.S. chargé d'affaires in Berlin, while Ambassador Dodd was on leave in the United States, and Mayer enthusiastically approved. Getting Lindbergh invited was not as complicated as it seemed. Like all senior Nazis, Air Minister Göring was desperately trying to "produce" famous visitors during the year of the Berlin Olympics. Smith thought of offering to ex-pilot Göring *the* Charles Lindbergh, the world's most famous pilot. He suggested the idea to a senior Air Ministry aide, who called a few days later to assure Smith that Minister Göring and State Secretary Erhard Milch would be delighted. Germany's new Luftwaffe would welcome Colonel Lindbergh and would show him anything he wished to see, including, of course, the Olympics. Göring could open all doors. He had even enlisted the partly Jewish Milch, who was a former Lufthansa chairman.*

Although it may seem strange that the Luftwaffe would reveal its secrets, the Nazi government was eager to impress other nations, to scare them and to warn them. Propaganda stood above secrecy. They could never deceive an expert like Lindbergh, so they would have to show him everything. (Almost everything: the one thing they never revealed was the experimental jet fighter 262 prototype being tested by Messerschmitt). Major Smith, who had never met Lindbergh, wrote to him via the assistant air attaché in London.

May 25, 1936

My dear Colonel Lindbergh:
Although I have not had the pleasure of your personal acquaintance, I feel free on account of my position in corresponding with you with respect to a possible desire on your part to visit Germany during your stay in Great Britain.

In a recent discussion with high officials of the German Air Ministry, I was requested to extend to you in the name of General Göring and the German Air Ministry an invitation to visit Germany and inspect the new German civil and military air establishment.[51]

The letter went on to offer an astonishing list of secret facilities the Germans were willing to show to Lindbergh. Lindbergh could "best preserve his incognito" by landing at military airfields. Smith wrote that the Germans would show more to Lindbergh than to anyone else and hinted at the "high patriotic value" of the visit. He then committed the embassy and himself to something impossible, which eventually would have painful results for the Lindberghs: "Mr. Mayer and I will arrange that no mention of your visit reaches either the American or German press."

The reply from Lindbergh on June 5 from Sevenoaks, England, accepted the invitation. He would fly to Germany with his wife in their own plane, which was then being completed in England. He was delighted about the promised anonymity: "What I am most anxious

---

*Göring gave Milch what was known in the Berlin vernacular as a Persil certificate. Persil was Germany's best-known laundry soap.

to avoid is the sensational and stupid publicity which we have so frequently encountered in the past and the difficulty and unpleasantness which invariably accompany it."

Characteristically, he added: "I hope General Göring does not feel it is necessary to provide any special entertainment as far as I am concerned . . . As a matter of fact I thoroughly dislike formal functions and have not attended one for several years."

This was the first of five visits Lindbergh paid to Germany. The information he obtained was invaluable. The promise of privacy was impossible to enforce; Lindbergh was too famous and Göring too eager to brag. The only embarrassing moment for the Luftwaffe came when the famous Colonel Ernst Udet, a World War ace, demonstrated the highly advanced Heinkel-112 fighter at Rostock. During a flat-out dive, the plane disintegrated and Udet had to bail out. He landed safely. The plane, presumably, was scrapped or redesigned. Udet was an exciting character, very similar to America's General Jimmy Doolittle. Like Doolittle, Udet's barnstorming and stunt flying for films made him widely known and liked. He eventually committed suicide in disgrace when Germany was at the end of the war.

On October 18, 1938, during a stag dinner, Lindbergh was suddenly presented with a high German decoration by Göring. The dinner was hosted by Hugh Wilson, the new American ambassador, at the American Embassy. Among the guests were Göring and Milch, the ambassadors of Italy and Belgium, Udet, all the U.S. military attachés, the American consul general, and the airplane builders Heinkel and Sikorsky. It came as a complete surprise to Lindbergh, and there was no way he could have turned it down without causing insult and creating a problem for the American ambassador. It was the same medal that was given to André François-Poncet, the French ambassador, and to Henry Ford, but it caused Lindbergh unending trouble in the United States.[52]

Lindbergh then had an exchange of letters with Ambassador Joseph Kennedy, warning of Germany's air strength; this may have reinforced Kennedy's isolationism more than any other source. Kennedy, quoting Lindbergh, ran afoul of his chiefs, Cordell Hull and FDR. Von Ribbentrop probably overrated Kennedy's influence after listening to diplomatic gossip about him and the power of America's isolationists. His self-delusion was encouraged by Lindbergh's international status.

The following assessment of Charles Lindbergh's years of visits to Germany is in the words of Major Truman Smith.

1. Lindbergh distrusted the Nazi government of Germany and found its anti-Semitic policies abhorrent. Nevertheless, he showed great curiosity about Hitler's personality, although he had no opportunity to talk with the Führer. Lindbergh admired most of the leaders of German aviation, its scientists, generals, and industrialists. As to Göring, his views about him were mixed, corresponding in general to those of the military attaché as set down in this record. ("Dangerous, a killer, some good sides, very clever.")

2. Lindbergh believed a war in Europe would be a catastrophe for the western world.

3. He thought that if such a war actually occurred, it would result either in a German victory or Russia's becoming the dominant power all over Europe.

4. Lindbergh hoped that if Hitler did launch a war it would be against Russia, and he believed that for France, Britain, and the United States the best policy would be to remain neutral while strengthening themselves militarily so that when Russia and Germany were mutually exhausted, the western powers would be in a position to dictate peace.[53]

Lindbergh was proved wrong, and his views, sacred to American isolationists, who appealed for his personal involvement, ruined his life. He joined the America First Committee, the most powerful of the antiwar groups. According to J. Edgar Hoover, it was secretly supported by Berlin with annual donations of one million dollars.[54] It was backed by General Robert E. Wood of Sears, Roebuck, Douglas Stuart of Quaker Oats, World War ace Captain Eddie Rickenbacker, Henry Ford of Detroit, New York Representative Hamilton Fish, Senator Burton K. Wheeler, Colonel Robert McCormick of the *Chicago Tribune,* William Grace, and Avery Brundage of the American Olympic Committee. Lindbergh became their star.

(In a speech on September 16, 1941, in Des Moines, he said that if America became engulfed in war, it would be "because of the British, the Jews, and Franklin Roosevelt." Was he anti-British, anti-Semitic, and anti-Roosevelt, or did he single out the three most obvious prowar factions? After Pearl Harbor, Lindbergh did courageous war duty, but much of America never forgave his apparent treachery.)

The time approached for the von Ribbentrops to become part of the London diplomatic scene. Until early 1936, von Ribbentrop had visited there often, alone or with Annelies, at first on private business and then, after 1933, on the semiofficial and official business of Nazi Germany. But he had barely touched the surface of the cynical, poisonous, charming, and witty world of London society. Not since Edwardian days had there been such a coterie of cynics. The von Ribbentrops probably thought they could cope with the international world because, after all, they had learned to deal with Berlin's fierce snobberies. But they were wrong. Few outsiders could hope to survive the acid-tinged Oxbridge purgatory of London's salons of the mid and late thirties.

The London faced by the von Ribbentrops was witty, acerbic, and difficult. No one was safe. Jew, Nazi, pretender, king — everyone was skewered by London's society's tongues. This should not have been a matter of moment to world history, but in the case of the vulnerable, ambitious, insecure von Ribbentrops, it was. Once they realized they were frequent targets, they despised the London people who were their torturers. Probably because of their London trials, they came to feel bitter toward the British and all things British.

On November 7, 1936, when von Ribbentrop was already in residence as ambassador to the Court of St. James's, he and Annelies were defined in the diary of Sir Henry (Chips) Channon, MP: "My feeling is that they will not be a social success in London, though at first I prophesied great things for them; but for all their ambition, they have not the well-bred ease which Londoners demand, and Frau von Ribbentrop really dresses too dowdily. She will be the liability, though he has not started off well, either."[55]

This was written after Channon and his wife had been the von Ribbentrops' delighted guests in Berlin during the 1936 Olympics, before von Ribbentrop had taken his post in London.

Adolf Hitler of course thought the von Ribbentrops were his perfect emissaries into the highest British circles, but the von Ribbentrops found a much more subtle world than they had ever faced, and were incapable of coping with it. Joachim, the impoverished young provincial who had married a rich and assertive wife and had then succumbed to a powerful national leader, was now to be overwhelmed once more, this time by a coterie of London society's insiders.

It was painful to the von Ribbentrops but only indirectly to Germany. Much more dangerous to Germany were Robert Vansittart and Duff Cooper, two influential men who were opposed in principle to any form of alliance between the British Empire and Adolf Hitler's Nazi Germany.

The more powerful was Sir Robert Vansittart, who had been the permanent under secretary for foreign affairs since 1930. He was suspicious of Germany, shocked by Nazi brutality, disdainful of Hitler, and pessimistic about the future of European peace.[56] His brother-in-law (their wives were sisters) was Sir Eric Phipps, the British ambassador in Berlin, who had become wholly disenchanted with the Nazis. Phipps was so filled with dislike for them that he was eventually replaced with a seemingly more amenable diplomat, Sir Nevile Henderson, when the last prewar prime minister, Neville Chamberlain, took office.

The other antagonist was Alfred Duff Cooper. He and his beautiful wife, Diana, were more worldly than Vansittart and held a place in society that was deceptive, because their salon life did not inhibit their influence. Alfred Duff Cooper, Oxford man, former Army officer, former member of Parliament, was secretary of war until 1937. He served as First Lord of the Admiralty from 1937 to 1938, and, from 1940, as minister of information. Lady Diana Duff Cooper, daughter of the Duke of Rutland, was a famous beauty and a stage actress. The Duff Coopers were powerful wheels in the machinery of London's society, known for their francophilia and anti-Nazi stand. In the case of Alfred Duff Cooper, the feeling was intense.

The Duff Coopers were often guests at homes where the von Ribbentrops had been invited, and that made for some tense evenings, although Lady Diana's legendary charm often managed to smooth things. They also disapproved of anyone in London society who accepted von Ribbentrop's invitations to the 1936 Berlin Olympics. It was a "show" year. For the foreign visitors' sake, there was reduced anti-Semitic display, "Jews not desired here" signs were hidden, and there was less talk against the west. Of course, it was all only temporary. Throughout the subsequent era of British admiration for Hitler's Olympics, the Duff Coopers remained steadfast anti-Germans.

In July 1936 the center of world attention had shifted to Spain. On July 17 and 18, General Francisco Franco launched the Spanish Civil War from Morocco at the head of Spain's rebel colonial army. This suited Adolf Hitler's anti-Communist paranoia. Here was an attack on one of the two supposedly Communist-influenced and Moscow-friendly regimes in the southwest sector of Europe; the other was France. Actually, the legal Spanish government and the French government were headed by moderate socialists. Hitler, as usual, began to fear a flood of red. He insisted that Germany was being "squeezed" between Czechoslovakia (through its Russian allies) and France and Spain.

Von Ribbentrop seemed to disagree. He was with Hitler at the Bayreuth Music Festival when word of the Spanish war reached them. Hitler, who was a guest of the Wagner family, told von Ribbentrop he had decided to help Franco. Franco had requested transport planes to shuttle troops from North Africa, and Hitler would provide them. In his memoirs, von Ribbentrop wrote that he suggested to the Führer that Germany stay out of Spain, there were "no laurels to be gained," and German intervention would have a negative effect in England. But Hitler insisted that he would not tolerate a Communist Spain. He had already ordered the planes for Franco. Von Ribbentrop wrote:

> Hitler rejected my objections. He said Spain's Prime Minister Negrin was a Communist, that his weapons came from Moscow, and that there was a close connection between him and Léon Blum in France . . . I saw things differently. I tried to argue with Hitler but found it too difficult. He reacted nervously and cut off the conversation. He said he had made his decision, this was "a matter of deep principle, and not of my sort of mundane foreign diplomacy."

Again Hitler was the ideologue while von Ribbentrop attempted diplomacy. According to von Ribbentrop, the Spanish matter "disturbed his mission" later when he was ambassador to London.

Hitler's unfriendly rejection depressed him; he fell into a black mood whenever he ran afoul of Hitler. His subordinates called it his "Tango Nocturno," and he took to his bed. But he was soon cured.

Apparently, Hitler's anger did not last. The day after the disagreement over Spain, von Ribbentrop was ordered into his Führer's presence. As von Ribbentrop told it, Adolf Hitler named him state secretary of the Foreign Ministry to succeed Bernhard von Bülow, who had died in June. Hitler congratulated him.[57] According to von Ribbentrop, he told Hitler it would be wiser to send him to England as ambassador than to appoint him state secretary in Berlin. "Despite Hitler's skeptical view of the possibilities of a bond with Britain, it seemed important to keep the Führer fully informed about the London situation. Also, although British Kings had little political influence, Edward VIII was friendly to Germany." This was written after Hitler's death, when his recognition of Edward VIII's lack of influence may have been a matter of hindsight.

Others viewed von Ribbentrop's London appointment quite differently.

Typically, the former Foreign Ministry official Dr. Paul Schwarz said von Neurath wanted to get rid of von Ribbentrop, who was a thorn in his side as long as he was in Berlin.[58] Erich Kordt's vacation in Greece was interrupted by a frantic phone call. Von Ribbentrop sent D-AMY to fetch him at once to Bayreuth. As a member of the Foreign Ministry, Kordt knew that von Neurath was eager to get rid of von Ribbentrop and probably had tried to prevent his appointment as state secretary. Von Neurath again threatened to resign, because he "could not personally work closely with von Ribbentrop." Now von Ribbentrop wanted Kordt to negotiate with von Neurath so that von Ribbentrop, in addition to keeping his London post, would be ambassador at large and would report directly to Hitler. The foreign minister agreed hastily and on July 27 he sent a request for acceptance of a proposed ambassadorship to London. It was granted on July 30, with unusual speed. Kordt claimed that many countries preferred Nazi ambassadors to Foreign Service professionals. Belgium turned down a top professional who had some Jewish blood, because a Nazi ambassador would guarantee the direct attention of Adolf Hitler.

At first von Ribbentrop refused to announce his London appointment, which probably confirms the Schwartz and Kordt views. Hitler then refused to receive von Ribbentrop's English guests, who were in Berlin for the Olympics. His adjutant told von Ribbentrop, "You announce the appointment, and the Führer will receive your guests," and that was exactly what happened. Von Ribbentrop's announcement of his appointment to London opened the doors to Hitler's levees for von Ribbentrop's guests.[59] Dr. Paul Schmidt, the interpreter, told how von Ribbentrop, on being congratulated after the announcement, responded with "a sour laugh."[60]

An apocryphal story of the day was that Göring told Hitler, "You cannot send von Ribbentrop to London." Hitler insisted that von Ribbentrop was the right man because "Ribbentrop knows the top people in England." Göring laughed and replied, "The trouble is that they also know him!"

The Büro remained intact, despite the bitter dislike of the professionals, who called it "full of overpaid playboys with London wardrobes and big expense accounts." Von Ribbentrop's eventual entourage for the London embassy was 120, many of them lower-rank SS men, some of whom did the flunky work and guard duty. The regular officials at the embassy were paid extra cash to bring their salaries up to the level of the newly imported SS officers. This money came from the mysterious so-called *Sonderfond des Führers*, the Führer's Special Fund, and it was flown in weekly from Amsterdam, where German marks had a good market.[61]

For the immediate weeks ahead, von Ribbentrop had "previous commitments" away from England, and the embassy in London was left without an ambassador for a discourteously long period of time. First the von Ribbentrops planned a vast party in Dahlem to entertain foreign visitors and leading Germans during the Olympic Games. The von Ribbentrop fête was one of three such stellar events. The other two were enormous entertainments given by Hermann Göring and Joseph Goebbels.

Another matter of priority was an anti-Comintern alliance with Japan, the "Aryans of the East," as Hitler called them. *Comintern* stood for the "Communist International," composed of the world's Marxist leaders, who met annually at the Comintern's headquarters in Moscow. Originally, there was some danger that such a pact would seem close to a declaration of war on Soviet Russia, but in November 1936, a clever legal expert at the Ribbentrop Büro, Dr. Hermann von Raumer, found a convenient technicality: Soviet Russia had denied responsibility for some controversial statements made by the Comintern's headquarters in Moscow. The Soviets had thereby removed themselves officially from certain directions they probably endorsed unofficially. This "loophole" allowed von Ribbentrop to formulate an anti-Comintern pact without officially involving Soviet Russia. The path was clear for von Ribbentrop's first attempt at Realpolitik with Japan. The whole subject of "race" and "congenial blood" soon came to haunt the conduct of Realpolitik. It caused problems for von Ribbentrop and his Büro, and it became an irritant for the supposedly principled and distinguished Foreign Ministry. Certainly with the approval of the opportunistic Konstantin von Neurath, the notorious department called Deutschland, its most Nazified wing, suggested on November 17, 1936, to the Nazi Party that it retain its racial policies in principle but avoid "damage in matter of foreign policy." The suggestion was turned down by the party on April 28, 1937.[62] Therein lies one of the secrets of Nazi Germany. Its evil men were usually more determined than those who considered themselves principled and decent.

August 1, 1936, marked the opening of the Olympic Games and the appearance of the many guests von Ribbentrop had invited. The huge party Annelies and he were giving was at hand. Earlier in the year, on July 14, the Duke and Duchess of Brunswick, both convinced Nazis, came to England for an Anglo-German Fellowship dinner. Brunswick had given up the British dukedom of Cumberland to declare himself the complete Nazi German. To schedule the dinner for Bastille Day, 14 July, was probably a deliberate anti-French provocation. The Fellowship meeting was chaired by Lord Mount Temple, who had a Jewish wife (a daughter of banker Sir Ernest Cassel). There were the usual pro-German speakers, the Lords Revell and Lothian and General Sir Frederick Maurice of the British Legion.

Many of these Fellowship guests had been asked by von Ribben-

Hitler's diplomat on the way to Buckingham Palace to present his credentials to King Edward VIII. The king had not yet been crowned, so the ambassador did not wear formal court dress. *Topham*

The special adviser shakes hands with his delighted chief, 1935. *National Archives*

Von Ribbentrop flanked by officials Karl Dietrich and Dr. Ernst Wörmann in front of the Carlton Hotel, London, March 1936. *Keystone*

In Rome with Japanese and Italian Axis partners, 1937. *National Archives*

The lavish Coronation Ball at the German Embassy in London on May 14, 1937. At center, with von Ribbentrop, are the Duke and Duchess of Kent. *Ullstein Bilderdienst*

An ad for Henkell champagne in *Berliner Illustrirte*, 1937.

Annelies as a young woman.
National Archives

Joachim and Annelies with Bettina, about 1932. *National Archives*

The new chief, dressed in
SS uniform, greets the
Foreign Ministry staff.
National Archives

Von Ribbentrop inspecting the Polish
guard of honor during a trip to Warsaw
to meet with Foreign Minister Josef
Beck of Poland, January 1939.
Der Spiegel

The Reichstag, February 20, 1938. Left to right: Goebbels, Frick, von Ribbentrop, Hess, and Hitler. *National Archives*

trop to the Olympic Games, as were Admiral Eyres Monsell of the Naval Treaty Agreement, the press Lords Rothermere and Beaverbrook, and Chips Channon and his wife. The least likely guests were Sir Robert and Lady Vansittart. She may have come to visit her sister, Lady Phipps. A startled von Ribbentrop said he was particularly happy to see them.[63] One Olympic guest, Lord Revell, wrote a letter to the *Times,* published on August 27, 1936, saying that "Hitler has removed the class divisions which hurt England," strange praise from a member of the peerage.

All guests were assigned Mercedes cars, driven by uniformed SS or men from the Nazi Party's motor corps, also in uniform. Everyone was impressed. Channon thought the "Horst Wessel Song" had "rather a good lilt."[64]

In total, the von Ribbentrops had asked six hundred people to Dahlem. A huge tent was put up over the gardens and the tennis court. There were water lilies in the swimming pool and rhododendrons everywhere. Milling among the guests were Göring, Hess, and their wives, and Himmler, who, as Martha Dodd, the American ambassador's daughter, reported, "wove his mincing, quiet, and menacing way through the crowd." There was a small crisis of protocol when the president of the International Olympic Committee, Count Balliet Latour, appeared uninvited. But, after all, it was the Olympic week and his reign.[65]

Barnabas von Geczy, one of Berlin's best band leaders, was hired to play, and the Vansittarts foxtrotted and tangoed and were among the last guests to leave. Von Ribbentrop remembered asking himself whether that was a good sign. The next day he had his answer. He lunched with Vansittart at the Hotel Kaiserhof, and tried to convince the British statesman of Hitler's peaceful intentions.[66] But he faced "a blank wall. There was no response, no reaction, only banalities." It was clear there was no approaching Vansittart. So much for late dancers!

In his Nürnberg prison memoirs, von Ribbentrop insisted that it was not true that Vansittart's anti-German views were the result of Adolf Hitler's policies. On the contrary, Hitler's views were the result of Vansittart's 1936 policies. Writing in his cell after he was condemned to death, von Ribbentrop insisted, "I am certain Adolf Hitler would have kept any pact with England," and "It is Vansittart who is largely to blame for the red incursion into Europe."[67] After all the broken pacts, the broken promises, with Germany in ruins, Hitler's spell still gripped his disciple Joachim von Ribbentrop.

Like many other guests at the von Ribbentrops' Olympics party,

Martha Dodd had congratulated von Ribbentrop on his appointment to the London embassy and he "accepted with a sort of pained graciousness, disdain, and bored *savoir faire*." Obviously it was not his favorite subject. Then Miss Dodd heard of Hitler's unique attitude to sports, sportsmanship, and the human race. One of von Ribbentrop's young assistants told her that Adolf Hitler considered Jesse Owens and other black American athletes unfair competition because "blacks were animals, non-humans, and to enter them in competition against whites was like entering fleet-footed deer, gazelle, or other species of speedy animals, and totally unsportsmanlike and unfair."[68]

After the Olympics, the von Ribbentrops had to plan all the details for their move to London. Joachim and Annelies separately went to see Pastor Niemöller, the decorated World War U-boat commander who now presided over the Dahlem congregation, one of the most fashionable Protestant parishes in Berlin. Niemöller was a German nationalist but a fierce opponent of National Socialism. He frequently preached sermons against the government's antireligious and anti-Semitic acts. Joachim wanted Niemöller, a world-renowned clergyman, to accept him back into the church he had left. He explained that the English "would expect that of him."

Niemöller told him that was not sufficient reason for confirmation, and turned him down.[69] Separately, Annelies had asked Niemöller to baptize her third child, Adolf, who was born on September 2, 1935, but Niemöller again refused unless von Ribbentrop returned to the church for God's sake and not for British society's.[70] Niemöller was denounced for his anti-Hitler attitude and was eventually sent to Dachau.*

Little Adolf von Ribbentrop was baptized elsewhere. Despite their misguided ambition, both von Ribbentrops were good parents.

In the meantime, the superb John Nash buildings that housed London's German Embassy were gutted, leaving only the façade. Annelies brought a Dahlem construction and furniture man named Martin Luther to London. He was hired to supervise the work of hundreds of imported German workmen. Luther, a tough Berliner and an old-time Nazi Party hand, remained a close associate of von Ribbentrop's and soon became his liaison to the "old fighters." Years later it was Martin Luther who represented the Foreign Ministry at the notorious Wannsee conference for the Final Solution of the Jewish

---

*Niemöller was arrested several times for his anti-Nazi sermons.

question, and it was Martin Luther who eventually landed in a concentration camp for betraying von Ribbentrop.

A story went the rounds of London during the embassy reconstruction that any German workman whose wife, back in Germany, gave birth to a male child could collect a three hundred-mark bonus if the baby was named Joachim. Supposedly, there were seven Joachims born during those months.[71]

While the construction work was going on, the embassy was temporarily moved into 17 Carlton House Terrace, and a Chamberlain family house on Eaton Square was rented as the von Ribbentrops' private residence.

The same Dr. Hermann von Raumer who had found the loophole for the Anti-Comintern Pact said that this was the pre-London briefing of von Ribbentrop by Adolf Hitler.

> Ribbentrop, bring me England into the Anti-Comintern Pact. That is my greatest wish! I'm sending you as the best horse in my stable. See what you can do . . . But if all efforts come to nothing, well, then, I'm prepared for war, though I'd regret it a lot, but if it has to be . . . But I believe it would be a short war and I'd offer generous terms to England, an honorable, mutually acceptable peace. Then I'd still want England to join the Anti-Comintern Pact. Ribbentrop, you hold all the trumps. Play them well. I'm prepared for an air agreement anytime. Do well! I shall follow you with interest.[72]

Meanwhile, preparation of the Anti-Comintern Pact with Japan went forward through the Japanese ambassador, Viscount Mushakoji, and his military attaché, Baron Oshima. Several things still stood in the way. The Japanese government was reluctant to commit itself too deeply. To them the three-year-old Nazi government was still a "new" friend, while the governments of Britain and America were well-known and familiar quantities. Another problem was China. Germany was trading with China and there was still a German military mission in China training Chiang Kai-shek's army.

Von Ribbentrop's ally in the pursuit of a treaty with Japan was the famous geopolitical scientist Professor Karl Haushofer, a former Tokyo resident and the mentor of Hitler's deputy, Rudolf Hess. Haushofer's political views impressed Hitler, who now conveniently discovered the similarities between the mythical knightly Wagnerian spirit of National Socialism and *bushido,* the warrior's way of the Japanese samurai. While the von Ribbentrops were preparing themselves for London, the Büro carried out the other von Ribbentrop function as Ambassador Extraordinary at Large and Special Adviser to the Führer. For von Ribbentrop the Japan connection was an exercise in old-time power politics as well as good business. For Hitler it was bathed in ideological blood and thunder, but above all, it was anti-Communist.

Surprisingly, on September 5, a few days before the party rally in Nürnberg, Germany decided to participate in the Nonintervention Committee, which had been formed in London to assure that no outside powers would intervene in the Spanish Civil War. This, after Germany had lent planes to Franco!

Finally came the 1936 party rally, which was to be named the Day of Honor. Among "Ribbentrop's Kindergarten," as the many British visitors were dubbed in Nürnberg, were Lady Redesdale, mother of the Mitford girls, two of whom, Lady Mosley and Unity Mitford, were quite at home in Nürnberg.[73] Lady Redesdale was there as a guest of Prince Bismarck, the former chargé d'affaires in London. Beverly Nichols in the *Sunday Chronicle* of September 12, 1936, wrote, "Such moral strength! So much that is beautiful!" Randolph Hughes in *The New Germany:* "Health, character and order. At home we have louts and hooligans!" Admiral Domville delivered himself of a little joke: "If I were named Solomon, I'd change my name to MacDonald and have a plastic surgeon change my face."[74] The party rally was deemed a post-Olympic success. However, the Diplomatic Corps of the western nations did not attend.

Then, at long last, von Ribbentrop assumed his post in London. The official announcement of his position as ambassador to the Court of St. James's and ambassador at large had been made on August 11, and the family finally arrived in London on October 26.

9

EMBASSY
1936, 1937, 1938

Our Fellows Look Terrific

ON SEPTEMBER 13, 1936, Heinrich Himmler promoted his friend Joachim von Ribbentrop to the honorary rank of general (*Gruppen-führer*) in the SS. So far, von Ribbentrop's year had gone well. His Führer seemed to trust him. Perhaps it was a disappointment that the Berlin post of *Staats Sekretär* (chief of staff of the Foreign Ministry) had escaped him, but Hitler had convinced him that he was, in Hitler's own words, the "best horse in the stable," sent to London to form an alliance despite British intransigence. Friendship with Britain seemed to matter immensely to Adolf Hitler, ever the ideologue, trapped by his "instinctive" ways of looking at the world and of making decisions. He was cynical about many things and most people, but he fed himself half truths to bolster his self-assurance. Hitler's Austrian soul probably considered the "Aryan brethren" across the Channel as even more "desirably Nordic" and coldly unreachable than his adopted Germans had once seemed. He wanted them.

Joachim von Ribbentrop, SS *Gruppenführer*, Ambassador Extraordinary to the Court of St. James's, Special Adviser to the Führer, and victor of the skirmishes at the British Admiralty in 1935, was ready to do battle. If he had any doubt about his lack of standing inside the Nazi Party, his absence from "court" in Berlin, or his possible rejection by Britain's people of influence, he hid it behind a newly assumed mask of gravity and purpose. As his battle flag he carried the unvarying message against Bolshevism. As his armor he had the memory of the day when he had told the British to "take it or leave it," and they had taken it. Besides, he had never lacked for the company of titled Englishmen when he was in London. Von Ribbentrop felt, right or wrong, that they respected him and the new Germany. And then, he always had Annelies by his side. Her taste and talent for entertaining would surely charm the most unbending Londoners. She had already worked wonders at the old embassy at Carlton House Terrace. Albert Speer, Hitler's favorite architect, was asked to help with the interiors of the rebuilt structure. The famous Professor Troost was designing special furniture. Martin Luther acted as contractor. Annelies even brought over some of her own valuable pieces of art from Dahlem. There were well-trained waiters, footmen, and guards, all SS men. Erich Kordt estimated that the total cost of the rebuilding was five million marks.[1]

Germany would be proud of the embassy and the new ambassadorial family, including the four children, Rudolf, Bettina, Ursula, and little Adolf. Feelers were put out to Eton for Rudolf, who was fifteen, but his parents decided on London's Westminster, a day school. Bettina was enrolled in a boarding school in Cornwall. Ursula, who was a delicate child, stayed in London, and Adolf was only a year old.

Rudolf had joined the Jungvolk (the "Cub Scouts" of the Hitler Youth) at the age of ten in Berlin. At fourteen he became a member of the Hitler Youth. His *Fähnleinführer,* a sort of Hitler Youth scoutmaster, a young man named Thorner, came to London with the von Ribbentrops as a secretary-aide to the ambassador, paid by the Büro.[2]

It must have been wrenching for young Rudolf to trade the hardedged, stiff Hitler Youth, with its brown uniform and shouted slogans, for the relaxed, top-hatted drawl of London's Westminster School. Thorner reported that Rudolf had several shouting matches at the Speakers' Corner near London's Marble Arch, where all one needs to this day is a soap box and a political cause. Rudolf howled "Bolshevist" at several speakers, who probably were.[3] The Austrian Reinhard Spitzy, also a secretary of von Ribbentrop's, said that Rudolf sometimes complained to him about his father, probably as the result of arguments with his schoolmates at Westminster, British schoolboys being unsympathetic to the Nazis.[4]

By the time the von Ribbentrops and their entire entourage, *Kind und Kegel,* as the Germans would say, arrived at Victoria Station on October 26, 1936, all seemed well in hand, organized and calm. Then the new ambassador decided, there and then, to apply the crude technique he had learned from Adolf Hitler and had used in the naval negotiations. On the station platform, dignitaries and embassy staff expected no more than the usual bland ambassadorial greetings. Instead, Joachim von Ribbentrop launched into an animated speech inviting Great Britain to join Germany in a crusade against "the greatest danger of the century, the Bolshevist menace."[5] Copies of the speech were handed out in mimeographed form to the press. Marked "Not Secret," Cable #237 to Führer and Reichskanzler and Reichsminister, dispatched at 17:34 hours London arrived 19:20 hours Berlin dated 26 October 1936, simply stated: "Arrived today. Took over business activities. Ribbentrop."

It was a supremely tactless way for a new ambassador to attempt to "manage" his host country's policy. Within the week, the influential Austen Chamberlain wrote an article in the conservative *Daily Telegraph,* complaining bitterly about this crude attempt to interfere in British affairs. He wrote "that neither the Nazi nor the Soviet faiths, both strange to Britons, are worth one British Grenadier's bones." Also, "while von Ribbentrop spoke of an anti-Communist alliance, Göring and Goebbels make speeches proclaiming that Britain has stolen Germany's colonies."

It was not an auspicious beginning.

As as opening gesture, perhaps to demonstrate his adherence to the new Germany's ways, von Ribbentrop decreed that the German Embassy's ladies would no longer curtsy to royalty and that all future embassy invitations would be worded in German instead of the language of the host country. An SS guard was posted in a sentry booth at the embassy entrance, also an unheard-of discourtesy. With one eye on Berlin, von Ribbentrop awaited the party's approval of the new German style he was introducing to stuffy old England. Nazi jargon such as "manly, direct, soldierly, forthright" was supposed to spring to mind. Instead, he had already been chastized by Austen Chamberlain and then dubbed "Brickendrop" by the widely respected cartoonist David Low, in the *Evening Standard* and *Manchester Guardian.* On hearing that only the raised-arm salute would henceforth be used by the embassy staff, Low drew a schoolroom, with one little boy who looks exactly like von Ribbentrop holding his arm in a Hitler salute. The teacher says, "Yes, von Ribbentrop, you may leave the room." A year later, during the coronation of George VI in Westminster Abbey, the ushers were instructed to guide straight to the cloakrooms anyone who raised an arm, "except His Excellency the German Ambassador."

The ambassador's urge to "Germanize" went far beyond the embassy. For many years a former German, Baron Bruno Schröder, a naturalized British subject and London resident, had financed London's German Hospital.[6] The Hamburg-born Schröder (a non-Nazi cousin of the Cologne banker Kurt von Schröder, who had called the 1932 meeting with Hitler and von Papen) devoted himself and his money to this charity clinic, which employed some Jewish physicians and had Jewish patients. Despite von Ribbentrop's personal urging, Baron Schröder refused to fire the Jewish doctors or discharge the Jewish patients. But to keep the appellation German Hospital, the administration had to fly the swastika flag, although there was still a small kosher kitchen for observant Jewish patients.

The new ambassador had the good fortune of having excellent staff members, since he needed frequent professional help. Erich Kordt was appointed first secretary, and Dr. Woermann became deputy to the ambassador, in charge during his frequent absences.

The ambassador refused to pay certain formal visits that were decreed by custom, such as the courtesy call to the financial secretary of the Admiralty, someone he deemed beneath his notice. The customary written self-introductions to other ambassadors were now in German, contrary to protocol. Said von Ribbentrop, "I don't care one whit about what used to be the custom." As a joke, the Turkish ambassador responded in Turkish.[7]

On October 30 von Ribbentrop, dressed in a morning coat, submitted his credentials to King Edward VIII.* The King was deep in his romance with Mrs. Simpson, which was about to bring a crisis of major proportions. How could a British sovereign, head of the Church of England, marry a foreign divorcée? What would happen if the German-friendly British King were forced to abdicate his throne? The dilemma presented itself to Adolf Hitler in these simplistic terms: a young King, a war veteran and a liberal, is prevented from marrying the woman of his choice by a "clique of reactionaries and Jews." Hitler thought the King should "tell these plutocrats and Marxists" that nothing would keep him from marrying a "girl of the people."[8] This was Hitler's lower-middle-class naïveté at its most conspicuous. In a misguided effort to show sympathy for the embattled King, he prevented the German press from reporting the entire matter. One wonders how Wallis Warfield Simpson of the International Best Dressed List would have reacted to the appellation "girl of the people."

The new ambassador's blunders were to be chided but not punished. Despite his careless and overbearing behavior, prominent Londoners, with few exceptions, were not willing to show anger. Only the press saw where von Ribbentrop was aiming and refused to follow. He stumbled on, overly eager to please Berlin and still impressed by his recent negotiating success. As a new senior diplomat, he was unsure of himself, so he used the weak man's way to bluff: press on

---

*Probably the presentation was informal, since the King was as yet uncrowned.

until someone calls a halt. Several subordinates, including Kordt and Spitzy, reported that whenever von Ribbentrop lost his temper, they could make him stop in his tracks by being firm with him. He became reasonable only after being confronted.

Meanwhile, preparations went ahead to solidify the Anti-Comintern Pact, and on November 25, barely a month after he became ambassador, von Ribbentrop flew to Berlin, where he signed the pact with Japan. It was a stormy, bouncy flight and the big Junkers passenger plane was tossed around, but there was no stopping von Ribbentrop, and D-AMY's Captain Zivina was one of the best.[9] Though this pact was duly signed by newly promoted Japanese Ambassador Oshima, the Foreign Ministry would have no part of it. So far as the professionals were concerned, the whole thing was a personal idea of Adolf Hitler's, negotiated outside normal diplomatic channels. From the point of view of the gentlemen of Berlin's Foreign Ministry, von Ribbentrop's signature gave Japan no valid treaty, nor was the pact taken as more than a gesture in Japan. Although the professionals in Berlin saw the pact as the "adventure of dilettantes," it created many fears of a future world conspiracy, particularly in Britain.

Adolf Hitler had personally visited Berlin's Japanese Embassy for the event, his first time in a foreign mission. Suddenly the Japanese had changed from the "culturally sterile race" of *Mein Kampf* to "a closely related race of heroes."[10] The pact also caused great anger in China, Japan's victim and Germany's old ally.

The Anti-Comintern Pacts were von Ribbentrop's pride until the Soviet Nonaggression Pact of 1939. Each anti-Comintern signing, country by country, was widely publicized, repeatedly featuring von Ribbentrop, the architect of the metaphoric fortification against Moscow.

This was the first of many times that von Ribbentrop left his post and traveled to the continent, and soon the British government took affront. In Parliament he was called "part-time ambassador" to the Court of St. James's. *Punch,* the satirical magazine, was to describe him as "the Wandering Aryan." It upset Whitehall that the man who was accredited as the ambassador to Great Britain negotiated an agreement like the Anti-Comintern Pact, which could be deemed dangerous to Britain and certainly to the allies of France and Britain.

He returned to London in December for a meeting of the Nonintervention Committee with Spain, presided over by Lord Plymouth. The two main opponents, von Ribbentrop and Russian Ambassador Ivan Mikailovich Maisky, both knew that no amount of work by the committee could stop intervention by Germany and Russia. Germany had already sent out "volunteers," the Condor Legion, who were all Luftwaffe pilots trying out their skills and equipment for things to come one day.

The ambassador instructed his staff to concentrate on the crisis of the King and his lady from Baltimore and on Mr. Stanley Baldwin, the prime minister who looked and talked like John Bull. The German Embassy expert in matters concerning royalty and its affairs of the heart was "Lu" Hessen, Prince Ludwig von Hessen, a great-grandson of Queen Victoria and a young official of the Ribbentrop Büro. The prince was told by the ambassador to stay as close as possible to Buckingham Palace and to report any rumors about the durability and future of the King.[11] While the British press desisted from any mention of King and country's dilemma, there were no holds barred when tackling the new German ambassador. The von Ribbentrops, in return for certain Nazi gestures meant to impress Berlin, became targets for London's gossip press. For instance, when Bettina was hurt in an accident at school, von Ribbentrop sought the advice of Professor Sauerbruch, Germany's foremost surgeon. Sauerbruch sent the family to an eminent specialist in Holland, a Jew, and Bettina was registered there under the name Henkell. The London papers found out and gloated.

Such Nazi manifestations as the Hitler salute, the use of German language in communications, the uniformed SS guard and waiters, the vast Mercedes limousine with its swastika flags (but London license plate CYF 3), the Jewish dentist who treated the von Ribbentrops in London,[12] the well-known D-AMY, which constantly ferried people between Berlin and London: all of these became the joy of gossip journalism reports. The von Ribbentrops were hurt by the sensationalized news coverage. Every time they left the embassy it was on a "mysterious mission." Every rumor was enlarged. Every visitor was a "mystery Nazi." What was surprising to von Ribbentrop, a man who had virtually grown up among English-speaking people, was the freedom of the press to publish rumor. His misjudgment was probably based on a false notion of his diplomatic immunity and the fancied respect due the senior official of a sovereign foreign nation. Several times he complained about the press to British government officials and even to the prime minister. It did not help him, because they could not help him. *Der Bo* (for *Botschafter*, or ambassador), as his staff nicknamed him, had to learn to live with it.[13]

Meanwhile, the imported SS staff was hard on Annelies. They thought of themselves as heroes, not as slaveys. An example was the case of SS Rottenführer (Corporal) Scharchewski, who got drunk, fell asleep on duty, and then lectured Annelies on "betraying Hitler's principles of equality." Before he was arrested and flown under guard to Berlin for his punishment, he told her to "kiss his arse."[14] The SS men were bored. Guard duty was one thing; scrubbing embassy floors was another.

On November 12, 1936, less than two weeks after von Ribbentrop had been driven to Buckingham Palace to present his credentials to Edward VIII, the King abdicated. It was a tremendous blow. Von Ribbentrop immediately informed Adolf Hitler and von Neurath of his view: the very pro-German King had been forced to abdicate his throne by reactionaries and Jewish plutocrats, using the Simpson romance as a pretext. It is hard to conceive that von Ribbentrop could have believed his own fairy tale. He was well acquainted with the Emerald Cunard set and other Windsor friends like Chips Channon. Surely he must have been told the constitutional facts long before the abdication. On his own staff, Ernst Woermann, his deputy, and Erich Kordt, the first secretary, were skilled diplomats, with connections in London. They certainly knew the truth, as did Chief of Protocol Count Dörnberg, the "red giant," who was a cousin of the Battenbergs (the name of the Mountbattens before the war).

Finally, Prince Ludwig of Hesse, who was related to the British royal family, must have told von Ribbentrop about the problems of a ruler who is also head his country's church: "No divorce and remarriage."

Perhaps von Ribbentrop fabricated the tale only to please his Austrian idol and then began to believe his own fabrication. He had done it before about the air treaty that never came about and about the unsuccessful attempt at postponing the Disarmament Conference.

On December 12, 1936, at a meeting of the Anglo-German Fellowship in London, von Ribbentrop made his first London speech since the much-noted arrival at Victoria Station in October.

Attempting a joke, he wielded a sledgehammer. He said that Lord Mount Temple was one temple that must not be destroyed because it was too useful, "despite the Lord's Jewish wife."[15] He then spoke unimpressively about Germany's need for her former colonies, the discarding of the "shackles of Versailles," the danger of the Comintern, and the tragic mistake of fighting each other in the World War. But, he said, if ever Germany were to re-enter the arena, "she would not allow herself to be threatened or menaced."

On February 5, 1937, came the notorious gaffe that shocked Britain's tabloid readers and caused anguish to Hitler's staff members in Berlin. It was a case of tactless, tasteless behavior, once again aimed straight at any doubting "old fighters" in Berlin.

The day had begun most decorously when the ambassador and some of his senior staff were driven to Buckingham Palace in the magnificent swastika-flagged Mercedes to attend His Majesty, King George VI, and to present the ambassador's credentials. The protocol was fairly strict. At the end of the formal handing-over of documents, the ambassador from Germany, dressed in knee breeches, hose, and buckled shoes, was to leave the audience chamber backward, stopping and bowing three times, according to custom. He did so, but each time he stopped to bow, he raised his right arm in a modified Hitler salute. Twentieth-century British court bows are not deep and never from the waist. They consist of no more than a dignified bending of the head. It was easy for the ambassador to raise his arm. Did he also shout "*Heil Hitler*"? No one can swear to it. Apparently the King smiled. The raised arm probably seemed "a bit rum" to him. But his entourage was less forgiving. They were mortified.

Reports reached the press, and they loved it. The Nazi salute to the new King! RIBB HEILS KING!

Low drew a cartoon of Soviet Ambassador Maisky in front of the King with the Russian's clenched fist under the King's nose, since Communists saluted with a raised fist. The caption read: EVERYONE SALUTES IN HIS OWN WAY.

The ambassador's staff members were as taken aback as the King's entourage. Reinhard Spitzy, von Ribbentrop's secretary, described the immediate aftermath of the Great Saluting Crisis, when the ambassador and his aides had returned from the palace to the embassy.

> Von Ribbentrop rushed into his office and turned on the DO NOT DISTURB light. Those who had escorted him stormed in, demanding cognac. Something awful had happened. [Erich] Kordt and [Prince] Lu Hessen fell onto couches, groaning. Then Hessen said, "Imagine, he greeted the King of England with the Hitler salute." Prince Lu smacked his forehead with his hand. Thorner gave a hollow laugh. Kordt's arm hung straight down. Woermann quietly cursed to himself.[16]

All German journalists in London were commanded to appear at the embassy to hear the "true story": the King had "smiled quite contentedly." Nevertheless, news of the gaffe quickly reached Berlin. Von Neurath was aghast. Even Hitler was critical.

During the War Crimes Trials in 1946, Göring said to the prison's junior psychiatrist, Dr. Douglas Kelley, that he had told Hitler von Ribbentrop's act was "like the Soviet ambassador greeting the Führer with a raised fist and yelling, 'Long live the World Revolution!'"[17] No one was more sensitive to British custom than London's young German professional diplomats, though they were not at all concerned about the thousands of German exiles and refugees who now lived hand-to-mouth in London, forced by British immigration policy to take menial jobs in order to be permitted to stay in Britain. Their fate was much more harmful to Germany's reputation than von Ribbentrop's gaffe. Architects were manservants; women university professors were children's nannies.

Everyone in London and Berlin took aim at von Ribbentrop. He had no one to blame but himself. The international businessman, in the guise of ambassador from a violent and revolutionary government, had been trapped by his own vanity and ambition. And those intelligent young German diplomats who worked for him and sat in judgment of him and who were paid by the same fierce master in Berlin, what of them? As Spitzy put it, "We continued because we were ambitious and enjoyed our careers."[18] Meanwhile, the brouhaha went on and on. There was even an amusing question in Parliament as to why the British ambassador in Berlin should not be instructed to shout "Rule Britannia" every time he saw Adolf Hitler.

Fear that damage may have been done to his standing with Adolf Hitler sent von Ribbentrop into panic. He was isolated from Berlin, where gossip and malice could bring quick reversals to the career of a senior Nazi. For this reason, 1937 became a year of frantic trans-Channel travel to perform "damage control" in Berlin.

The embassy's massive reconstruction was nearing completion just in time for a lavish ball planned for May 12 to celebrate the coronation of George VI and his Queen, Elizabeth. Everyone in London was waiting to see the new Frankfurter Hauptbahnhof (Frankfurt Central Railway Station), as the embassy was known among Mayfair wags.

D-AMY became a veritable taxi. Captain Zivina brought everyone from Baron Steengracht and his beautiful wife, who became Annelies's assistants and helpers because they knew London society, to Rudolf Likus, an old friend of von Ribbentrop's since elementary school days. The semiliterate Likus became his factotum and party contact. To please his friend von Ribbentrop, Himmler made Likus an SS colonel, and he was frequently sent to Berlin as a gossip collector and spy. Dozens of friends and party bigwigs went to and fro. Captain Zivina also ferried custom shirts from the Berlin haberdasher Jacquet and cologne (straw-bottled bay rum). But the most frequent passenger was the ambassador. Nothing tells the tale better than his schedule for 1937.

2/2/37 Return Berlin to London
3/1 Speech in Leipzig
3/5 Opera-Munich with Hitler
3/10 Return to London
4/16 German Navy training ship at Torquay
5/19 Spithead to see fleet review
6/5 Berlin
6/8 London
6/24 Berlin
6/25 Dresden (Autobahn opening)
6/28 London
8/12 Vacation — England
8/14 Germany — vacation
8/28 Kiel — funeral
8/29 Stuttgart — conference: Germans Living Abroad
9/13 Party rally — Nürnberg
9/14 With Japan's Prince Chichibu — Berlin
9/25 Mussolini in Munich
9/26 With Mussolini for Army Maneuvers
9/28 With Goebbels at reception for Italians
9/30 London
10/4 Berlin
10/15 London
10/17 Berlin
10/19 Munich
10/20 Berlin
10/21 Munich
10/22 Rome with Mussolini and Ciano
10/24 Berlin
10/25 Londonderry
10/26 London — Parliament opening
10/26 Nonintervention Committee — London
10/29 Nonintervention Committee — London
11/4 Rome
11/5 Rome
11/6 Rome-Japanese Treaty
11/7 Meeting — Mussolini
11/9 London
12/3 Lunch with Lord Mayor — London
12/3 Dinner — German Chamber of Commerce
12/3 Anglo-German Fellowship
Rest of month — Berlin and Dahlem[19]

Von Ribbentrop clung to his master, but his absences raised more resentment in London, where it was felt that the Court of St. James's was entitled to more than a part-time ambassador.

Earlier in 1937, on January 30, Hitler had made a Reichstag speech in which he emphasized that there would be "no more surprises," but several major conflicts with Britain remained, such as the colonial question, the Spanish Civil War, and the persecution of the Jews. Added to these was the heightened persecution of the Protestant clergy. On July 1, 1937, Pastor Niemöller was arrested for the fifth time, but this time he was not released after the usual few days of interrogation. The Church of England launched no immediate official complaint. The Anglo-German relationship was sensitive.

The embassy began to make more than the usual routine contacts with Germans who were living in Britain but who were neither Jewish refugees nor non-Jewish political exiles. By German law, every passport-bearing German in Britain, Jewish or not, had to report to the nearest German consulate every six months, or else his passport would be canceled, thereby invalidating his British residential visa. This applied to exiles and "good" German citizens alike, including the hundreds of German domestic servants and waiters who worked in London's hotels, restaurants, and homes. A former Navy captain named Karlova, who worked as the resident SS police agent in the embassy, tried to organize an espionage ring of German servants.[20] Karlova's idea was probably von Ribbentrop's tithe to his friend Himmler, who by then had placed SD (*Sicherhertsdienst*) police agents in all German embassies and missions worldwide.

Captain Karlova also made contact with all German organizations that were not out-and-out Nazi groups. Several old-time German "Kränzchen," coffee-and-cake *gemütlich* associations, were warned of dire consequences for their relatives in Germany unless they "*equalized*," the Nazi term for becoming National Socialists.

There were thousands of recent German-Jewish exiles in London, most of them still shocked and bewildered by the strange new English world and language, and often degraded into menial jobs. For these people, the obligatory semiannual visits to the German Embassy were like trips to hell. Their German passports carried swastikas on the dull brown cover, and they received no smiles of warmth from the dour German passport clerks. Yet there was no way even the refugees could avoid this unpleasant task, because an invalid passport meant the loss of residency visa or work permit. Still, London's refugees found their own little Germany. Undaunted by what happened to them, they clustered together in middle-class London neighborhoods like Hampstead, where German accents became quite common. Some began businesses. The Kempinski family, once the owners of the famous Berlin delicatessen carrying their name, opened a small restaurant on Swallow Place just off Regent Street. Several tiny Berlin- and Vienna-style cabaret theaters sprang up. The sons of German and Austrian refugees appeared at a few of the old public schools. At St. Paul's School in London, Freud's grandsons became schoolmates of the son of Putzi Hanfstaengl, by then estranged from Hitler.

Germany's great stage star Elisabeth Bergner and Berlin's Shakespearean actor Fritz Kortner were invited to work in London. The young Lili Palmer and the boy André Previn were among London's Germans in exile. Erich Pommer, the producer, made films in partnership with Charles Laughton. Ludwig Stein directed films.

An apocryphal story is told about Kortner. Try as he would, he could not learn to play Shakespeare in English, which broke his heart, since he was a famed Shakespearean in Germany, where the Bard is as beloved as in England. Kortner was invited to the Dorchester Hotel suite of Erich Pommer. There, Pommer accused Kortner of cowardice for not playing Shakespeare in English. While they were arguing, the phone rang, and the desk clerk told Pommer that Vivien Leigh was waiting downstairs to see him.

"Good," said Pommer in English. "Send she up."

Kortner gently admonished Pommer: "Erich, it's not send *she* up! It's send *her* up."

"Vell," said Pommer, shaking his head in disgust, "if you're going to start *that* way, you'll *never* play Shakespeare!"

This little London-German world stayed very much alive until 1939, when many of its members were interned, ironically as "enemy aliens." Most were soon released, but many were shipped to the Isle of Man, to Canada, or to Australia. One group's ship was torpedoed by a U-boat on the Atlantic. Many found their way to the United States. Some joined the British army's Pioneer Corps.

In the memoirs written by former members of von Ribbentrop's London embassy staff, mostly well-educated young Foreign Office or Büro members, there is never any mention of these German residents of London. Most of the writers were concerned only with the embarrassment von Ribbentrop was causing Germany, when the true shame for Germany lay in the refugee world all around them in London.

The question of Germany's former African colonies was quite another matter. The return of the colonies was more hotly pursued by those who wanted to return them than by those who claimed them.

Britons who, in letters to the *Times*, advocated their return included Lord Astor, Bishop Carey (he was the chaplain of Eastborne College and principal of Ely Theological College), the Bishop of Southampton (he was the former Bishop of Johannesburg), and Lord David Cecil.[21] Most of these men felt it was just and fair play and no reason to go to war.

Two enemies of von Ribbentrop were about to be removed. On February 2 the British ambassador in Berlin, Vansittart's brother-in-law Sir Eric Phipps, a great Nazi antagonist, was posted to Paris. Then the American ambassador, William Dodd, took a leave of absence from his post and did not return, probably in protest against his instructions from Washington to attend the Nürnberg party rally in September. Until then no western ambassadors had attended.

On May 11, 1937, the day before the coronation in London, Sir Nevile Henderson, the new British ambassador to Berlin, submitted his credentials to a very disturbed Adolf Hitler.

The Führer had just learned that the airship *Hindenburg* had burned and crashed in Lakehurst, New Jersey. He told Henderson that several warnings about sabotage had been received.

Now all those in London who wished to appease Hitler, but also those who wanted to delay while Britain rearmed, had the right man. Henderson was a Foreign Office professional like Phipps, but unlike Phipps, Henderson appeared neutral and friendly. He was able to carry out a brief that some described as sympathetic to Nazism and collaborative. Others saw Henderson as the hero who held Hitler at bay while stalling for time so that Britain could rebuild her arsenal and, most important, strengthen her will.

Sir Nevile Henderson was despised by many as Great Britain's "Nazi ambassador," but to others he was the twilight hero of what he himself eventually described as a failed mission. The eagle-nosed, mustachioed, graying Henderson was the quintessential diplomat in looks and action — calm, charming, and stylish. Von Ribbentrop so dreaded any direct contact in Berlin between the new ambassador and the Führer that he tried at once to discredit Henderson in Hitler's eyes, even in small ways. For instance, von Ribbentrop knew perfectly well that Englishmen of the thirties wore chalk-striped suits, brown suede shoes, and carnation boutonnières in the style of Edward VIII. So it was an obvious act of malice to tell the unworldly Hitler that Henderson was being "disrespectful" when he wore a carnation to meet the Führer. The Führer's limited experience had never presented him with the more stylish manifestations of the extraordinary species known as the British Gentleman. Certainly, according to his memoirs, Henderson often thought disrespectfully, but he would never have dressed disrespectfully. Would he have behaved in a disrespectful manner? Probably not. But to demonstrate how exasperated even Sir Nevile Henderson became with the German dictator in the last days before the war, at a meeting with Hitler he once actually pounded the table! He also stood red-faced and angry in von Ribbentrop's office, ready for fisticuffs with an equally red-faced and yelling von Ribbentrop. The interpreter Paul Schmidt sat between them, wondering whether diplomatic protocol called for him to stand, too. He decided to sit until the storm had passed.[22]

Meanwhile, Henderson became a new irritant for von Ribbentrop. He was an unknown quantity, an Englishman, a "new broom," and, worst of all, he was in Berlin, where he could establish direct contact with Adolf Hitler. Certainly von Neurath would have no compunctions about bypassing his hated ambassador in London.

Using George VI's coronation as an opportunity, von Ribbentrop planned the great Coronation Ball at the "new" German Embassy. Newly promoted Marshal von Blomberg, tall, gray-haired, and gray-uniformed, and his aides were to represent Adolf Hitler, Germany's chief of state, at the coronation. It was a strange choice, but a clever one. Von Blomberg, Germany's top soldier, came from the sort of old German stock the British could appreciate. Titled British gentry had always felt a kinship with their German opposite numbers. After all, the Windsors were basically German; old Queen Victoria had been married to a German consort; former German families like the Mountbattens were very much part of British society. "German" did not necessarily mean "evil" to the British upper classes.

Somehow, instinctively, Adolf Hitler knew that Germany's *Adel*, its old aristocratic families, were more like their British counterparts than like Germany's bourgeoisie or workers. The *Adligen* had a bond with Germany's farmers and peasants that was almost paternal. At the level of equals they identified with the ideas, customs, and manners of the families of the British counties, and they were frequently related to them by marriage. Toward the end of the war many German officers who had British relatives (*Fremdverwandt*), even wearers of the coveted Knight's Cross of the Iron Cross, were disqualified from holding command.

On a more threatening note, von Blomberg's martial presence would serve to remind London that there was a new, well-run, well-armed, and well-led German Army.

Buckingham Palace was ready for the coronation. So was the German Embassy.

Reinhard Spitzy's memoirs told about the colorful, braid-trimmed uniforms of the empire's troops and its dignitaries, including bejeweled Indian maharajas, "a picture from a Thousand and One Nights." He used the breathless German vernacular of the time: "And then this sparkling picture is interrupted by a field-gray fog. The crowd's cheering dies down. Impressed, everyone's eyes are fastened on the simple appearance of the German delegation, Blomberg accompanied by his military aides . . . all in field gray and wearing steel helmets. They are tall men, walking with dignity. There is only a slight clink of spurs and rattling of sabers. Their only decorations are those from the World War . . . It was like a cold gust of air which gave a hint of future battles between the two nations." Spitzy may well have accurately gauged the crowd's hushed reaction.

Also among the spectators were exiles from Nazi Germany who had once worn those same field-gray uniforms in the same war. An apocryphal Kafkaesque refugee story of that time was told about two former German-Jewish officers, then refugees in England. As they looked at the small field-gray delegation from Nazi Germany, one of the refugees said with tears in his eyes, "Our fellows look terrific!" ("*Unsere Jungens sehen schneidig aus!*")

The motives for the Coronation Ball given at the German Embassy to celebrate the crowning of George VI and his Queen were tainted both with admiration and with disdain, with hatred and with longing, in fact with von Ribbentrop's very own complexes both of inferiority and superiority. It certainly would never have been Adolf Hitler's idea to invite twelve hundred foreigners to London's German Embassy for a lavish *fête*, catered by Horcher's, Berlin's finest restaurant. Supper was flown in. Also Berlin's finest dance band and stars. Hitler's Potsdam days were far behind him. His adoration for Kings and Emperors had ended. He would never have chosen a royalist occasion as the reason for celebration. The anniversary of the January 30 Nazi takeover? Yes! But a royal coronation? Never! Hitler was and remained a revolutionary. Deep down he was contemptuous even of Germany's own imperial house, the Hohenzollerns, though he still made occasional use of their pathetic Prince Auwi.

The ball must have been von Ribbentrop's idea or, more likely, Annelies's. She had played a major part in devising and executing the whole venture. She would show Britain's society women!

Invitations to the Diplomatic Corps were sent out in German, "10³⁰ *Uhr Anzug: Frack-Uniform-Orden*" (10:30 P.M. Dress: Full Dress, uniforms, decorations), with the resultant Babel of multilingual responses. Who at the embassy spoke Turkish or Finnish? There was a frantic search.²³

To assure themselves of those acceptances which were difficult to obtain, each invitation carried a handwritten note above the swastika-and-eagle escutcheon at the top: *K.K.H.H. der Herzog und die Herzogin von Kent haben ihr Erscheinen zugesagt* (Their Royal and Imperial Highnesses the Duke and Duchess of Kent have confirmed their acceptance).

Among others expected were Churchill, Baldwin, Eden, Lord Halifax, the Vansittarts, and the Archbishop of Canterbury. The presence of the Kents guaranteed a flood of guests; also, London was curious to see the inside of the renovated embassy. The menu for the light midnight supper, again swastika-headed, was:

> *Langouste tail en croute*
> *Salad*
> *Baby Peas*
> *Mocha and frozen dessert*
> *Parmesan cheese croquettes*
> *Peaches*

Since it was served after 12:00 P.M., it was dated May 15, 1937, with typical German efficiency.

As Spitzy pointed out, "British society laughed that the invitation went out in German." Obviously, no one laughed hard enough to send regrets. The guest list was "sparkling."

Besides the Duke of Kent and his beautiful duchess, Marina, *née* Princess of Greece, there were Prince Chichibu of Japan, General Maurice Gamelin, the French chief of staff, one of Ibn Saud's sons, and most of the other princes and dukes who had assembled in London for the week of coronation celebrations. Cranach's famous painting *Suicide of Lucretia Borgia* was a much-admired part of the embassy's décor, and the ambassador and his staff were convinced that the ball showed everyone that the new Germany was civilized and worldly and culturally up to the level of the other great powers.

It was probably the von Ribbentrops' final attempt to impress German society. After the Dahlem Olympic party, this was their second try for a wider audience of the British ruling classes. Curiously, in his 1986 memoirs Spitzy insisted that immediately afterward von Ribbentrop sent anti-British dispatches to Berlin, lest the German

delegation under Marshal von Blomberg throw doubt on von Ribbentrop's adequacy as Germany's representative.

But if the von Ribbentrops had not wished to solicit British good
will, why did they throw the big embassy party? In fact, Spitzy himself
wrote that after the coronation party, the von Ribbentrops' popularity
was partly restored.[24]

Invitations to the embassy were accepted at the last minute by Sir
Alexander Cadogan, the new foreign secretary, and even Churchill,
whom the von Ribbentrops considered a less than gracious guest. On
May 21, 1937, he came for lunch and to discuss an anti-German
article he had written for the *Evening Standard*.[25] Von Ribbentrop
bluntly offered a promise from Adolf Hitler to guarantee British security. An angered Churchill growled that the Royal Navy "had been
doing that for centuries and needed no help." Undeterred, von Ribbentrop pressed on. Germany would guard Britain's interests if Germany could have a free hand in the east of Europe. He showed
Churchill a wall map, pointing at Polish, Ukrainian, and Byelorussian
Lebensraum for Germany, five times the size of its own territory.
Churchill said the British would never tolerate this, even though they
hated Communism. Von Ribbentrop turned away abruptly and said,
"In that case, war is inevitable. The Führer is resolved. Nothing will
stop him or us." Churchill replied, "Do not underrate England, and
do not judge her by the present administration. England is very clever.
She will again bring the whole world into the war to help."

Von Ribbentrop replied heatedly, "England may be very clever, but
this time the whole world won't help her."

Churchill said privately he knew of the proposal "from Vansittart's
agent in Göring's office."

The rest of June 1937 von Ribbentrop frantically chased between
Berlin, whence came his support and sustenance, and London, where
his duties forced him to be.

By now both of the von Ribbentrops must have realized that their
London dreams of social and political acceptance were never to be
realized. There was no question that the embassy ball had been a great
success, but it took only a few days for tensions to return. Between
June 5 and 28, von Ribbentrop's plane flew from London to Berlin to
London to Berlin to Dresden to London. His mind was not on London, although on June 15 he did attend a meeting of the cynically
named Nonintervention Committee, despite the bombardment of
Guernica by the Condor Legion on April 26 and the naval bombardment of the Spanish port of Almería by the German Navy. The Almería "punitive" action was ordered because Spanish Loyalist planes

had bombed the German battleship *Deutschland* while she was in their enemy's repair yard on the island of Ibiza, held by Franco's forces. Thirty German sailors were killed. News of this event reached von Ribbentrop, his family, and aides while they were on a golf vacation in Cornwall. It was also at this time that the SS discovered that Thorner, Rudolf's former Hitler Youth supervisor, now von Ribbentrop's London secretary, an SS captain, and Büro employee, had one-eighth Jewish blood. The frightened, shocked, pale Thorner told Spitzy behind locked doors about this disaster and his immediate discharge from the SS, which would lead to his removal from his London post. Von Ribbentrop, who was usually loyal to subordinates, attended the opening of the Dresden Autobahn on June 2 ; and persuaded the Führer to be generous with Thorner "due to years of membership and Hitler Youth duty."[26] The Führer "graciously permitted Thorner's transfer to the embassy in Stockholm."

Obviously, even Hitler did not wish to interfere with many decisions of the SS, which was rapidly growing into a separate state, a reservoir of Teutonic myth. The short, owlish Himmler, as unlikely a physical specimen as his Führer, was just as besotted with the notion of the tall, blond, blue-eyed Aryan. As if to frustrate Himmler, even the tall, blond Reinhard Heydrich, his monstrous chief of the Gestapo, whom he considered the perfect Aryan specimen, was known to have vast hips and a fat rear. He was also said to have Jewish blood.

During July von Ribbentrop spent some time in Britain, because his assistants at the embassy had heard too many rumblings from affronted Whitehall. Meanwhile, his Japanese friends chose that July to launch a massive attack on China. Following an armed clash — or "incident," as international politics would have it — on Marco Polo Bridge in Peking, they seized the old Imperial capital as well as Tientsin. Chinese troops soon abandoned the port of Shanghai to the Japanese, who then attacked British and American ships near Nanking. The American gunboat *Panay* was sunk with a loss of American lives. Apologies were offered by the Japanese government and restitution paid, but it was the beginning of Japan's road to war with the west. In London, von Ribbentrop was visited by a young Japanese diplomat, dispatched from Berlin by Japanese Ambassador Mushakoji. Von Ribbentrop, very much out of the picture, asked, "Will the Japanese soon defeat the Chinese?" and received a polite Japanese nonreply.

Kordt and his Foreign Ministry associates were now witnesses to a power play within the Japanese government parallel to their own. Their Japanese counterparts in London told them that the Japanese

Foreign Ministry was rapidly losing its control of policy, and nation-alist politicians and the military were taking charge. A friend of Kordt's at the Japanese Embassy launched into uncharacteristically frank complaints about the situation in Tokyo, but von Ribbentrop remained totally unaware. He was concentrating on his empty seat "at court" in Berlin. His old elementary school friend from Metz, the party hack SS Colonel Likus, had become a fixture at the embassy but could do little to reinforce him in absentia. It was important for von Ribbentrop to be physically present in the anteroom of the Chancel-lery in Berlin each day before 2 P.M. That was when Hitler usually appeared and chose his luncheon companions by pointing at those waiting for "the call." "You, Herr X, sit on my right, and you, General Y, on my left, and the rest of you gentlemen may choose your own seating." Those who were named were deemed to be in special favor, but one had to be present to get chosen.[27]

In August the von Ribbentrops reluctantly decided to take a short vacation in Britain. No doubt the ambassador would rather have been in Berlin.

August 3, 1937
To Führer and Foreign Minister

According to permission given me by the Führer [I am] going to Scotland to regain my health. I intend to stay in Scotland in August to be available in case of developments in nonintervention matter. End of August I shall be in London for a short stay and then go to Germany to undergo cure. Minister Woermann will represent me. Assuming that the Führer and Foreign Minister agree, I shall then give personal report from Berlin.
  Ribbentrop
  (handwritten) note R567G
  We request that day of beginning and end of vacation be given to us by embassy.
  Bavarian Vacation: Feldafing,
  Hotel Empress Elisabeth, near Starnberg.[28]

They motored to Gleneagles in Scotland in two Mercedes behe-moths. One of the cars developed some mechanical problems, so the three-motor D-AMY flew from London to Germany to take aboard a Mercedes mechanic. The other plane passenger was SS General Wolff, Heinrich Himmler's aide, requested by von Ribbentrop for "important consultations."[29] It must be assumed that von Ribbentrop wanted to reinforce his conduit to Heinrich Himmler and that Wolff's trip was probably trumped up. The landing of the large, lumbering D-AMY on a small Scottish airfield apparently caused eyes to pop. Actually the plane was ideal for the purpose, slow and powerful. For this reason, the JU-52 became Germany's main troop transport and parachute plane.

In mid-August, unable to stay away any longer from his Führer's side, von Ribbentrop brought his family and part of his staff to the hotel at Feldafing on Starnberg Lake, near Berchtesgaden and the Berghof. They continued their vacation, except for a trip to the Navy port of Kiel for the funeral of recently promoted Admiral Wassner, the true architect of the Naval Agreement. Then a short trip to Stuttgart to meet the *Auslandsdeutsche,* delegations of "German-blooded" people from all over the world. Von Ribbentrop was busy looking busy. (The *Auslandsdeutsche,* people of German descent who lived abroad, became Hitler's constant excuse to interfere with other countries. They were all *his* Germans. Today this heritage has come to haunt the German Federal Republic, which would probably prefer to think of them as foreigners.)

The 1937 party rally in Nürnberg began on September 8, and, to the joy of Adolf Hitler and Joseph Goebbels, the two leading western ambassadors did attend. Sir Nevile Henderson, Neville Chamberlain's new Berlin "accommodator," signaled his acceptance, and in order to "keep the appearance of solidarity," André François-Poncet of France also attended. The disgusted departure of Ambassador Dodd left the new American ambassador, Hugh Wilson, not yet willing to accept, though he was authorized to do so.

Henderson and François-Poncet agreed to limit themselves to two days in Nürnberg. (The full rally lasted a week.) Their reactions were divergent. Henderson, a newcomer to Nazi Germany, thought the rally "indescribably picturesque, of grandiose beauty. Hess, aloof and inscrutable. Supper in the SS tent sinister and menacing. For Hitler: [The Germans had] idolatry."[30]

François-Poncet was not overwhelmed. Long familiar with Adolf Hitler and the National Socialist style, he was the "featured" speaker at a reception for foreign diplomats at the Hotel Deutscher Hof. He told Hitler, in front of the other diplomats, "Your propaganda minister must be wrong, because you invited us despite the fact that Goebbels said we, the democratic peoples, are calves who chose their own butcher."[31] François-Poncet was quoting an excerpt from a Goebbels warm-up speech at the beginning of the rally. Goebbels fumed. Hitler grinned.

As usual, the rally had a theme; Goebbels had named the 1937 event the Rally of Labor. It became the stage for announcing the Four-Year Economic Reconstruction and Rearmament Plan, slated to be administered by Hermann Göring.

As soon as the Nürnberg rally ended, von Ribbentrop rushed back to Berlin. His next plan did not include London. Mussolini was on his way to pay a five-day state visit to his ally, Germany, which would precede the signing of von Ribbentrop's Anti-Comintern Pact, supposedly now a powerful bloc comprising Germany, Italy, and Japan. For von Ribbentrop the foremost aim was the building of these political blocs. Hitler thought in terms of an ideological brotherhood of National Socialism, Fascism, and *bushido*. For him power-bloc thinking was reactionary and dated, but he decided to humor his touchy adviser. Whitehall's patience was wearing thin. Why should the ambassador to Great Britain dance attendance on Italy's chief of state? But von Ribbentrop paid no attention.

At 9 A.M. on September 25 the special train carrying the Duce, accompanied by his tomcat foreign minister and son-in-law Count Ciano, known as the Ducellini, arrived in Munich. The train also carried Dino Alfieri, his propaganda minister, and one hundred of the Duce's staff.

After a visit to Hitler's private apartment on Prinzregentenplatz, Mussolini, the man who had first used the term Axis, was presented with an immense parade of SA and SS on Königsplatz, the open Munich square. Mussolini was trying to be "more Prussian than the Prussians" in his newly designed, ribbon-encrusted uniform.[32] In Bologna he had bragged about the "olive branch of peace growing from a forest of eight million bayonets." He had seemingly overcome his 1934 disdain for Germany's Führer and had told John Whitaker, of the *New York Herald Tribune*, that he would "invite Hitler to make Austria German."

There was no doubt in von Ribbentrop's mind. He had to be there. He had to be part of the event. This was history in the making. The stakes were high and the penalty for absence was steep. The fact that he was still ambassador to Great Britain and that the proper escort for Mussolini and Ciano was Germany's ambassador to Italy, Ulrich von Hassel, gave him no pause. He hounded Mussolini and his aides for the full five days of their state visit. From Munich to Essen to Berlin he chased after them by supercharged Mercedes or on one of the special trains.[33] His chauffeur, Brütgam, was ordered to cut in ahead of von Hassel's Mercedes when everyone was traveling in convoy. At Mecklenburg they watched Army maneuvers. At Swinemünde there were mock naval attacks. At Essen, the Krupp works displayed their weapon-building steel muscles. Von Ribbentrop was always right there. Then, finally, on to Berlin on September 28. For the last few kilometers to the capital, Mussolini's and Hitler's special trains ran precisely side by side on twin tracks in a dazzling theatrical demonstration of parallel Italo-German aims and loyalties.

Six hundred and fifty thousand Berliners assembled on the May Field outside the Olympic Stadium to hear Hitler and his top dignitaries declare their faith and trust, a marriage of Fascia and Swastika.[34] When it was Mussolini's turn to speak from the thirty-five-foot-high concrete podium, the heavens opened up in a deluge of September rain. Within minutes Mussolini's notes lay dissolved in soggy tatters. His uniform was soaked, and the water-logged microphones projected only high-pitched gibberish while the Roman dictator gesticulated wildly. Had they not been drenched and standing in mud, the cynical Berliners would have had a hard time suppressing their laughter. It was a good thing the flagpole with Hitler's *Standarte* was manned by sailors who were used to the soaking.

The way back to Berlin became a nightmare of jammed traffic and mud-spattered sliding and tottering dignitaries from generals to Gauleiters trying to find their parked, mired cars. Annelies von Ribbentrop was never even able to leave her big Mercedes stuck in a muddy parking lot at the edge of the May Field. She was supposed to have joined Joachim. Her husband went back to Berlin in a car Spitzy requisitioned from a minor party functionary by howling at the top of his lungs in the Prussian military manner about the importance of his Chief, the Ambassador Extraordinary and SS General. Among the sopping dignitaries was Franz von Papen, dressed in a Kaiser-era uniform with all his World War decorations and sashes. On his head he wore an old-fashioned, spiked helmet. Göring greeted him with an ironic "Heil, Herr Old Reichs Chancellor!"

Mussolini as honored guest was quartered in the former Presidential Palace, once the crown prince's. When the shivering Mussolini asked for a hot bath, he found out that Prussian efficiency was not infallible. There was no hot water for the lavish rococo bathtub. *Freddo, freddo, freddissimo!* was the plaintive call of the Duce's aides. The drenched and freezing Mussolini had to take a frigid bath before rushing for his mountainous and regal bed.[35]

Despite this minor failure, Mussolini was impressed by Hitler's ways. He returned to Rome with some poisonous souvenirs. He would now reshape his empire in the image of Hitler's Germany, everything from the goose step to anti-Semitic "blood" laws.

His oldest Fascist associates were aghast. Even the most banal of Nazi manifestations were resisted. The goose step, or *Parademarsch,* now became the Passo Romano. His most heroic soldier, Marshal Emilio de Bono, protested, "Since the average height of the Italian soldier is five foot five, we shall have an army of stiff-necked dwarfs!"[36]

The advent of anti-Semitic laws raised a much bigger furor. Many Italian Jews were old Fascists and supporters of Mussolini, and Italians were by nature brotherly with their Jewish compatriots. Many Italian-Jewish families dated from the days of the Roman Empire. In a demonstration of protest, Marshal Balbo, Italy's air hero, famed pilot, and one of Mussolini's closest friends, flew himself from Libya to Ferrara. In that ancient center of distinguished Italian Jewry, he made it a point to visit every leading Jew and then to dine with Ferrara's Jewish mayor in the city's finest restaurant.[37]

A veritable deluge of Italian decorations accompanied Mussolini's visit to Germany. Even the hall porter at the Hotel Vier Jahreszeiten in Munich was awarded a knightly cross.[38]

The von Ribbentrops and their retinue returned to London on September 30. Once more, it was a short visit. Other matters were in the offing elsewhere. First, the signing by Italy of the Anti-Comintern Pact — now, with Japan, a three-power agreement — was to take place. The Ribbentrop Büro's clever Herr von Raumer, whose research had originally produced the technicality that removed the Anti-Comintern Pact from being a virtual declaration of war on Russia, was still the pact's chief architect.

On October 4 von Ribbentrop was in Berlin. He stormed over to London on the fifteenth and then immediately back to Berlin, to the Berghof, and finally to Rome. The meetings with Mussolini and Ducellini Ciano went smoothly, and all was prepared for the gala signing, scheduled for early November in Rome.

Next, no sooner had Rome said "si!" when von Ribbentrop again rushed back to Berlin, there to protect the tenuous bond originally tied with the help of the late Ambassador von Hösch at an Emerald Cunard soirée, where von Ribbentrop had met the famous couple now known as the Windsors.[39] Their 1937 trip to Germany had been arranged by a charming but shady Franco-American then called Charles Bedaux, an expert in industrial efficiency, whose automated production systems were said to have been the inspiration for Charlie

Chaplin's film *Modern Times*. Bedaux had advised German industry for years. Surprisingly, although they were not intimate friends, the Windsors had accepted Bedaux's offer of his château in France for their wedding and honeymoon.

The Windsors ostensibly wished to study social conditions in the "new" Germany. Dudley Forwood, the duke's aide, said that the German-speaking Duke of Windsor was fully aware of the potential for Nazi propaganda and was extremely careful.[40] He even avoided any arm gesture that might have been photographed to resemble the Nazi salute. Still, some reporters made the unlikely claim that he rendered a full Nazi salute to Adolf Hitler and to a Death's Head SS parade.[41] True or false, the resultant uproar forced the Windsors to cancel a trip they had planned to the United States.

By the time von Ribbentrop saw them in Berlin, the Windsors had already visited the Berghof for tea with Hitler. Paul Schmidt, the interpreter, reported that the duke had been noncommittal to the Führer. Forwood reported that when the duke criticized something, an interpreter gently modified it for Hitler to avoid annoying the Führer. The duke then shouted in German, "*Falsch übersetzt!*" (Wrong translation!)[42] In Berlin the von Ribbentrops gave a dinner for the Windsors at Horcher's. The other guests were the Himmlers, Marianne Hoppe, a well-known film actress, and Gustav Gründgens, the famous actor and Nazi puppet on whom the 1980 film *Mephisto* was based. The duke, on being introduced, gently tapped his heels together in the old-fashioned, pre-Nazi manner, which amused some of the Nazis.[43] They considered it "reactionary."

Von Ribbentrop made a token return to London on October 26 for two events: the first was the opening of Parliament, which foreign ambassadors viewed from a special gallery. At noon exactly, the slow procession of the royals, with Lord Halifax carrying the Sword of State with his one and only hand, moved through the sea of robed peers. According to Chips Channon, the King had overcome his stammer and spoke well. Then came a session of the Nonintervention Committee with all of its empty discussions. The die had long before been cast in Spain, and Franco was winning. Germany and Italy were helping and the Russians were withdrawing their support from the Republicans. It was a heartbreaking time for the many international volunteers, like America's Abraham Lincoln Brigade, fighting on the side of the Loyalists. Ernest Hemingway learned firsthand the price paid by those who hesitated to oppose the appetites of dictators. François-Poncet once described Hitler as a *Nimmersatt*, the German word for someone who is insatiable, and Mussolini had already begun his own masticative process in Ethiopia.[44] Now both he and Hitler sharpened their appetites for future feasts by joining hands over Franco Spain. For these two it was to be what François-Poncet called a fatal friendship. Mussolini's early unpunished aggression in Africa encouraged Hitler. Hitler's unopposed threats to the western powers misled Mussolini. Only Franco remained the enigma among the dictators. Adopting all the usual fascist trappings, including the raised-arm salute, he established an absolutist regime and kept it out of World War II. He guided it through the very decades when dictatorships in Germany, Italy, and Japan were crushed, toward constitutional monarchy and then democracy. During World War II he rejected any major collaboration with Hitler or Mussolini, with the exception of a limited number of volunteers. He kept his borders inviolate and permitted no back-door access to the Mediterranean, the Atlantic, or to vital Gibraltar. He so exasperated Hitler that even Goebbels, in sheer disgust, condemned Franco throughout his diary.

To prepare the way for von Ribbentrop's Italo-Japanese Anti-Comintern plans, Hitler ordered withdrawal of all help to Chiang Kai-shek's China. Germany was now in Japan's camp.

On November 4, a Friday, von Ribbentrop arrived in Rome. Foreign Ministry officer Prince Philipp of Hesse* had returned from Rome after testing the waters for Hitler. He had succeeded with Mussolini but encountered some reluctance from Ciano, who was not prepared to trust this von Ribbentrop out-of-channels treaty. For the same reason, the Ambassador Ulrich von Hassel had gone to Berlin to get clarification. Von Neurath and the ministry were wary of the entire Anti-Comintern Pact. They were afraid Germany might bind herself to the adventures of her new cosignatory. Besides, it was not *their* idea, and a depressed von Hassel told Kordt that no one had been able to stem the flow of events. Hitler was in favor of the pact. Von Ribbentrop had gained his victory over the professionals. To assuage the old diplomat von Hassel, Kordt pointed out that the treaty "contained mainly nonsense." Von Hassel agreed. Nevertheless, he worried about the future undertakings of Italy and Japan.

Among von Ribbentrop's Berlin allies for the Anti-Comintern Pact was Ambassador Walther Hewel, the charming and skilled diplomat whom von Ribbentrop had appointed as the Büro's liaison man at the

---

*Philipp was of the minor branch of the family of Prince Lu Hessen, who served in the embassy under von Ribbentrop. Philipp was married to Princess Mafalda of Savoy and was therefore the Italian King's son-in-law. He was used by Hitler as a contact with Rome. He probably had ambitions to climb above his secondary Hessian status.

Reichs Chancellery. Adolf Hitler was extremely fond of Hewel, but Hewel stayed a loyal subordinate of von Ribbentrop's. He reassured von Ribbentrop that Adolf Hitler favored the Anti-Comintern Pact in spite of von Neurath's opposition.

The pact was duly signed on November 6 in Rome, and the large state dinner that followed involved the Special Ambassador Extraordinary in a battle of precedence with Ambassador von Hassel, who was technically *in loco* Germany's head of state. To complicate things, Rudolf Hess arrived from Berlin. Hess was senior to von Ribbentrop within the Nazi Party, since the Büro was technically part of Hess's Deputy of the Führer organization.

The Italian protocol people enjoyed much glee while watching the German titans in undignified combat over precedence. They then tactfully solved the dilemma by deciding on round tables without seating by rank. These small skirmishes between old and new were constant, and Adolf Hitler relished them. He was getting his revenge over the Prussians and their aristocracy. Potsdam lay far behind.

The euphoric events of Rome made von Ribbentrop careless. On several occasions he had said publicly that he was destined to become foreign minister in 1938, when von Neurath's age would force his retirement. He did not know that Hitler had given von Neurath his personal assurances that in his case the age limit would be waived. Ambassador von Hassel immediately informed von Neurath of von Ribbentrop's Roman indiscretions, and when von Ribbentrop returned to Munich, expecting his Führer's enthusiastic congratulations, he was pointedly ignored and had to stay in his hotel, cooling his heels. He had no warning that a rockslide of anger was about to come down on him. When von Ribbentrop was finally ordered to report to his Führer at 9 A.M. on November 8 at the Führer's private apartment on Prinzregentenplatz, he and his secretary, Spitzy, both wearing full black SS uniforms complete with dress swords, arrived punctually. Von Ribbentrop received a vicious and audible tongue lashing behind the Führer's closed study door. Hitler was furious because von Ribbentrop had bragged that he would soon be foreign minister. Hitler asked, "*Was bilden Sie sich eigentlich ein?*" which is the German equivalent of "Who the hell do you think you are?" He continued, "No, Herr von Ribbentrop. We don't behave that way! And particularly not in front of foreigners!"

A whipped, wounded, and meek von Ribbentrop beat a hasty retreat to the Hotel Vier Jahreszeiten, where he retired to the safety of his bed in a darkened room, suffering a heavy attack of "Tango

Nocturno."[45] According to Spitzy, von Ribbentrop moaned that "it was all finished" and that he would now volunteer to fight in Spain; he asked Spitzy to join him. The young SS captain was less than enthusiastic about seeking a heroic death and gave a noncommittal answer.[46] A lengthy phone call to Annelies in London restored some of the ambassador's equilibrium, and he returned to England the following day.

A tragedy that soon occurred showed that Joachim von Ribbentrop still had a normal human side when his day was untouched by Adolf Hitler. His young Büro aide Prince Lu was about to marry an English girl in London. His whole family, all the Hessians, were to be flown by a special Lufthansa plane to London for the wedding. The Duke and Duchess of Kent had agreed to be the best man and matron of honor for their young cousin.

The plane crashed on takeoff after refueling in Brussels, and everyone aboard was killed, including a sister of the Duchess of Kent, the Grand Duchess of Hesse. It was a great tragedy. Even the most cynical members of his staff said that both Joachim and Annelies were kind and supportive. The young couple decided to go through with the sad wedding, and the Kents, Mountbattens, and von Ribbentrops helped them. At times, the von Ribbentrops could still muster those expected decencies which were part of their upbringing. In fact, in matters of their own family, their children never lacked for affection. A human tragedy in their immediate surroundings could bring the von Ribbentrops to free themselves for the moment from the strings that made them Hitler's marionettes. But it happened rarely.

At about the time the Rome Anti-Comintern Pact was signed, Adolf Hitler had a confidential meeting with Göring, von Blomberg, Army Chief of Staff von Fritsch, Admiral Erich Raeder of the Navy, and Foreign Minister von Neurath. Supposedly he outlined his plans for the takeover of Austria and the conquest of Czechoslovakia. He believed that Britain would fight Italy but not Germany. At this meeting Göring asked for an end to the involvement with Franco, but obviously without success.

The meeting, recorded by Hitler's military aide, Major Friedrich Hossbach, became well known later from the Hossbach Memorandum of November 5, 1937, because it seemed to prove how early Hitler had planned the Anschluss and the conquest of Czechoslovakia, the country that was to move to center stage in 1938. This document has occasionally been discredited; some historians claim that several of the participants could not have been present due to other commitments. However, it became the *bête noire* of German diplomats, who often heard about it from their foreign colleagues.

According to the German military agenda, there actually was a secret review of Case Green at the War Ministry on December 21, 1937. Case Green was the code name for the eventual invasion of Czechoslovakia.

Early in December in London von Ribbentrop was a brief and perfunctory speaker at the London meeting of the Anglo-German Fellowship, attended by the usual group and also by the unlikely Sir Robert Vansittart. Von Ribbentrop's attention was diverted by the visit which Lord Halifax, one of the participants at the dinner, had just made to Adolf Hitler at the Berghof, with von Neurath in attendance. Von Ribbentrop knew none of the meeting's agenda, and it took a full month before he had to embarrass himself by requesting a report from von Neurath. Hitler had not asked von Ribbentrop, his "England expert," to attend the Halifax meeting, nor had he responded to a request for an audience in early January. From November 1937 until February 1938 von Ribbentrop was clearly a man out of his master's favor, and Adolf Hitler was eager to mollify von Neurath.

Others had absolutely no problem learning about the Halifax-Hitler meeting. On December 5, 1937, Chips Channon's diary reported:

> I had a long conversation with Lord Halifax about Germany and his recent visit. He described Hitler's appearance, his khaki shirt, black breeches, and patent leather evening shoes [*sic*]. He told me he liked all the Nazi leaders, even Goebbels, and he was very much impressed, interested, and amused by the visit. He thinks the regime absolutely fantastic, perhaps even too fantastic to be taken seriously. But he is very glad that he went, and thinks good may come of it. I was rivetted by all he said and reluctant to let him go.[47]

Channon made no comment of his own.

Von Ribbentrop's days as Hitler's favorite now seemed to be numbered, and von Neurath was someone Hitler was not ready to discard. That chance would soon come, brought on by a series of events that once and for all let Hitler vent his hatred of most aristocrats, particularly those in the Foreign Ministry. He was sure the nobles had always been his enemies. Along with Jews, Bolsheviks, and Masons, *Die Reaktion,* the reactionaries, were the objects of his most bitter ideological enmity. There were those words in the Nazi Party's anthem,

"The Horst Wessel Song": "*Kameraden die Rotfront und Reaktion erschossen . . .*" (Comrades who were shot to death by the Reds and the reactionaries).

Meanwhile, though von Ribbentrop had to suffer his beloved Führer's rejections, he refused to blame Hitler, and he said to Spitzy, "The poor Führer has fallen into the hands of evil advisers and saboteurs."[48]

From the day he met Adolf Hitler to the day he died on the gallows, even at those times when he received shabby treatment, Joachim von Ribbentrop never showed a moment of disloyalty to Adolf Hitler. In his Nürnberg cell, after he was condemned to death, he proclaimed his eternal, personal devotion to Hitler. With the exception of Joseph Goebbels, he was the most steadfast of the top Nazis. It was this unwavering loyalty which Adolf Hitler sensed and used, and it would become von Ribbentrop's death sentence, passed on that day in 1932 when he first met Hitler in Berchtesgaden. Von Ribbentrop was indeed the son of an officer in the Kaiser's Army; blind loyalty was the German officer's religion. His father had ruined his own career out of loyalty to the great Bismarck. The son would lose his life for being unquestioningly faithful to an evil man.

Although von Ribbentrop believed that he had fallen from the Führer's grace and favor, he decided to perform one final task to demonstrate his undying loyalty to Führer, Reich, and party. He began a major evaluation of the Reich's future relations with Great Britain, a long and complicated document eventually labeled Ambassador's Report A5522. It took him weeks to complete. Annelies helped him.*

A5522 was rambling and unfocused, but in the main it stated that Britain was trying to catch up by rearming as quickly as she could, that she thought time was on her side, and that the Halifax visit was only a smoke screen. Also, Britain did not trust Nazi Germany and would fight as a last resort, and Germany should continue an open show of conciliation while maintaining an Italian-Japanese coalition against Britain. He asked rhetorically, "Will France and Britain go to war if Germany goes to war in Central Europe?" He suggested that he preferred to make an oral report about the matter directly to the Führer. He was convinced Britain would fight if the British Isles were threatened. He reported that Edward VIII had had to leave the throne

---

*There are several accounts of the days when Joachim and Annelies von Ribbentrop scrambled on hands and knees on the floor of their bedroom, sorting the hundreds of drafted pages.

because he was too friendly to Germany. "We must think of England as our most dangerous enemy."

While he slaved over this paper, helped only by his wife, Adolf Hitler and Benito Mussolini prepared a new and harsher plan for future international dealings. On December 11 Mussolini's Italy withdrew forever from the League of Nations, and Hitler announced that Germany would never again return to Geneva.

10

EMBASSY — MINISTRY — MUNICH — KRISTALLNACHT 1938–1939

Will My Adorable Austria
Become Nazified?

THE DOWNHEARTED and pessimistic von Ribbentrops returned home for Christmas and New Year's of 1937–1938. They were accompanied by a substantial group from the embassy. An expense voucher of March 1938 notes that Mitropa, the German sleeping-car company, had charged the Foreign Office for thirty first-class tickets and sixteen second-class tickets. The tickets cost 3166 marks.[1]

Christmas was spent at Sonnenburg, the country estate the von Ribbentrops had just bought near Berlin. There was never any shortage of money. Between the von Ribbentrop Büro and the embassy, most of their travel, entertainment, and living expenses were paid, including the constant use of D-AMY. At the same time, the wine business still flourished. The von Ribbentrops were a wealthy couple. Much of their money was earned privately and not through the party, in contrast to other party people.

Hitler made a vast fortune through the massive forced sales of *Mein Kampf.* Göring earned large sums for administering his party-sponsored industrial complex, the Hermann Göring Works, with its 600,000 employees, founded in July 1937.[2]

Certainly the purchase of the Sonnenburg estate caused no financial strain, but von Ribbentrop was always careful to play down his personal fortune in front of the Nazi elite. He was willing to boast of his political or party achievements and power, but never of his personal wealth.

A few months later, after he became foreign minister, he was lunching at the Führer's table in the Chancellery with a group of Nazi highnesses, including Dr. Goebbels. Reinhard Spitzy, hovering dutifully in the background, overheard the following interchange:

> GOEBBELS: Herr von Ribbentrop, is it true that you just bought a grand estate and you are now going to renovate it?
>
> VON RIBBENTROP: Yes, the place must be straightened out agriculturally and the house should be renovated if I want to use it for some of my work as foreign minister, or if I should wish to vacation there.
>
> GOEBBELS: Oh, agriculture? Do you know anything about it? For instance, can you tell an ox from a steer?
>
> Grins appeared around the table while an amused silent Hitler bent over his dish of noodles and poked around. Ribbentrop gave a pained laugh and tried to be a good sport.
>
> GOEBBELS: Herr von Ribbentrop, you seem to be making quite an investment. Is it true you are building a private golf course?

This did not sit too well with the Nazi bigwigs at the table, who had little patience with such plutocratic affectations.

> VON RIBBENTROP: Well, it's only a few holes and greens, hardly worth mentioning. I need it for those guests who like to play golf, and it relaxes me after the office routine.
>
> GOEBBELS, going for the jugular: And all this on a government salary?

There was much laughter until Hitler, smiling briefly, changed the subject while Ribbentrop stared angrily at the table and stopped participating in the conversation. He left soon after.

The von Ribbentrops probably bought Sonnenburg with their own money, so why did von Ribbentrop not tell Goebbels to go to hell; how he spent his own money was nobody else's business? The reason was obvious. He would not play the role of rich man among these revolutionaries. He wanted to be one of them, accepted as an "old fighter." He had a lot to overcome: his good looks and careful grooming, his title, though "adopted," his international life, his beautiful houses, his aristocratic friends, his rich wife, and his money. Among the Nazi Party stalwarts, he was still an outsider.

Goebbels once said, "Ribbentrop bought his name, married his money, and cheated himself into his job."[3] But it was a jealous Goebbels who said so, always eager to be foreign minister, always hating anyone Hitler admired.

After weeks of being ignored by Hitler, in those first days of 1939, von Ribbentrop might have thought his career was over. His patron had turned from him. But the fates had worse in store for him; soon they would return him to the very center of Adolf Hitler's favor and attention.

It began on January 12, oddly enough at a wedding. That day, in the presence of the Führer, Field Marshal Werner von Blomberg, minister for war, was married to Miss Eva Gruhn, his former secretary. Miss Gruhn was not really a suitable match for the aristocratic von Blomberg; she came from a simple, lower-middle-class Berlin background. Nevertheless, everyone approved of the decision of the tall, sixty-year-old marshal, long a widower and known as a great flirt. He adored beautiful young women, and now he was about to marry one. His friends smiled and shrugged their shoulders. Why keep him from a chance to regain his youth? Even Göring had urged him to go ahead with the wedding, though Miss Gruhn was known to have had several affairs in the past. According to the historian Joachim Fest, Göring even paid off a rival for Miss Gruhn's affections to clear Blomberg's path.[4]

Within a few days, police files revealed that the new Frau von Blomberg was not only a *femme fatale,* but had actually practiced prostitution and had been arrested after posing for pornographic photographs, now in the possession of a Belgian military attaché.

It was a major dilemma. The Führer had given his tacit blessing to this *mésalliance* by being present at the wedding, and the military leadership of the Reich was now in the hands of a man who had shown a complete lack of judgment in the conduct of his personal life.

After originally expressing uncertainty about the Nazis, von Blomberg had often demonstrated his loyalty to Hitler. He helped to plan the Rhineland occupation and after von Hindenburg's death had approved switching the military oath of allegiance from the Reich to the person of Adolf Hitler. Hitler had always been able to count on him, but that was no longer enough. Now von Blomberg had offended Hitler's lower-middle-class prejudices. A German aristocrat did not marry a prostitute. And how dare von Blomberg make him, Adolf Hitler, an unwilling partner to such immorality! There was also the satisfaction of teaching all those gentry in Army headquarters who was really in charge. He would make the noble generals shake in their well-polished boots. If only Röhm had not been such a clumsy fool! Of course, Röhm was absolutely right. Germany needed a new people's army.

But through all the anger, the romantic Hitler's tear-filled eyes saw the "besmirching of the noble German military spirit." Now, fifteen days after he had witnessed von Blomberg's wedding, Hitler told his war minister, "It is time for us to part," and von Blomberg was summarily dismissed. The von Blombergs stayed married. They went off for a honeymoon.

The world of the generals would undergo yet another jolt, this time delivered unintentionally by General Werner von Fritsch, the chief of staff. Von Fritsch, one of the architects of the new German Wehrmacht, had backed Adolf Hitler in the Röhm action, but after the meeting documented by Major Hossbach on November 5, 1937, von Fritsch feared that Hitler's plans of eastern conquest were premature and precipitous. Von Fritsch had counseled moderation, and his influence among senior Wehrmacht officers had to be considered. Then, suddenly, came a Gestapo report stating that von Fritsch had engaged in "offenses against paragraph 175," the coy German way of referring to homosexual acts.

Von Fritsch stood accused by a homosexual blackmailer and prostitute who was serving time in jail. The report had first landed on Göring's desk. Göring advised the Führer. Von Fritsch was secretly warned by newly promoted Colonel Hossbach, Hitler's military aide, who respected the general. Of course, von Fritsch insisted on facing Hitler and Göring. He rushed to the Chancellery, where he was kept waiting for several hours. As if they were small-time detectives, they produced the accuser, who had been temporarily freed for the purpose of confronting von Fritsch.

"Is this the man you saw?" they asked the shaken crook, who immediately said, "That's the man!" No one knows what the Gestapo had done to him or had promised him.

The shocked von Fritsch did something Hitler observers judged a great mistake. Instead of howling his defiance, breaking his sword over his knee, and throwing it at Hitler's feet, which would have impressed the Führer, von Fritsch calmly denied everything. Hitler never understood understatement, as the British were to learn.

Hitler immediately passed summary judgment instead of waiting for the Military Court of Honor, which was to convene later. Von Fritsch had to retire and "go on a long vacation." Later, the disgraced von Fritsch was acquitted by a military tribunal, but it was too late. In 1939 during the attack on Poland he was killed while leading a regiment of artillery.[5] Most German military men said he was seeking death. As a postscript, Colonel Hossbach, who had warned von Fritsch, was dismissed.

Hitler appointed a new head of the Army, General Walther von Brauchitsch, and General Wilhelm Keitel became Hitler's chief of staff and his perfect instrument, but now Adolf Hitler himself assumed the post of commander-in-chief of the entire Wehrmacht. Keitel, a passive, servile man, was soon called Lakeitel, a play on the German word Lakei, "lackey." He was a cynical flunky who never disagreed with Hitler, endorsed all measures taken by the increasingly cruel party, and was hanged at Nürnberg. He died with more dignity than he had lived.

The armed forces, always Hitler's main instrument of policy, were now entirely in his hands. All opposition had been silenced, all reason was ignored. Generals and admirals would be instruments of Adolf Hitler and the party. The Luftwaffe was Göring's creation.

Not all of them were automatons. There were still senior officers who opposed Hitler, and who had not buried their morality, but most leading officers of Germany's armed forces were now Hitler's property. He promoted his generals when he needed them, discarded them when they no longer suited his purpose, or decorated them and even gave them cash bonuses in the manner of a feudal lord. Some generals who had managed to preserve their integrity were seduced when Hitler's early wartime generalship seemed brilliant. Only a handful remained their own masters.

Now that the Wehrmacht had been brought to heel, only the Foreign Ministry remained a stronghold of the old guard. Time and again they had acted as brakes, slowing Hitler's plans. He was sick of what he considered their air of superiority, their vacillation, their lack of flexibility and imagination. He had to persuade and convince von Neurath and his diplomats each time he wanted to step outside the path of conventional policy. From Rhineland to Naval Agreement to Anti-Comintern Pact, the Foreign Office professionals had consistently been nay-sayers.

The conciliatory year of the Olympics was now in the past. The friendly King Edward VIII was gone. The attempts to deal with Britain were stalled. Italy and Japan had become closer allies. France had stayed placid no matter what the provocation. Germany no longer needed the League of Nations, whose system of sanctions was impotent and ineffective.

Von Neurath had not made any plans for dealing with upcoming problems such as the former German port of Danzig or guaranteed access by road and rail across that "Versailles abomination," as he called the Polish Corridor, or the return of the former German port of Memel.

Von Neurath was reluctant to look east. Hitler had always insisted that was where Germany's future lay, in Poland and Russia. Von Neurath even failed to acknowledge the alleged "danger" that the Franco-Russian treaty had brought by way of Germany's southeastern neighbor, Czechoslovakia.

And did von Neurath really understand Austria's hunger for union with its German "brothers?" Adolf Hitler had reasons to doubt it. All of von Neurath's demonstrated allegiance to National Socialism seemed opportunistic. It is odd that Hitler unknowingly agreed with François-Poncet, who called von Neurath "not frank, but lazy, a liar, and lacking in moral courage."[6] Von Neurath did not join the party until 1937, and his general's rank in the SS was Himmler's gesture to him as a government minister. He did get involved in anti-Semitic measures and antichurch measures, but that took little National Socialist conviction or personal courage.

Hitler needed a young, imaginative, flexible internationalist, someone totally loyal and aggressive who would agree with Führer policy, Führer plans, Führer wishes. Since his earliest days of political combat, Adolf Hitler had been completely sure of his own political credo. He rambled and meandered when he wrote *Mein Kampf,* but he had not changed one scintilla of his views. He now needed a new foreign policy executive.

He made an unlikely choice for foreign minister because he had only the narrowest list of candidates: Rosenberg, Goebbels, and Göring. Alfred Rosenberg had failed on his London mission in 1934. He preferred that Goebbels concentrate on propaganda. Göring was already too powerful. Most top ambassadors, like Ulrich von Hassell in Rome and Herbert von Dirksen in Tokyo, were professional diplomats, not in the least different from von Neurath. Von Papen could not be taken seriously. He too was an opportunist and, as a Roman Catholic, too closely tied to the Vatican. Hess had never expressed great interest in the job. So Hitler chose von Ribbentrop, his adviser on foreign policy since 1932 and his ambassador to Germany's most important adversary.

Konstantin von Neurath was completely unaware of his impending dismissal. He was sure that Hitler trusted him and depended on him. Hitler had time and again backed him against von Ribbentrop's attacks, although von Ribbentrop's Büro was still active and had often briefed Hitler before meetings on foreign policy. Von Neurath had put up with the Büro. Anyway, it did much of the dirty work, like bribing foreign journalists and recruiting shady agents, and it was welcome to such functions. The gentlemen of the Foreign Ministry preferred to keep their hands clean.

Besides, the Führer had just celebrated von Neurath's sixty-fifth birthday by personally coming to congratulate him and to present him with a superb piece of medieval art. As von Neurath had told his former colleague Paul Schwarz, "I always respected the amount of knowledge a simple man like Hitler was able to accumulate, without the right schooling and the right opportunities. If Hitler had the chance for traveling abroad, if he had received proper education, he really would have become one of the world's greatest statesmen."

On the morning of February 4, 1938, von Neurath was a contented man. Lulled by the recent birthday celebration and gift, the von Neuraths decided on a holiday on their estate, Leinfelderhof, in Württemberg, in the south of Germany. His wife began to pack for the trip. At noontime of that day, the Führer's state secretary informed von Neurath that Hitler wished to see him at 3 P.M. He attended a long meeting with the Führer on foreign policy; von Ribbentrop was present. When it was over, von Neurath walked through some gardens to his ministerial villa, accompanied by Hitler's and von Ribbentrop's best wishes for his holiday. When he arrived at home there was a message asking him to return "for a few minutes" to the Chancellery. Hitler met him in the garden behind the Chancellery, linked his arm through von Neurath's as they strolled together. In gentle tones he said that von Ribbentrop would be the new foreign minister, and that von Neurath would become president of a secret privy council, which had just been created. "This is my fondest wish," said Hitler.

The stunned von Neurath returned to his villa, no longer the foreign minister. Two days later, Frau von Neurath was told that her servants were to report to the von Ribbentrop villa in Dahlem and that the tableware was property of the Reich. Then von Ribbentrop's people asked when the villa would be vacated.

It is difficult to muster sympathy for von Neurath, because his presence contributed little to what remained of German sanity. Von Hassell and dozens of others had first served their strange and vicious new master and then rebelled against his monstrous ways. Von Neurath simply went along. He was a man of the world, *un homme du monde*. He knew right from wrong, and he willingly continued to serve the wrong. His subsequent career as Protector of Bohemia and Moravia and his occasional "housekeeping" stints in the field of diplomacy reflected no honor on him. He was eventually sentenced to fifteen years as a war criminal.

Suddenly, after thirty days of abject depression, during which he had neither word nor gesture from his master, the emotionally drained and embittered Joachim von Ribbentrop found himself foreign minister, and Annelies was the wife of a man of cabinet rank. In Wiesbaden, Käthe Henkell would ask, "Why did the most stupid of my sons-in-law achieve the biggest success?"

Many things needed to be arranged. The entire London household had to be returned to Berlin. A new ambassador had to be assigned to London. What was to become of the Büro? The short month of February was crowded with the new foreign minister's unfamiliar duties. Von Neurath made absolutely no provisions for his former subordinates in the ministry, and these gentlemen now awaited the new regime of party stalwarts with much anxiety. It fell to Kordt to handle the details of the transition as best he could. Along with von Neurath's came the dismissal of several aristocratic ambassadors, among them von Hassell.

Adolf Hitler's attention now focused on his homeland, Austria. Almost as a side issue he ordered the diplomats to prepare Germany's recognition of Manchukuo, Japan's new puppet state in China. It was also propitious that Anthony Eden, now the "difficult" British foreign minister, was replaced by the easy-to-please Lord Halifax, or Lord Halali as the Berliners called him ("*Halali!*" was Germany's old hunting yell, and Halifax had recently been Göring's guest for the hunt.) But no matter what happened elsewhere in the world, nothing would or could divert Hitler's attention from Austria.

A week after his appointment, von Ribbentrop attended his first international meeting as foreign minister. An urgent call from the Berghof told him to report immediately to his Führer at the Bavarian retreat for a meeting with Austria's Chancellor Kurt von Schuschnigg and the German ambassador to Vienna, the indestructible Franz von Papen.

Von Ribbentrop was in the dark about the state of German-Austrian affairs, and quite unprepared for the meeting. Curiously, von Papen had only just been fired from his Vienna ambassadorial post, along with all the other dismissed nobles, but since it was he who had arranged the von Schuschnigg meeting, he was reinstated. Luring von Schuschnigg to Hitler's Berghof, and into the lion's den, had been no small achievement. Von Papen deserved credit of sorts. As Sir Nevile Henderson wrote, "Going to Berchtesgaden at all was the first of von Schuschnigg's mistakes."

Meanwhile, the new foreign minister was on his way south to do the Führer's bidding. He was accompanied by Spitzy, and they were joined by a senior SS officer named Wilhelm Keppler, who was Hitler's expert on Austrian political and economic matters. Arriving in Berchtesgaden, they met with von Papen, who showed them his draft for an Austro-German agreement, but von Ribbentrop knew next to nothing about the subject of Austria. Nevertheless, according to Spitzy, von Ribbentrop took von Papen's draft and "hardened" it from the German standpoint, since one "never did oneself harm with the Führer by being aggressive."

They arrived at the Berghof on February 12, promptly at 10 A.M. Next came von Schuschnigg, who was met halfway up the flight of stairs by his host. The pale and tired Austrian chancellor was introduced to Hitler's associates, and the two chiefs of state then retired to Hitler's study. Several generals, led by the newly minted Führer-supported chief of staff, Keitel, had also been ordered to attend, supposedly to discuss Spain, but more probably to project a military threat.

February in the Bavarian Alps can be cold, gray, and whipped by snow-seeded mountain winds. It must have been a threatening scene for the Austrian chancellor, his foreign minister, Guido Schmidt, as well as Schuschnigg's secretary, who was an officer of the Austrian Guards Regiment, and an Austrian detective. Also on the scene, and most unwelcome to von Schuschnigg, were two semi-uniformed (they wore white stockings) representatives of the thirty thousand illegal Austrian Nazis now living in exile in Germany.* Spitzy, who reported on the conference, was also an "illegal," as the exiled Austrian Nazis were called.

The paladins of both sides could do nothing but sit around and wait. Conversation between the exiled Austrian Nazis and the Austrian government officials was halting at best. No doubt their minds were not on their conversation, but on the two men locked in agreement or in combat somewhere upstairs in the sprawling Berghof. Both protagonists were Austrians, one from a titled family, the other from the simplest of backgrounds, and they were playing poker with the lives and fates of their fellow Austrians. Most observers believe it was a harsh meeting and that von Schuschnigg was threatened and browbeaten.[7] He had to accept measures and conditions that must have

---

*Austria's Nazis were banned and could not wear uniforms. They improvised by wearing white farmers' stockings instead of brown suits.

been repugnant to him. Probably to ease his pain, Hitler later made a well-publicized declaration that he wished an *evolutionary* solution to the Austro-German future, and he replaced the head of Austria's Nazi Party.

Von Schuschnigg was forced to add the Austrian Nazi politician Arthur Seyss-Inquart to his cabinet. Hitler also bludgeoned von Schuschnigg into granting amnesty to all Nazis imprisoned in Austria, and insisted on free return for all "illegal" Austrian Nazis, as well as compensation for them. At one point during the conference, Hitler made a big show of consulting privately with General Keitel just out of von Schuschnigg's hearing, but not out of sight. It was certainly an implied threat. At 10 P.M., the end of that disastrous day for von Schuschnigg, his Austrian detective bade his German hosts goodbye with "*Heil Hitler!*"

Eventually, von Schuschnigg could not and would not go through with the odious deal that had been foisted on him. On March 9 he declared a national Austrian plebiscite to determine whether Austrians preferred their independence or wished to become part of the German Reich. Word of the unexpected plebiscite soon reached Hitler in Berlin and set off an attack of Hitlerian rage. His victim had dared to betray him! The deal was unraveling. Austria now had only a few days left to live as an independent nation. Austrians played a curious but important role in the life of National Socialism. The popular notion in Germany was that Germans made better Nazis but Austrians made better anti-Semites. Quite aside from their Austrian Führer and his German brand of spoken Austrian, with its rolled *r*'s and anachronistic style, they had strong influence. They were only 8 percent of the total German population, but they were 14 percent of the SS. The Einsatzgruppen, the SS death squads, had more Austrians than Germans. Forty percent of the extermination camp staff members were Austrians.[8]

Colonel Adolf Eichmann, the SS "Jew expert" who organized the execution of the Final Solution, had been reared in Austria. Seventy percent of his staff was Austrian. Chief of the SS–SD (the party section of the Gestapo) Ernst Kaltenbrunner was an Austrian. Odilo Globocnik, overall commander of the death camps in Treblinka, Sobibor, and Belzec, was an Austrian. General Alexander Löhr, a war criminal who had ordered the murder of Greeks, Slovakians, Yugoslavs, and Jews, was Austrian.

(There were also great Austrian heroes. Among them were Anton Schmidt, an Army sergeant in Vilna, executed for helping Jews, and Ewald Kleisinger, an Army officer who hid Jews in Warsaw. Fifty

Austrians were declared Righteous Gentiles by Israel, the highest acclaim given to those who braved the Nazis.)

After the von Schuschnigg meeting, it was back to Berlin for von Ribbentrop, where he attempted to fit himself into his important new post. Fortunately for him, he got professional help in the person of Ernst von Weizsäcker, a former Navy officer and Foreign Ministry professional. Von Weizsäcker, who had been chargé d'affaires in Switzerland and then head of the political department of the ministry, was promoted to state secretary, a post similar to London's permanent under secretaries or Washington's assistant secretaries of state. If there was any chance to conduct professional, international diplomacy, it would be due to von Weizsäcker, who was appointed at the urging of Erich Kordt and others. Von Ribbentrop was forced to trust them because of his own lack of experience and training. Later, constantly battered by the insecure "loose cannon" von Ribbentrop and the influential Annelies, and, most of all, by the aims of Adolf Hitler, von Weizsäcker did what he could to soften the shocks, ease the pain, and divert the harm. In time he found it impossible, and asked to be relieved. He was sent to the Vatican as ambassador at the end of the Nazi regime.

Some of the filth that splattered everything surrounding the person of Adolf Hitler also tainted von Weizsäcker. In fact, all professional diplomats whom von Ribbentrop drew close to himself quickly became "Ribbentrop people" in the eyes of many of the Wilhelmstrasse ministry offices. Most of the professional people chose to forget that Erich Kordt and those he brought to the office of the foreign minister were originally proposed by the distinguished State Secretary von Bülow, who hoped they would be "observers and restrainers." It was virtually impossible for anyone, no matter how opposed to his ways, to work for Adolf Hitler without becoming part of his evil. The men who mounted an unsuccessful attempt on Hitler's life on July 20, 1944, had come to the conclusion that Germany herself could never survive in Hitler's filth. Yet there is strong evidence that if they had succeeded in killing Hitler, Germany might have been plunged into civil war while the Allies were still tearing at her flanks from east and west. To the end, Hitler, who was willing to destroy every German as "unworthy," was adored by the majority of Germany's people.

Von Ribbentrop witnessed the first act in Austria's eventual tragedy without being able to contribute the slightest piece of advice or expertise. On returning to Berlin, he ordered a ceremony that must have shaken quite a few Foreign Service veterans. Everyone had to assemble for a quasi-military "mustering" and a banal Hitler-loyal speech from the new minister, who was dressed in his SS uniform. By now, von Ribbentrop had worked out a makeshift persona for himself, somewhat in the imagined style of a statesman in ancient Rome: dignified, measured, stern, assured, and a devoted servant of Adolf Hitler and of National Socialism. His staff at the London Embassy had often heard his dinnertime harangues, proclaiming the need for a "new nobility" in Germany, a new elite, founded on Aryan roots and on National Socialist teaching.[9] The old titled families who considered the Foreign Service their private club had to relinquish command. He insisted, "It is not so important to speak foreign languages. The others will soon have to learn German." Both his adopted dignity and seeming assurance were soon to be put to the test. Von Weizsäcker and Kordt persuaded him to return to London in order to take his formal leave of Whitehall after his sporadic and careless performance as ambassador to the Court of St. James's. Perhaps they felt a courteous gesture might salve wounded British feelings.[10]

While he was back in London, he met with Lord Halifax and asked him to tone down unfriendly newspaper pieces. Amazingly, Halifax did try to reason with the papers. On the same day, Kurt von Schuschnigg suddenly announced his plebiscite and a furious Hitler unleashed his troops.

The day after, von Ribbentrop appeared at Buckingham Palace to bid a formal farewell to the King, this time without any Hitler salutes. At this exact time, far to the east, von Schuschnigg announced a postponement of the referendum on Austrian independence and his own resignation. It can only be assumed that von Ribbentrop had paid no attention to events in Austria. Certainly he was not informed, although Kordt, who was with him, seemed *au courant*. Exactly one month had passed since the cruel Berghof meetings with von Schuschnigg. On March 11, von Ribbentrop was attending a luncheon at 10 Downing Street, hosted by Neville Chamberlain, the new prime minister, and his senior cabinet ministers. Winston Churchill was also there. Suddenly news of the German military entry into Austria was handed to Mr. Chamberlain. Understandably, the luncheon soon ended, but there was no discussion of these events. Every British official present must have thought that Foreign Minister von Ribbentrop knew exactly what was happening in Austria and was playing the innocent, and one can imagine their disgust with him. No one would have believed that von Ribbentrop had been purposely left in the dark by Hitler or that the military move had been a sudden whim of the Führer's and that there was no way that word could have reached his foreign minister, who had been visiting all over London.

Hitler knew how insecure von Ribbentrop was. He wanted to prevent the foreign minister's sudden departure from London. He needed his "England expert" to be near to 10 Downing Street so that he could gauge the British government's reaction to the Anschluss (Unification).

He had virtually trapped von Ribbentrop in London.

To add insult to injury, von Neurath was instructed to be caretaker at the Foreign Ministry in Berlin.

Lord Halifax paid a visit to the German Embassy in London after the luncheon at 10 Downing Street and expressed his deep concern to a falsely cheerful and reassuring von Ribbentrop, who asked when next he might see Halifax in Berlin. "Lord Halali" answered tersely, "I doubt if there'll be a hunting exhibition soon."[11]

A thoroughly nervous, disturbed, and anxious von Ribbentrop was now stuck in London while his place at the Führer's side was being filled by others. He had left Spitzy behind in Berlin to look after some of his interests, but Adolf Hitler's decision to reactivate von Neurath during these events seemed ominous. What did "temporary charge" mean? Von Ribbentrop was still not aware of Hitler's strategy. A letter from the Führer had been carried to Mussolini by Prince Philipp of Hesse to make sure of Mussolini's friendly reaction to the Anschluss, because the Duce had played Austria's "protector" for years. Now Hitler wanted to keep von Ribbentrop in London so that Mussolini would think an accommodation about Austria was being worked out with Chamberlain.

As he had so often, von Ribbentrop felt isolated and feared he had lost the Führer's confidence. The morning after these events, he begged Kordt, almost tearfully, to fly to Berlin to "save what he could." Von Ribbentrop whined, "Please see that Neurath is no longer involved." Kordt flew to Berlin, but von Neurath was nowhere in sight.

Von Ribbentrop finally managed to phone Spitzy, who, it turned out, had accompanied Hitler to Vienna. The young former "illegal" Austrian Nazi could not resist his Austrian Führer's personal invitation to join him. They were now two returned patriots. Vienna's Cardinal Innitzer greeted Adolf Hitler with the Nazi salute one day after his arrival and assured him of Catholic support if the church received "the same freedom as the German Catholic churches."[12] (He was referring to the concordat of September 10, 1938, between the Catholic Church and the Nazi regime, which was eventually breached by Hitler.)

Spitzy obtained Hitler's permission for von Ribbentrop to leave London and return to Berlin. Most officials of the Foreign Ministry were ordered by von Ribbentrop to greet him at the airport, a forced show of false devotion and loyalty designed to assuage his wounded ego. But before leaving Britain, von Ribbentrop had to wait for the arrival of Spitzy, who carried a personal order from Adolf Hitler requesting von Ribbentrop's equally personal report of British reactions. It was a bitter pill for the foreign minister: at the moment, even his young secretary was closer to the Führer than he was. That may have been why he ordered the full Foreign Ministry reception committee.

First reports of the brutal treatment of Vienna's Jews, of old Jewish men forced to scrub the streets on their hands and knees while the crowds jeered and spat on them, soon reached London.[13] It reduced former British sympathizers of Adolf Hitler's Germany to those who only wished to appease. What remained of British enthusiasts for Hitler soon shrank to a tiny hard core. The *Times* of March 15, 1938, headlined THE RAPE OF AUSTRIA, and reported the debauches against both anti-Nazis and Jews.[14] Even the pacific Lord Lothian called for conscripted National Service. Only a few diehard British apologists still carried on.[15] Lord Redesdale said in the House of Lords on April 15, 1938, "Hitler avoided civil war and bloodshed in Austria," and Lord Londonderry blamed Britain because "we failed to hold out the hand of friendship." Chips Channon, now a parliamentary aide, heard the news in 10 Downing Street. He considered it a setback for the Chamberlain government and then, reverting to the sophisticated traveler, asked, "Will my adorable Austria become Nazified?" And, prophetically, "People are saying Czechoslovakia will be next."[16]

By the time von Ribbentrop reached Vienna, he was part of the "second wave." Hitler and Göring had already left. Only Schacht was still there to deal with immediate financial and economic problems. The Austrian official who greeted von Ribbentrop was Guido Schmidt, von Schuschnigg's former foreign minister who had been to Berchtesgaden with him. Schmidt was now devotedly on the side of the Germans while his former chief was on his way to Gestapo jail and then to a concentration camp. Eventually, Guido Schmidt was appointed to run the immense Hermann Göring Industrial Works for the fat marshal, a profitable reward for his treachery. Von Ribbentrop quickly visited the Austrian Foreign Ministry, took charge, and appropriated the great Metternich's world globe for removal to his Berlin office.

André François-Poncet reported one of the most startling reactions to the Anschluss. According to him, Eduard Beneš, the Czechoslovak president, said, "I'd rather see the Germans in Vienna than the Haps-burgs."[17]

Ambassador Sir Nevile Henderson, the man so often accused of Nazi sympathies, now wanted to make a gesture of protest against the invasion of Austria. He decided to boycott the annual Heroes' Me-morial Day Parade in Berlin, the March 13 ceremony usually attended by all ambassadors and foreign envoys. Instead, with Union Jacks flying from the embassy's Rolls-Royce, he had himself driven to the Austrian Mission in a show of British sympathy. He could have saved himself the trouble. The Austrian minister, in full diplomatic uniform, was on his way to attend the ceremonies, where he saluted with "*Heil Hitler!*"[18]

During the first days of the Anschluss, much of Austria's popula-tion went on a rampage of antidemocratic, anti-Communist, antireac-tionary, anti-Semitic "revenge." Many Austrians now insisted that they had been Nazis all along. Not only did they, in the words of Dr. Joseph Goebbels, "wish to go home to the Reich," but they delivered themselves of a shamefully amplified imitation of the wildest SA debauches of 1934. In Während, a prosperous section of Vienna, wealthy Jewish women were forced to scrub the street while wearing their fur coats. Some of the spectators then urinated on their heads.[19] (Jews who were arrested by the Gestapo were forced to sign papers before they were released attesting to the good treatment they had received. Dr. Sigmund Freud wrote, "I am happy to give the Gestapo my best recommendation.") Eleven hundred Viennese Jews killed themselves after the Anschluss.

While the Viennese were committing their *vox populi* street perver-sions, the German SS and the Gestapo's leather-coated agents roamed throughout Austria as Himmler's angels of death, seeking anyone who had ever opposed the Anschluss or wished to protect and preserve Austria's independence as a Christian democratic nation. Even those who had compromised their democratic principles by backing the rightist regime of Dollfuss now became targets for the Gestapo.

This SS–Gestapo sweep produced one murder that benefited the von Ribbentrop family and was counted in their disfavor by many Austrian and German nobles. The SS took over a charming lakeside castle called Fuschl, near Salzburg, after arresting its owners, the von Remitz family. Herr von Remitz, an Austrian patriot of the highest order, was sent to Dachau and executed. Fuschl was handed over to Joachim von Ribbentrop.

Over the following years, Annelies, Joachim, and the children used it extensively. Fuschl became the place where von Ribbentrop would await the call from the nearby Berghof, his master's call. Frau von Remitz, a niece of the leading German industrialist Fritz Thyssen, and her children were left to fend for themselves. When von Ribbentrop was host to Mussolini in 1942 at Fuschl, he spoke of it as "his father's castle."[20]

Some Austrian Nazis were shocked because everything "Austrian" was now stricken from view. Even the name *Austria* became *Ostmark*, or "eastern province." Reinhard Spitzy bemoaned the loss of Austria's old traditions. He was not alone.

In return for Mussolini's apparent approval of the takeover of "his" Austria, Adolf Hitler bartered away the mostly German-speaking lands and people of the mountains of South Tyrol. This region, the domain of ancient Austro-German families like the von Wolkensteins, von Enzenbergs, and von Trapps (of *The Sound of Music*), was released to Italy without any regard for the Tyroleans' wishes. Thousands of these people from the high mountains were forced to resettle in southern Italy or flat East Prussia. As Hitler declared on May 19, 1938, "The Tyrolean question has ceased to exist."

These decisions were made without so much as a moment's consultation with the new foreign minister. It seemed von Ribbentrop would never be able to initiate foreign policy or execute it independently. The vainglory would still be his, but the policy would be Hitler's.

The first four "problems" Hitler had originally outlined to his foreign minister on the day he was appointed were Austria, the Sudetenland, Memel, and Danzig. Austria was now "solved." In his memoirs, von Ribbentrop wrote that it was always his task to offer the diplomatic solution.[21] The military people were instructed to prepare the military solution. Neither side knew the contents of the other's plans. Hitler would make the choice. This time Hitler had made the military choice.

It was, in the words of von Ribbentrop, "hard to make one's point against such a strong personality. Every man who worked for Adolf Hitler had this experience. No one could change his mind once it was made up."

Von Ribbentrop claimed that three separate times he tried unsuccessfully to resign and to be transferred to the Army for combat duty. Although he had become a pampered man who loved his comfort, it is possible that this claim was true. Someone who drove bobsleds as a youngster, went halfway around the world to serve as a combat soldier, and was willing to brave many a storm-tossed flight in the primitive passenger planes of those days probably did not lack physical courage.

Neither did he lack vanity. To von Ribbentrop, appearance was vital, and he complained that Germany's diplomats made a poor appearance because they had no special diplomatic uniforms like other nations. Von Ribbentrop himself often wore his SS general's uniform, complete with sword of honor, black tunic and cap, Sam Browne belt, black riding breeches, and shiny black riding boots. It pleased him to wear it. It also pleased his friend SS Chief Himmler. However, the SS uniform would not do for many international diplomatic occasions. It was too martial, and besides, it was not the uniform of the German Diplomatic Corps. When a forthcoming state visit to Rome was announced, an urgent call went out to Benno von Arent, a famous theatrical designer who had staged many Nazi events. Von Arent designed a sort of "admiral's" uniform with "piston rings" on each sleeve to denote rank. Here, too, Adolf Hitler, the artist-architect *manqué*, had his say. He approved it.

Until then, most members of the Foreign Ministry had appeared in conventional cutaway coat and striped trousers or in white tie and tails. They were often ordered by an angry Hitler to "get into uniform," and for this reason many were given honorary ranks in the SS. Kordt became an honorary SS colonel, as did Schmidt the interpreter.

However, for the state visit to Rome in May they now got their new German diplomatic uniform in several versions for diverse occasions. In a childish act of competition, von Ribbentrop engaged in a struggle for insignia with State Secretary Meissner, who ran the Führer's Chancellery. Meissner felt he was entitled to the same number of sleeve "piston rings" as the foreign minister. Then von Ribbentrop designed a special Eagle-and-Swastika-Over-the-Globe emblem for his own sleeves, trumping Meissner. According to Spitzy, on the morning of May 3, when the Führer's party of six hundred was leaving for Rome, Göring saw von Ribbentrop at the railroad station wearing his new diplomat's uniform. Göring laughed and yelled, "Herr von Ribbentrop, you look like the doorman at the Rio Rita Bar." Von Ribbentrop "chose not to hear him."[22]

A predator, Adolf Hitler waited for whatever he could designate as a provocation. Like the gangster with a loaded gun who asks his victim to "please, oh, please, make just one little move," Hitler's every action was preceded by the provocation he had chosen for the purpose. The Rhineland militarization was "provoked" by France's extended duty for conscripts. Almería was bombed after a German ship lying in a Franco harbor was bombed for being where it should not have been. Austria had been invaded because her chancellor, after being bludgeoned into an impossible agreement, decided to call for a referendum. He had consented only under duress and had a perfect right to test the will of the constituency within his own country.

Joachim von Ribbentrop had no wedge, no leverage, no strength to oppose Hitler's decisions, even had he wished to do so. He was entirely dependent on his Führer's whim-driven benevolence. The party's old-timers still thought von Ribbentrop an interloper. The aristocrats considered him a *parvenu*. The Army called him Hitler's puppet. He was shackled by ambition or an ill-conceived sense of duty or both.

To keep Adolf Hitler's favor became his twenty-four-hour task, because even those who had long-term claims on Hitler's loyalty and gratitude could find themselves ignored or discarded without warning. Men like Alfred Rosenberg and Baldur von Schirach, the Hitler Youth leader, frequently drifted in and out of the Führer's current of good will. The Jew baiter Streicher was now ignored as a fossil, an anachronism. Probably the four men who were most secure were Göring, Goebbels, Himmler, and Hess. But even Göring was often powerless to change Hitler's mind, and, despite strenuous efforts, Goebbels had failed to expand his own area of influence beyond that of propaganda and the creative arts.

Himmler collected secrets about the Nazi hierarchy, hoping by a show of devoted Teutonism and faithfulness to dazzle his suspicious Führer; Heydrich, the cold and dangerous policeman, became Himmler's life insurance policy. Hess, who was one of Hitler's oldest comrades and his party deputy, would soon strike out on a dangerous venture of his own.

While von Ribbentrop was still a young businessman in Berlin, in search of commercial success and acceptance in society, these men around Hitler were outcasts, strange disciples of an obscure Munich political zealot. While the von Ribbentrops decorated their beautiful new house in Dahlem, tried to join good clubs, hoped for invitations to prominent Berlin homes and society parties, Hitler's revolutionaries lived the dangerous lives of political activists. They were shot at by the police, by the Communists, and by the reactionaries. They were arrested, jailed, vilified in the press. They were ridiculed and denounced by most decent and serious people. Their experiences were worlds apart from those of the von Ribbentrops.

Despite his rank as foreign minister, von Ribbentrop had a lot to learn, and might never be able to catch up. Meanwhile, he was useful to Adolf Hitler and fulfilled his purpose. Every time one of the old party faithfuls criticized the foreign minister, Hitler, who often joked about him, rallied to his defense. Though it is probably apocryphal, several sources claim that Hitler called von Ribbentrop the "second Bismarck." This is either a form of self-congratulation ("Any man who works for me becomes a great man") or Hitler's sign of disdain even for his nineteenth-century predecessor, Prussia's Iron Chancellor.

When von Ribbentrop had been in office a mere three months, he realized that the Foreign Ministry's organization needed rudimentary patching. Hans Georg von Mackensen, who had preceded von Weizsäcker as state secretary of the Foreign Ministry, was appointed ambassador to Rome. He was von Neurath's son-in-law, and von Ribbentrop was suspicious of him but found him pliable. Dr. Woermann, who was von Ribbentrop's deputy ambassador in London, now became head of the political department of the ministry, replacing von Weizsäcker. The bespectacled, schoolteacherish-looking Herbert von Dirksen was shifted from the embassy in Tokyo to the Court of St. James's. Von Dirksen was related to the chairman of I. G. Farben Industry, Georg von Schnitzler, and came from an old diplomatic family. In London he found a difficult atmosphere. After two years of von Ribbentrop, London was suspicious of the "new" German style of diplomacy. Von Dirksen would soon have to face the shock of events to come, such as Germany's grim November pogroms, while he tried to maintain some semblance of amity with his British hosts. In June 1938, Albrecht Haushofer, a friend of Hess and the son of Professor Karl Haushofer, the political thinker who had been a major influence on Hitler, sent a pessimistic memorandum to the Führer and his foreign minister. He flatly stated that the chances for Anglo-German rapprochement were slim and fading fast.[23] His opinions were dismissed; knowing this, von Dirksen found it more diplomatic to play the optimist for Berlin. Von Ribbentrop's "ear" at the Chancellery was still Walter Hewel. Everyone liked Hewel, but he was weak and had fallen totally under Hitler's influence.

The actual running of the Foreign Ministry was the job of the new state secretary, von Weizsäcker. Von Ribbentrop rarely attended the morning meetings of the department heads because that was the hour of his attendance at the Chancellery, where the Führer usually made his first daily appearance around 11 A.M. The men in Hitler's coterie had to be present to guard their precarious place. As Erich Kordt wrote, "If a minister was not present, an assignment could go to the competition."

Of the "problems," the "return to the Reich" of Austria had now

been achieved by its most notorious son. The "problem" of the Sudeten Germans of Czechoslovakia came next. To Hitler, the Czechoslovak Republic represented everything he despised about the time of
Versailles. The new country had been formed in 1918 out of parts and
parcels of the old Austrian Empire. Czechs, Slovaks, Germans, Hungarians, Poles, and Ruthenians, held together by a newly created
democratic form of republic, were asked to live in harmony. This was
not an unlikely notion, since the fledgling republic was comparatively
rich in minerals and had strong industry and agriculture and therefore
a good basis for economic existence.

In 1918, everyone tried to follow the American example: Americans of diverse national and religious backgrounds seemed to be able
to live together in a brand-new nation. But Europe was different. Old
hatreds, both ethnic and religious, persisted. Countries were small and
crowded. Perhaps if the different components of Czechoslovakia had
been reassembled three thousand miles away in a vast country like
America, the Czechs could have had their wish. Meanwhile, underneath the appearance of a successful new nation, the dream of its
founder and first president, Tomáš Garrigue Masaryk, was full of
cracks and fissures.

Much of Czechoslovakia's German-speaking population lived in
the Sudetenland, the mountain range called the Erz Gebirge, just south
of the German border. There were ancient hatreds. During the First
World War, Czechs had fought on the Allied side. The mutual dislikes
of Czechoslovakia's Slavs, Hungarians, and Germans were as old as
their mountains. The Czechoslovak Germans were often accused of
arrogance. Indeed, the city of Prague and its ancient university were
jewels of the German-speaking world and a source of German pride,
though not of arrogance. It was said that some upper-class Czechoslovaks avoided speaking their own language, particularly in Prague or
international resorts like Karlsbad and Marienbad, to "avoid being
taken for servants." The Czechoslovak Germans, in turn, felt that they
were discriminated against by the Slavic government and that they
were entitled to better representation.

As is often the case in political disputes, there was some basis of
truth in each of the accusations. Mutual antipathies simmered and
grew. German-speaking Czechoslovak citizens, encouraged by blatant
propaganda from the German side of the border, decided that their
day had come. After all, they were, in their eyes and in the eyes of
their "brothers" across the border, superior people, neat, clean, conscientious, hard-working, educated — in a word, German. The German pejorative term for something slovenly and inefficient is "Polish

farm" (*Polnische Wirtschaft*). This was the classic anti-Slav slur. Another term for a mess was *Böhmisches Dorf,* a Bohemian village.

The Sudeten Germans had chosen a leader, the head of the SdP, the Sudeten deutsche Partei, a former gymnastics teacher named Konrad Henlein. Under his leadership, the SdP represented the majority of Czechoslovakia's German-speaking, non-Jewish citizens. By 1935, the SdP had become the second biggest party in Czechoslovakia. The country also had an ancient Jewish population, who spoke careful High German, unlike the regional accents of the Sudeten Germans, and were among the country's leading citizens.

Henlein's original profession was no coincidence. Gymnastics (*Turnen*) implied much more than mere exercise. It was also political. The gymnastic movement begun by Friedrich Jahn in the early nineteenth century represented a pre-Hitler, pre-"Aryan," idealized picture of the battle-hardened German. It was a derivative of the Greco-Roman *mens sana in corpore sano* concept and usually closely blended with German nationalism. For Henlein, the German ideal was the Nazi, so the SdP became a Czechoslovak Nazi party after the Czechoslovak government banned Czechoslovakia's German Nazi Party.

Hitler fanned the flames of the dispute. He considered himself the destined champion of all Germans, no matter where they lived. On March 3, 1938, Henlein paid a secret visit to the Berghof and then returned to his home country, reinforced both ideologically and financially by the big brother at Obersalzberg. As Hitler once said, "Wherever in the world there is a fire, I shall use it to warm the German soup." Henlein's demands multiplied. He insisted on self-rule for the Sudeten Germans, though still within a loose Czechoslovak federation. He also hinted broadly of threats from the bully across the border.

The Czechoslovak government reacted sternly. There were bloody clashes between Sudeten Germans and the Czech police, particularly in the resort town of Teplitz.

Following another Henlein visit, Hitler announced, on March 28, that he intended "to solve the Czechoslovak question in the near future." He urged Henlein to stiffen his demands still more. Von Ribbentrop had attended the Henlein meetings, and now he entered the arena. On the thirty-first he informed Czechoslovak Ambassador Vojtech Mastny that Germany did not intend to interfere directly, but "that the fate of the Sudeten Germans must change radically." Then the Czechoslovak stew was allowed to simmer quietly on the back of the stove. There were more pressing matters at hand. On April 16, the

Italians signed a Mediterranean naval agreement with the British. The rumor was that the French would be next. Obviously, Mussolini was still nursing the pain of the Anschluss.

The state visit to Rome by Adolf Hitler lay just ahead. Elaborate safety preparations were taken by Reinhard Heydrich of the Gestapo long before May 3, 1938, when Adolf Hitler set foot on the platform of San Paulo station in Rome, which had been especially prepared for this visit. Six thousand suspects had been arrested by the Italian police, some of them German Jews in exile.[24] Heydrich's foreign specialist, Walter Schellenberg, was sent to Italy, where he traveled every yard of the route the Führer was to take with Mussolini. Eighty Gestapo plainclothesmen were placed at key points. The preparations also gave Heydrich a chance to infiltrate Italy with German agents. Schellenberg devised teams of linguists to travel through Italy in the guise of tourists.[25]

Hitler had accepted the new Foreign Ministry uniforms for the trip, but he insisted that no one in his delegation wear a white tunic lest it seem that the Germans were treating the Italians as "exotic or colonial."[26]

On arrival, Hitler, von Ribbentrop, Goebbels, Hess, Himmler, the legal aide Hans Frank, SS General Sepp Dietrich, General Keitel, and the German press corps were met by the King and the Duce. Hitler seemed shocked that the King and his entourage greeted him while Mussolini stood off to the side in respectful attendance. Who was running Italy? This was not how Hitler had envisioned Mussolini's place in the Roman scheme of things.[27]

Mussolini at last greeted the Germans, and Hitler stepped into the King's horse-drawn parade carriage ahead of the sovereign, raising the ire of the little King, who disliked having to entertain the former corporal. Without speaking, they rode through Rome, lighted into an artificial ocean of flame and fire. At the huge old Quirinal Palace, there were no Fascist uniforms in sight, only court liveries and the courtiers of the royal family.

The Italian royals barely hid their distaste for the visiting Nazis, and Mussolini constantly deferred to his King, heightening Hitler's disdain. There was no place in his revolutionary's mind for the regal trappings of the ancient House of Savoy. Long after the visit, Hitler complained that he was "compelled to have contact with the arrogant idlers of the Italian aristocracy." The British politician and historian Ivone Kirkpatrick wrote that whenever Hitler was accused of keeping his Italian allies in the dark, he invariably blamed it on the Italian royals and their lack of dependability.

The King called Hitler a psychopath and spread a story that the Führer insisted he could not sleep unless a woman had made up his bed instead of the male servants of the royal family. So Hitler watched while a maid borrowed from a nearby hotel made his bed in the early hours of the morning.[28]

L'Osservatore Romano, the Vatican newspaper, pointedly ignored Hitler's visit. The Pope closed the Vatican to all visitors and moved to Castel Gondolfo, his summer residence.[29] "A cross other than Christ's Cross has been raised over Rome," the Pope complained. He also felt that "the air in Rome was difficult to breathe." The Holy Father and Cardinal Innitzer of Vienna seemed to disagree. Certainly the Pope, a former Papal Nuncio in Berlin, was familiar with the Nazis.

The next day Mussolini mounted a vast parade. Italian troops were now goose-stepping in the Italian version of the German *Parademarsch.* Curiously, there were still Jewish officers among the parading Italian units.[30] Italian Jewry's archenemy, Roberto Farinacci, a leading Fascist anti-Semite soon to be minister of state, had not yet convinced his Duce of the "dangers" of Italy's Jews. On May 8, Farinacci was awarded the Grand Cross of the Order of the German Eagle by his German friend Adolf Hitler, and his star was on the rise.

The vast caravan moved on to Naples, where everyone witnessed an intricate and picturesque naval review. Hundreds of Italian submarines dived and surfaced in unison. That night, an immense HEIL HITLER signal shone from the Naples waterfront. Italian Fascism was very operatic.

At the end of that day came Hitler's great "debacle of the full dress suit." He attended the opera with the King. Shortly after the end of the performance he was scheduled to be in the stand at a military parade. Twenty minutes and a special private room had been set aside at the Opera House so that he could change into his Nazi uniform to review the Italian troops. But the royal chief of protocol apologized abjectedly that there was not enough time for Hitler to change clothes, and a fuming Hitler found himself reviewing the troops while wearing his civilian evening suit. The old combat soldier had wanted to present a properly martial appearance, and there he was, garbed in a tailcoat like a gigolo at the Eden Hotel in Berlin, while the King at his side pranced around in his marshal's uniform with all his ribbons, sashes, medals, and crosses.

Von Ribbentrop, who had stayed glued to his Führer's side during the trip, bore the brunt of the explosion that followed. Back on their private train, he was called into Hitler's private car and berated for his carelessness and lack of attention to detail. He managed to channel the Führer's fury toward an old friend, the hapless Vico von Bülow-Schwante, the Foreign Ministry's chief of protocol, who was immediately relieved of his duties. Von Dörnberg, the tall, red-haired "Sandro" who had handled these things at the London Embassy, became the new chief of protocol on the spot.

On May 9 the Italian royals stayed in Rome while Mussolini, Hitler, and their retinues traveled to Florence. Now that he was no longer in the hated royal presence, Hitler's enthusiasm knew no bounds. He lavished praise on Florence, Mussolini, Italy, Fascism, architecture, and scenery.

Hitler had hated the antique horse-drawn carriages of the King. ("Will it take fifty years for the King to discover the internal combustion engine?")[31] He now admired the antiquities of Florence.

At last, Hitler was temporarily happy, but von Ribbentrop was not. Even while dancing attendance on Hitler, he had tried to use the visit to obtain a military treaty from Mussolini. During a short pause in the trip an outline of this Italo-German pact was handed to Ciano. Despite the Anti-Comintern Pact of 1937, Italy was not yet Germany's military ally. Hitler insisted that it was time to make final such an alliance, but every attempt to discuss the forthcoming Czechoslovak "problem" was politely bypassed by Mussolini and Ciano. When von Ribbentrop stole another half-hour between banquets, parades, receptions, and performances, the smiling, smooth, almost handsome Count Ciano once again said that surely the warm friendship between Italy and Germany made it unnecessary to sign a formal treaty. He promised, however, that he would study von Ribbentrop's proposals.[32]

When another short meeting was arranged, von Ribbentrop, with his usual unwavering persistence, badgered Ciano. Usually, this worked for him, but Ciano smiled again and once more expressed his doubt of the need for a formal treaty. It seemed to Schmidt, the interpreter, that the Italians were still under the shock of the Anschluss and all the cruel things that had followed in Austria.[33] Besides, Italy was not ready to cut its bonds with the western allies, following the April 16 Anglo-Italian Treaty.

The disappointed and embarrassed von Ribbentrop had to return to Berlin without fulfilling the Führer's greatest wish, a military alliance with Mussolini.

At the final banquet in Palazzo Venezia, Hitler said, "It is my unshakable will and my testament to the German people that the mountain border that nature provided for us shall never be violated."

He was speaking of the line that crossed the Brenner Pass and of the German-speaking Italians of Austrian descent in the South Tyrol, whom he had permanently abandoned. Mussolini was sure of the Tyrol for the time being. How sure could he be of the future?

For Hitler, the Czechoslovak drama of early 1938 opened prematurely. Austria's Anschluss still needed some digesting.

Until May 1938, Henlein, drunk with Berghof power, had pushed and badgered Prague with an eight-point program of demands presented at a conference in Karlsbad, but President Beneš was in no hurry to accept Sudeten German self-government. This understandable dragging of feet caused Henlein to overwork his sense of duty to the Führer and to the Reich. He organized Sudeten German demonstrations that, in turn, brought about Czechoslovak governmental retaliation. Heads were broken. Blood was spilled. People were arrested. As usual in a clash between civilians and armed police, the civilians were the losers. It made for unpleasant newspaper reading and began to embarrass the man from the Berghof, who had styled himself the protector of all Germans. Goebbels's German press howled. Henlein even traveled to London, where he met, mysteriously, with Churchill on May 13. Chips Channon asked in his diary, "What is he [Churchill] up to?"

Rumors were plentiful in Prague that the German Army was posed to repeat its Austrian blitz action, this time toward Czechoslovakia. The whispers finally reached the presidential residence on Prague's Hradcany Hill, where they were taken seriously. On May 20 President Beneš ordered a partial mobilization of the Czech forces to counter the perceived German threat. Perhaps it was a hysterical act; perhaps it was for internal political consumption and meant to divert the Sudeten Germans from their demonstrations. Would Sudeten Germans consider themselves citizens of Czechoslovakia once they were in uniform? The horror of international dispute is that it often reflects the whims and conceits of a few powerful individuals. Was Masaryk's heir, President Beneš, a great man? Probably not. But the power over Czechoslovakia lay in his hands, and he had mobilized with the approval of his cabinet.

Officially, the Czechs had based their mobilization on reports of German troop movements near their border. In fact, most neutral sources denied there were any such troop concentrations. Ambassador Henderson, after meeting with General Keitel while von Ribbentrop was absent, dispatched two military attachés to the disputed area. They found nothing to indicate that German troops were massing. Traveling separately, two British attachés between them covered twelve hundred miles of Saxony and Silesia on May 21 and 22, and came up troop-less. Nevertheless, Henderson asked State Secretary von Weizsäcker to request of General Keitel an official denial of the invasion rumors; von Weizsäcker obtained it. An earthquake followed; von Ribbentrop was furious. According to Kordt: "Sir Nevile Henderson had been instructed [by his government] to inquire officially if Germany was massing troops and to convey British warnings about any use of force. Von Ribbentrop was outraged by this 'presumptuous' British inquiry. He treated Henderson in a decidedly unfriendly manner. Talking himself into a rising temper, he said he would instruct all German government officers to refuse further replies to questions of this sort."[34]

Schmidt, who did the interpreting at the meeting, saw things less diplomatically:

> On May 21 I interpreted a stormy discussion between Ribbentrop and the British Ambassador Sir Nevile Henderson, which dealt with Czechoslovakia. Von Ribbentrop began "You, Mr. Ambassador, inquired from General Keitel behind my back about alleged German troop movements on the Czechoslovak border!" The foreign minister looked furious. They were seated in Bismarck's historic office in 76 Wilhelmstrasse. Von Ribbentrop continued, "I shall see to it that in the future you will receive no information whatsoever about military matters."
>
> Henderson replied, with an unusual show of temperament, "I shall have to inform my government about that. I must draw the conclusion from your remarks that the information given to me by Keitel did not conform to the truth!" Henderson then hinted that Britain would not stand by idly if France got involved.
>
> "If there is a war," said von Ribbentrop, "then France will have provoked it and Germany will fight as a she did in 1914."[35]

Sir Nevile Henderson's own view of the contretemps is much more diplomatic. The ambassador wrote of "a certain amount of acrimony" on both sides. Von Ribbentrop, after threatening to delay military information to the ambassador, "turned in wrath" to the accidental killing of two Sudeten Germans and used "the most reprehensibly bloodthirsty language about the Czechs . . . They would, he assured me, be exterminated, women and children and all . . . I believe that the unsuitability of his language on this occasion earned for him a reprimand from his master."[36] The rumors of German troops massing at the Czech border were not true, but the results were calamitous.

Hitler, furious when he learned that the western press reported he had pulled back because the Czechs had mobilized, ordered Case Green (invasion of Czechoslovakia) to be readied at once.

When this order was received on May 30 by General Ludwig Beck, the Army's chief of staff, it did not have the effect Hitler desired. General Beck, a devoutly anti-Hitler officer, realized that the time had come for a military revolt against the man he detested. Like many other senior officers, Beck had begun the Nazi era by enthusiastically applauding Germany's rearmament. He hoped that his country would once more become a great nation, with strength and dignity. Then he recognized Hitler's voracious appetite for conquest, and he wanted no part in furthering his ambitions.

Beck now became the center of the anti-Hitler opposition in the military. He tried to convince von Brauchitsch, the Army's commander-in-chief who had followed the disgraced von Fritsch, but he got a tepid response. Six years later, the anti-Hitler plotters even slated Beck to become Germany's head of state.

As soon as Hitler ordered Case Green to be readied, von Brauchitsch asked for a meeting with von Ribbentrop, from which the latter emerged depressed and nervous. Von Brauchitsch had told him the German Army was not ready for military confrontations. Kordt also begged von Ribbentrop to influence the Führer to pull back. "You are the foreign minister! You know the French and the British. For heaven's sake, tell him to keep the peace!"[37] Von Ribbentrop shuddered at the idea of being made responsible for influencing Hitler's decisions. "The Führer will know what to do!" he said. Later, he complained that Kordt was "a good diplomat but lacked nerve."

Von Ribbentrop and Kordt rushed to where Hitler was in residence. A letter arrived from Lord Halifax, earnestly urging that "nothing irreparable be done." Von Ribbentrop and his aides returned to Berlin without any notion of Hitler's plans.

Only a few Germans were openly distressed by Hitler, although the Nazis' control over "Aryan" Germans had tightened. Many people learned to glance over their shoulder in cafés, restaurants, theaters, and hotels. Had anyone overheard what one had said? Could it be misunderstood? One could get into a lot of trouble, even at a friendly dinner party.

Jewish citizens were subjected to far more painful degradation, and it intensified each month. Even former combat soldiers were harassed. Their appeals for help, if any appeals could be made, were usually to former regimental comrades or commanders. In a sense, the Jewish former front-line soldier was one of the Nazis' most pathetic victims. The percentage of German-Jewish soldiers who had died in the First World War exceeded that of their Christian comrades, and a large number had been decorated for bravery. In a country where combat soldiering brought lifelong respect and admiration, the Jewish veterans were barely able to comprehend that their sacrifices had been for nothing. The actual figures tell the story. During the First World War:

100,000 German Jews (about 18 percent of the total Jewish population) were soldiers;
80,000 were front-line soldiers;
35,000 were decorated;
25,000 got field promotions, of whom
2000 became officers;
12,000 were killed in action (about 12 percent).
Many of these former combat soldiers died in Nazi concentration camps.[38]

During 1938, further cruelties were added to the many that had been imposed since 1935. Jews had to declare all foreign holdings. This pertained as well to non-Jews married to Jews. Jews could no longer attend universities. All Jews who had ever been convicted of any offense were arrested. Jews were barred from all financial exchanges. Jewish physicians were decertified. Newborn Jewish babies could no longer be given "German" first names, such as Arnim, Siegfried, or Sieglinde. Those who already bore such names had to add *Israel* or *Sarah* to their given names. Jewish lawyers were decertified. The passports of all Jews were stamped with J. Even German-Jewish exiles had to preserve their German passports to validate their residency as exiles in their host countries. The passports, which had to be revalidated by German consulates every six months, were to have *Israel* or *Sarah* added, and the photo page was to be marked with a large red J. Every such addition was dated and initialed by a consular clerk. This was the responsibility of the Consular Service of the Foreign Ministry, so von Ribbentrop was surely aware of it.

Worse things were to follow, but by the time of the Czech crisis many Germans knew of all these measures. They were published in the *Völkische Beobachter*, the party paper, read by almost every German. Most people realized the pain these measures caused but chose to shrug their shoulders; "it was not their concern." Fewer than one of each hundred German citizens was Jewish. What happened to this minority was of small concern to most German citizens. But the von Ribbentrops had Jewish relatives in the Henkell family; that should have given them reason to think carefully about what was happening. Yet Hitler's furious reaction to von Ribbentrop's Hotel Aldon luncheon for his Jewish acquaintances in April 1933 must have smothered sympathy for the Jews. The von Ribbentrops were neither brave enough nor secure enough to risk the Führer's displeasure.

Austria seemed orderly and manageable. Now the Führer could turn his full attention to Czechoslovakia. At a tense meeting on May 30, he advised all his senior staff that it was his "unshakable intention to wipe Czechoslovakia from the map."

General Beck then composed a paper, which he distributed to other senior generals, asserting his disagreement with Hitler's decision, and expressing his anger that the Army could be committed by one man without consulting Germany's military leadership. By mid-July several officials of the Foreign Service also voiced their resistance to Hitler's goals. The lead was taken by State Secretary von Weizsäcker and Captain Fritz Wiedemann, ex-Corporal Adolf Hitler's wartime company commander. In an ironic reversal of roles, Wiedemann was now one of the Führer's aides. The wartime relationship gave him a certain leeway with his former company runner. To von Weizsäcker, a man of judgment and common sense, it was clear that Hitler, intent on conquest, was willing to provoke a war, and that such a war would be fatal for Germany. He had no doubt about what should be done, only about how to do it. In the classic manner of the diplomat, he began with all the leverage available to his position. He drew Erich Kordt into his confidence; then he suggested to Sir Nevile Henderson and to Bernardo Attolico, the respected ambassador from Italy, that Hitler intended conquest. He also indicated that tough words from London and a firm "don't" from Mussolini might have desirable results. He convinced some diplomats in Hungary of Hitler's lust for war and got their assurance that they would never help the Führer, although he had asked for their collaboration.

Von Weizsäcker also met with Generals Beck and Halder and with Admiral Wilhelm Canaris, the head of Military Intelligence, and briefed them about his diplomatic efforts. He wanted to discredit Hitler by showing him to be the war-lusting Tartar he was, and he hoped for a military boycott to back up his effort. But the plan began to collapse when the conciliatory Chamberlain asked for a meeting with Hitler.

The brothers Erich and Theo Kordt had done their best to stiffen London's attitude toward Berlin. At great personal risk, they had appealed to senior politicians, but to no avail.

William Manchester wrote that Henlein, before his "mysterious" visit to Churchill in May 1938, was briefed by von Weizsäcker on how to reassure and calm British fears. That is not likely. It is probable, however, that Henlein on his own, or under orders from Hitler, played down the demands made on Beneš. Henlein may have been invited to London at the suggestion of Vansittart, seconded by a well-meaning von Weizsäcker. From August 18 to 24, there was in incognito visit to London by Ewald von Kleist-Schmenzin, a Pomeranian noble, who took a great risk. The message he carried from General Beck was: "If England is willing to fight, I shall end this regime." He met with David Lloyd George, Robert Vansittart, and Churchill. But his visit came to naught. Chamberlain, who did not meet with him and who was briefed verbally by others, would not or could not give the response General Beck had requested.[39]

Meanwhile, Beneš offered Henlein a role for his country modeled on the Swiss cantou, but it was not enough.

Earlier that year Fritz Wiedemann had made his own effort at conciliation.[40] As Hitler's aide-de-camp, he flew to London on a well-publicized "fact-finding" mission, and returned to say the British were prepared to negotiate or, if necessary, to fight. Hitler and von Ribbentrop were not happy with his report. The visit had been initiated by the controversial but well-connected Princess Stephanie Hohenlohe, the very handsome Captain Wiedemann's lover and a friend of Göring's. She used the good services of her friend Lady Snowden, who had Halifax's ear. The Viennese Princess Hohenlohe, daughter of a Jewish dentist, was an ugly but charming woman, and an enigma. Captain Wiedemann lied to Hitler that the British had made contact with him through the princess, but Göring had been told the truth by her, and he cooperated to assure that every effort was made for a peaceful solution. Wiedemann, in turn, implied to Halifax at the latter's 88 Eaton Square residence that he was there at Hitler's suggestion. Everyone was prepared to use whatever influence he could.

An angry von Ribbentrop, who scorned these extracurricular efforts, immediately discredited Captain Wiedemann with information supplied by the Gestapo. He felt that Wiedemann was using his connections as a Hitler intimate to meddle in foreign affairs. After all, he had brought the Jewish Princess Stephanie Hohenlohe into Hitler's Aryan presence. In fact, Hitler had spent a lot of time on several occasions in conversation with the amusing Princess Steph.

On his return from London, Captain Wiedemann was immediately removed from the Führer's presence and sent to San Francisco as consul general. Was he to build an espionage network? Was he to help Lindbergh and the isolationists? Or, most likely, was the move just to get him out of Adolf Hitler's and von Ribbentrop's way?

Now the Kordt brothers made another desperate attempt. They assured Vansittart that there actually was opposition to Hitler, a military one. They told him that Hitler would not hesitate to deal with the hated Stalin, but that if Britain pre-empted him by making an Anglo-Russian pact, Hitler would pull back from his schemes of conquest of Czechoslovakia and Poland. They explained that they preferred the risk of committing treason to the risk of Germany's destruction through Hitler. Vansittart assured the Kordts that Britain would "soon conclude a pact with the Soviets," and the Kordts were relieved.

Strangely, at the War Crimes Trials in 1946, Vansittart attacked the Kordts and von Weizsäcker for reporting that Britain would manipulate the Soviets, but the International Military Tribunal did not acknowledge his accusation.[41]*

Even Göring made an attempt to clip Hitler's claws. He went to the Berghof confident that he would prevail; he returned to Berlin deflated, having been accused of cowardice by his old party comrade.

Private British efforts to promote friendship with Germany were waning. Only members of the Anglo-German Fellowship still planned to attend the September 1938 party rally in Nürnberg with Sir Nevile Henderson. Ambassador François-Poncet once again spoke for the Diplomatic Corps attending the rally. He hoped that "Hitler would do nothing to bring tears to a mother's eyes," a hint that Hitler ignored.

Even Henlein began to have fears that the Sudeten dispute could bring about a world war. On July 23 in Bayreuth he had asked Hitler to desist from a military solution. Karl Herrmann Frank, the Nazi Sudeten German whom Hitler had chosen as a possible replacement for Henlein, also tried in August to prove to Hitler that war was not necessary.

By now the *soigné* Sir Nevile Henderson was describing the foreign minister's comments as "ill tempered" and his manner as "truculent."[42] Obviously, the two men had developed irreversible mutual antipathies. Also in July, the British government, purportedly at the request of the Prague government, dispatched an "impartial" fact finder, Lord Runciman. The mission was pointless, with Runciman out of his depth. Along with everyone else, von Ribbentrop ignored the whole thing as a "British matter." Even Beneš was unimpressed.

The Army coup planned by General Beck and supported by General von Witzleben was now set for the day Hitler had slated for

---

*Vansittart may have been hoping to placate the Soviet members of the tribunal.

mobilization, October 28, at noon. (Later, when asked who the coup's targets were, General Hans Oster, an elegant and witty co-conspirator, in a singsong answered "Hi-Gö-Rib-Hi-Hey," for Hitler, Göring, Ribbentrop, Himmler, and Heydrich.[43]) But the military opposition to Hitler and all hope for long-term peace was undone when a cable arrived in Berlin on the morning of September 14, 1939.

> In view of the increasingly critical situation I suggest that I visit you at once in order to attempt to find a peaceful solution. I can come to you by air and shall be ready to travel as of tomorrow morning. Please advise the earliest time when you can receive me and indicate a place for the meeting. I should be grateful for a prompt reply.
>
> Neville Chamberlain[44]

By now Joachim von Ribbentrop seemed to be a vessel adrift, with no chance of the anchor catching hold as he was pulled into deeper and deeper waters. All his judgment seemed suspended; all his personal tradition abandoned. In an August discussion, he told von Weizsäcker that Hitler had made the firm decision to solve the Czech matter by force of arms.[45] The deadline, he said, was the middle of October, because flying weather would deteriorate after that. He was sure no other nation would lift a finger. If anyone did, they would be badly beaten. When von Weizsäcker voiced doubt, von Ribbentrop insisted that "von Weizsäcker was responsible only to him and that he [von Ribbentrop] was responsible only to the Führer, who was the only one responsible to the German people."

And then came the credo that von Ribbentrop followed for the rest of his days. He told Kordt "that the Führer had never been mistaken and that his most difficult decisions and actions, such as the Rhineland, now lay behind him. One simply had to believe in his genius, as he, von Ribbentrop, had learned to do over the years." He said "that I would regret not accepting this if facts proved later that I had been wrong." Von Ribbentrop declared that the Führer would ride into Czechoslovakia in the leading tank with his foreign minister at his side, and that von Weizsäcker, not von Neurath, would run the Foreign Ministry in his absence.

Chamberlain's cable brought an instant and positive reply from Adolf Hitler. It destroyed for some time to come the notion that Britain would raise a fist to strike at those who threatened her allies. Britain wanted to *talk*. So much for General Beck's coup. Disgusted, Beck on August 28 asked to be relieved of his command.

Chamberlain's cable also brought embarrassment to all those, like the Kordts, von Weizsäcker, and von Kleist, who thought Britain was done with talking. One of Chamberlain's greatest admirers in the forthcoming months of appeasement was Joseph P. Kennedy, the United States ambassador in London. The Boston multimillionaire who had made his fortune in the stock market, films, liquor-importing business, real estate, oil, and corporate acquisitions, was an early Roosevelt supporter when America's upper classes were against "the man with the income tax." Perhaps that was his revenge for social snubs he had suffered. Kennedy served Roosevelt as chairman of the Securities and Exchange Commission and the Maritime Commission. In 1937 he was appointed ambassador to the Court of St. James's as a political reward.[46]

He was a strange and careless choice. The son of a saloonkeeper and liquor dealer, he harbored instinctive and vestigial suspicions of anything British. His background had taught him to "take care of his own," and his plans for his nine children, for his personal fortune, and the fortune of his country did not include war, certainly not on the side of the English. Nor could he muster enough dislike for anti-Bolshevist Nazi Germany to warrant the drawn American sword.

Charles Lindbergh's urgent and expert warnings had made a deep impression on Kennedy, and he did his best to flood the occupant of the Oval Office with dire warnings. He insisted that Britain was unprepared for a fight with Germany, that America had to avoid backing a loser; he advocated strict neutrality and accommodation with Adolf Hitler. In 1939 he said in Boston, "There is no place in this fight for us." (While Kennedy was ambassador, his second son, John, was studying with Professor Harold Laski, a Socialist, at the London School of Economics. His third son, Robert, was attending London's Westminster School, like Rudolf von Ribbentrop.)

Ambassador Kennedy must have given much false hope to Joachim von Ribbentrop. Herbert von Dirksen, who followed von Ribbentrop at the embassy in London, reported to his chief that Kennedy had shown a degree of sympathy for the anti-Semitic views of Nazi Germany. This was later strongly denied by Kennedy.

(Joseph Kennedy resigned his ambassadorship in 1940, to the evident relief of President Roosevelt and Secretary of State Hull.)

Annelies and Joachim von Ribbentrop must have danced with delight. The arrogant British wanted to parlay, to palaver, to shirk a fight. Once more, the Führer was right. By now there were banners all over Germany saying *Der Führer hat immer Recht* (The Führer is always right). Also, what a setback for the reputation of the "reasonable" top Nazis, such as Göring and Hess, not to speak of reluctant Army generals like Beck, von Witzleben, Halder, and even von Brauchitsch, the Army's commander.

During the summer of 1938, the Westwall, later nicknamed the Siegfried Line by British wags, was built and expanded. This was a curious anachronism, since it was a defensive fortification, while the art of modern tank warfare being adopted by the German Army was offensive, with coordinated tank and armored infantry movement, air support, and paratrooper drops into the enemy's rear. This new form, called blitzkrieg, lightning war, had no need for defensive installations. Building the Westwall was probably a patronizing act, as if to say, "Here, you idiots, we'll do it your way to lull you. You cannot understand what will happen to your beloved Maginot Line once our Stukas and panzers get moving." But since the Germany Army had never fought a blitzkrieg, the new Westwall was also a sop for those in Germany who were thinking in old-fashioned terms.

Ironically, the demands of the Sudeten Germans included the line of mountain fortifications in the Sudetenland that were the keystone of Czechoslovakia's defense. After the Sudetenland was ceded to Germany, Czechoslovakia was helpless against conventional old-fashioned attack; certainly it could never have held against blitzkrieg tactics. But the loss of their fortifications became a major morale killer of the Czech soldiers. Europe was deluded by defense walls like the Maginot Line. Even the lay architect Hitler was personally involved in the design and planning of the senseless Westwall. He must have known it was a military anachronism, but he could not resist the silent call of the blueprint. He would see no one during the time of construction, sending von Ribbentrop once more into "Tango Nocturno."

The meeting with Chamberlain was fixed for September 15, 1938, in Munich. The aging British prime minister, who had never before traveled by air, arrived in Munich on a gray, choppy day in a small, twin-engined Lockheed Electra. With him was his confidential adviser Sir Horace Wilson, whom Churchill detested, and also William Strang, a Foreign Office expert on central Europe.

It was the consensus in Britain that Chamberlain was doing a very courageous and "English" thing, taking the bull by the horns, getting to the heart of the matter, risking his health and his life to deal with this chap Hitler. On Chamberlain's part there was the absolute conviction that if he could speak with this fellow, man to man, he could, like the good businessman he was, stuff some common sense into him. So off he went, ready, as he said later at the airport in London, to put to work the things he had learned as a small boy and "try, try, try again." It was a noble and courageous performance — by a man in his late sixties who looked much older, with his unfashionably high collars. In fact, he looked like the headmaster of a second-rank, small private school.

There was no way the Austrian former corporal could have penetrated past this neo-Victorian mask to the sporting soul of Neville Chamberlain. It was difficult for Adolf Hitler to see beyond the umbrella. Nothing in his experience had taught him about this species of externally eccentric British statesman. Meanwhile, von Ribbentrop, who lumped Chamberlain with the leisurely upper-class group in Whitehall which he detested, had no intention of "selling" Chamberlain to Hitler. But it is doubtful whether he could have made a difference, or whether von Ribbentrop had more than marginal influence on the *Nimmersatt* plans of voracious Adolf Hitler.

Von Ribbentrop still had some helpers in Great Britain, people who, for reasons ranging from blind anti-Semitism and anti-Communism to deep British patriotism, joined groups like Sir Barry Domville's Link. This group grew between March 1938 and June 1939 from eighteen hundred to forty-three hundred, though it contained many of the same English names and faces that had been staunchly pro-German since the Nazis came to power.[47] But they were only a small voice, only a small minority of votes.

Adolf Hitler had the advantage of the revolutionary. He was willing to gamble. Like the street drifter who accosts the well-dressed man, he counted on the self-protective instincts of the other. Britain was tired of war and of losing her young men in battle. Her wish for peace was real, and her leadership expressed that wish. Germany's masses were no different. They too wanted to live in peace, but they were dazzled by their powerful leader, who seemed to achieve *without bloodshed* everything he had promised. Their self-preservative instincts were dulled by propaganda and all the trappings of nationalistic success and blind faith. Hitler was their hero, their shining knight. Yet the average roadside citizen of Munich cheered Chamberlain with much enthusiasm because he was their *Friedensbote,* their messenger of peace.[48] Dr. Paul Schmidt wrote that they cheered Chamberlain more than they had cheered Mussolini in 1937.

Chips Channon's reaction to Chamberlain's mission was typical of London society's prejudice, snobbery, and cheerful innocence.

> *15 September.* This morning Neville, accompanied by one or two experts, left London for Berchtesgaden. Of course, some Jews and

many of the shady pressmen who hang around Geneva are furious. No war. No revenge on Germany — and they say that Hitler will insult, browbeat him as he bullied Schuschnigg. No fear.

This evening I dined with Maurice de Rothschild at a dinner of seventeen in his rich house, full of amazing Boldinis and medium Tiepolos. Dinner was indifferent but the wines staggering. One claret was sixty-nine years old, the same age as Neville, as I pointed out. Everyone was a touch tipsy with Rothschild wine and admiration, even hero worship, for Chamberlain.

Hitler's special train came to Munich to fetch Chamberlain and his group as well as von Ribbentrop and Nevile Henderson. By coincidence or design, the train was continually passed by armored troop trains. Waiting in the fog and drizzle, the Führer greeted the British prime minister at his mountain chalet. In a symbolic gesture of respect, Adolf Hitler stood at the very foot of the long flight of stairs to lead Chamberlain from the big Mercedes up to the Berghof. As soon as they had doffed their coats and hats, after a short exchange of halting banalities about the weather and the views from the Berghof, Hitler asked whether he could speak to Chamberlain alone, with only the interpreter Schmidt present. This, according to Schmidt, had been secretly worked out by von Weizsäcker and Ambassador Henderson long before the meeting, to avoid the presence of von Ribbentrop. The plan had the full knowledge of Hitler, who feared that von Ribbentrop might be a disturbing influence. It also had Göring's enthusiastic endorsement.[49]

Schmidt, the only eyewitness to the first Chamberlain-Hitler talks, wrote about the moment when the irascible Hitler threatened to solve the Sudeten question "one way or the other" (Schmidt's translation of Hitler's much more ominous *"so oder so"*). Chamberlain reacted with uncharacteristic firmness. "As I understand it," he said, "you intend to move against Czechoslovakia one way or the other. In that case I may just as well return to England. There doesn't seem to be much left to be done here." To Schmidt's amazement, Hitler immediately reacted. Suddenly calm, he said that he "would be satisfied with a solution to the Sudeten problem."[50]

That night at the Grand Hotel in Berchtesgaden, when Schmidt tried to practice a routine diplomatic courtesy by turning over a copy of his notes to a foreign negotiating partner, an angry von Ribbentrop appeared in his room and rudely told him not to give the notes to the British. "You are no longer in Geneva, where everyone was chummy. Your notes are for the Führer only!" With great regret, Schmidt informed Chamberlain and Henderson of his new instructions. Understandably, Chamberlain complained bitterly. For the next meeting, the British delegation would certainly bring its own interpreter.

These instructions to Schmidt were typical instances of pettiness. Von Ribbentrop had been bypassed, and now he was getting even. It was the revenge of an insecure man giving no thought to the harm he could cause an already strained relationship.

Chamberlain's plane left Munich exactly twenty-four hours after it had arrived. He was on his way to ask cabinet approval for recommending a separate Sudetenland to the Czechs.

This was the first of the three momentous September meetings that came to be known as the Munich Conference of 1938.

The second took place at Bad Godesberg, the old Rhine resort near Bonn. Neville Chamberlain now made the third flight of his life. He was installed high on a hill in the Hotel Petersburg, a ferry ride across the Rhine from Bad Godesberg's Hotel Dreesen, where Hitler usually stayed. Curiously, perhaps ominously, four days before this second meeting, Hitler had met secretly with the Polish foreign minister and the Hungarian regent at his Berghof.[51] Both Poland and Hungary insisted that they too had long-standing territorial claims against Czechoslovakia, because some Czechoslovak citizens had once been Poles and Hungarians.[52] (The great Tomáš Masaryk's dream of a new nation was based on the American example, made up of diverse nationalities and regions.)

Hitler was delighted to take note of these Polish and Hungarian claims on Czechoslovakia. They served to legitimate his own demands. To add to Hitler's fuel, Sudeten Germans now began to rush across the border into Saxony, inside Germany. About 250,000 of them were temporarily received as "brothers," although the Reichs Germans were inclined to look down on them. They were not *Reichsdeutsche,* only *Volksdeutsche,* and they often spoke German with strange Slavic accents.*

Ever the old-school man, Sir Nevile Henderson, described the ferry traffic from Hitler's hotel to Chamberlain's hotel as "varsity boat race day," because of the large numbers of spectators ashore, the Germans' field glasses focused on the occupants of the ferries. Hitler had always loved the Hotel Dreesen. Most memories were good, although it was there that he had been forced to decide on the Röhm bloodbath.

Now, in a conference room on the main floor, the Führer and the prime minister once more quickly came to grips. Chamberlain was

---

*Today the descendants of the *Volksdeutsche* are again entering an even more reluctant Germany.

pleased to inform Hitler of success. He had even persuaded the French to urge the Czechs to hand over the Sudeten territories to Germany. The Czechoslovaks' agreement in principle seemed assured.[53]

Chamberlain had done what he had promised in Berchtesgaden. He was therefore shocked when Hitler said, "Extremely sorry, but that is no longer acceptable," and insisted that the claims of Hungary and Poland must be added to the agenda. Hitler also rejected Chamberlain's timetable for the ceding of the Sudetenland "because of the urgent dangers now facing Czechoslovakia's Sudeten Germans." An outraged Chamberlain returned across the Rhine to his hotel, accompanied by his advisers. The next morning he sent a letter rejecting Hitler's additional demands. A conciliatory note from Hitler in room 108 of the Dreesen, carried by the interpreter Schmidt, soon came back across the Rhine. In their turn, Henderson and Sir Horace Wilson carried Chamberlain's reply to von Ribbentrop, who had finally become involved. At the next meeting in Hitler's hotel at 11 P.M., all the second-level participants from von Ribbentrop and von Weizsäcker to Henderson and Sir Ivone Kirkpatrick were present. It was a stormy meeting. Hitler's forty-eight-hour deadline for the ceding of the Sudeten territories, which Chamberlain angrily called an ultimatum, was described as *Ein Diktat* by the German-speaking Henderson. In the middle of this angry impasse came the explosive news that Beneš had fully mobilized the Czech Army. Silence fell on the conference room; everyone waited for Hitler to react with his usual fury. Schmidt described it as the silence that follows the crash of tympany in a concert. Then gently, uncharacteristically, Hitler spoke: "I shall still keep my promise to you, not to take any action." He seemed willing to make concessions about the schedule. It was 2 A.M. They all parted in a friendly way. The following day, Chamberlain and his group returned to London.

Sir Horace Wilson flew to Berlin on September 26, bringing Chamberlain's letter. It said that, as he had warned, the Czechs had balked and rejected the terms discussed at Bad Godesberg. Now Hitler threatened, "If the Czechs do not get out by the first of October, we shall march across the border."

Wilson calmly and firmly said that if France got involved in hostilities against Germany, the United Kingdom would feel obliged to help France. Schmidt remembered giving the translation somber emphasis.

An angry Hitler said he took note of the statement, and then, raising his voice, said that if France and Britain felt they had to attack Germany, he "did not care one way or the other." Hitler almost lost control. In front of von Ribbentrop, Wilson, Sir Ivone Kirkpatrick,

Henderson, and Schmidt, he rushed to the door of his office, yelling at the top of his lungs, "There is no sense continuing with this!" Then he stopped and returned slowly, like a naughty child realizing that his behavior was unacceptable. Sir Nevile Henderson and von Ribbentrop had their own "heated discussion" over Beneš, whom von Ribbentrop called a warmonger and terrorist.[54] The meeting soon broke up, the mood tense, as Hitler was about to make a major speech at the Sportpalast later that day.

In that address he threatened Beneš but assured Chamberlain that Germany's involvement would cease once the Czechoslovaks had dealt with the problem of their minorities. This was his last territorial demand. "We do not want any Czechs!"

After the Sportpalast speech, the exchange continued. Wilson, still in Berlin, received instructions from London to state that Britain would guarantee the Czechoslovak withdrawal from the Sudetenland if Hitler guaranteed not to use force. Hitler, sensing that London was softening, turned this down, with his usual threats, but strangely, that very night, Schmidt had to translate a conciliatory letter to Chamberlain. What had changed Hitler's tune?

The explanation given by the majority of contemporary witnesses is that earlier on that dull, drab autumn day, in a demonstration of martial might, or perhaps as a trial balloon, Hitler had ordered a combat-ready panzer division to move through central Berlin, engines roaring and tank tracks clattering on the asphalt. It made its menacing way along the Wilhelmstrasse and past the British Embassy. To Hitler's shock, as he watched from a Chancellery window, the Berlin crowd was apathetic. He had expected wild cheers for these fierce panzer warriors in the *Balkenkreuz* and swastika-decorated tanks and trucks, cannon and machine guns uncovered and ready for action. In 1938, Hitler's instincts had not yet been dulled by the isolation that is the fate of all dictator warlords. Hewel, von Ribbentrop's man at the Chancellery, reported that Hitler, disillusioned and disappointed by the lack of enthusiasm, declared, "I cannot yet fight a war with this people." He revised his aggressive posture.

But the mobilization date of September 28 stood unchanged. That day there was the unending coming and going of ambassadors at the Chancellery, beginning with François-Poncet, who, speaking in perfect German, assured Hitler that an attack on Czechoslovakia would set fire to all of Europe (*Stecken Sie damit ganz Europa in Brand*).[55] Von Ribbentrop tried to interfere by urging that the Führer was right, that if war came it would be a Franco-British war, but François-Poncet dressed him down. That day General Beck, who had not yet resigned, and General von Witzleben were again poised for a coup should the mobilization go into effect.

Göring also went to see Hitler, along with von Neurath, who had not been invited. When von Ribbentrop asked for his support for the Führer, Göring yelled that he knew all about war, but if the Führer said "March," he would be in the leading plane, "provided Ribbentrop was in the seat next to him." He was said to have called von Ribbentrop a "criminal fool."[56]

The key visitor that day was the tall, heavyset, bespectacled ambassador from Rome, Attolico. This respected diplomat now rushed Mussolini's message to the Führer: "I have been asked by Chamberlain to help negotiate. Please accept me as part of the negotiating process." Hitler, softened by François-Poncet and not too sure that the Italians would help in case of war, was ready to talk. Besides, after witnessing the tepid Berlin reaction to the armored division, he was subdued. When Henderson brought yet another message that Chamberlain was ready to return to Germany, Hitler told Sir Nevile that "to accommodate the wishes of my great friend Mussolini, I have postponed mobilization for twenty-four hours."[57]

In Parliament on the twenty-eighth, the prime minister told the packed House that there would probably be mobilization of Germany by 2 P.M. Suddenly a message was handed to him, and he told the hushed chamber that Mussolini had accepted his request to negotiate. In the absence of mobilization on September 28, the Beck-Witzleben military coup stood down once more.

The stage for the third and final conference in this series was now set, and the military revolt dissolved under the seemingly peaceful events that took place in the newly finished neo-Classic Führer Building on the Königsplatz in Munich on September 29.

This time the number of participants was substantial, because of the Italian group that accompanied the "great conciliator" Mussolini and Ciano on their special train. Von Ribbentrop was only one of many participants. Unhappy with the negotiations, he was not convinced of its advantages. To show the direction he preferred, he had ordered new uniforms for the Diplomatic Corps — field gray this time — which he wanted his people to wear at Hitler's military headquarters.[58] François-Poncet sent a message to the Quai d'Orsay that *"Ribbentrop poussait le Führer visiblement à la résistance"* (Ribbentrop is visibly urging the Führer to be obstinate). Von Ribbentrop was obviously upset by the course of things. To the last moment he tried to create obstacles. Von Weizsäcker, Kordt, and Attolico, among others, were astonished and aghast that von Ribbentrop was so openly eager to save "his" war.[59] He did not succeed. Czechoslovakia's Sudetenland was amputated.

Munich drowned in beer when the pact was announced. As the joyous taxi driver told Kordt on his way to the Hotel Vier Jahreszeiten, "Sale of beer has been incredible ever since they announced there would be no *Schlamassel*," which was, ironically, the Yiddish word for misfortune. The street in front of the Vier Jahreszeiten, which housed senior Nazis as well as Édouard Daladier, the French prime minister, was besieged by crowds shouting the rhyme *"Daladier! Vive la paix!"* Daladier, with tear-filled eyes, stood at his window overlooking the Maximilianstrasse.

Looking into the future, Sir Nevile Henderson wrote to Chamberlain:

> Millions of mothers will be blessing your name tonight . . . oceans of ink will flow hereafter in criticism of your action. The day may come when we may be forced to fight Germany again. If we have to do so, I trust that the cause may be one in which the morality of our case is so unimpeachable [and] the honour and vital interests of Britain are so clearly at stake, as to insure us of the full support of the united British people, of the Empire, and of world opinion.

Sir Nevile concluded that this would not have been the case in 1938.

Shortly before he returned to London, Chamberlain had asked Hitler, at the end of the meeting in the Führer's private Munich apartment, to sign a note declaring that all future Anglo-German disputes would be resolved through peaceful negotiations. Hitler shrugged and signed. It was this paper which Chamberlain triumphantly waved when he spoke the famous phrase "peace for our time." Spitzy reported that a short while after the agreements were concluded and the "paper" was signed, he followed Hitler and von Ribbentrop down the stairs at the Führerbau. He was close enough to overhear them. Von Ribbentrop petulantly criticized the agreement and the special "paper" for Chamberlain, whereupon Hitler said softly, "Well, you don't have to take it so seriously. This paper is really of no great importance" (*Ach, das brauchen Sie nicht alles so ernst zu nehmen. Dieses Papier hat doch weiter keinerlei Bedeutung*).[60] Spitzy, a long-time Hitler worshiper, was stunned.

This is the text of the famous "Peace for our Time" paper:

> We, the German Führer and Chancellor and the British Prime Minister, had a further meeting today and are agreed in recognizing

that the question of Anglo-German relations is of the first importance
for the two countries and for Europe.

We regard the agreement signed last night and the Anglo-American Naval Agreement as symbolic of the desire of our two peoples
never to go to war with one another again.

We are resolved that the method of consultation shall be the
method adopted to deal with any other questions that may concern
our two countries, and we are determined to continue our efforts to
remove possible sources of difference and, thus, to contribute to
assure the peace of Europe.

Adolf Hitler
Neville Chamberlain
December 30, 1938

Von Ribbentrop remembered things quite differently. He was
asked at the Nürnberg trials whether "the Führer was very unhappy"
that there was agreement at Munich, because Hitler "did not get his
war." Von Ribbentrop replied, "There is not a word of truth in that.
The Führer was very satisfied with Munich and I never heard so much
as a hint to the contrary from him."[61]

"Like jackals," in Churchill's words, Hungary and Poland now
were lusting to seize the territories they had discussed earlier at the
Berghof. It was the year of the political cynic. Still, Chamberlain and
his signed "letter of agreement" brought cheers from most corners of
Britain. People were not ready to fight a war.

President Beneš had quit. Frantisek Chvalkovsky, the Czechoslovak foreign minister, was a weak, conciliatory man. Czechoslovakia
waited, relieved. But Hewel at the Chancellery told Erich Kordt in
confidence that the danger of war had by no means passed. Over at
the Abwehr (Armed Forces Intelligence) Headquarters, where the
anti-Hitler military conspiracy was now centered, General Hans Oster, Admiral Canaris's chief aide, confirmed to Kordt and his friends
that all planning for the military takeover of the rest of Czechoslovakia had been ordered and initiated. Just when Kordt and the other
staff members were delighted and relieved to pack away their new,
wartime gray Diplomatic Corps Uniforms! It was obviously premature to put their fears in mothballs.

The month of October 1938, following close on the heels of the
Munich Agreement, seemed to demonstrate that Hitler could count
on greed and fear to motivate most nations. On October 2, the Poles
unilaterally had marched into the Olsa district of Czechoslovakia.
There was no objection from Hitler.[62] At that time he still considered
Poland a potential ally against Russia.

The interpreter Schmidt, present in Hitler's personal apartments when Chamberlain had asked him to sign the "peace paper," could not understand why the Führer seemed gloomy and depressed after his negotiating triumphs. Then Hitler's fierce speech of October 9 at Saarbrücken made things clear. It destroyed the notion that the Munich Agreement guaranteed peace. Hitler was infuriated that Daladier and Chamberlain were now under heavy criticism in their own countries. He yelled, "We are not the Germany of 1918. If Herr Duff Cooper or Herr Eden or Herr Churchill would come to power in England, we know that he would immediately aim for war with Germany. We must maintain constant vigilance and guard the Reich!" He had no faith in the durability of a battered Chamberlain. Hitler was angry with all those in his own camp, like Göring, who had counseled restraint. Von Ribbentrop had emerged as a firm and stalwart ally, but several members of his old guard had, in his eyes, been cowardly.

Spitzy wrote that Annelies von Ribbentrop insisted it was an error to "settle" at Munich.[63] This would have been the best time for a military confrontation, with an unsure and poorly armed Britain. Several other contemporaries have mentioned her involvement in her husband's political world. Hitler's SS aide Heinz Linge was sure that Annelies von Ribbentrop often saw important dispatches before her husband did.[64] One of Hitler's private secretaries said that Walter Hewel insisted Annelies von Ribbentrop played an important role behind the scenes in foreign policy and that she was von Ribbentrop's evil genius.[65]

This would contradict many of Hitler's associates and von Ribbentrop's contemporaries who portrayed the foreign minister as "Hitler's parrot," and Adolf Hitler as a willing prey of abject flattery. Eyewitnesses often reported von Ribbentrop's toadying manner, his *"Ja, mein Führer, nein, mein Führer"* servility.

It was easy to hate the von Ribbentrops. They had not endeared themselves to contemporaries. Their arrogant style had caused much bitterness among their subordinates. Their success brought jealousy from their equals, such as Goebbels and Göring, and their tactlessness, derision from foreigners. But it would be a mistake to underrate Adolf Hitler's ability to judge others. No doubt he knew little about the *haut monde* of Britain, France, and America, but lower-middle-class Austrians were born to cynicism. It was his uncanny ability to gauge German-speaking people, both individually and *en masse,* that had enabled this uneducated Austrian to climb to the leadership of Germany, one of the great nations of the world. He has often been described as a brilliant mimic, an actor *manqué*. Cynicism and mimicry are not the mark of the man who is easily fooled by playacting and open flattery. There is an American expression: "Never con a con man."

Something more fundamental about the von Ribbentrops must have appealed to him and made him seek their collaboration. Obviously, von Ribbentrop was not a master of statecraft, but to discard his seeming anglophobia as a matter of personal spleen may be a mistake. It is possible that he was convinced that an early war was the best way to solve Germany's problems and was close enough to Hitler to back his view, which was similar. Hitler's jugular instincts probably sensed the weakness of Britain and France, and he hated to let them wriggle off the hook.

Similarly, Churchill, Duff Cooper, and Eden embraced the "early war" option.

The fundamental differences between Adolf Hitler, the avid revolutionary, and von Ribbentrop, the pragmatic *haut bourgeois débrouillard*, still existed, but on the subject of war with Great Britain, they were in agreement. Curiously, both continued to be admirers of Albion, though they saw Britain as the enemy. Victory over England would have been their ultimate and optimal act of faith in Germany's future.

The Poles had grabbed Olsa without consultation. Now the Hungarian claims of Czechoslovakia needed settling. Von Ribbentrop flew to Rome and asked the Duce to let him create an Italo-German "jury," with himself and Ciano as judges. They would decide the merits of each party's claims in the dispute. Austria's new chief, Seyss-Inquart, was enlisted as host. Castle Belvedere in Vienna was dusted off and requisitioned. A dinner for the Italians was laid on at a restaurant on the Kobenzl mountain of north Vienna. Spitzy, and his brother who lived in Vienna, became the impresarios. The prettiest Viennese girls were produced for the flirty Ducellini, Ciano. The ladies were all required to greet von Ribbentrop with a genteel Hitler salute. Annelies, who had stayed in Berlin, quickly got wind of the festivities and expressed her displeasure over the telephone.

Knowing that Hitler hated the Hungarians even more than the Czechoslovaks, von Ribbentrop more or less "took the Czechoslovak side" in this sham; Ciano had more sympathy for the Hungarians. Smiling ironically, Ciano said to von Ribbentrop, "If you keep defending Czechoslovak interests, Hacha [the new Czech president] will give you a medal."[66] Between them, the Italian and German "judges" changed people's fates and lives with the stroke of a fat pencil on the large map of poor Czechoslovakia spread before them. Eventually, Hungary received her booty, though it was smaller than she wished.

On November 7, 1938, a murder took place in Paris that set off a series of events which would shock the civilized world. That day, Herschel Grynszpan, a seventeen-year-old German-born Jewish refugee, shot and killed a German Embassy official named Ernst vom Rath. Grynszpan was born in 1921 in Hannover, where his Polish-Jewish parents had moved to escape Polish anti-Semitism. To help their son evade the Nazis, the Grynszpans sent Herschel to Paris in 1936. The senior Grynszpans stayed behind, hoping for the best, until the Nazis passed a law that Polish-born Jews, even if they were nationalized German citizens, would be expelled to Poland. But the Jew-hating Polish government refused to readmit them.

Thousands of these unfortunates were left to fend for themselves in the icy fields and woods of the no man's land along the Silesian border with Poland. They were virtually nonpersons, victimized by both German and Polish frontier policy. It was brutal and inhuman. Herschel Grynszpan's parents were among those expelled. Young Grynszpan heard about their fate and decided to avenge them. He planned to shoot the German ambassador in Paris, where he was living the precarious life of the refugee, subject to the chauvinistic Paris *flics,* who issued the sainted, obligatory *carte d'identité* of the French government. It was grim irony that the inexperienced young Grynszpan mistook vom Rath for the ambassador when he was shown into the minor official's office in the embassy and that at the time vom Rath was under Gestapo surveillance as "politically unreliable."

Most 1938 observers blame the events that followed on the "poisonous dwarf" of the Nazi hierarchy, Dr. Joseph Goebbels, and on the cooperation of the SA commanders. There were also some SS involved, although Himmler seemed unhappy with the spectacle of his "black knights" performing these vulgarities side by side with the SA. He need not have been so squeamish. A year later Himmler's SS would begin to perform tasks that revolted even some top Nazis with cast-iron stomachs.

On November 9, 1938, starting early in the morning, Nazi bands roamed throughout Germany and set fire to 171 synagogues, broke the windows of 7500 Jewish shops and department stores, wrecked homes and apartments, murdered 91 Jews, and arrested 26,000 others, who were transported to concentration camps. The shattered glass shards in city streets from broken windows and storefronts were the cause for the bitter black-humor term Kristallnacht, an ugly joke. All of this destruction was a "spontaneous demonstration" of the "righteous anger of the people because of the foul murder committed in Paris."

Jewish citizens were paid insurance compensation of about a hundred million marks, which they had to turn over to the government. Next, the sum of a billion marks was demanded from Germany's Jewish community as "penalty" for the murder of vom Rath.

Although several senior Nazis, including Göring and von Ribbentrop, uttered faint protests against these actions, they did so only because they feared upsetting foreign business and diplomatic dealings. No one questioned the moral issue. The pogrom continued through the tenth of November.

Most of the Jewish men who were sent to concentration camps on that November 9 were battered and beaten but eventually released. Even the most optimistic and proud Jews in Germany now tried to flee the country of their birth.

The pogrom represents one of the ugliest stains on the honor of Germany, although it was but a gentle hint of things to come. Yet according to a recently published eyewitness report, an infuriated Goebbels called in Count von Helldorf, Berlin's police chief, and howled at him that this sort of crude nonsense "is not the way to solve the Jewish problem." He blamed the debauches on "that thick-necked moronic idiot in Munich [Streicher], the schizophrenic vulgarian. Because of him Germany has made a fool of herself all over the world."

Crystal Night was not ignored abroad. On November 15, Chips Channon chronicled from Belgrave Square, "The pogroms in Germany and the persecutions there have roused much indignation everywhere. I must say Hitler never helps, and always makes Chamberlain's task more difficult."[67] One of the foulest of Adolf Hitler's crimes was the subversion of ordinary German decency. From a non-Jewish, British eyewitness* in Berlin:

> The streets were a chaos of screaming, bloodthirsty people lusting for Jewish bodies. I saw Harrison of the *News Chronicle* trying to protect an aged Jewess who had been dragged from her home by a gang. I pushed my way through to help him and between us we managed to heave her through the crowd to a side street and safety. Next, the object of the mob's hate was a hospital for sick Jewish children, many of them cripples or consumptives. In minutes, the windows had been smashed and the doors forced. When we arrived, the swine were

---

*A British journalist, probably a Scot.

driving the wee mites out over the broken glass barefooted and wearing nothing but their nightshirts. The nurses, doctors, and attendants were being kicked and beaten by the mob leaders, most of whom were women.[68]

Disgusted foreign correspondents like the American Louis Lochner reported the bestiality despite Gestapo censors.

President Roosevelt recalled Ambassador Hugh Wilson in protest.*

This time there were hundreds of outraged newspaper editorials all over America. The *New York Times* of November 11, 1938, wrote about "scenes witnessed yesterday . . . which no man can look upon without shame for the degradation of his species."

One of the few whimsical results of the terror: Mayor Fiorello LaGuardia of New York, who was half Jewish, assigned a twelve-man squad of Jewish policemen, commanded by Captain Max Finkelstein, to guard the German consulate.

The newly named National Conference of Christians and Jews founded the Volunteer Christian Protest Committee to boycott Nazi Germany, although, despite editorials and threats of boycott, the United States did not increase its immigration quota for the German refugees (about twenty-seven thousand to thirty thousand Germans annually).

Isolationists, like the anti-Semitic, anti-Roosevelt "radio" priest Father Charles Coughlin, grew even stronger. Coughlin's national weekly broadcasts had a wide audience. Another clergyman, the Reverend Gerald L. K. Smith, and his hate sheet *The Cross and the Flag* also prospered.

Eventually, in what was described as a tawdry public relations move, President Roosevelt called for an international conference on the Jewish refugee problem.[69] Representatives of thirty-two nations convened at Evian les Bains, the old French spa, between July 6 and 14, 1939, but the conference led nowhere. No one agreed to accept immigrants from Nazi Germany. Each government, beset with its own economic ills, was fearful of adding foreigners to its population. Eventually only the British took steps, and admitted about forty thousand. Franklin Roosevelt, the man who had called the conference, refused to antagonize his domestic opponents, the isolationists.

---

*The recall was postponed for four days pending the results of a public opinion poll. It showed that four out of five Americans did not wish to admit immigrant refugees from Germany. Nevertheless, at the urging of Sumner Welles, the number two man in the State Department, the recall was carried out.

One curious reaction to Kristallnacht came from Reform Rabbi Ferdinand Isserman of St. Louis, Missouri. He called on Jews to forgive and reconcile with Nazi Germany "so that the minds and hearts of the persecutors may be changed."

Aligned with the America First Committee, Father Coughlin, and the Reverend Gerald L. K. Smith was the German-American Bund. On March 29, 1936, Fritz Kuhn, a forty-one-year-old, Munich-born Ford worker, was elected the Bund's leader, and opened its headquarters at 178 East Eighty-fifth Street in Manhattan's Yorkville. The Bund had training encampments where the men played at being Storm Troopers. One, Camp Siegfried, was at Yaphank, Long Island. Others were in Philadelphia and Pontiac, Michigan. Many of their expenses were underwritten by Berlin and doled out by the Foreign Ministry's Hans Thomsen, special assistant to Ambassador Hans Dieckhoff. (The Norwegian-born Thomsen, tall, blond, very "Aryan," and his beautiful wife, Bebe, tried hard to entertain, influence, and even bribe American lawmakers.[70])

By 1938 the Bund claimed 100,000 members and sympathizers. Then in December 1939, Fritz Kuhn was sent to Sing Sing, the federal prison at Ossining, for misappropriations of the Bund's funds.

America First, Coughlin, Smith, and the Bund represented the extreme right wing of isolationism. Many other Americans, though not organized, were in sympathy. They had no wish to focus on bad news from Europe. They listened to the new Glenn Miller band, read Hemingway's short stories, and loved the book about China by Nobel Prize–winner Pearl Buck. Bob Hope sang "Thanks for the Memory." Don Budge won the Grand Slam, and Orson Welles petrified the country with his radio broadcast about invaders from Mars. In 1938, Thornton Wilder won the Pulitzer Prize for *Our Town,* and Shaw's play *Pygmalion* became a film. Daphne Du Maurier published *Rebecca,* and Roosevelt signed the Wage and Hours Act, raising the minimum hourly wage to forty cents, and limiting the maximum weekly working hours to forty-four. The only sounds and laws from Germany were martial and cruel.

It was impossible for the von Ribbentrops not to have known the brutal details of Kristallnacht, but now, more than ever, they were accomplices. Joachim von Ribbentrop's businessman's soul was sold to the barbarians around him.

Besides, his plans were prospering. Hungary, the country that had slavishly accepted its Czechoslovak booty from the Rome "jury" of von Ribbentrop and Count Ciano, added its signature to the Anti-

Comintern Pact on November 25. As usual, the ceremony was lavish and well publicized, with special acclaim for the creator of the pact, von Ribbentrop. On his orders, a glossy, trilingual magazine was prepared in Berlin, glorifying the pact; it was called *Berlin-Rome-Tokio*. A hundred thousand copies were printed and distributed among all German embassies and missions. The magazines were difficult to give away, but the embassies asked for more for obvious political reasons.[71]

Early in December 1938, von Ribbentrop went to Paris on a formal state visit for the signing of the Franco-German Treaty of Nonaggression. To the participants, the treaty looked like a cynical gesture, a holding action. Despite such French courtesy as a special Pullman car, built for the British royal visit, which was sent to collect von Ribbentrop, neither the diplomats nor the French spectators had faith in the enterprise. For von Ribbentrop's ceremonial wreath-laying at the grave of the Unknown Soldier under the Arc de Triomphe, an immense German wreath was ready, but without its swastika-festooned ribbon, which was left behind in Berlin and had to be rushed to Paris on a Luftwaffe plane.

Though most foreigners were shocked by the barbaric events that took place in Germany in early November, a surprising number of intelligent Germans still did not realize the enormous harm that had been done to the image and reputation of their country. One month after Kristallnacht, a senior German diplomat, a non-Nazi, insisted on speaking to Sir Ivone Kirkpatrick, then a senior official at the British Embassy in Berlin, who was being transferred back to London. In the strictest of confidence, the German told Kirkpatrick that Hitler had instructed the Luftwaffe to prepare plans for a sudden peacetime attack on London. He did not know whether or when the plan was to be carried out, but he felt that the British government had to be informed. His reason was that "I and my friends are appalled at Hitler's barbaric idea. Moreover, we don't believe that an air attack would be decisive. It would merely blacken Germany's name for centuries and range the whole world against her."

Obviously, the man was unaware that the barbaric acts of November had already irreparably stained Germany's name.

All this was ignored by the von Ribbentrops. Because of some differences between Goebbels and Himmler, over Kristallnacht and other matters, von Ribbentrop saw a chance to consolidate his position as a party stalwart; it called for using his only friend in the leadership echelon, Heinrich Himmler of the SS. He began to "donate" some of his own senior Foreign Ministry officials to Himmler. In April 1938, at von Ribbentrop's request, von Weizsäcker and Woermann became honorary senior SS colonels, though they had no specific duties in the black-coated fraternity and certainly felt no affection or loyalty for it.[72] Soon, several other senior Foreign Ministry officials found themselves wearing the black uniform. Of course, it was possible to refuse the "honor," but that took men who had not yet been pushed beyond the limit of their morality. Most senior ministry officials accepted SS membership, rationalizing that the unwanted SS rank would provide them with a valuable party listening post and a certain amount of leverage.

Probably some of this justification was valid. By 1939 even the most experienced Berlin diplomats were isolated from the world's attitudes. There was no more free exchange with foreigners — diplomats, journalists, or just friends. The number of foreign visitors from London, Paris, and New York had shrunk. Besides, any German diplomat who wore an SS uniform, no matter how seldom, alienated visitors from the democratic countries. By now, through its police functions and concentration camps, the SS had become a symbol for brutality and a cause for fear even among many Germans. Fear of the SS went everywhere, even to California. There was barely a Hollywood film about the new Germany without that symbol of horror, the SS man. It could not be blamed on the "Jewish film clique," although Goebbels's Propaganda Ministry trumpeted this as the explanation. The horror of the SS came from the true tales of its surviving victims and from the eyewitness reports of foreign journalists like Shirer and Lochner. To the world outside, an SS captain was a ruthless man, no matter whether he wore "honorary" rank or was an SD man and part of the Gestapo, with the dread SD "diamond" insignia on his left sleeve. The Sicherheits Dienst (Security Service) of the SS was the direct instrument of the Himmler-Heydrich-Kaltenbrunner triumvirate. The SD sought, arrested, held, tortured, imprisoned, condemned, and executed almost at will. There were occasional hints of decency to be found among the men, particularly former professional policemen, of its sister organization, the Gestapo. There was none of it in the SS. Most of the world did not distinguish between the "weekend" soldier of the SS and the captain of a concentration camp guard company. As a well-known German aristocrat and former Army officer put it, *"Man schauderte wenn die SS Uniform dabei war"* (One shuddered when one saw an SS uniform).[73] Some decent men who worked for von Ribbentrop were tarred with this brush to satisfy his party ambitions.

The empty drive to reassure the world continued. Following the hollow state visit to Paris, the von Ribbentrops, accompanied by Paul Schmidt, took a private train to Poland for a state visit with Colonel Josef Beck, the Polish foreign minister, and his associates. Poland was still treated as a potential anti-Russian ally, but there were specific German "requests" on the agenda.

Earlier in January, Colonel Beck, unable to dodge it, had accepted an invitation to the Berghof. Among the requests made by Hitler, against the background of majestic mountain views from his windows, was the return to Germany of Danzig. In exchange, Poland could use the city as a free port. Hitler also wanted an "extraterritorial" right-of-way for an autobahn and a railroad line across the Polish Corridor to German East Prussia. He virtually wanted to carve a slim strip of German territory across Polish soil so that Germany and East Prussia, now separated by Polish territory, could be connected. No more Polish frontier police, no more Polish customs, no Polish uniforms on German trains. The ideas were rebuffed by Joseph Beck. No matter how powerful his host and how beautiful the scenery, the suave Colonel Beck made it clear that Danzig would "stay Polish" and that cars and trains would have to submit to Polish law when crossing Polish soil.

On January 26, the von Ribbentrops' train pulled into the swastika-festooned Warsaw main station. Flowers were presented by Mme. Beck to Frau von Ribbentrop. (Mme. Beck was used to making such gestures. Her husband, the colonel, had a reputation for philandering.) The German national anthem was played, as was the Polish one, von Ribbentrop's party at the stiff Hitler salute. The foreign minister then inspected a smart honor guard of Polish infantry. He strode slowly and with much dignity, as suited a man of his station. A state dinner followed. Its toasts and mutual compliments were empty. Von Ribbentrop had only two aims: Danzig and the autobahn strip. Now von Ribbentrop heard the echo of the Berghof "nay" repeated in Warsaw. Once more the answer from Poland was a firm and polite no. On the second day of the state visit, proceedings were cut short by a "bad cold" that Beck developed overnight.[74]

Hitler was infuriated by these two failures, and von Ribbentrop was mortified. According to Schmidt, he had already used hours of his famed perseverance at the Berghof to change the mind of Colonel Beck, but without an iota of success. He thought he could improve on his Berghof performance during the Warsaw visit, but he was disappointed once more. It angered him that Hitler had supported Poland's claims against Czechoslovakia and her seizure of Olsa. Was Poland still to be pampered because she was a potential ally against Soviet Russia? In von Ribbentrop's view, Poland had exhausted her credit. He had other initiatives in mind, which might involve an alliance with the devil, an unthinkable notion: *a deal with the Soviets.* Poland would no longer be needed except as a buffer area, a margin of safety. The idea would have been inconceivable for men who had grown up with Nazi ideology and who considered *Mein Kampf* their bible, but von Ribbentrop was enough of the international businessman to remain unhindered by such ideological instincts, and Annelies was in complete agreement. They awaited only the supreme opportunity.

According to Annelies in the von Ribbentrop memoirs, which she edited after his death, on the train back to Berlin from Warsaw Ribbentrop told his staff, "Now all that remains is to make an agreement with Russia if we want to avoid being completely surrounded."

Was Hitler ready for this hateful solution? Was he prepared to parlay with the Satan of his nightmares, the dragon he had sworn to slay since the beginning of his political life? Or was this sort of power-block thinking only the businessman's despised way of international diplomacy?

Before turning to this problem, Hitler had to deal with the correction of an error he had made in 1938: the Munich Agreement. It had not sated his appetite to solve the "problem" of Czechoslovakia. The Sudetens were now "free." The Poles and Hungarians had received their territories through the Vienna "jury." Even the Slovaks had formed a separate republic in Bratislava on October 6, 1938, under a Slovak priest named Father Josef Tiso. Tiso had asked for and received German backing. His violently anti-Prague views led to deep conflict with the Czechoslovakian government. "Offenses" against German-speaking people of the area were drummed up in the German and Austrian press as preparation, once again, for conquest.

Father Tiso's rule, encouraged by Hitler, was so inflammatory toward Prague that the Czechoslovak government occupied Tiso's capital, Bratislava, on March 10, 1939, and substituted another, more reliable Slovak named Karol Sidor to head the new Slovak republic.

On March 11 in Berlin, Tiso requested Hitler's help and patronage after being persuaded by von Ribbentrop to do so. Then, "in order to avoid further Slovak-Czech conflict and to stop further violence against Germans living in the remainder of Czechoslovakia," Hitler agreed to meet with the current Czechoslovak president, a former judge named Emil Hacha, a meek, tired, and ill man with the thankless task of shepherding an ailing, crippled nation. Hacha had requested the meeting through the German chargé in Prague, who forwarded it to von Ribbentrop. Of course, von Ribbentrop received Hitler's instant agreement. When Hacha and Foreign Minister Chvalkovsky arrived in Berlin, this was the course of events, according to von Ribbentrop's memoirs:

> Hacha told me the fate of Czechoslovakia was in the hands of the Führer. That very night at the Chancellery the Führer told Hacha that he intended to send his troops into Bohemia and Moravia. Foreign Minister Chvalkovsky agreed to the decision. Hacha then received approval by telephone from Prague and instructed his cabinet to receive the German troops "in a friendly manner." No protest was raised from the Czechoslovakian side. The occupation then took place immediately and without incident.

To von Ribbentrop, it was as simple as that. The next day Hitler entered Prague in his usual gray, six-wheel, cross-country Mercedes, license WH 32288. In Prague, von Ribbentrop was ordered to read "a proclamation that made Bohemia and Moravia into a German protectorate." Again, according to von Ribbentrop, it was all very pleasant and calm.[75]

The truth was more brutal. At 10:40 on the night of March 14, the train with Emil Hacha, his daughter, who was his nurse-companion, and Chvalkovsky, pulled into cold Berlin. Even before they inspected a menacing-looking SS honor guard, they were told by Czech Ambassador Mastny that German troops were already crossing the border into what remained of Czechoslovakia. They were immediately taken to the Hotel Adlon near the Brandenburg Gate, where they waited until 1:15 A.M., when they were driven through snow flurries to the newly designed Reichs Chancellery. Hitler's office was an immense, lavish, and gloomy wood-paneled hall with the desk at the very end of the long, thick carpet. To the side of the desk was a square of upholstered sofas and couches around a low table where they were asked to sit. Hacha himself had begun to question the *raison d'être* for Czechoslovakia. He and his foreign minister sat motionless as mummies. As Schmidt described it, "Only their eyes gave proof that they were living people. Göring and Ribbentrop were in attendance."

Hitler came straight to the point. "The movement of German troops cannot be halted. If you wish to avoid bloodshed, call your minister of war and instruct him to avoid all resistance." That ended the conversation for Hitler, who then left. Göring took Hacha into a nearby room while telephone connections with Prague were attempted, but the lines were not open and no amount of yelling by von Ribbentrop to "get the Reichs postal minister out of bed to do his job" worked. Göring tried to chat with the shaken old man; Chvalkovsky stayed with von Ribbentrop. Still no telephone connection, and the danger of a military confrontation between German and Czech troops grew. Meanwhile, the text of a document was drafted and typed; it said that to preserve law and order the fate of Czechoslovakia had "been voluntarily put into the hands of the German Führer. The Führer had accepted the Czechoslovak request." Suddenly, Göring came out of the neighboring room bellowing, "Hacha has fainted. Fetch Dr. Morell at once!"

Morell, an expert on stimulants, was rushed to Hacha's side. He injected the old man, who recovered quickly, and when telephone connections were established, Hacha and Chvalkovsky, in turn, yelled in Czech to instruct their government to accept the inevitable and avoid the loss of Czech lives. The text of the communiqué was finally signed at 3:55 A.M. by von Ribbentrop and Chvalkovsky. The exhausted participants left the grandiose Chancellery, which Albert Speer had probably designed for more lofty purposes than the rape of a small country and the bullying of a sick old statesman.

According to yet another view, the actual signatures were written only after Göring and von Ribbentrop literally chased Hacha and Chvalkovsky around the table, holding out pens to them. It was then that Hacha had his fainting spell. This is possible, though the usually reliable Schmidt mentioned only a "calm conversation between Hacha and Göring."[76]

It was later that day that Hitler left his special train at the border station Böhmisch Leipa, got into his Mercedes, and entered Prague. According to the proclamation about Bohemia and Moravia read by von Ribbentrop, Konstantin von Neurath was to be Reichs protector of the new protectorate. Von Ribbentrop's memoirs failed to mention the last sentence of the proclamation: *"Die Tschechoslovakei existiert nicht mehr!"* (Czechoslovakia has ceased to exist). So much for Hitler's claim that "we want no Czechs."

No British or French threats or reactions were heard. No doubt von Ribbentrop slept well. Once more his master was right.

On March 17, the day after Hitler and von Ribbentrop awakened in Prague, a grim Neville Chamberlain made a speech in Birmingham, asking bitterly whether anyone could ever again believe promises made by Hitler. In Paris, an angry Daladier told German Ambassador

Count Welczeck that Hitler had betrayed him and had made a fool of him. Schmidt doubted whether Hitler ever saw the translation of Chamberlain's Birmingham speech, hinting that von Ribbentrop did not provide it or had sidetracked it. Notes from the British and French governments delivered by hand to the Foreign Office were discarded unread by von Ribbentrop.[77] Warnings of this sort had been delivered after the takeover of the Rhineland, the Anschluss, and Kristallnacht. They had come to mean very little. An Anglo-German industrial conference scheduled for the day of Hitler's proclamation in Prague went ahead as if nothing had happened. Von Ribbentrop felt only contempt, buttressed by other unavailing British and French efforts at conciliation, and he refused to listen to any of the signals from across the Channel. The Wilhelmstrasse had become isolated, because men like von Dirksen, the ambassador in London, refused to sound warnings that might have made him seem faint of heart and displeased his chief or the Führer.

It is understandable that von Ribbentrop ignored whatever warnings might have come to the Foreign Ministry from the United States. America seemed blissfully unaware of the gathering thunderheads in Europe. Even Roosevelt's request for a 535-million-dollar military appropriation (over two years) seemed more pro forma than threatening. The United States was more concerned with the launching of the film of Margaret Mitchell's *Gone With the Wind* and the hiring, by Harry James, of a young singer named Frank Sinatra. Congress did repeal the prohibition against the export of arms, obviously with Britain and France in mind as friendly cash customers, but that seemed mild enough. There were no storm warnings from the German Embassy in Washington. Who wanted to be the bearer of bad tidings? Besides, only the "Jews around Roosevelt" like Judge Sam Rosenman and Henry Morgenthau made noises. The rest of America seemed blissfully isolationist. Ambassador Hans Dieckhoff in Washington seemed to be on safe ground when he reassured the Wilhelmstrasse.

Friend and foe alike were shocked by the Prague invasion and by Hitler's faithlessness. The reaction of Sir Nevile Henderson, who had been sent to Berlin to accommodate Hitler's foibles and was probably the longest-suffering messenger of the policy that became known as appeasement, wrote in his memoirs, "The Germans are a strange people. They seem utterly incapable of seeing any side of a question except their own or to understand the meaning of civilized decency and moderation." To Henderson, generally a man of objectivity, Hitler, von Ribbentrop, and the German people had now become one and the same despicable thing. He was soon recalled to London in a gesture that could only be interpreted as Downing Street's attempt at a change of policy.

Then on March 22, Chips Channon chronicled, "Memel was today ceded by the Lithuanian Government under threats of invasion and aerial bombardment. Memel, not in itself very important, is the camel-breaking straw, and the cabinet is now unanimous that 'something must be done.' And Lord Halifax . . . is beginning to hate the devil more than his works."

Memel, the port on the Baltic Sea, was part of the Memel region, independently governed but federated with Lithuania. About half of the Memel population of 140,000 spoke German, half Lithuanian, but most of Memel's legislators were German-speaking, and there were tensions with the Lithuanian government. Hitler simply ordered a warship to threaten the port, and Memel joined the Third Reich on March 23, one week after the end of Czechoslovakia.

Von Ribbentrop seemed completely puzzled by the reactions of England and France. At first, he thought London was "reasonable and positive" because Chamberlain declared in the House of Commons that Hitler's move into Prague was not a breach of the Munich Agreement: "The guarantee was given to Czechoslovakia, but now that country has ceased to exist." Then, a few days later, "influenced by the opposition," a storm broke loose. Even the peaceful Lord Halifax, as von Dirksen was forced to report from London, had become "totally negative." Later, von Ribbentrop claimed this confirmed a prediction he had made to his Führer on March 14. In hindsight, despite his self-imposed blinkers, he was to claim that he had "warned that there would be a penalty for the move into Czechoslovakia."[78]

While Europe looked east, the next announcement came from the southwest. Franco, the enigmatic, uncooperative, tiny Caudillo, announced that Spain was now securely in the hands of the Falange, that all Republican resistance had ceased, and that a Fascist government had been installed. It was small comfort to Hitler and Mussolini. Franco had accepted their help but given little in return. The road to Gibraltar and the Bay of Biscay remained barred behind the Spanish border. Still, in the Nazi-Fascist view, it was also a defeat for Communism, because it denied the Communists the "back door" to France and the possibility of naval bases and airfields.

It is amazing to learn what shocked the von Ribbentrops. The plural is indicated because by 1939 Annelies no doubt was privy to all matters of policy that reached her husband's private office in the

Wilhelmstrasse or, for that matter, in the Speer renovation of Berlin's former Presidential Palace, which von Ribbentrop was soon to use as his official residence. After Hitler's open breach of the 1938 Munich Agreement, von Ribbentrop was shocked when Polish Ambassador Lipski arrived with a message from Warsaw that "brusquely" turned down Hitler's Danzig and Polish Corridor suggestions and even declared that "any further pursuit of these German plans, particularly those concerning Danzig, would mean war."[79] He gingerly told Hitler about this "threat," but, uncharacteristically, Hitler asked him to put it to the Polish ambassador that no form of settlement would be found if the word "war" was mentioned.

When the Poles concluded a preliminary mutual defense agreement with Britain on April 6, von Ribbentrop was doubly shocked. After all, it was Chamberlain who had insisted on and drafted the very paper which stated that Germany and Britain would not enter future political agreements without mutual consultation.[80]

Apparently von Ribbentrop had not been listening carefully when his Führer assured him in Munich, on the steps of the Führer Building, that this paper "meant next to nothing." But now it puzzled von Ribbentrop that Chamberlain, the man who had complained so bitterly in his Birmingham speech about the betrayal of the Munich Agreement, had signed a Polish agreement without consultation. Britain also planned to introduce conscription, more loftily known as National Service, probably yet another blow to the closed-eyed and closed-eared Joachim von Ribbentrop. He would have been even more surprised if he had learned of the convoluted untruths and failed purposes that preceded the British guarantee to Poland.

Both Lord Halifax and the prime minister firmly believed that Poland was a first-rate military power, able on its own to rebuff any German assault. That was their first miscalculation, largely the result of the swagger of Colonel Josef Beck, Poland's foreign minister. Beck assured them that Germany had never been truly insistent about Danzig and had never contested Polish rights there: another delusion.[81] Chamberlain had also hoped that a guarantee given to Poland would ensure Polish help in defending neighboring Romania, but Beck would promise no such thing.

As William Manchester wrote, His Majesty's Government "had been had!" The fate of Britain's vast empire, from a military standpoint, was now in the hands of little Poland.[82]

Worse, knowing that the eventual political guarantee against German aggression would need the cooperation of Soviet Russia, Chamberlain and Halifax now discovered Beck's implacably anti-Soviet stance. His attitude was: "Fighting with Germany might cost us our land. Collaborating with the Soviets would cost us our soul."

On April 7, to avoid being outshone by his former protégé, Hitler, Mussolini invaded Albania. It was cheap victory against a tiny country. King Zog fled, and Italy had her conquest. Mussolini could now present himself as a conqueror and could dream his dreams of invading Greece from the new Albanian base. This was his reply to Hitler's Austro-Czechoslovakian incursions.

Shortly after Mussolini's Albanian adventure, one of the most acerbic exchanges of prewar diplomacy took place. Roosevelt wanted, once and for all, to demonstrate that the United States, though far away, was closely involved in the fate of Europe. In a personal letter to Hitler, he asked the German chancellor to commit himself to the freedom and integrity of some thirty European and non-European countries. He named each one in his letter to the Führer. Hitler responded in a savage and ironic speech that is seen whenever German newsreels of 1939 are shown again. He stood in front of his adoring, party-uniformed audience, hands on hips, bobbing up and down on spread legs, pronouncing "Herr *Roose*velt" with the unmistakable sound of the German name Rosenfeld, which is often, but not always, carried by German-Jewish families.*

Reading aloud Roosevelt's letter, he made his points as if he were reading the statements of a demented person. With a grin, he read every one of the thirty countries Roosevelt listed, until the audience burst into howls of derisive laughter. Hitler then went on to say that he had taken the trouble to ask all of these countries whether they felt threatened. "In each case, the answer was in the negative and, occasionally, quite harshly so!" The audience roared its outrage at Roosevelt's "presumption and impertinence." In the same speech, Hitler unilaterally announced the cancelation of the Anglo-German Naval Agreement of 1935, von Ribbentrop's first diplomatic triumph. The foreign minister must have flinched, but broken treaties had become the norm.

Amazingly, von Ribbentrop and most of the other senior Nazis were not targets for assassination, nor is there any record of attempts on von Ribbentrop's life. But the so-called Reichs protectors in conquered countries — like Heydrich, who was assassinated in Czechoslovakia — who were *in loco* Adolf Hitler outside the Reich, were

---

*Like Alfred Rosenberg, many Germans and German Jews have names that are interchangeable.

constantly on the alert. In contrast, there were over forty documented attempts on Adolf Hitler's life. A very eccentric one was planned for his fiftieth birthday, on April 20, 1938.[83] The man who conceived of the deed and wanted to execute it was Colonel Noel Mason-Macfarlane, military attaché at the British Embassy in Berlin, a leather-tough son of a military family. Painful polo and automobile injuries had almost crippled him but never kept him from living an energetic life.

The colonel knew that a vast review of troops and party formations was planned for the occasion and that the reviewing stand would be a short 110 yards from his flat on Sophienstrasse. This stand was traditionally where Hitler received the birthday salute of the parading units. Enormous crowds always massed all along the route of march, climbing onto anything from tables to tree limbs. The colonel thought that, under the cover of these yelling crowds, he could shoot Hitler from the flat's bathroom window. He had no trouble finding a hunting rifle with a telescopic sight and a silencer. Even a poor shot could not miss at such short range, and Mason-Macfarlane was an expert. Ever the loyal soldier, he went to London to seek permission from Whitehall. The idea was turned down as "unsportsmanlike." The details are in the colonel's notes on deposit at the Imperial War Museum. Obviously, Chamberlain was not the only representative of the Victorian view of the world.

Probably to clear up any further designs Mussolini might have after his first Balkan conquest, von Ribbentrop attempted to convince Prince Paul of Romania and his prime minister to enter the German camp, but the Romanians managed to evade him. Next came Turkey. An even more forceful session of wooing and coercion took place at the von Ribbentrop country estate, Sonnenburg. Schmidt, who was there to interpret, described the almost athletic agility with which Memenencoglu, the Turkish foreign secretary, eluded his persistent host's thrust.

Then, at last, something to present to the Führer. On May 22 in the Great Hall of the new Chancellery, with Hitler in godfatherly attendance, von Ribbentrop and Ciano, the Ducellini, signed the ill-named Italo-German Pact of Steel.

It was Hitler's countermove to the newly revived Anglo-French friendship, and it probably frightened every Italian except Mussolini. Even Ciano was described as looking "scared of his own courage,"[84] and he spoke to Hitler and von Ribbentrop of "a future peace-filled, three-year cooperation." In what must have been a supremely cynical mood, Hitler congratulated von Ribbentrop on the swift conclusion of nonaggression pacts with Denmark, Estonia, and Latvia, probably to put the lie to the accusations in Roosevelt's letter. One wonders whether the Latvian, Estonian, and Danish governments were all living in a vacuum or had decided to ignore Hitler's Prague breach of promise of March 15.

Both Germany and her opponents now realized the importance of Soviet Russia, and each of them set out to woo the bear. Britain needed a second-front ally; Hitler needed a safe back.

The British historian Margot Light, an expert on modern Russia, pointed out that 1939 to 1940 was the only span of Soviet history not revised later by Stalinists. The Soviet attitudes and accounts of the time are, therefore, accurately reflected in their histories.[85] As viewed from Moscow, British and French appeasement wrecked all Soviet initiative to create an anti-Nazi security bloc. The Soviets had not even been invited to participate in the Munich negotiations over Czechoslovakia, although their vital interests were also at stake. They tried after Hitler's March 15 seizure of Prague to invite France and Britain to another joint security conference, in fact to form a tripartite pact, but they were ignored. Britain gave Poland its guarantee, but the Soviets did not believe the British would ever honor this promise.

In May 1939 there finally seemed to be some Anglo-French interest in alliance. The Soviets wanted to include Belgium, Greece, Turkey, Romania, Poland, Latvia, Estonia, and Finland in a treaty, but British reaction was lukewarm. Nevertheless, the Soviets invited Halifax to Moscow; he declined. Instead, a Moscow meeting took place on June 14 between William Strang, a Foreign Office official, and Vyacheslav Molotov, the new Soviet foreign minister. Then came several weeks of stalling over definitions and responsibilities. The Soviets were convinced that the British and French were still trying to make some sort of a deal with Hitler, and were using the renewed Soviet talks as leverage. Moscow became even more resentful when an Anglo-French military delegation, which arrived on August 11, comprised delegates who had no powers to negotiate. The senior British delegate, a retired admiral named Reginald Drax, was, politically speaking, a eunuch. The Russians gave full powers of representation to Marshal Kliment Voroshilov, their defense commissar. The problem of defending Poland and Romania was self-evident. The Russians would have to enter them in order to defend them, but neither the British nor the French had obtained permission from Poland or Romania for such action. Frustrated and then infuriated, the Russians called a halt to the talks.

Meanwhile, the Germans sent urgent signals through their Moscow embassy that they wanted to talk. Probably the Soviets were aware that they could never achieve real peace with Nazi Germany and that sooner or later the Germans would attack, but they needed time to prepare themselves.

When they agreed to von Ribbentrop's arrival in Moscow on August 23, there was still no progress in their meetings with the Anglo-French delegation. Anglo-French indecision brought on the Soviets' decision. This, in outline, was the Soviets' rationale for the pact with Hitler.[86]

Soviet distrust of Britain and France was probably justified. Churchill's friend Robert Boothby, MP, said that, with the exception of the *Daily Telegraph,* the British press, led by Geoffrey Dawson of the *Times,* was "bright yellow."[87] In fact, the BBC's Sir John Reith still barred the former ambassador to Berlin, Sir Horace Rumbold, and Harold Nicolson from the air because they were anti-German.

Besides, there were signs that Chamberlain was at the edge of a breakdown. When news of the April 7 Italian invasion of Albania reached London, Under Secretary "Rab" Butler rushed to Chamberlain's small private study at the top of 10 Downing Street, bearing the dispatch. Chamberlain, who was feeding the pigeons through an open window, barely took notice of the startling news.[88] He brushed off Butler's mention of the danger. "Don't be silly," he said. "Go home and go to bed." Then he continued feeding the pigeons like a man in a trance. William Manchester wrote of stress and of a "personal tragedy" overcoming the seventy-year-old Chamberlain during the summer of 1939.

A different view of Chamberlain, one in which he had resigned himself to war, was given to the anti-Nazi German official Adam von Trott zu Solz, who went from Berlin to England on a secret mission to persuade London to speak up and offer clear warnings. Von Trott began at Cliveden, to which he was invited by Lord and Lady Astor. From there he was invited to meet Chamberlain on June 7 at 10 Downing Street. Chamberlain wearily told him Britain was through "warning"; she would fight. The Prague invasion had finished any conciliatory talk.[89] Chamberlain would no longer appease Hitler, and yet he would not negotiate decisively with the Soviets.

The courageous Trott zu Solz was later executed by the Germans as a traitor.

Poland never gained true British sympathy. Czechoslovakia, though sacrificed reluctantly, was widely considered a democratic country. Poland was not. The historian A. J. P. Taylor has pointed out that there was not a single demonstration in London advocating "Let's stand by the Poles!" Czechoslovakia, however, always had a certain amount of popular support. It seemed to make sense to protect Poland through a Soviet alliance, but the conservative and deeply religious Halifax, among others in the British government, could not persuade himself to do more than nod toward such an alliance. In fact, the British delegation to Moscow had been sent out via slow boat almost as if to prove that its presence would be halfhearted. Taylor speculated that when Marshal Voroshilov asked Admiral Drax for his credentials, the admiral probably said, "Frightfully sorry, but I think I left them at the club." Two days were spent wiring to London for such credentials. Drax's French opposite number, General Doumenc, was also a nobody, but at least he carried credentials. If the Russians soon got fed up with the vague style and shallow content of the negotiations, London was not disturbed. From Britain's perspective, it was most unlikely that there were other bidders in this particular auction. Certainly it considered Russia's archenemy Hitler an unlikely prospect. England was wrong. The Germans were avidly eager to bid, and Stalin was willing to listen.

The logical idea of an agreement or a pact with the Soviets had come early to von Ribbentrop. It may also have occurred to Adolf Hitler but only as a last resort. No matter how often von Ribbentrop had advanced the solution, it took an agonized decision by Hitler to set it in motion. The key man chosen to prepare the way was Germany's ambassador to Moscow, the splendid Count Friedrich Werner von der Schulenburg, a handsome and elegant silver-haired Saxon, a professional diplomat, and a great ladies' man. His appearance and manner could have served as a textbook example for young students of diplomacy. The count was first sent to Moscow by von Neurath in 1934 to counteract some of the adverse effects of the anti-Soviet propaganda emanating from Germany's new Nazi government. As proof of his skills, von der Schulenburg managed to keep alive some measure of rational diplomatic dialogue between Moscow and the Wilhelmstrasse. How ironic that a right-wing, revolutionary government would dispatch an old-line, superbly mannered and trained aristocrat of the old school to deal with a left-wing revolutionary government. It was like sending a Nobel Prize–winning physicist to mediate between two angry pugilists. It was not the only time a German patriot found himself serving the cause of the Nazis. Usually those who did so chose to wear blinkers, like von der Schulenburg, and like so many of Germany's generals, who despised the *canaille* that governed Germany but were impressed with its victorious ways (and also with the many promotions it was handing out). But unlike them, von der Schulenburg did not serve the Nazis out of opportunism. His love was for Germany, even if she had an evil master. He would have done anything to keep Germany safe from war with Russia. He probably had hopes of saving whatever he could of the country he had loved as a young man.

Four years later, when the German Army lay bleeding in the snow on the Russian front, he joined Claus von Stauffenberg's rebels, and they slated him to become the foreign minister once they had exterminated Hitler. It was not to be. At sixty-nine, the handsome Count von der Schulenburg was hanged by his Nazi masters like a common criminal at Plötzensee prison in Berlin.

But in 1939, before war came, von der Schulenburg was overjoyed to hear a speech of Stalin's at the Eighteenth Communist Party Congress in March, in which he expressed Russia's unwillingness to "pull British and French chestnuts out of the fire."[90] Another sign of Russia's willingness to deal with Germany was the substitution of the Jewish foreign commissar, Maxim Litvinov, with party stalwart Vyacheslav Molotov. Known among Russia's elite as Kamenaya Poposatka, or Iron Ass, for his dour style, the short, brush-mustached Molotov was a member of the Politburo, and therefore closer to Stalin than Litvinov had been. Molotov was a machinelike party functionary who never made a decision on his own. He invariably deferred to Stalin, which often delayed results. Adolf Hitler, an impatient long-distance participant in the upcoming negotiations, could not have known that it was Molotov's deference to Stalin and nothing else that often slowed Russian decisions.

The first real feelers were to be in the field of trade. One of von Ribbentrop's trade specialists, Dr. Julius Schnurre, was sent to Moscow. The meetings were tentative. Molotov insisted that "until we have political rapprochement, we cannot talk about trade agreements." Also, the Anglo-French team had only just arrived, and Molotov still did not want to upset any potential western agreements in return for a small trade deal with Schnurre. According to Hans von Herwarth, the postwar German ambassador in London who was then a young deputy of von der Schulenburg's in Moscow, it was Britain's guarantee to Poland, added to the arrival of the Franco-British negotiating team, that had caused Hitler to rush into full negotiations with the Soviets. Through von Ribbentrop, Hitler began to put heavy pressure on von der Schulenburg to secure an early date for a Moscow visit by von Ribbentrop. The whole matter was to be described to Molotov as extremely urgent and extremely confidential.

No one in London, Paris, or in Washington would have guessed that the leopard could have changed his spots, that Adolf Hitler, Communism's blood enemy, was about to negotiate with Josef Stalin, the Nazis' bitterest foe. On the face of it, the possibility was out of the question. Not so for Hitler or von Ribbentrop. Hitler saw the entire project as vile but necessary; von Ribbentrop saw it as necessary and wonderful. It would be his crowning diplomatic achievement and a stroke of genius if he could provide his Führer with safety from the east.

Young "Johnny" von Herwarth's conscience as an anti-Nazi soon forced him to draw others into his confidence. Perhaps rumor could foil the negotiators. He saw the danger of a Soviet treaty: it would free Hitler to launch a war. He began by speaking to a friend in the Italian Embassy, who could hardly believe his ears. A pact between Hitler and Stalin? Never!

But negotiations went ahead. In a secret telegram of May 25, von Ribbentrop assured Molotov that even if Germany and Poland went to war, "Russia's special interests would be taken into consideration." By now, Ciano had become involved, briefed by the Italian friend of von Herwarth's. Then Georg von Mackensen, the German ambassador in Rome, reported to Berlin that even the Duce thought it not a bad idea to conclude such a pact. Von der Schulenburg, in Berlin for consultations, was asked to explain how Mussolini got wind of the whole thing, but of course he had no explanation. How could he have known that one of his own best men, Hans von Herwarth, had leaked the facts? Von der Schulenburg passionately wanted to forge again the bonds between his country and Russia, severed by the outbreak of war in 1914.

For a brief moment in June, von Ribbentrop hesitated out of fear that word of a treaty with Soviet Russia would upset the honorary Aryans of the east, Germany's new Japanese allies and Russia's enemies. But he paused only for a moment, and by July the pressure was on again. At the end of the month Hitler politely turned down an offer from Mussolini, à la Munich, to help negotiate a Polish pact. Hitler did not wish to offend Moscow and put Soviet sensibilities ahead of Rome's. Times were changing.

On August 21, 1939, at 10:50 A.M. a teletype letter arrived at the Berghof signed *Stalin*: "The Soviet Government has instructed me to say they agree to Herr von Ribbentrop's arrival on 23 August."

Hitler immediately ordered his press chief, Otto Dietrich, to announce the forthcoming trip. He told Dietrich, "Now we can spit in anyone's face" (*Jetzt können wir jedem ins Gesicht spucken*).[91]

On Monday, August 21, von Ribbentrop also broke the news to his friend Ambassador Oshima of Japan that he was heading for

Moscow to negotiate a treaty. Oshima was aghast, as was Tokyo when the news reached there. The German ambassador to Japan, General Ott, was equally surprised, unpleasantly so. At a Propaganda Ministry briefing in Berlin, the angry correspondent of the Japanese news agency Domei behaved so badly that a complaint was sent to his embassy. Oshima, feeling he had failed to warn Tokyo, resigned.

Von Herwarth now decided to involve a non-Axis western diplomat, his young American friend Charles (Chip) Bohlen, who served in his country's embassy in Moscow. According to his memoirs, Bohlen immediately telegraphed a skeptical Washington. It is equally certain that Washington then briefed 10 Downing Street. The news did not seem to stir up much action in London or Paris. The same halfhearted, slovenly efforts were continued by the Anglo-French "negotiators" in Moscow.

Only Sir Ivone Kirkpatrick later believed that Anglo-French efforts to close a Soviet treaty were bound to be stillborn. For the Soviets, the Anglo-French negotiators offered the prospect of war, no discussion of the Baltic states nor of any territorial gains for Russia. In contrast, the Germans offered peace, a part of Poland, and the three vital Baltic coast countries. The German deal was much more palatable. Kirkpatrick's view is not the majority's, but it has great validity.

On August 22, a shocked, helpless von Herwarth was ordered to fly from Moscow to Königsberg, in East Prussia, to accompany Joachim von Ribbentrop on the last leg of his journey to Moscow.[92] They all arrived at the Soviet capital about noontime on Tuesday, August 23. Von Ribbentrop was greeted by a Soviet delegation and by Ambassador von der Schulenburg and his staff.

A German Embassy friend of von Herwarth's pointed at a group of plainclothes Gestapo men who walked down the ramp of the big four-engined German plane and were immediately greeted with warm handshakes and fraternal smiles by a group of Russian Secret Service men. The attraction of kinship.

The streets on the drive to Moscow were decked with swastika flags, which had been hard to find in Moscow. The Soviet protocol people were frantic until somebody remembered that an anti-Nazi film was being shot in a studio near Moscow. The street sets of the film were decked out with hundreds of swastika banners. Presto! Swastika flags! These were requisitioned and the filming was suspended.

After a hasty meal at the German Embassy, von Ribbentrop's delegation was driven to the Kremlin for a meeting with Molotov. No one in the German party had slept the previous night, because von Ribbentrop kept everyone awake to help him assemble his notes.

The meetings began at once. Schmidt's chief Russian language expert, Gustav Hilger, did the interpreting. Schmidt himself remained at the German Embassy, because von Ribbentrop wanted "the fewest faces" to simplify dealing with the Russians.*

To everyone's surprise, Stalin appeared in Molotov's office. Even von der Schulenburg was stunned. He had served in Moscow for four years but had never spoken to Stalin. Stalin, shorter than everyone had assumed, was dressed in his simple high-buttoned tan twill jacket, smoking a cardboard-tipped Russian cigarette. At Stalin's gesture to Molotov to lead off the meeting, Molotov deferred, and, shrugging his reluctance, Stalin took charge, as was predestined.

Poland was split in half like a melon, on a north-south axis, and then apportioned to each party in the negotiations. Every Russian "suggestion" was followed, and twice von Ribbentrop had to use the telephone to get permission from the Führer, specifically for the secret "assignment" of Finland, Estonia, Latvia, and Bessarabia to the Soviets. Hitler was agreeable; he wanted the treaty signed and sealed. He was in a hurry.

Late that afternoon von Ribbentrop and his delegation went back to the embassy for a hasty meal. The foreign minister was enthusiastic about the men around Stalin: *"Die Männer mit den starken Gesichtern"* (The men with the strong faces).

Later, in Berlin, he would tell the story of his Moscow triumph and say how much he felt at home with the men in the Kremlin. "They were," he told several Nazi Party stalwarts, "wonderful fellows. It was like being among old party comrades!" The comparison was not appreciated by the old party comrades. The diplomat clearly hadn't learned diplomacy with his own people.

After the snack, Ribbentrop and his men returned to the Kremlin. At 6 P.M. the broad-shouldered commander of Stalin's bodyguard conducted them up narrow stairs to the long office where Stalin and Molotov stood waiting once more.

Since this was, in many ways, the apex of his career, his most important achievement, von Ribbentrop's memoirs told the story of the two days in some detail.[93] He began by insisting that at first he had asked his Führer to send someone else to Moscow, possibly Göring, because he thought of himself as badly compromised by his years of anti-Bolshevik speeches and his friendship with the Japanese.

---

*Russian was one of the few languages Schmidt did not command.

But Adolf Hitler insisted that von Ribbentrop "understood these things best" (*die besser verstünde*). Until von Ribbentrop left for Moscow, he claimed, he "knew nothing about an alleged decision of Hitler's to attack Poland," although he acknowledged that Hitler had mentioned "a definite solution to the Danzig and Corridor problems." His impression was that the Polish problems would be solved peacefully, through diplomacy. The outline for the Soviet pact was not sketched until the plane ride to Königsberg and Moscow. The Russians had prepared no draft at all.

According to von Ribbentrop's recollections, at 10 P.M. there was a late supper for four, at which Stalin rose and spoke of a friendly new phase, as did Molotov. After much haggling and several concessions by telephone from Hitler, the treaty was signed, at 2 A.M., Wednesday, August 24. The fate of Estonia, Latvia, Finland, and Bessarabia (Lithuania was eventually to follow) as "assigned to the Soviet sphere" was contained in a separate secret protocol.

Von Ribbentrop was impressed by the affable, quietly dressed, and plain-spoken Stalin. During an early morning photography session by Heinrich Hoffmann, Hitler's photographer, Stalin made it a point to tell von Ribbentrop that this was the first time a foreigner had been permitted into the Kremlin since the Soviet takeover. Then he refused to be photographed in the reactionary act of drinking Crimean champagne, which must have dismayed von Ribbentrop, the old champagne merchant. The next morning von Ribbentrop noticed there were faces staring at him through the open window of one of the buildings across from the old Austrian Embassy, where the Germans were quartered. He was told they belonged to the Anglo-French team.

Von Ribbentrop probably had no idea that Hoffmann, an old friend (Eva Braun was an assistant in the Hoffmann studio when Hitler first met her), had special instructions from the Führer: he was to photograph Stalin's ears so that Hitler could judge whether they looked Aryan (loose) or Jewish (supposedly indicated by attached lobes).

Von Ribbentrop also did not mention that when he wanted to introduce the text of the treaty with some lofty phrases of mutual admiration and respect, Stalin stopped him and said, "We have been pouring buckets of manure all over each other for years. So let us tone down the praise."

At a final serving of caviar and champagne, Stalin toasted Hitler "because the German people love him."[94] Von Ribbentrop shook hands warmly with Trade Commissar Lazar Kaznovich, a Jew. The

Muscovites had created a little song to celebrate the German foreign minister:

Spassibo Jasche Ribbentropu
Shro on otkryl akro w Jewropy

(Thanks to dear little Joachim Ribbentrop
for opening the window to Europe.)

It was a parody of an old verse about Peter the Great. For the moment, everything German was "ruled" popular in Moscow. There was even a Wagner concert.

The Lithuanian section of the Secret Protocol of 23–24 August was not signed until September 28, during a return visit to Moscow by von Ribbentrop.[95] Now all the Baltic states had been "donated" to Stalin. They would stay part of the USSR for over fifty years, with varying degrees of bitterness. In their hatred for Soviet Russia, many Baltic groups became fruitful recruiting grounds for the SS after the Russians were pushed out in 1941. Some of the most cruel Death's Head SS troopers, NCOs, and officers, the concentration camp guards, came from the Baltic republics. They were often found in the murderous Einsatzgruppen, the roaming SS execution battalions far behind the combat lines in Poland and Russia.

Certainly the ecstatic von Ribbentrop could never have guessed what Molotov said about him, once he had flown back to Berlin: "We were immensely pleased when we found out through his chatter how stupid the Reichs minister was."[96]

On the flight home aboard the big Condor aircraft, Joachim von Ribbentrop was euphoric. He had been in Moscow only twenty-four hours, but he had concluded one of the world's most historic treaties.

The four-engine Condor was escorted by fighter planes of the Luftwaffe, because Polish antiaircraft guns had begun firing at Luft-hansa planes.[97] To avoid Polish flak, the planes took a long loop out over the Baltic. Polish-German railroad connections had already been suspended, and war was near. They landed in Königsberg, where Erich Koch, the Gauleiter of East Prussia, hailed von Ribbentrop as a hero and presented him with an amber-encrusted case containing copies of all the treaties he had negotiated. Later, Hitler was amused to learn that all but one of these had long been broken.

Earlier that day, at 3 A.M., when von Ribbentrop had reported via telephone that the pact was signed, Hitler put down the phone, turned, and said, "It will hit like a bomb!" He hammered the wall with his fists and yelled, "Europe is mine! The others can have Asia!"[98]

He, the teetotaler, even sipped a bit of champagne while his subordinates toasted him, but Alfred Rosenberg, the fanatic of the Nazi Party, the unwavering National Socialist, a Balt who hated the Soviets, was deeply distressed.

His diary recorded: "I had the feeling that the Moscow Pact would one day turn and take revenge on National Socialism [*sich irgend wann am National Sozialismus rächen wird*]. How can we talk of saving Europe when we have to beg for help from those who would destroy it?"⁹⁹ Rosenberg remained the only senior Nazi who was a purist.

This was not a step Hitler had freely taken, but a plea by one revolution to the head of another revolution, the defeat of which had been a primary goal of twenty years of struggle.

Hitler flew from the Berghof to Berlin, where he greeted his "Bismarck." The von Ribbentrops must have savored their triumph. Only twenty months earlier, they thought their political years were over and that their Führer had turned his face from them.

That August 24 when von Ribbentrop relished his triumph, a disillusioned Johnny von Herwarth asked his chief, von der Schulenburg, to release him from the diplomatic service so that he could join the Army. At first, von der Schulenburg tried to dissuade him. "Come on now, Johnny, are you sure? Think it over!" But then the old veteran had a clairvoyant moment, one of incisive self-chastisement. "Perhaps you're right," he said. "I have tried with all my strength to work for good relations between Germany and the Soviet Union. In a way I've achieved my goal. But you know perfectly well that in fact I've achieved nothing. This pact will bring us a second world war and plunge Germany into disaster."¹⁰⁰

While von Ribbentrop was signing the treaty in Moscow, Sir Nevile Henderson was delivering an urgent letter from Neville Chamberlain to Hitler at the Berghof. The letter stated that Britain would support Poland but would still help to find a solution for Anglo-German differences if Germany was prepared to open such negotiations, and that Britain was anxious for a truce while Polish-German differences regarding the treatment of minorities were being discussed.

Hitler's first reaction was intemperate and negative. His second reaction was calm and negative. For the patient Henderson, he trotted out the false allegation that 100,000 "Germans" had now fled from Polish brutality, and once again presented himself as the world protector of all people he alone decided were "Germans," no matter how remote their national or racial bonds. He said he realized it might mean war to "protect German interests," but he would rather "fight a war at fifty than one at fifty-six."[101] He hinted that Britain had incited Czechoslovakia and was doing the same to Poland. While von Ribbentrop was proposing friendly toasts in faraway Moscow, Ernst von Weizsäcker and Walter Hewel were in the Berghof as witnesses to this display of Hitler's intransigence.

Sir Nevile Henderson's memoirs treated the German Führer with more objectivity than he deserved. He wrote, "When Hitler comes up before the bar of the Last Judgment, he will certainly argue with apparently complete self-conviction that he could have spared the horrors of war if the Poles had accepted his reasonable and generous conditions. It will, I submit, be false." The British guarantee to Poland of earlier in the year was transformed into a full treaty on August 25, and Hitler originally planned Case White, his invasion of Poland, for August 26.

A sad Erich Kordt had waited and waited after Vansittart predicted that an Anglo-French pact would be closed. Admiral Canaris, head of German Army Intelligence, told Kordt he was naïve. "Kordt, how can you believe that? Emil is cleverer than you think!" *Emil* was Canaris's code name for the despised Hitler.[102]

Part of the Soviet treaty was kept hidden from the world, especially the protocols about the Baltic countries. On August 24, a tired von Ribbentrop swore the reluctant German Embassy staff in Moscow to absolute silence, "on Adolf Hitler's life," about the special "deal" made for the Baltic republics.

On that same day in London, Ambassador Joseph Kennedy told Chamberlain's right-hand man, Sir Horace Wilson, that it was all useless. Poland could not be saved. "The Poles can only fight in revenge and plunge all of Europe into destruction.[103]

Von Ribbentrop must have been shocked when his finest achievement, which would clear the path for the Führer's master plan, seemed suddenly to be blocked by outside interference. Now that Hitler's back was secure, his partner was fading. After all the time he had spent with Ciano and the Duce, getting assurances of alliance, a letter from Mussolini to Hitler arrived at 6 P.M. on August 25: "This is one of the most painful moments of my life, but I must tell you that Italy is not ready for war. My chiefs of staff advise me that our fuel reserves would last only for three weeks. Please understand my position."

This letter was carried by Ambassador Attolico, and reached the Führer at the Chancellery shortly after Henderson had once again paid another visit in the hope of reaching accommodation. He was becoming somewhat of a joke in Hitler's circle. Von Ribbentrop, delighted as the results of his Moscow diplomacy became manifest, gloated over Henderson's unseemly urgency. But now came the shock of that whimper from the Villa Torlonia. Hitler's reaction was cold and angry, and Attolico was dismissed like a schoolboy.

François-Poncet's successor, Ambassador Robert Coulondre, came to try his turn that evening, but Hitler simply yelled about the Poles.* He would guard German interests, no matter what the British or French threatened. After all, had he not given up all claims to Alsace-Lorraine? He had done his best to stay friendly with France. Once more, von Ribbentrop was encouraged. His Führer stuck to his convictions, even if the Duce had turned into a weakling. Schmidt reported that Hitler said, "The Italians are behaving just as they did in 1914." Everyone in the Chancellery spoke of the unreliable Axis partners.

The scene was almost operatic. The immense anteroom was crowded with Nazi courtiers. In his vast, gloomy inner sanctum, Hitler walked to and fro, meeting a constant flow of visitors and aides, pulling all the strings of events as he saw fit. He was watched by von Ribbentrop, Hewel, Schmidt, like witnesses in an operating theater. At first, Hitler had shrugged his shoulders in anger at Mussolini's cowardice, but now the import sank in.

He shouted, "Keitel! I want to see Keitel!" When Keitel rushed in, Hitler snapped, "The attack must be recalled at once!" Keitel, in turn, yelled instructions at his aides. Another down swing for von Ribbentrop. Why did his Führer pull back again? The rumor he had heard must be true. The attack had been scheduled. In the anteroom, an Army major said to Schmidt, "It's all the fault of the diplomats," and Schmidt privately agreed. He had to rush back into Hitler's office to translate a teletype letter from the Führer to the Duce into Italian, a cold letter in which Hitler asked Mussolini to keep secret the fact of Italy's neutrality in order to avoid encouraging the British and French.

Attolico soon brought Mussolini's reply: "I promise."

Henderson arrived with another scheme from London. Chamberlain had earlier been offered a quasi-deal by Hitler: "You run your part of the world and I'll run mine, and we'll stay out of each other's way." Now Chamberlain replied: London regretted that Britain could not accept a separate proposal. She had treaty obligations to her allies. But Chamberlain guaranteed he would produce a "Polish representa-

---

*François-Poncet had been posted to the embassy in Rome.

tive for full discussions." It was August 28. Hitler immediately told
Henderson that the Poles were to have their man in Berlin by August
30: "The barbaric treatment of Germans in Poland cries to high
heaven. This cannot wait!" Sir Nevile complained strenuously: "The
Poles barely have twenty-four hours! It's an ultimatum!" Hitler
warned that "Polish atrocities" might bring matters to a boil long
before then. There was no time. He yelled, "You don't give a damn
how many Germans are mauled by the Poles!" Henderson had just
returned from London, tired and worn-out. He had bathed, changed
clothes, and drunk a half-bottle of champagne. His limit had been
reached. He lost his temper. He pounded on the table and yelled
his anger and defiance at Adolf Hitler, the man he had once tried
to trust. It was to be his final meeting with the Führer.[104] Hitler
would have accepted the gesture of a Polish negotiator, but one never
appeared.

More interference with von Ribbentrop's area of responsibility
and, as he saw it, with the Führer's own plans came from an old von
Ribbentrop enemy, the powerful Hermann Göring. An old friend of
the Reichs marshal's, Birger Dahlerus, a Swedish industrialist, thought
he could use his London connections to defuse conditions. Von Ribbentrop was outraged by this unsolicited offer. Nevertheless, Dahlerus
traveled between Berlin and London a number of times. He did his
best but was generally ignored as an amateur without credentials. He
began to pout and withdrew from the task, but not before shopping
for some special teas at Fortnum & Mason in London. This last
initiative of Göring's soon dissipated, leaving von Ribbentrop once
more in command of the field.

Göring was apoplectic with anger at the "champagne salesman."
He was convinced that von Ribbentrop was a warmonger and had an
evil influence on Hitler. Hermann Göring was always willing to see
the best in his old comrade Hitler and to distrust the newcomer to
National Socialism, a man he believed ill qualified to be foreign
minister.

The avalanche of conferences, telephone calls, and teletype mes-
sages of those last two days before Hitler attacked Poland were like
the "fast forward" on a modern video cassette. The number of events
was almost unaccountable by location and content. The arrival within
twenty-four hours of a Polish negotiating team with full plenipotentiary powers became more and more unlikely. Colonel Beck, the Polish
foreign minister, was as stiff-necked and stubborn as the German
Führer. Beck was absolutely sure of Poland's military strength and

more than eager to hold Britain and France to their promises. Hitler counted on Beck's immovable attitudes and on his arrogance, and he was right. Ambassador Lipski told Dahlerus in Berlin on the day before war broke out that from the Polish side there was not the slightest interest in any German proposals. After five years in Berlin, said Lipski, he knew Germany well, and in case of war "the Germans would overthrow their government and the Polish Army would then march into Berlin."[105] So much for Polish political judgment.

Poland mobilized on August 30. Sometime that day Schmidt was suddenly asked to translate yet another final proposal from Adolf Hitler to Great Britain, France, and Poland. To Schmidt's amazement, the draft he read was logical, reasonable, sensible, and constructive. Not since the days of the League of Nations had he seen anything as conciliatory. Then he realized it was a complete sham, set against the never-to-be-observed Polish deadline, a bitter joke to make Hitler seem a statesmanlike, judicious man, who had proposed these solutions but had been rebuffed. How could Hitler help it if the Poles had failed to keep their appointment? Later, Hitler said in the presence of Schmidt, about this "reasonable" draft, that he needed an alibi to show the German people he had done everything in his power to avoid war.

Late that night, just before the Polish deadline of midnight, von Ribbentrop asked Sir Nevile Henderson to the Foreign Office, where he read the full text of the "reasonable" proposals. The startled British diplomat fancied he knew German well, but a treaty and all its technicalities, orally delivered, tested his linguistic skills. He began to interrupt and ask questions and then asked to read the paper himself. Von Ribbentrop at first refused, but then tossed it on the desk. Contemptuously he said, "There! Go ahead. It's no good, though. The deadline for the Polish negotiator has come and gone." Schmidt told the story of this, "the most stormy meeting he had witnessed in his years as a diplomatic interpreter."[106] Von Ribbentrop started to yell at Henderson, who took what the German foreign minister was dishing out until von Ribbentrop yelled that the matter was damned (*verdammt*) grave. That breached Henderson's limit of self-control. Sir Nevile, red-faced in his turn, shouted, "You have used the word damned (*verdammt*). That is not the language of statesmanship in this grave situation." It sounds mid-Victorian by today's standards, but Sir Nevile had a strict sense of what was decorous and what was unseemly in diplomatic conduct. Von Ribbentrop was struck dumb for the moment. This cowardly British aristocrat had dared to speak to

him as if he were a schoolboy? Both men jumped to their feet, tempers
flaring. Schmidt, not believing his eyes and ears, lowered his head.
Courtesy demanded that he stand up with the disputants, but good
sense dictated otherwise. Finally he heard them breathe easier and saw
them resume their seats. Schmidt, who was known for his sense of
humor, saw nothing funny in this moment. Too many lives were at
stake.

All this took place late on the night of August 30 in the historic
office of Germany's great Iron Chancellor, Prince Bismarck.

Historians will not allow the memory of von Ribbentrop to reach
above Bismarck's ankle. Yet both men were ambitious builders of
power structures. Both found war to be the final instrument of their
achievements. Neither one understood the strength of persuasion, the
power of reason, or the sanctity of life. In this way, perhaps, Hitler
was not too far afield when he called von Ribbentrop the "second
Bismarck."

Late in the afternoon of the following day, August 31, the last day
of peace, Ambassador Lipski of Poland went to see von Ribbentrop at
the Foreign Ministry. He expressed Poland's interest in pursuing the
points of the final German proposal. He said that an answer was
forthcoming from Warsaw. "Are you empowered to negotiate?" asked
von Ribbentrop. "No," said Lipski. That ended the meeting, the short-
est of the Polish crisis.

That same night, there was one last Allied attempt. Ambassadors
Henderson of Great Britain and Coulondre of France asked to be
jointly received by the German foreign minister to hand over their
governments' notes. Von Ribbentrop refused a joint meeting but gave
Henderson a 9:30 P.M. appointment and Coulondre one at 10:00.
Henderson's note warned once more that His Majesty's Government
would carry out its international obligations. The French note was
almost identical. A cold von Ribbentrop insisted on oral translations
of each ambassador's statement, as if he spoke neither English nor
French. He told each that he had no authority to give a reply and
would refer their notes to the Führer.

Another desperate attempt was made by Ambassador Attolico.
The plump, elderly man rushed back and forth between von Ribbentrop's Wilhelmstrasse office and the British and French embassies. At
8 P.M. Attolico gave up. No one would accept Mussolini's offer
to mediate. The British and the French mobilized their armies. At
4:45 A.M. on September 1, Case White, the invasion of Poland, was
launched.

Directive OKW/WFA No. 170/39 g.k. Chefs. LI, issued in eight copies, dated 31.8.39 Berlin, marked "Secret," issued at 12:40 P.M. was signed by Adolf Hitler as commander-in-chief of the armed forces. He stated: (1) He has decided, after trying all peaceful means, to change the intolerable conditions on the eastern frontier through the application of brute strength (*Gewaltsame Lösung*). (2) The attack will be called Case White and will take place on September 1. (3) It is to be left to the French and British to open hostilities in the west. The neutrality of Holland, Belgium, Luxemburg, and Switzerland is to be scrupulously observed. "Air attacks against London are to be left at my discretion. Attacks on the British Islands are to be planned, assuring that sufficient forces are involved to avoid partial success." Distribution: Commanders-in-chief of Army, Navy, Air Force, and General Headquarters.

An "incident" fabricated to create a typical Hitler propaganda episode was planned by the chief of the SD and Gestapo, Reinhard Heydrich. An SS captain, Alfred Naujocks, was ordered by Heydrich to "capture" a German radio station on the Polish border at Gleiwitz, using SS men in stolen Polish uniforms. The radio station was then to broadcast a Polish-language appeal. The men were to dress dead concentration camp inmates in Polish uniforms (the Gestapo called the cadavers "canned goods") and leave them around the radio station's grounds as if they had been killed by German border police during the skirmish. The attack was made, and Naujocks was the moment's SS hero. The German police reported the attack and said that some Polish attackers were shot by German frontier guards. The *Völkische Beobachter* bellowed, POLISH PARTISANS CROSS GERMAN BORDER. As Naujocks said much later, "The closer you were to Heydrich, the more you learned to fear him."[107]

What could have been Adolf Hitler's frame of mind those final days before he loosed the storm, and how did Joachim and Annelies von Ribbentrop feel? Hitler must have been absolutely certain that his destiny was to fight the war. He was a superstitious man and a creature of whim. In the manner of a balky child, he always resented any denial, any interdictions of his pet ideas or his favorite dreams. One of his Army aides, Major Engel, wrote in his diary on August 27, 1939:

Führer wants to bet Hewel that England will not interfere in case of war with Poland. Hewel disagrees avidly and says, verbatim, "My

Führer, don't underestimate the British. When they know there is no
alternative, they become stubborn and go about their business. I think
I know a lot more about that than my minister [Ribbentrop]." Führer
very annoyed. Broke off conversation.

Hewel meant that his having dealt with the British for years, while
he was in self-imposed exile, gave him more knowledge about them
than von Ribbentrop had, which may have been true. Also, as a 1932
fellow fighter of Hitler's, one who had been jailed with his Führer, he
had the freedom to speak up when it mattered. (A loyal man, he
committed suicide in Berlin on May 3, 1945, when the city fell.) But
Hewel could not budge Hitler from his point of view in 1939. Hitler
brooked no disagreement even from an old comrade.

Hitler never lost sight of his beginnings and of his penniless days
as a vagrant, living in public shelters, trying to sell his paintings. Later,
everyone who knew him spoke of the evenings and nights when Hitler
told stories about his Army service as a simple soldier, unable or
possibly unwilling to raise himself to higher rank. His commander
had stated that Hitler "was extremely courageous but could not be
trusted with command responsibility." He had won the Iron Cross
First Class, which was rare among the lower ranks, and still he had
stayed at the bottom of the military heap. Now he was the master of
an empire. He had learned that he could manipulate, command, cheer,
horrify, teach, lead, destroy, almost at will. He often must have asked
himself what it was that brought him from nothing to the very peak,
and the only answer he probably found was that it was destiny. His
every decision, it seemed to him, his every judgment, had been guided
by fate, along the path laid out millennia before in some book that
guides the gods. He had once been weak, like others; then fate lifted
him above his station. Now he could recognize each weakness in
others and use it against them. Nations were like men. And he sensed
an "old rich man" weakness of Britain, the country with false teeth.
Their language simpered: "Oh, I'm afraid that I . . ." Their umbrellas
kept their heads out of the clean, storm-driven rain. They no longer
deserved to rule the world. He, Adolf Hitler, and his Germany, did!
What had he said to Dahlerus? "My people love me. When they have
no butter, I'll eat no butter. They will follow me. I can outlast the
others by one year, no matter how tough." He would win. It was so
written.

And the von Ribbentrops? They had now drifted very far and had
changed completely from the people they were only a short seven
years before. They had tied their lives to this man Adolf Hitler. There

was no way out and no way back — and why would they have wanted a way out or back? They were idealists, freed from catering to the cheap, material world. They had become one of the most powerful couples in one of the most powerful countries in the world. Joachim and Annelies, who had once longed to be invited to Berlin's "better" homes, now commanded the presence of kings and presidents, prime ministers, and captains of industry. The man who had trusted them and through whose genius they had come to this high station now wanted to make war against Poland. Surely he was right. Surely England would not interfere. Hitler was always right. The von Ribbentrops were willing to encourage their eldest son, their firstborn, Rudolf, to join the elite fighting Waffen SS as a private soldier. He was bound to be in combat soon.

What ever had happened to Berlin's worldly, wealthy, young von Ribbentrops, who had loved being invited to sophisticated little dinners by Freddy and Lali Horstmann? Dahlem was only a short car ride from the Chancellery. To the von Ribbentrops, it had become a thousand-mile journey.

On September 1, 1939, Adolf Hitler spoke to the Reichstag. The gist of what he said was contained in one sentence; it incorporated all his subversion of morality. He, the aggressor, said, "Since 5:45 we have been returning their fire" (*Seit 5:45 Uhr wird jetzt zurückgeschossen*). The *Völkische Beobachter* headlined: THE FÜHRER DECLARES THE FIGHT FOR THE RIGHT AND SECURITY OF THE REICH.

On September 2 Sir Nevile Henderson was instructed by Lord Halifax to request "that the United States chargé d'affaires be good enough to take charge of British interests in the case of war."[108] All ciphers and confidential documents were burned, and the embassy staff left their residences and moved into the Hotel Adlon next to the embassy. Now, in Sir Nevile's calm words came a diplomat's equivalent of shipwreck:

> In the early hours (4 A.M.) of September 3 I was accordingly instructed by His Majesty's Government to arrange for a meeting with the Minister of Foreign Affairs at 9 A.M. There was some difficulty in establishing contact with the ministry at that hour, but I was finally informed that Dr. Schmidt was authorized by the minister to accept on His Excellency's behalf any communication which I might make to him. I accordingly handed to Dr. Schmidt precisely at 9 A.M. the final ultimatum from His Majesty's Government . . .
>
> Dr. Schmidt received the communication and undertook to deliver it at once.

The hour for war or peace was 11 A.M., as the ultimatum stated. It was close at hand.

In Schmidt's words:

> On Sunday September 3 I awoke late because of the strenuous days I had behind me. I rushed in a taxi to make it to the Foreign Ministry and as we crossed Wilhelm Square I saw Sir Nevile Henderson walking into the historical entrance of Wilhelmstrasse 76. I took a side entrance and, promptly at 9 A.M., stood waiting for Henderson in von Ribbentrop's office. Punctual to the minute, he was announced by one of the clerks. He entered, his face very grave, shook hands, but refused a seat at a small table in a corner of the room. Instead he stood in a solemn, ceremonial manner in the center of the room. With an emotional voice, he said, "I am sad that my government has instructed me to deliver an ultimatum to the German government . . ."

He then gave the terms: If there is no withdrawal by 11 A.M., a state of war exists between Britain and Germany. Schmidt remembered that "after these words he handed me the fateful document and said good-bye. 'I am truly sorry,' he said, 'that I had to hand over this document to you of all people. You have always been so helpful.'"

Schmidt continued, "I also expressed my regrets and directed some heartfelt words of farewell to the British ambassador, whom I had always respected, as I said previously."

Schmidt put the paper into his briefcase and walked from the Foreign Ministry to the adjoining Chancellery, where everyone was expecting him. There was much tension as he elbowed his way through the unusually large and visibly nervous throng of uniformed and civilian party eminences milling around in the Führer's anteroom. Several functionaries shouted, "What's the news?" But Schmidt shrugged and said, "No school today," an allusion to the many informal briefings he had given in this anteroom in former days.

He stepped into Hitler's office. The Führer sat at his desk. Von Ribbentrop stood to his right near a window. Both were riveted on Schmidt. He stopped some distance from Hitler's desk and began slowly to translate the ultimatum. When he had finished, there was a silence that seemed to Schmidt like the silence after the "crash of tympany" at the Godesberg Conference.

> Hitler sat there as if he had turned to stone, staring straight ahead. He did not lose his composure, as some said. He did not rave, as others would have it. He sat at his desk, completely immobile. After some time, which seemed to me like an eternity, he turned to Ribbentrop, who stood frozen at the window.

"What now?" Hitler asked his Foreign Minister, with a furious look in his eyes, as if he wanted to make it clear that Ribbentrop had given him false information about the reaction of the English. Ribbentrop said in a soft voice, "I assume that the French will give us an identical ultimatum within the hour."

Schmidt then withdrew. He told the surging crowd in the anteroom about the British ultimatum. There was dead silence. Göring turned to Schmidt and said, "If we lose this war, may heaven have mercy on us." Goebbels stood in a corner, looking *"wie ein begossener Pudel"* (like a wet poodle).

The French delivered their ultimatum an hour later.

BOOK III

11

WAR
1940

*Is He Trying to Bore Us
into Peace?*

THE FIRST GERMAN to fire a shot in the Second World War was Lieutenant Albrecht Herzner, a young officer in the Brandenburg organization, the secret sabotage unit of Admiral Canaris's Abwehr. The shots were fired inside Poland on August 26, six days before Germany actually attacked.

Herzner, a typical intelligence "freebooter," was such a bitter anti-Nazi that in 1938 he had volunteered to assassinate Hitler. But he was a German officer, and now he had been given orders to assemble a small team of Poles of German ancestry in ragtag uniforms and secure an important mountain pass, Jablunka. He was then to capture a railway station at nearby Mosty. The mountain pass and the station were vital tactical points for the coming armored drive. Lieutenant Herzner, with his corporal and ten men, Combat Group Jablunka, quickly took charge of the pass and the railway station from frontier guards and were amazed by how easily they did so. They had only one wounded man. Then they found out, by asking a Polish colonel whom they captured, that there was no war. Case White must have been postponed. Herzner reached his headquarters on the normal phone; indeed, no German attack had taken place. He managed to make his way back to the German frontier with his swastika-armband-wearing, German-Polish "partisans." This ended the first attack on Poland.

In the textbook definition of intelligence agents, there are commercial, patriotic, and coerced ones. The commercial agents are skilled but unmotivated, the coerced ones are unreliable, and the patriotic ones are amateurish but loyal. Herzner's big chief, Canaris, who ran an excellent intelligence organization, preferred the patriotic variety. There were German Military Intelligence agents in the most unexpected places and guises. Usually they were separatist patriots in foreign countries motivated politically, not financially. For instance, among Canaris's Egyptian agents were Lieutenants Nasser and Sadat, both patriotic antiroyalists and therefore anti-British. Canaris's organization also was the heart of the early wartime anti-Hitler conspiracy and the military opposition to Hitler.

Erich and Theo Kordt, Count Schwerin, Colonel von Kleist, State Secretary von Weizsäcker, Generals Beck and von Witzleben, General Oster, all of them men who wanted to remove Hitler and avoid needless war, depended on the silver-haired Admiral Canaris to lead their effort. He was cooperative but not active. He was a cynic. He knew human nature and the vicious men around Himmler and the Führer. Many histories of the early days of World War II speak of the 1938 rebellion that was supposed to have taken place inside Germany in order to prevent war.

Joachim von Ribbentrop blamed the halfhearted German opposition groups for falsely stiffening the backs of the Chamberlain group and reinforcing the arrogance of the Poles. "They squelched all our attempts to find a peaceful solution."[1] It never occurred to von Ribbentrop that the world at last became ashamed of accommodating the men who had unleashed such horror in Germany, Austria, and Czechoslovakia.

On April 20 he was promoted to SS Obergruppenführer, the third-highest SS rank. Perhaps this clouded his vision about that black-uniformed fraternity and its crimes, the subversion of individual rights, the suspension of due process, the mass arrest, torture, and repression of racial minorities, and the black plague of Gestapo and SS that swamped Germany and each place Germany now dominated.

Until September 2, 1939, this SS flood of horror had not followed combat troops, bombers, and tanks like a pack of scavenging hyenas. Germany and Austria were wealthy, well-organized countries, and even small Czechoslovakia was wealthy, worldly, and industrialized. SS and Secret Police functioned in these countries, but covertly. It was different in devastated Poland, with its mud-caked villages, churchgoing peasants, and clustered Jewish settlements, which became SS machine gun–controlled hells long after the Stukas had finished their bombing, the panzers had done their mauling, and the armored infantry had mopped up and passed through. In the wake of the German Army men, who wore the new Germany's eagle and swastika insignia on the right front of their uniforms, came those who wore this insignia on the left sleeves, the SS and its Einsatzgruppen.

The German historian Heinz Höhne, a leading expert on the SS, told the story of these ruthless groups.[2] Reinhard Heydrich, Gestapo and SD head, formed five of the Einsatzgruppen, or "attack groups." During the Polish campaign, they were attached to each German field army. Every Einsatzgruppe contained four Einsatzkommandos of a hundred to a hundred and fifty men. Each small, vicious Kommando was assigned to an Army corps. At first, trying to keep track of what the SS Kommandos were doing was like keeping an eye on a group of ten men in a crowded sports stadium. But while they were carrying out their supposed mission of suppressing anti-Reich and anti-German elements, they became extremely noticeable. These Einsatzkommandos were often assisted by Poles of German ancestry taking revenge on the Slavic Poles who had hounded them earlier. These "racial German self-defense organizations" soon were shooting untold numbers of Poles and Jews. One of their leaders was SS Colonel Rudolf von Alvensleben of the family that had once attracted the young Ribbentrop brothers to seek adventure in Canada. On April 20, 1940, the first Jewish ghetto was formed in Lodz. The special SS men with the SD diamond patch on their sleeves began to commit such acts of brutality and bestiality that word soon reached the top echelons of the Army.

Then, to the deep shock of the SD and its chief, Reinhard Heydrich, Colonel General Johannes Blaskowitz, the Germany Army commander in Poland, interfered. He would not permit the Army to be complacent witnesses and passive collaborators in things that the general considered abominable. He had many reports of shameful acts. He collected these and sent a written protest about the mass murders and other SD debauches to the Army chief of staff.

General Blaskowitz said it affected Army morale to witness this SD swinishness. The memorandum was read by Adolf Hitler on November 18, 1939. He was furious with the general, but Blaskowitz was undeterred. The field generals under his command continued to report SD atrocities all over Poland. Poles were shot arbitrarily. Jews were beaten, humiliated, and killed, men, women, children, and babies, sometimes in their synagogues. There was rape and looting.

Blaskowitz's next memorandum stated that "the attitude of the troops toward SD and police alternates between abhorrence and hatred. Every soldier feels disgusted by these crimes committed in Poland by nationals of the Reich and representatives of our state."

Several generals at Hitler's headquarters joined Blaskowitz in expressing revulsion. Army officers at Blaskowitz's headquarters would no longer shake hands with SS officers. Himmler finally had to order an investigation, but it was a sham. Blaskowitz was relieved of his command in 1940 by Adolf Hitler and never promoted, although as a talented general he was given a command in the western campaign. In a bitter stroke of irony, he was arrested by the Allies at the end of the war and charged with war crimes. It was too much for him to bear. He committed suicide in a Nürnberg prison in February 1948.

The era of Heinrich Himmler and the SS mass terror was at hand. They grew in power until they became an empire within the Hitler empire. The further Hitler's Army ranged, the wider the black shadow of the SS that followed them. Their Death's Head units dominated all prison systems from concentration camps to Gestapo jails. The SD began to swallow up the old Gestapo and its functions. Beginning with Poland, the SD's Einsatzgruppen sent their bands of killers all over the eastern campaigns, including the Baltics and Russia. Another branch of SD took over some espionage work. On October 26, 1939, it became part of each embassy and ministry, invading von Ribbentrop's field. In a rare conciliatory gesture, von Ribbentrop approved. After all, Himmler was powerful. The SD even asked for and got diplomatic status from the Foreign Ministry as so-called police attachés.[3] Many of these SD police attachés reported directly to Heydrich and Himmler and even to Hitler, which did not endear them to the foreign minister.

Eventually, this led to a showdown between the two former close friends, von Ribbentrop and Himmler. A *modus vivendi* was created: SD would report directly to chiefs of mission like ambassadors and chargés d'affaires and would avoid interfering in matters of policy.

Probably the "purest" form of SS, or the least besmirched of the entire foul order, was the newly created Waffen SS. The organization was an expansion of Hitler's own bodyguard; it was formed into a separate army on September 27, 1939. The Waffen SS, all fiercely motivated Nazis, became a fanatical fighting army of armored and infantry divisions. It also raised almost twenty units of volunteer non-German Nazis, mainly from the occupied countries. There were Norwegians, Belgians, Frenchmen, Spaniards, Russians, Dutchmen, and even Arabs who wore Waffen SS uniforms. Many Waffen SS atrocities were later committed against German Army soldiers whom the SS deemed cowards or shirkers. At the end of the western war, hanged Germany Army soldiers were found by Allied troops. Often there was a notice pinned to a body: "This man was a coward! SS Division of the Reich." In the last days before the total collapse, German soldiers were often more afraid of the SS than of Allied troops.

From the day Mars helped Hitler draw the sword, the use for diplomacy, statesmanship, deal making, power-block building, and treaty signing was waning fast. In war, generals do the talking and diplomats the listening, but during the Polish campaign, at the very beginning of the long war to come, von Ribbentrop was still unaware that his days as Adolf Hitler's most precious minister and adviser would soon be over. Now the priorities shifted. Important were the Air Force (Göring), Munitions (Todt), Intelligence (Himmler), Police (Himmler), Party (Hess), Propaganda (Goebbels), and above all Hitler's generals and admirals. Diplomacy could wait and, all too frequently, so would Joachim von Ribbentrop in the six years to come.

Most of Hitler's courtiers now moved into two special trains. (Göring had his own train.) Hitler's was his usual private train, *Adler* (Eagle). The other was called *Heinrich*, after Heinrich Himmler. It included Himmler's car, a lavish antique, von Ribbentrop's sleek, streamlined one, and the car of State Secretary Hans Lammers, who now ran the Chancellery for his Führer. It must have peeved the acclaim-conscious foreign minister that the train had been named after Himmler. The few Foreign Service people who accompanied von Ribbentrop were quartered in a standard civilian Mitropa sleeper attached to *Heinrich*. All meetings were held in an old wooden dining car next to von Ribbentrop's vehicle.[4] Whenever the train stopped overnight on its way into Poland, von Ribbentrop spent hours in the office section of his car, speaking on the phone to the Wilhemstrasse, screaming his annoyance and giving his instructions.

The train's batteries often ran down, and then candles were lighted. The "cowardly pacifists" of the ministry, as von Ribbentrop called them, thought it was like being in a combat dugout. To the more courageous officials it looked like the chic, candle-lighted Café Savarin in Berlin.

Von Ribbentrop ruled over the Foreign Ministry from his car, and poor Paul Schmidt, as a senior ministry official, had to carry out his master's instructions to phone Berlin and "tell that horse's ass to . . ." (translated into "The Reichs Minister would be grateful if . . .") At the slightest holdup in the Wilhelmstrasse, von Ribbentrop let fly his disdain for the "cowards," "loafers," and "know-nothings" who "did not seem to realize there was a war on."

Each morning Schmidt, carrying a military map under his arm, had to climb across the rails and gravel of the open railway yard to the Führer's train, *Adler,* where he attended a briefing on the military situation. Schmidt then returned to *Heinrich* to give a briefing to von Ribbentrop and his people, using the same sweeping gestures that soon earned him the nickname "Napoleon." Reluctant ministry staff members were instructed in the loading and firing of two small anti-aircraft guns, one at each end of *Heinrich*. Fortunately for them, their gunnery was never needed.

In Poland, the *Adler* was Hitler's temporary command post. Later, various Führer headquarters were built, both in the west and the east. They usually had Teuto-romantic war names like Wolfsschanze (Wolf's Lair). The men around Hitler knew how to satisfy his Wagnerian taste for Germanic folk tales and myths. Other headquarters were dubbed Felsennest (Rock's Nest) and Wolfsschlucht (Wolf's Gorge).

There was much nighttime work on *Heinrich* in the early hours of September 18. At 2 A.M. von Ribbentrop finally went to sleep in his car, as did Schmidt and the other staff members in theirs. The foreign minister had spent hours on the phone, fighting to bar Propaganda Minister Goebbels from seizing charge of the field of foreign propaganda and in pursuit of evidence of Goebbels's incursions into his own sacred territory. At 5 A.M. the tired Schmidt was awakened and told that the Russians had begun their entry into Poland toward the agreed line of demarcation between the two armies.[5]

He waited until 8 A.M. to tell von Ribbentrop, who was shaving. Dressed in his underwear, the apoplectic foreign minister, his soap-flecked face purple, waved his razor at Schmidt and howled, "Because you're too damned lazy to come to my bedroom, you've now interfered with history! You're too young to do that! What if there were clashes between their troops and ours?" Schmidt tried to calm him. After all, the line of demarcation was well known to both German and Russian troop commanders. But von Ribbentrop did not quiet down, probably because he was sure the hated Goebbels had already broadcast the news of the Russian advance. That honor belonged to the press chief of his own Foreign Ministry.

On September 19 they left *Heinrich*, and temporary headquarters was established in a beachfront hotel of the Baltic Sea resort Zoppot. They were still in Zoppot when Poland surrendered, divided now between Germany and Russia.

Von Ribbentrop returned to Berlin. On September 26 he flew to Moscow, this time to sign away Lithuania. It was the final section of the secret protocol to the Soviet treaty of August.

Ciano arrived in Berlin on October 1, representing Italy, the "cowardly shirkers." At dinner in Dahlem, von Ribbentrop, now very much the superior after the Soviet treaty and the Polish victory, patronized

233

the Ducellini, told him the tale about the "strong faces" of Moscow, and even compared the Kremlin military guards to the Duce's guards, causing the usually garrulous Ciano to sink into an icy silence. Relations between Berlin and Rome had cooled, and Ciano had obviously been sent to remove some of the chill. Mussolini was infuriated by the Soviet treaty, and much of the Italian public felt betrayed by it.

Back in Rome, Ciano made a speech that sent several stiletto thrusts toward Germany. On January 3, 1940, Mussolini wrote to Hitler: "You will not be surprised if I tell you that the German-Russian agreement has had painful repercussions in Spain. The earth which covers the dead — yours and ours and the Spanish — is still fresh."[6] He wrote that he realized the necessity for the pact, "since Ribbentrop's efforts toward the nonintervention of the French and the British were not realized," thereby taking a slap at his least favorite German.

Then there followed the bitter complaints of a friend betrayed: "But I, a born revolutionary who has not modified his way of thinking, tell you that you cannot abandon the anti-Semitic and anti-Bolshevist banner, which you have been flying for twenty years and for which so many of your comrades have died. You cannot renounce your gospel, in which the German people have blindly believed."

He suggested that Germany's territorial needs still lay in Russia, and suggested reconciliation with the "courageous Poles, liberated from the Jews." He said he approved of Hitler's plan to concentrate the Jews in a large ghetto in Lublin. Obviously the views he had expressed five years earlier had deserted him by 1939.*

Almost in response, on October 6 Hitler made a lengthy speech at the Kroll Opera House in Berlin, supported by his usual audience of *Sieg Heil* yellers, offering European peace in the vaguest of terms. It was his usual procedure: to follow punitive measures with soft talk until the next aggressive act. It was roundly ignored by the Allies, who had taken the measure of his duplicity. On October 21, a statement released by von Ribbentrop said the Allies had ignored the Führer's offer and had thrown down the glove of challenge.[7]

Now it was von Ribbentrop's turn to go to Rome to patch the cracks in the Hitler-Duce base and also to make sure that Mussolini's weakness-induced neutrality did not widen. As if to help von Ribbentrop regain Italian loyalty, the British had imposed a sea blockade of all coal shipped by Germany to Italy, raising great bitterness in coal-

---

*On November 13, 1934, Mussolini berated the visiting German Jewish leader Nahum Goldmann, accompanied by the Chief Rabbi of Rome, for being afraid of Hitler. "You will long survive him."

starved Italy. Despite Mussolini's disgust with the Soviet treaty, von Ribbentrop's mission was easier to accomplish than he had anticipated. Also, the Duce was himself mortified by his neutrality and hungry to prove himself an equal to the man in the field-gray uniform. Hitler had donned his new gray uniform jacket with a gold eagle and swastika on the left sleeve (in the SS manner) on the day Poland was invaded. "I have," he declared in a speech, "once more put on my favorite coat, that of the soldier, and I do not intend to take it off again until victory is won." It sounded portentous. Actually, it was only a change in color from his usual tan Nazi Party jacket. Hitler liked symbolism.

Late in February 1940 there came one of those curious interludes which occur when well-meaning but unauthorized people attempt to play peacemaker. Sumner Welles, under secretary of state for Cordell Hull, persuaded President Roosevelt, who was a personal friend, to let him go to Europe on a fact-finding mission. The trip was a precursor of the many political "fact finding" junkets that are so popular among U.S. congressmen. Welles, a tall, calm diplomat from the patrician equestrian village of Bernardsville, New Jersey, soon met with every available Italian and German senior official, including Hitler and Mussolini. His memoirs reflected shock that Mussolini, whom he knew, had deteriorated physically and looked bloated, clumsy, and ten years older than his fifty-six. He also chronicled his frustrating interviews with von Ribbentrop. The latter was unsmiling and curt, and "refused" to understand English, insisting on an interpreter. All the Nazi bigwigs, according to Schmidt, who interpreted these meetings, told Sumner Welles identically warlike and unconciliatory things and all in the same words. Welles returned to Washington, having learned only the truth: Germany wanted to fight on, and Italy would probably join in. Welles spoke of a split between Mussolini and Ciano, but he knew who was the boss. By unhappy coincidence, his visit to Rome coincided with the British coal blockade.

On March 10, 1940, when in his turn von Ribbentrop arrived in Rome to woo Mussolini, his private train disgorged an entourage of thirty-five, including legal and economic experts, two hairdressers, a masseur, a doctor, and a gymnastics coach. He carried an "exceedingly long" letter from Hitler, which rebutted the Mussolini assertion that Germany had attacked Poland through some sort of miscalculation about London and Paris.[8] Instead, Hitler wrote, he wanted to involve himself in war with the west earlier rather than later, a point of view he had presented to others. Finally, he wrote what amounted to: "Duce, all is forgiven. I understand why you could not go to war.

But now it is time to share in the fight so that you can share in the spoils." Von Ribbentrop was certain to fan anti-British feeling by expressing Hitler's outrage over the coal embargo. When von Ribbentrop was confronted once more with the Duce's doubts about the Soviet treaty, he trotted out the argument he had devised for Hitler and all other senior Nazis except Rosenberg: "The Soviets were no longer exporting world revolution. Stalin was just a Russian patriot, concerned with the fate of Soviet citizens." Mussolini was skeptical, but he had made up his mind. Yes, he would join Germany. But not yet. No matter how persistently von Ribbentrop tried to press him for a definite date, Mussolini remained vague. To avoid returning to Berlin emptyhanded, von Ribbentrop quickly arranged a meeting between Führer and Duce, to take place at the Brenner Pass around March 19. If this was acceptable, von Ribbentrop could give the cosmetic semblance of success to his inconclusive Rome efforts.

It pleased Mussolini that the German delegation was also invited to the Vatican. The conversation between Pope Pius XII, the former Cardinal Pacelli and papal nuncio in Berlin, seemed cordial enough. However, Cardinal Secretary Maglioni, mincing no words, probably gave true expression to the Vatican's point of view. Von Ribbentrop complained that "if Cardinal Maglioni had continued to talk as he did, I would have stood up and left. I was ready to reach for my cap!" He did not reach for his cap. Instead, he seems to have discounted any comfort he may have received from the cordial Pius XII.

Von Ribbentrop faked the results of his Mussolini meetings, but so did Mussolini. After the Germans departed, he tried as well as he could to retreat from his promise to make war. The Italian newspapers were warned by his press aides to dampen the Duce's martial sounds and saber rattling. *Piano, piano!* Sumner Welles returned to Rome on March 16 and reported to Washington that Mussolini seemed more at ease now that he had postponed entry into the war and "had not determined to cross the Rubicon."

Berlin phoned, "Is March 18 for the Brenner Pass acceptable?" Mussolini, annoyed at being pushed, balked but agreed.[9] Ciano thought that by now Benito Mussolini was too cowed by Adolf Hitler to say no to him ever again. On the agreed day, the trains of the two dictators stopped on neighboring tracks in the deep snow of the mountain pass at the little station near the German-Italian border. Mussolini and Ciano welcomed Hitler and von Ribbentrop on the icy platform and escorted them to the Duce's well-heated salon car. In an informal photograph of the conference, Hitler sits at a narrow lace-covered table in Mussolini's lavishly paneled custom carriage. At his side, the Duce shows a heavy-chinned, bulldog face, darkened with the shadow of the heavily bearded. Ciano, sitting across the table, is a handsome man with slick hair, who has been fattened and softened by a sybaritic life. Both of the Italians are wearing the gray uniform of the Fascist senior echelon, chests covered with decoration ribbons. They are both in dark shirts and ties. Hitler, sitting between them, looks embarrassed and reluctant to be photographed. His uniform appears to be his standard new field-gray jacket with gold party badge, Iron Cross First Class, and World War Combat Wounded Badge. The glittering Italians seem very much in command, but the appearances in the photo are deceiving. Hitler immediately launched into an extended, unstoppable monologue to justify the Soviet pact ("Stalin has become a nationalist patriot"). If Italy wanted to be number one in the Mediterranean, she would have to fight England and France, whether she was ready or not. In any case, Germany would not postpone her timetable. France and Britain would be attacked as planned.

Pushed hard, Mussolini agreed to a plan that would allot a limited number of Italian divisions to a joint attack on southern France. The entire Italian Army would enter the battle if the Germans gained early victories.

Even though Italy's senior army commanders turned it down, the plan was to stand. Mussolini would become a combatant, and von Ribbentrop and Ciano became recalcitrant harnessmates. Ciano hated von Ribbentrop, and his diaries reflected the feeling: "Everyone in Rome dislikes Ribbentrop."[10]

Shortly before the Brenner Pass meeting, SS Chief Himmler met with the senior generals of Army Group A at their Koblenz headquarters to deal with their outrage over the excesses of the SS in Poland and Danzig. In the case of Danzig, where Gauleiter Forster had complained that the Army interfered with his brutal "pacification" methods, Army troops had been moved out so that the SS were no longer under their control. In Poland that did not apply. The Army was still there, and in great numbers, commanded by very senior generals who could not be bullied. After his initial annoyance, listening to Himmler's report, Hitler's reaction to General Blaskowitz's complaint was simple. How could an Army command be entrusted to a man who was so childish? At Koblenz, the complaints about the SS Einsatzkommandos were brought to a painful head when Himmler told the generals, "Everything I do is done with the full knowledge of the Führer."[11] The implications were inescapable. Like all German officers, the generals had sworn their personal allegiance to Adolf Hitler. If, as Himmler said, Hitler knew of these crimes, how could they continue to serve him? But, having sworn their oath, how could they refuse? Three years later, at the time of the slaughter of Stalingrad, Erich von Manstein, who was desperately trying to stave off military disaster, was asked by the military rebels under Colonel von Stauffenberg to join their ranks. Von Manstein, Germany's most talented strategist, knowing that a great German disaster was at hand, replied, "German field marshals do not mutiny."

The 1940 generals had complained only about the blot on Germany's honor, a much smaller cause for rebellion than the Hitler-directed catastrophe of 1943. In 1940, they did nothing. Instead, they went away, grumbling. Besides, new glory was close at hand. They would soon shake the dust of Poland's villages from their riding boots and leave everything in the evil charge of the SS. All except General Blaskowitz. He never forgot the horror.

The curtain now rose for the next act.

Friday, May 10, 1940. *Das Oberkommando der Wehrmacht gibt bekannt* (The High Command of the Armed Forces announces): In view of the widening of the war by our enemies onto Belgian and Dutch soil and the resultant threat to the Ruhr area, the German Army attacked at dawn across the western German frontier on a wide front.

This was a triumphant report about an "easy victory."

June 5, 1940. Report on western operations. *Wehrmacht HQ:* Losses of the Wehrmacht, May 10 to June 1.

Heldentot (Died heroically): 10,232 officers, NCOs, and other ranks.

Missing: 8463

Wounded: 42,523 officers, NCOs, and other ranks.

Aircraft lost: 432

The overture to the attack in the west ended quickly. While Poland was being crushed by German panzers, infantry bombers, and Stukas, Britain did little, and France, under its weak Army commander, Gamelin, did even less. The attitude in Britain was curious. No one seemed to wonder why Britain had not launched bombing raids against the Ruhr industrial region, or had not planned an attack on the ground, no matter how limited, while German forces were committed in Poland. There was indeed a British bomber campaign, but the planes dropped propaganda leaflets, not explosives. Channon's November 4 diary entry expressed this inexplicable lack of aggressive spirit. He seemed to believe, along with others in Britain, that attacking was a German prerogative. He wrote, "There is no real war. Hitler is indeed shrewd. Is he trying to bore us into peace?"

One man was certainly not bored. Ribbentrop's enemy Winston Churchill, the First Lord of the Admiralty, planned the first imaginative moves, mainly, an attack through Narvik in Norway on neutral Sweden to deny Sweden's iron ore to Germany. The other Norwegian ports were to be mined to prevent German interference. It was all very Winston, filled with drama and *panache*. He had regained center stage. Unfortunately, some of the plans became known in Berlin and became the excuse Hitler needed: a "pre-emptive" attack on Denmark and Norway was prepared and executed. Denmark, undefended, was invaded on April 9. This gave Hitler airfields to help German ships and troops invade Norway. To help little Norway's six divisions, British, French, and Polish troops were landed on Norwegian soil, and German mountain troops and Marines were in some difficulty until the invasion of the Netherlands and France forced the withdrawal of Allied units for use on that front. Norway surrendered on June 9. The Norwegian Vidkun Quisling, a Nazi leader whose name became synonymous with treason, was superseded as Norway's new chief by Hitler's own man, Gauleiter Josef Terboven of Essen. King Haakon, and many Norwegians with him, fled to England to fight on from there. These, in brief, were the military events of early April 1940.

On the afternoon of May 9, von Ribbentrop called together the heads of the Foreign Ministry's press, broadcast, and interpreter sections and informed them, matter-of-factly, that the attack on the west "between the Swiss frontier and the North Sea" would take place the following morning. He told them just as calmly that the Führer had stated that anyone who allowed word to leak out would be shot.[12]

"I swear to you," said von Ribbentrop, "that I would not be able to save you." The meeting was in the lavish old Presidential Palace farther down the Wilhelmstrasse that had been expensively renovated by Speer as the von Ribbentrops' official residence, at the cost of millions of government marks.

Very late that same night, German Intelligence intercepted a message from the Dutch ambassador to his government warning of the attack. No one knew where the leak had occurred, and von Ribbentrop was worried that the culprit was someone in his ministry. A special detective checked the entire staff, and no one was found. Von Ribbentrop was safe.

On May 10, he gave official notification of the invasion to the Dutch and Belgian ambassadors — while their countries were being attacked. Then he boomed out to the assembled foreign press the declaration that the attack had been launched "to forestall a wild act of desperation on the part of the Allies" by their "new conscienceless leader . . . Churchill."

Winston Churchill, former First Sea Lord, was at last Britain's prime minister, the very Churchill who had ranked second only to Robert Vansittart on the list of Joachim von Ribbentrop's British enemies. Churchill was now promoted to the most hated. Immediately after he announced the German invasion of the Netherlands and Belgium, von Ribbentrop swung to a black mood. He had to listen to his bitter party foe, Joseph Goebbels, read on the radio the very statements von Ribbentrop had just devised for the whole world to hear. How dare Goebbels pre-empt the right of Germany's foreign minister to announce this historical attack of May 10, 1940, the attack by which Adolf Hitler would avenge Germany's defeat and disgrace of 1918? Von Ribbentrop was furious. He screamed at Schmidt that the entire broadcast section of the ministry was to be fired.[13]

Holland and Belgium were only the anterooms of the west. The inner sanctum was France and its army, as well as the Expeditionary Forces of Great Britain on the continent of Europe. Perhaps now Chips Channon and his friends would no longer feel that Hitler was trying to bore them into making peace.

In his turn, buoyed by Germany, Mussolini was ready to take the plunge. François-Poncet, in Rome, was asked to come to the Italian Foreign Ministry. Ciano greeted him formally and said, "Perhaps you can imagine why I have asked you to call on me." A sarcastic François-Poncet replied, "Though I have never thought of myself as particularly intelligent, I am able to grasp that you wish to declare war on us." Reports of this haughty response set off some anti-Ciano glee in Berlin's Foreign Ministry.[14]

Heinrich the train was reactivated for the beginning of the western campaign.[15] It transported the same eminences, Himmler, von Ribbentrop, and Lammers, and their staffs, housed in eight sleeping cars and salon cars and two dining cars that were used as offices. The members of the triumvirate had friendly afternoon teas in the von Ribbentrop salon car. Tea party chatter: Himmler was happy that the Queen of

Holland had not surrendered. It would have been a nuisance if Hitler had had "to be nice to the old lady." Von Ribbentrop said the British "would be more sensible once they had been chased back to their island." He was upset because the Führer's new headquarters, Felsennest, was across the Rhine from *Heinrich,* and that Göring's train, standing in a raid-proof tunnel in the Eifel hills, was closer to Felsennest. Von Ribbentrop was anxious because lately he had not been able to see his Führer often enough. He had managed to visit him at Felsennest only twice.

Meantime, most of the old-time diplomats were recalled from the German embassies in Oslo and The Hague so that they would not embarrass the new military occupation authorities by their judicious presence.

Von Ribbentrop finally got clearance to join Hitler's field headquarters at the luxurious Château d'Ardenne near Dinant. In some ways he would regret leaving *Heinrich.* The hotel, once among the continent's best, had fallen into disrepair. Nothing seemed to work. There was only intermittent water and electricity and absolutely no service.

After the last Brenner Pass meeting, von Ribbentrop had got rid of one of his annoyances, Ambassador Attolico, who had tried so often to preserve the peace. Attolico was transferred to the Vatican, and Dino Alfieri, an old Fascist and a close friend of Ciano's, took his place.

The Germans sliced toward Paris. The French government ran away and settled temporarily in Bordeaux, and on June 17 Marshal Henri Philippe Pétain asked the Spanish ambassador to France, Felix de Lequerica, to mediate a request for a truce. Hitler, accompanied by von Ribbentrop, flew to Munich on June 18–19 to meet with Mussolini, their new fellow warrior, at the Führerbau, where Neville Chamberlain, Édouard Daladier, and the two dictators had negotiated the Sudetenland hand-over in 1938. Schmidt translated into Italian for a surprisingly pacific Hitler, who claimed that he wanted to offer France gentle armistice terms. Mussolini, suddenly ferocious, insisted on the surrender of the French fleet, but Hitler rejected this "energetically." "If you make that demand, the entire French fleet will defect to the British." Hitler also refused when Mussolini asked for a joint German-Italian negotiating team to deal with the French. Later he told von Ribbentrop, "Why should I burden our negotiations with Franco-Italian animosities?"[16]

The Führer was clearly in the midst of one of the periods of calm after his furies. His serenity manifested itself in many areas. He had interfered directly with the Army High Command and ordered the troops to hold up the attack on Dunkirk. Now he said, "Why destroy the British Empire? It still represents a great force for world order." And he was almost calm about the Jews. During the discussion of France's colonies and their future, he asked Mussolini, "Why not begin an Israelitic [*sic*] state in Madagascar?"

At von Ribbentrop's instructions, this Madagascar idea was later promoted and pursued at length by some senior officials of the Foreign Ministry. Originally, it was conceived of by the eccentric German Orientalist Paul de Lagarde, at the University of Göttingen. He had been a pupil of one of the Grimm brothers. His convoluted racial theories were later adopted in part by Alfred Rosenberg and also became part of the Nazi credo. His plan to create a Jewish island-nation on French colonial Madagascar, which was being investigated by the Nazis, eventually foundered because of the Royal Navy's blockade, the Vichy government's reluctance, and the difficulties of the German Army in Russia.

Despite his bluster, Mussolini had come to Munich with empty hands. When the Germans occupied Paris on June 14, the Duce instructed Marshal Pietro Badoglio to launch a June 18 attack on the south of France. It was a disaster. His troops, commanded by the Italian Crown Prince Umberto, got stuck in the mountains and stopped at the small Riviera town of Mentone. Mussolini was not in a position to demand much at Munich, although he wanted Nice, Corsica, and Tunisia. The performance of his troops had been abysmal.[17]

Taking his lead from the Führer, von Ribbentrop comported himself as a moderate, temperate, peace-seeking victor. When Ciano, according to his memoirs, asked von Ribbentrop whether there would be more war, von Ribbentrop immediately said, "Peace."[18]

On the night of Thursday, June 13, two French officers and a trumpeter had met a German delegation at Sarcelles, a few miles north of Paris, to negotiate a truce for Paris, which had been declared an open city (to the relief of the French and the Germans). The French government moved to Vichy, the old spa. On July 10, by a vote of 569 to 80, they gave ruling power to old Marshal Pétain, who then administered about 40 percent of France. It became known as the Vichy government and was entirely dependent on the Germans.

The fall of Paris began one of the strangest chapters in von Ribbentrop's career. Although he was very much in evidence at the signing of the armistice on June 22 in Compiègne, he did not set foot in Paris during the entire German occupation of France.[19] Visiting a conquered

Paris should have been his second greatest personal triumph. (The first would have been to go to a conquered London.) How much it might have meant to Annelies and Joachim von Ribbentrop to appear, victorious, in Paris. Yet, for unknown reasons, he was one of the few top Nazis to stay away from the occupied city. The overjoyed Göring made innumerable art-hunting trips to the Luftwaffe's Parisian headquarters in the Rothschild house on Avenue Marigny and to the Palais Luxembourg, where he kept a suite. But von Ribbentrop stayed away. Perhaps it was Adolf Hitler's own unexplained reluctance to be in Paris that influenced von Ribbentrop.

Hitler visited once, on June 23, the morning after the signing at Compiègne. He was driven on a dawn tour of the main tourist attractions. His caravan of open Mercedes cars carrying his military aides, and also the architect Speer and the "court" sculptor Arno Breker, rushed around an empty, early morning Paris. When they reached the Opéra, Hitler told everyone he had studied the building's plans as a young man and admired it extravagantly, "Glouglou," the Opéra's caretaker, switched on the stage lights for the Germans but turned down a tip. By noontime Adolf Hitler was back in his field headquarters at Bruly de Pêche in Belgium.

Few *citoyens* had followed Charles de Gaulle into exile. A handful took a more lethal escape; the mayor of Clichy, Maurice Naile, and the head of the American Hospital, Count de Martel, both committed suicide.

The apex of von Ribbentrop's 1940 must have been his witnessing the armistice with France. The ceremony took place in a clearing in the woods of Compiègne, using 2419-D, the salon car of Marshal Foch, where Germany had hurriedly signed the surrender papers of 1918.

Hitler, Göring, Hess, and von Ribbentrop sat like ramrods in the crowded car. The photo has often been printed. The actual signing was done by the mustachioed General Wilhelm Keitel and the bitter-faced French General Charles Huntziger. Part of the truce agreement committed France to hand over its many German exiles, a stroke of the pen that doomed thousands of German-Jewish refugees who had fled to the safety of France.

Von Ribbentrop's new Paris representative, Emissary Otto Abetz, stood outside in the clearing in front of the railroad car with a small group of friends he had brought from Paris following an "armistice" luncheon at the barely reopened German Embassy on the rue de Lille. Abetz told his guests that he had already met with fifty French politicians, forty-nine of whom had asked him for extra gasoline or coupons or special permits. One had asked him about the fate of France.[20]

If Abetz was swamped with favor seekers, how the Parisians would have fed the von Ribbentrops' self-esteem. They would have been the toast of *le tout Paris*. If one reads the names of those who followed Marshal Pétain's request to collaborate with the new masters, it is difficult to understand so many claims of "resistance." Or perhaps it is human nature to keep on living as normally as possible, even after *l'affreuse chose c'est réalisée*, as the Paris police prefect had called it in his diary.

The first German commander, General Bogislav von Studnitz, opened events by giving a reception at the Hôtel Crillon for the dignitaries of the city. Next came a victory parade on Champs Élysées, which was less than formal, an entertainment rather than a drama. Later, standing in front of the American Embassy on the Place de la Concorde, Robert Murphy, the deputy to anti-German American Ambassador William Bullitt, watched as motorized German Army columns passed by. One stopped, and a young German lieutenant walked over and asked Murphy for a good hotel. Murphy suggested several, as if the German officer were a tourist. Shortly after, Murphy was sent to the Crillon to "see what was happening." As a neutral diplomat, he was welcomed by General von Studnitz. The German Army made a big show of courtesy and manners.

Many Parisians who had fled the city before the truce now returned, but some of the famous internationalists who considered Paris their home left for the duration. The Windsors hurried from their house on Boulevard Suchet. The Aga Khan, James Joyce, Daisy Fellowes, Peggy Guggenheim, the Princess de Polignac, Gertrude Stein and Alice Toklas, René Clair, Louis Jouvet, Jean Renoir, André Maurois, Fernand Léger, Elsa Maxwell, Sir Charles and Lady Mendl, Vladimir Nabokov, Marc Chagall, André Malraux, Henri Matisse, André Gide, had all left for the unoccupied zone or for other countries.

But Paris was by no means emptied of the famed, the mighty, the notorious. De Gaulle was broadcasting from London, but his appeals did not stop Sacha Guitry or the dancer Serge Lifar from being acclaimed by the Germans. Lifar performed for Hitler, Goebbels, and Göring during three trips to Germany. The couturière Coco Chanel was having an affair with a very senior German Nazi.* She "holed up" (as the historian David Pryce-Jones reported it) at the Ritz with

---

*The consensus points to Walter Schellenberg, the Gestapo–SD espionage head.

her National Socialist paramour and appeared only occasionally at parties to spew forth anti-Semitic tirades.[21]

Perhaps it is fair to offer the names of some who stayed in Paris during the occupation, if only to balance Britain's prewar appeasers. Colette, Cocteau, Georges Duhamel, Georges Simenon, and Jean Giraudoux functioned as before. Braque, Vlaminck, and Laurencin painted, as did Picasso, who returned to Paris during the occupation and remained there until the Allied victory. Jean Berard stated that "Fascist and Hitlerian doctrines are today championing civilization."[22]

Herbert von Karajan came often to Paris to conduct, but Wilhelm Furtwängler, the most patrician of Germany's conductors, refused to come while there was a military occupation.

Mistinguett, Edvige Feuillère, and Edith Piaf were performing in Paris, as were Maurice Chevalier and Piaf's newest protégé, Yves Montand.

In literature and the arts, the American Sylvia Beach continued to run her bookshop, Shakespeare and Company, where Joyce was once published and Hemingway had often roamed. Also among those propagating Franco-German friendship were Marie-Laure de Noailles, the Duchesse d'Harcourt, and Marie Louise Bousquet, who became the postwar doyenne of the Paris office of New York's *Harper's Bazaar*.[23]

The couture was open for business. Balenciaga, Nina Ricci, Paul Poiret, Lucien Lelong, and Jacques Fath catered to rich clients, mostly German.[24] Of course the House of Chanel was open.

The Hotel Majestic (later General Eisenhower's Supreme Headquarters) became German Army headquarters; 72 Avenue Foch was turned into Gestapo and SD offices. Maxim's was run by the management of Berlin's Horcher restaurant. Much seemed to be functioning as usual in non-Jewish Paris. Porfirio Rubirosa, the Santo Domingan playboy-diplomat who later married, successively, Doris Duke and Barbara Hutton, was giving all-night parties to the music of Django Reinhardt's jazz (Le Hot Club of France) and selling visas to Santo Domingo for much money to wealthy refugees who needed to escape from the Nazis.

Otto Abetz, who, at thirty-seven, was von Ribbentrop's careful choice for "ambassador" to occupied France, was a believer in Franco-German amity. A francophile since he was a very young man, he had taught art, knew France well, and spoke excellent French. He was also married to a Frenchwoman, Suzanne de Bruyker. Von Ribbentrop had recruited Abetz into the Büro before the war and sent him to Paris, attached to the embassy. The French expelled him in 1939 with vague accusations of espionage, which brought a storm of unpleasant newspaper publicity. His diplomatic status had saved him from jail. Now, back in Paris, Abetz understood he was to watch over von Ribbentrop's interests, although running occupied France was actually the business of the military and of the many French collaborators who — collaborated.

The SD had their own harsh job: the Nazi-style boundaries of everyday life, the racial laws, the political consensus. Abetz's function eventually evolved into becoming the catalyst for society, the arts, industry, education, and, above all, propaganda. He assembled a team of journalists and academics. In the former German Embassy, where he entertained often and in regal style, he soon became known as King Otto I.

Otto Abetz was one of the few German functionaries who admired and respected von Ribbentrop. He blamed most of the foreign minister's failings on the immense pressures and endless tasks that were part of the 1936–1943 period. By the summer of 1942, von Ribbentrop told Abetz that he preferred separate field headquarters, because being near Hitler was "too strenuous and abrasive."[25] But Abetz's memoirs throw little light on the puzzling reason for von Ribbentrop's absence from Paris.

Occupied France, especially Paris, became a hunting ground for Nazi and French opportunists, who indulged their conceits and vanities. Typical was Göring, with his collection of stolen art assembled in the Jeu de Paume, much of it taken from Jews and Gaullists. In Göring's view, "They are a defeated nation. Let Herr Abetz worry about their sensibilities."

Alfred Rosenberg, licensed by Adolf Hitler to do so, conducted his own hunt for art. Rosenberg's inventory was meant to be used as a bargaining tool with the French. By 1944, 21,900 pieces of art had been "curated" by Rosenberg's staff.[26]

In 1940, the occupation was still in its infancy. Much horror, debauch, and degradation, some of it self-inflicted, was yet to come. In 1940, there remained a semblance of German "correctness" and good manners; the true evils of collaboration were not yet apparent. The line between unwilling acceptance and enthusiastic, self-promoting cooperation with the Germans had not yet been crossed. The mass deportation of Jews, the murder of hostages, the recruiting of French volunteers for the SS, and all the other French debasements were still in their cocoons. Some of it began with the Statut des Juifs, issued on

October 3, 1940, in Vichy, which legislated, in effect, that Jews were second-class French citizens. Some earlier regulations cleared the way for newspapers to attack Jews and limited the rights of naturalized French citizens.

By July of 1940, three thousand Alsatian Jews were deported from their homes to the unoccupied zone.[27] On August 8 a German police major, Walter Krüger, sent fourteen hundred German-Jewish refugees from the occupied north of France into the unoccupied zone and "freedom." They were arrested by the Vichy police and interned at Saint Cyprien on the Spanish border. Sadly and not surprisingly, the former Germans, all Jews, appealed to Berlin to "save them from humiliation by the French enemy."

In October 1940, 1504 Jews were rounded up in the German provinces of Baden and Saarpfalz, and dumped into unoccupied France at Lyons. Each was allowed only one hand parcel. According to German records, the oldest deportee was ninety-seven, and hundreds were over sixty. Many were children. This, according to the historians Michael Marrus and Robert Paxton, was the beginning of a plan to dump 270,000 Jews from Germany and the former Austria into unoccupied Vichy France. It also marked the founding of the notorious French concentration camp at Gurs, near the Spanish border. Sealed trains of cattle cars delivered detainees, some already dead, to Pau, the nearest railroad station. Pau was the little resort town where, in 1938, René Dreyfus, the French auto-racing champion of Jewish descent, had defeated the Mercedes-Benz racing team to the wild applause of the French spectators.[28] Now, dead Jews were unloaded from cattle cars where the French had once cheered themselves hoarse.

Unfortunately for those who wanted to think of France as a reluctant victim, these acts were committed under the auspices of a new "nationalist" (read fascist) government. Among its characteristics were hatred for Britain, disdain for de Gaulle and his followers, and a frantic search for union and equal status with Hitler's plenipotentiaries north of the demarcation line in occupied France. There were acts of compassion and decency in Vichy France, but they were relatively few.

While Abetz in Paris tried to further his chief's interests among the other officers of the Wehrmacht, party, SS, Luftwaffe, and Propaganda, von Ribbentrop became part of one of the most bizarre schemes of the war: persuading the Duke and Duchess of Windsor to lend their presence, if not their support, to the German cause. It is even possible that the aim was to place the former Edward VIII once more on the throne of Great Britain, after Britain was invaded and defeated. But any use of the Windsors, no matter how passive, was the sort of laughable plan the Berliners called a *Schnapps Idee* (a notion found at the bottom of a glass of brandy).

Having left Paris to avoid the Germans, and unwilling to deal with the vagaries of "unoccupied" France under Pétain and Laval, the Windsors arrived in neutral Spain on Sunday, June 2. It was the duke's forty-sixth birthday.[29]

A rudimentary explanation of Franco Spain can be given only in broad outline. General Franco seemed neutral, neither pro-Axis nor pro-Allies. He was careful and judicious. The second most powerful man in Spain, the interior minister and a Franco in-law, Ramón Serrano Suñer, was pro-Axis, but Spain's foreign minister, Colonel Juan Beigbeder, was in sympathy with the Allies. Representing the Nazi side in the seething, spy-ridden, rumor-swilling Spanish capital was the German ambassador, Eberhard von Stohrer, lukewarm toward the Nazis, disliked by von Ribbentrop, despised by Hitler. Von Stohrer's beautiful and unfaithful wife, Marie Ursula, had great influence with certain gentlemen of Spanish society. On the Allied side was the new British ambassador, a former Chamberlain colleague, Sir Samuel Hoare, a man who seemed to be so stuffy that he was described as "descended from a long line of maiden aunts." He was, however, an accomplished politician and diplomat. After presenting his credentials to Franco, he wrote about the Caudillo, "There was obviously more in him than met the eye, or how else could this young officer of Jewish origin, little influence, and unimpressive personality have risen to the highest post in the State?"[30]

Spain was waiting particularly to see some signs of the future, although the Germans had squashed France and the British had fled for their lives from Dunkirk. Britain's long history should have been proof to Spain of her resilience, but unless Churchill could convince Spain that Britain still had the will to fight, Spain would ally itself with the Axis. Sir Samuel Hoare's brief was brutally simple: convince the Spaniards that Britain will fight and fight and fight!

The duke's arrival could have been either godsend or disaster, depending on his frame of mind and strength of devotion to his country. The duke had been treated coldly by his brother, King George VI. The duke was also in search of a decent war job, and he wanted the royal family to accept his American duchess as a part of the House of Windsor. How would he behave?

Ambassador Hoare need not have worried. The duke, who was popular in Spain and was related to the House of Bourbon through his great-grandmother, Queen Victoria, played his role to perfection. At a vast embassy party on Saturday, June 29, for a thousand prominent Spaniards and members of the foreign Diplomatic Corps, the duke exuded confidence and reassurance about the future of Great Britain. No matter how deep the divisions between himself and Buckingham Palace, his duty was clear and his loyalties were unshaken. Any doubts were carefully tucked away behind his sun-tanned, smiling face and well-tailored front.

However, Madrid was Madrid, and Madrileños gossiped. The duke would grumble in private, and some of his old Spanish friends would tell about it. Among the "leakers" was his old friend Miguel Primo de Rivera, a Spanish government official. The duke was sick of the close surveillance by the British Secret Service. The duke was distressed by his bad treatment and the snubbing of his wife. The duke was upset that his friend Winston Churchill had not found him important war work in Britain and had sloughed him off with the governorship of the Bahamas. Perhaps the duke's private grumblings were justified, but nothing would lead him into public disloyalty.

Three days after the British Embassy party, German troops paid "fraternal" visits to several Spanish border towns, and Foreign Minister Beigbeder, still sympathetic to the Allied cause and prodded by the British ambassador, launched a firm protest to Berlin.[31] The Germans withdrew their military version of innocent tourism, but the danger was too near. The Windsors prepared to go to Portugal as quickly as possible, waiting only for the departure of the Duke of Kent from Lisbon. Kent, the Duke of Windsor's favorite and youngest brother, was in Portugal for a "show the flag" visit, and Windsor would no doubt have loved to see him, for the first time in three years, but his presence in Portugal might have interfered with Kent's mission. Again, the Duke of Windsor knew his duty.

On July 2, Kent left Portugal, and that same day the Windsors set out for Portugal. Their destination was Estoril and the seaside home of their friend, the banker Dr. Ricardo Espiritu Santo e Silva, a great British sympathizer, well known in London Intelligence circles as the "Holy Ghost." The Portuguese dictator, Antonio Salazar, was also pronouncedly pro-British, so the Windsors could feel safe in Portugal. To help confuse the Germans, Beigbeder had circulated a rumor that the duke would later return to Spain to hunt. Now the Windsors could relax temporarily while the duke continued his long-distance struggle with London to be assigned important war work.

The German ambassador to Portugal, Baron Oswald von Hoynigen-Huene, a distinguished and worldly diplomat, sent a most unlikely telegram to von Ribbentrop; perhaps Hoynigen-Huene wanted
to ingratiate himself with the foreign minister. He reported that the
duke was in Portugal to postpone his undesirable appointment to the
Bahamas, that war could have been avoided had he been King, that
bombing would make Britain sue for peace, that he was being kept
from England because he was on the side of compromise.[32] Perhaps
Hoynigen-Huene indulged in the old diplomatic ploy of "looking
busy" by sending gossip-filled, confidential dispatches to his ministry.
This time, the idle gossip raised hell. The cable reached von Ribbentrop at Fuschl, and he swallowed it completely. He immediately telephoned von Stohrer in Madrid: "Persuade Windsor to stay in Spain.
Keep him there. Tell him of peace efforts. Ask his help. Tell him he is
to be assassinated in the Bahamas."

Von Stohrer saw Serrano Suñer, who was willing to send Primo de
Rivera to invite Windsor back to hunt in Spain and to warn him of a
Bahamas plot. Serrano Suñer thought the whole thing a bit silly, but
he was willing to help von Ribbentrop in this trivial matter to defuse
their many other tensions.

The next to get involved was Walter Schellenberg, back from Paris
and Chanel, Heydrich's chief of espionage and foreign counter-intelli-
gence. Schellenberg, a former medical and law student, was a crudely
handsome thirty-year-old, multilingual protégé of Heydrich's. Schellenberg was a roué and a talented intelligence operative.

In his memoirs, Schellenberg told how one day he heard the "sono-
rous" voice of von Ribbentrop on the phone: "My dear fellow, would
you please come to see me right now? No, I cannot give you details
over the phone!"[33]

Anxious to avoid jealousy, Schellenberg first cleared the visit with
his wolf-faced chief, Heydrich, who called von Ribbentrop an idiot
but told Schellenberg to find out the details. A grave von Ribbentrop,
after outlining all the usual theories about why the Duke of Windsor
had been dropped from British favor, said that the duke now was
virtually a prisoner of the Secret Service, eager to be free. He then
announced that Hitler thought the duke could be offered a sum of
fifty million Swiss francs over twenty years to sustain his friendly
relations with Germany. He could live in a neutral country like Switzerland.

The British Secret Service was to be prevented by force from interfering with this plan. Should the duke seem to hesitate, he was to be
persuaded to "help things along," if necessary, with some force. When

Schellenberg asked about the source that reported the duke's dissatisfaction, he was told "the highest Spanish circles."

Von Ribbentrop then flatly announced, "This order is now given to you by the Führer. You will carry out the mission."

Minutes later, on an extension phone, Schellenberg heard the unmistakable gravel voice of Adolf Hitler tell von Ribbentrop, "Schellenberg must be sure to gauge the duchess's attitude (*Frau Herzogin*). She has much influence on the duke."

Schellenberg cleared the mission with a skeptical Heydrich and immediately flew to Spain; even Heydrich could not abort a Führer-ordered mission. In Madrid von Stohrer confirmed rumors about the duke's unhappiness with the Bahamas job. He offered to introduce Schellenberg to Spanish social circles so that he could get his own reading of the story. But most of all, von Stohrer poured out his complaints about von Ribbentrop. The Herr Minister hounded him each week to urge Spain to join the war, but the Spaniards were in deep economic trouble and unable to jump into the fray. Von Stohrer had been instructed to treat the Spaniards with "sovereign hauteur" because of their lack of comradeship. How could he now woo them?

However, none of this was Schellenberg's problem. He went to Lisbon, where he made contact with an old associate, a professional espionage agent who was Japanese. Schellenberg needed the details about the duke's living quarters in the borrowed home of the Holy Ghost in Estoril. The Japanese agent was brilliant; Schellenberg got all the details. From then on, not a single word uttered by the duke went unreported. All the house servants were "bought."

Schellenberg also met with Hoynigen-Huene, the chic ambassador whose gossip had set the whole thing in motion and who now quaked at the thought of violence or any breach in Portuguese-German relations. Totally convinced that the entire mission was nonsense, Schellenberg, with the help of his Japanese colleague, faked a few quiet scare tactics, knowing they would not work. A stone was thrown through the window. A letter "from an admirer" was sent, warning the ducal pair of the "murderous" British Secret Service, of a bomb on the ship to the Bahamas, of an assassination attempt in Nassau. Of course, there were no results. The duke was made of firmer stuff. Although the duke still argued by letter with Churchill and sent back two flying boats that had been dispatched to Estoril to return the Windsors to Britain, he finally decided to accept the Bahamas governorship. "Poor Bahamas," Lord Halifax wrote to Sir Samuel Hoare, his ambassador in Madrid.

The whole sorry affair almost came to a boil when a telegram ordered Schellenberg to "prepare for abduction." Fortunately, Schellenberg seemed to have been spotted by the British Secret Service. Guards were tripled, and his Portuguese contacts refused to help him any further. He reported the setbacks to Berlin and was instructed to "use his own judgment."[34]

Having wriggled off the hook, he returned to Berlin to face von Ribbentrop, who said, "The Führer was disappointed but approved of your decision to let the matter drop." Later, Heydrich shrugged and said Schellenberg should never have accepted the mission. During his trial at Nürnberg in 1946, Schellenberg found out "that no one in British Intelligence knew of his presence in Portugal," although that is most unlikely.[35]

Thus ended a silly episode after the many cruel ones of 1940. The last telegram sent by Schellenberg from Portugal was "Willy [code name for Windsor] not willing" (*Willi will nicht*).

On July 19, 1940, von Ribbentrop alerted everyone in the Foreign Ministry that Hitler would deliver a speech in the Reichstag that was to contain an "offer of peace."

It contained nothing but empty verbiage. "I speak as a victor, not as a victim, and I appeal to reason . . ." No concrete proposal, not even the suggestion of a plan. (The speech was soon forgotten, but Paul Schmidt introduced the new radio technique of voiceover translation while the speech itself was heard in the background. It is still a popular form, used for many of today's television speeches.)

In a broad sense, the speech may have contained little of substance, but for Joachim von Ribbentrop and Annelies, it was Nirvana. Hitler said, "I cannot finish this day of honor without thanking the man who made my plans into realities through years of loyal, unceasing, and self-sacrificing work. The name of Party Comrade von Ribbentrop is for all time linked with political rise of the German nation." Was this a job-well-done or the gold watch given before retirement?

The Hungarians and the Romanians were feuding again. So on August 30 von Ribbentrop and Ciano returned to Vienna for another session of "judging" Hungarian-Romanian frontier demands. The urgent matter for Hitler and Mussolini was to make sure that Romania's oilfields were secure for aircraft fuel. "All I need," Hitler had told von Ribbentrop and Ciano at the Berghof, "is two weeks of good flying weather to wreck the British fleet and prepare the invasion."

New borders were drawn in Vienna, and, fatefully, Germany and

Italy now "guaranteed the integrity of the Romanian frontier." This would not please the Russians, who had already occupied some small Romanian islands in the Danube delta. Germany also sent "training battalions" to Romania. Tension was rising between the unconventional partners of August 23, 1939.

Von Ribbentrop's persistence was famous. Franco's lack of enthusiasm did not prevent von Ribbentrop from assuring Mussolini in Rome, on September 19 and 20, that Spain would soon enter the war.[36] He obviously wished to ignore the only valid signal to come out of the "Willy" embarrassment: Franco was not about to rush to the German-Italian side.

In the same euphoric flow of wishful thinking, von Ribbentrop assured the Duce that the invasion of Britain was imminent, and would be so easily performed that a single German division would cause British defenses to collapse. Ciano reported this exact sentence, and Schmidt noted in his memoirs that this was a typical Ribbentrop statement and that he, Schmidt, had translated hundreds like it. "I got the impression that most people no longer took him seriously." Obviously, Mussolini was one of them. He looked at von Ribbentrop "amusedly and incredulously."

Serrano Suñer, about to become Spanish foreign minister, came to Berlin late in September to represent his side of "the Spanish question" and to prove that von Ribbentrop had been wildly optimistic. From Hitler and von Ribbentrop's point of view the key was the infuriating lack of enthusiasm Franco showed for combat against England and her empire. Schmidt reported the scene in von Ribbentrop's office in front of the windows giving onto the old park behind the minister's renovated Wilhelmstrasse office. A map of France's colonies was set on an easel, and what von Ribbentrop said to Serrano Suñer boiled down to "Do help yourself to some colonies!" The visitor was not shy. He immediately chose Oran in Algeria, all of Morocco, sizable stretches of desert, and the French West African colony of Rio de Oro. Von Ribbentrop was "selling merchandise he did not own." All he asked for in return were some German submarine support bases in Spain; Serrano Suñer agreed to only a few.

There now followed a diplomatic maneuver that was to become a millstone around Germany's neck. In Berlin on September 27, 1940, the seventh year of National Socialism, the seventeenth year of Fascism, the ninth month of the fifteenth year of Emperor Hirohito's reign, the tripartite military agreement between Germany, Italy, and Japan was signed. Within fourteen months it would force Germany to declare war on the United States, certainly not von Ribbentrop's foremost wish in December 1941, following the "date which will live in infamy." Nor did Germany think she would have to send General Erwin Rommel to Africa. So much for the advantages of alliances with Japan and Italy.

Another Brenner Pass, two-train, traffic-jamming meeting took place on October 4.[37] In a three-hour monologue, Hitler told Mussolini about his plans for the fate of the British Empire and his quandary. Where to begin? Should he attack them in the islands or in the Mediterranean? Once more, Mussolini was only a listener, not an answerer. He could have asked embarrassing questions about the Luftwaffe. But at least this time he was kept informed.

A four thousand-mile trip lay ahead for Hitler and von Ribbentrop during October. Their purposes: to persuade the reluctant Franco to join the Axis powers, to persuade the reluctant Pétain to join the fight against Britain, to persuade hungry Mussolini to cancel his rumored plans to attack Greece.

The entire trip was a diplomatic shipwreck. On October 23 Hitler awaited Franco at the small railroad station at Hendaye, on the border between Spain and France. Franco was an hour late, but the good weather kept Hitler cheerful, which, in turn, cheered von Ribbentrop. When Franco finally appeared, at 3 P.M., Hitler offered him Gibraltar and even the conquest of its fortress by Germany Army specialists. He also offered some African colonies. The shrunken, somber, terse Franco was not interested. Speaking in a low voice, he catalogued all his own problems, from food to fuel. He pointed out that he would have to defend an immense coastline, would lose the Canary Islands, and, as a Spaniard, could never permit foreign troops to take the fortress of Gibraltar. North Africa would be immensely difficult to attack. As an old North Africa soldier, he knew this. Britain might fall, but she would surely move her government and her fleet to North America and fight on. He said all this in, as Schmidt described it, a "quiet, near-Islamic singsong."

An irritated Hitler stood up and, in a typical display of temper, said there was no use continuing the conversation. Then he sat down, but by then the meeting had virtually ended. With the dictators dead in the water, von Ribbentrop and Serrano Suñer tried to carry on some dialogue in von Ribbentrop's private train, but this time there was no offer of French colonies. Instead, Spain was told it could have them once the French were compensated with captured British colonies. It all fell on deaf Spanish ears. There followed a formal dinner in Hitler's special banquet dining car, with its brilliant indirect lighting and luxurious appointments. At table there was some desultory talk. The two dictators' trains then left, and von Ribbentrop's stayed behind. The next morning, Schmidt reported, an infuriated and short-tempered von Ribbentrop broke off what remained of any working structure with Serrano Suñer.

The angry foreign minister then rushed to Bordeaux and barely reached the Pétain meeting. The weather was foul, and Hitler's own pilot, the bibulous Captain Bauer, a veteran of many stormy landings, only just managed to get von Ribbentrop and Schmidt safely onto the runway at Tours. From there, the two men rushed to the Führer's train at Montoire.

Sitting opposite Hitler, the old marshal seemed tall and austere and assured, while little Laval was unsure and fidgety. Hitler went into his monologue. France would have to reconquer her own colonies if they had switched to de Gaulle, and protect the ones that had not. "We have already won this war," he said. "Either France or England will have to pay the costs. It is up to you to put the burden on England."

Pétain quickly answered that France was not in a position to fight a war; he sensed that Hitler was trying to enlist France to fight Britain. Pétain asked for a formal peace agreement with Germany "so that two million French prisoners of war can return to their families."[38] Laval added that France would help in every way except fighting.

Hitler did not acknowledge Pétain's request, and Pétain would not speak about joining the war against Britain. Schmidt claimed that on the same day, October 24, while Pétain resisted Hitler's urgent suggestions, an emissary of Pétain's, a Professor Rougier, was with Churchill in London. Rougier assured Churchill that France would never willingly do anything dishonorable toward her former ally. As the two gloom-filled special trains rolled back to Berlin, the third purpose of the trip was being negated. Word came of Mussolini's foolhardy attack on Greece. The Duce's not forewarning the Führer was revenge for the cavalier way his German allies usually dealt with him. On to Italy! Perhaps they could still persuade the Duce to draw back. The Alps were already covered with snow, not a good sign for the attacking Italian troops in mountainous Greece on the other side of the Adriatic. In Florence, the strutting Duce told them that the "victorious Italian Army has crossed the Albanian border into Greece," and he meant, *Basta!* Nothing was to be done. Hitler heard the news with a grim smile. He was not delighted but kept it to himself. He and von Ribbentrop left for Berlin, back across the snowy Alps, with three diplomatic debacles to show for their four thousand miles. If Hitler was grim, von Ribbentrop was even more so. The process of diplomacy seemed to crumble.

Von Ribbentrop was not in a victorious mood when the most important meetings of 1940 began. On the morning of November 12, a train bearing Molotov and his staff pulled into Anhalter station in Berlin. Schmidt, there to keep the record of the coming conference, drew a stern glance from von Ribbentrop when he suggested that the Russian national anthem, the Communist Internationale, be sung by many of the Berliners lining the square in front of the station. It was best forgotten how many Nazis were Communists long before Hitler came to power.

Von Ribbentrop need not have worried. The only music was a martial tune played while Molotov inspected the honor guard. The station was decked with hammer-and-sickle emblems and banners, and the ceremony was the usual routine, including the open-car caravan into the city. But there was no cheering, because no one had "instructed" the crowd to show enthusiasm. (The young Foreign Ministry wags called Wilhelmstrasse, often lined with organized "cheerers," the Via Spontana.)

The first conference was in von Ribbentrop's office in the former Presidential Palace. He was forthcoming, but Molotov was laconic, and his associate, the Kremlin's German specialist, Vladimir Dekanozov, was grim.

Von Ribbentrop opened with "England is beaten. It is only a question of time until she admits it. The Axis powers are trying to end the war as quickly as possible."

Next, he suggested friendship with Japan, which was now looking south, not west, and would spend decades colonizing Asia. Germany too was looking south to Africa, not east (toward Russia, as Hitler had said in *Mein Kampf*). Why would Russia not look south toward the open sea? "Which open sea?" asked Molotov. "The Gulf of Persia and the Red Sea," said von Ribbentrop. He next brought up a new agreement about the Dardanelles and then an invitation for the Soviet Union to join the three-nation Axis as a fourth, the treaty perhaps to be signed in Moscow by Germany, Italy, Japan, and Russia. Finally, a suggestion that there be rapprochement between Chiang Kai-shek and Japan, mediated by Germany.

Molotov responded to none of these schemes. However, he asked for the meaning, precisely, of the Greater East Asia Co-Prosperity Sphere, which Japan had recently proclaimed.

"It has nothing to do," hurried von Ribbentrop, "with the Russian sphere."

The gong rang for a late breakfast.

End of round one.

The afternoon discussion, this time with Adolf Hitler, was a crushing series of questions and answers, a fierce and cold debate about conflicts of interest openly displayed and resented by both disputants. From Finland to Romania, from the Baltic to the Dardanelles, Hitler and Molotov disagreed on every subject and their tone was frigid. Von Ribbentrop was silent.

That night there was a banquet at the lavish old Russian Embassy on Unter den Linden. The meal was cut short by air-raid sirens, and von Ribbentrop, shepherding Molotov to his own shelter, had the embarrassment of explaining why British bombers were overhead while "England had already lost the war." Molotov was unimpressed by von Ribbentrop's explanations.

Von Ribbentrop's greatest achievement, the Nonaggression Pact with Soviet Russia of August 1939, began to unravel, and Adolf Hitler found himself once more on old, familiar ground: hating Bolshevists. No doubt he felt relieved, and no doubt von Ribbentrop felt devastated.

Besides Greece, where the Italians were now floundering, 1940 brought yet another Mussolini-engineered disaster. Aiming at one of Napoleon's geographic goals, and eager to rival his Austro-Teutonic competitor, the Duce sought Cairo, the Suez Canal, and the Nile. Across the Mediterranean in Libya was Mussolini's army of 200,000 men, commanded by one of Italy's best, the tall Marshal Rodolfo Graziani. "Attack!" said the Duce. "Bring me Cairo." And Graziani had attacked in September, pushing east toward Egypt and Britain's troops. They did not get far. By October they were bogged down only fifty miles inside Egypt near the Mediterranean at Sidi Barrani, with hundreds of miles still to go to Cairo. There they said they would stay until 1941, "waiting for spring." Mussolini turned down Hitler's offer of German troops.

Hitler, still furious about the Greek adventure, took offense. In November he told Keitel, "No help in Greece. No help in Libya."[39] By Christmas, General Sir Richard O'Connor, the British commander in North Africa, rammed the Italians back to Bardia inside the Libyan border. O'Connor was no great military star, but he was good enough to stop the Italians with ease. Later, General Erwin Rommel seized O'Connor's command vehicle (along with O'Connor). He named it Mammut (Mammoth) and used it all through the African campaign. O'Connor's truck became as famous as Rommel's captured British goggles.

By December the Italians were hanging on the ropes, and by January 22 they had lost Tobruk, fifty miles inside the Libyan border.

The best thing to happen to the von Ribbentrops during 1940 came in the very last week. Their youngest son, Barthold, named after an earlier Ribbentrop ancestor, was born, on December 26. His godfather was the Führer. In most other ways, for the von Ribbentrops 1940 had been severe and filled with somber signals, though it is unlikely that Annelies and Joachim von Ribbentrop wanted to heed them.

12

1941–1942

Unsung Heroes Doing
the Reich's Dirty Work

FOR THE PROTAGONISTS, most views of international politics were myopically self-serving. Von Ribbentrop began the new year disgusted with the Italians and furious with the "ungrateful" French. His view of the Pétain meeting at Montoire differed substantially from that of Schmidt, who had portrayed "its abrasiveness." Von Ribbentrop's memoirs reported it as a peaceful German offer of help to Pétain, open and candid. In von Ribbentrop's hindsight, Serrano Suñer lusted for French colonies while he, von Ribbentrop, backed by the Führer, had protected the French against the avaricious Spaniard. How ungrateful the French had been! In his memoirs, he contrasted Germany's "honorable" behavior toward the French leadership with the unchivalrous treatment later accorded the senior Nazis at Nürnberg. He also insisted that it was at *his* suggestion that the body of Napoleon's beloved son, L'Aiglon, was transferred from Germany to be entombed next to L'Empereur in the Invalides. It was a gesture meant to demonstrate Hitler's gallantry.

The arrival of the SD and the Gestapo at 72 Avenue Foch removed any notions of chivalry as soon as they began their cruel business. To von Ribbentrop's annoyance, Pétain had canceled his promised attendance in early December 1940 at a ceremony at Napoleon's tomb, and Otto Abetz was delighted that Hitler had allowed the ceremony to go on despite the marshal's intransigence. There seemed to be no overt petulance or opposition by most French citizens. Obviously the many French *collaborateurs* had clouded Abetz's vision.[1]

The rattled von Ribbentrop then had to face the Duce's undesirable invasion of Greece and the harm it had done to Germany's friendship with Yugoslavia. Seeing an opportunity to woo the Yugoslavs in February 1941, Roosevelt even sent Colonel "Wild Bill" Donovan to Belgrade.[2] When the angered Yugoslavs finally joined the Tripartite Alliance on March 24, 1941, it looked, Hitler said, "like a funeral."[3]

More trouble: the Japanese, whom von Ribbentrop had enticed into the alliance in the hope of keeping Roosevelt from threatening Germany, now caused unnecessary tension with the United States. When Matsuoka, the new Japanese foreign minister, had visited Berlin (the Berlin crowds loved to yell the melodic sound of his name: MAT-SU-OH-KAH), all seemed fraternal, but now Japan's policies were a disappointment to von Ribbentrop. The Japanese occupied French Indochina, thereby alarming the United States and raising some eyebrows in Berlin. After all, France and its colonies were Germany's beaten foes. Von Ribbentrop's memoirs even agreed with General George C. Marshall in his writings about Japan, and quoted him in English: "Japan acted unilaterally and not in accordance with a unified, strategic plan." Both of Germany's partners in the pact seemed bent on undermining its function and purpose (*"Starke Kräfte an der Aushöhlung der Automatik dieses Vertrages"*). Alas for von Ribbentrop. The French did not want to accept decent treatment, the Italians indulged in disastrous rampages in Greece and North Africa, and the Japanese brought the Americans closer to war on the Allied side. The senior generals of the Army had raised hell about the brutality of the Polish SS actions, the Spaniards did not want to risk their necks, and even the Duke of Windsor indirectly refused offers of money and friendship. Worst of all, the Russians were no longer the jovial friends of 1939.

The only one of his representatives von Ribbentrop could trust was Abetz in Paris. He was fed up with the old aristos, but the bureaucrats in the Foreign Office were proving difficult to discard. He had prepared retirement certificates for two hundred of them (including Kordt and von Weizsäcker), but the Führer had stopped him. Once again Adolf Hitler preferred dual teams.

By now, it must have occurred to von Ribbentrop that his diplomatic efforts were faltering, that the Führer would soon be ready to scrap his crowning achievement, the Moscow pact, and that the men of the Army and of the party were now in power. The Army conducted the war; the party ran the conquered territories. Where could diplomacy still play its part? He should have remembered April 17, 1940, when Stalin bitterly complained to him directly because German troops had occupied an oil region of Poland at Drohobycz in breach of the agreed demarcation line. When a mortified von Ribbentrop complained to the Führer, Hitler had shrugged. He was on the side of the military. "Whenever diplomats make errors in wartime they always blame the soldiers," Hitler said. Germany's allies were fascinated by Germany's military victories, not by her diplomatic ones. Even Britain, German's only remaining intact combative enemy, would no longer accept diplomatic overtures, no matter how precarious her position. The two greatest powers, Russia and America, loomed as possible enemies. The Russians were growing aggressive, Adolf Hitler was hardening his position, and America was being inexorably drawn into conflict by the warm friendship between Roosevelt and Churchill, and also by Japan's risky forays in the Pacific. Only the forceful and sizable isolationist movement in America deterred Roosevelt from extending immediate naval support to the British.

On the face of it, von Ribbentrop should have relished the patriotic glory of it all: most of western Europe and Scandinavia was in German hands. Britain was under fierce air attacks and "nearly beaten," with much of her equipment and some of her pride left on the bombed beach of Dunkirk, all of Czechoslovakia and half of Poland were in German hands, including Danzig, the Corridor, and Memel. For the time being, Russia was neutralized by a treaty. Mussolini was on the march in Greece, the Balkans, and North Africa. The Germany Army remained intact and powerful. The Luftwaffe was pounding British coastal cities and airfields, seemingly still preparing for an invasion, and the Americans were busy worrying about Japan. The new German order, National Socialism, was being installed in the conquered nations, and Germany's "abused" minorities abroad had been reunited with their "homeland."

However, it is more probable that von Ribbentrop remained too much the businessman to swallow Goebbels's advertising slogans. By early 1941 he must have sensed that National Socialist Germany's high-water mark had been reached, and that his own days as a master diplomat were beginning to run out.

Hitler grew ever more paranoid about the Russians. Those old Nazi comrades who had warned him about the alliance with the Soviets became more insistent. They blamed von Ribbentrop, the *nouveau* Nazi, for the dilemma. It still infuriated Hitler that he had been "soft," and that now Latvia, Estonia, and Lithuania were part of the USSR, all because of the hastily approved Secret Protocols. He probably blamed von Ribbentrop for having pushed him into approval of this give-away. Forgotten was his own haste.

Molotov's November 1940 visit was meant to relax these tensions, but it did exactly the opposite. Finland, recently a Soviet victim, became another bone of Soviet-German contention. "In spring 1941 Hitler became much more negative about Russian questions," said von Ribbentrop's memoirs.[4]

On April 6, von Ribbentrop, attending a conference in Vienna, was ordered to join the Führer on the nearby train *Adler.* That day Hitler told his foreign minister that he had decided to invade Russia.[5]

The shaken von Ribbentrop offered to make one final attempt to defuse matters in Moscow; everything he had worked for was collapsing. But Hitler, in a fit of temper, prohibited any such move. "Discussion will rob us of the element of surprise!" he yelled. "One day the west will understand why I attacked the east!"

Hitler's reasoning was that the United States and Britain would soon combine to attack Germany with the Russians as their ally. Britain had already begun negotiations with Russia; Sir Stafford Cripps, the new British ambassador, had visited Moscow to work out a trade agreement. As far as Adolf Hitler was concerned, the time for negotiating with Russia had passed.

Like a shipwrecked sailor trying to bail out a leaking lifeboat with his hands, von Ribbentrop saw the water rise inside the hull. Control was slipping away. The Führer had decided on war. But first, some patching had to be done.

As expected, Mussolini's adventures had failed. The Greek campaign was a disaster, and the Libyan attack had turned into a debacle. Adolf Hitler, an angry, unwilling, I-told-you-so Adolf Hitler, had to come to his black-shirted ally's help. The whole thing was, as usual, dressed up in heroic terms. A directive announced on February 5: "Fighting shoulder to shoulder with our allies in the Mediterranean [German troops] must be conscious of their lofty military and political mission. They have been selected to lend valuable assistance in a psychological and military way to our allies who in every theater of war are struggling with a numerically superior army and who are insufficiently equipped with modern weapons because of Italy's limited productive capacity."

To run the campaign in North Africa, General von Brauchitsch chose the tough young Erwin Rommel, who was put in command of the DAK (Deutsches Afrika Korps). Rommel, a World War I winner of the Pour le Mérite, Imperial Germany's highest military decoration, was a modernist, a tank man, a blitzkrieg expert. He had once been the commander of Hitler's personal army guard battalion. Rommel was Hitler's sort of general: no title, no affectations, a tough, imaginative tactician and panzer soldier. He was a self-made man, without estates or noble ancestry, much like Richard Ribbentrop. On February

14, the first German combat troops landed at Tripoli.[6] On February 24 near Agedabia, an advanced German unit ran into two troops of British armored cars from the Dragoon Guards and a troop of Australian antitank guns. The Germans destroyed one armored car, one truck, two armored reconnaissance cars, and disabled one armored car they then took in tow. A British crewman was killed in the skirmish. No German was killed or wounded. The action appears in the Wehrmacht report of Wednesday, February 26, 1941. The report adds that some British prisoners were taken.[7] Rommel, who had wondered how his men would do in desert surroundings, had his proof. They would be fine . . . and so would he. Other Wehrmacht reports of that day noted that:

> Over Malta, German planes shot down an RAF Hurricane.
>
> Hull, Harwich, and Great Yarmouth were attacked, as well as airports in the east of Britain and factories in Ipswich and Norwich. An unsuccessful RAF attack on the Channel coast was repelled. Three RAF planes were downed. RAF bombers dropped high-explosive and incendiary bombs in western Germany, doing only slight damage. Flak shot down one RAF bomber. A U-boat sank an armed merchantman of approximately six thousand tons. Southeast of Britain, a British destroyer was sunk by a German torpedo boat.

It was a quiet day, but many men had died.

The fighting was going well for Adolf Hitler's soldiers, sailors, and pilots, but that left little room for Adolf Hitler's diplomats. Rommel had a "direct line" to the Führer in the person of Hitler's military aide, Colonel Rudolf Schmundt, who flew to Tripoli with him and then rushed back to the Berghof to report that Rommel was the perfect man for the job. Hitler congratulated himself on his brilliant judgment. "Anything Rommel wanted, anything at all . . ."

The historian David Irving reported Hitler's anger at Mussolini's arrogance and impotence. "The lunacy of it all! On the one hand, the Italians are screaming about their shortages of arms and equipment. On the other hand, they are infantile and find the use of German soldiers and equipment repugnant. Mussolini probably wants us to fight in Italian uniforms."[8]

It was the soldiers' year. Their days would wane, but in 1941 the soldiers outshone the diplomats.

Two months later, on Sunday, April 6, 1941, the Wehrmacht HQ announced:

> Because of the penetration of British amphibious troops from Greece to the north making connections with the Yugoslav Army, German

troops went on the counteroffensive this morning. The Greek and Serbian frontier was crossed at several points. The Luftwaffe attacked Fortress Belgrade, and Italian fighter units successfully attacked targets in southern Yugoslavia.[9]

Having come to Mussolini's aid in Africa, Hitler had to bail out his stalled and faltering troops in Greece, now that the Greeks and their British allies had mounted a forceful counteroffensive. But Hitler's mind was elsewhere. His key thought bore the code name Barbarossa, the planned attack on the Soviet Union.

The one ally that could have helped bear the weight of the immense adventure was samurai Japan, which was admired by Adolf Hitler. On March 26, 1941, many of the Reich's ranking people awaited their favorite Japanese diplomat, Foreign Minister Yosuke Matsuoka. The Berlin crowds had seen him before, and once again they liked his melodic name, his minuscule figure, and the fact that his warlike country was on Germany's side.

Following the perfect halt of the train at the station platform's red carpet, the Japanese minister inspected the stiff SS guard of the Leibstandarte Adolf Hitler. Then, after the two national anthems had been played and speeches made, he stepped into the obligatory black Grosser Mercedes open phaeton for the "triumphant" drive to the Chancellery through cheering crowds, past rising-sun and swastika banners. At his side in full field-gray diplomatic uniform was the foreign minister of the Greater German Reich, Joachim von Ribbentrop. Nothing had gone wrong. Last time, a Berliner had yelled, "Make sure the little feller don't slip under the wheels!" as they climbed into the car, and recently the special train had made a jerky stop and a certain foreign dignitary had cracked his head against the frame of the train window. But this time all went well, and Yosuke Matsuoka seemed pleased. Hundreds of photos were taken. The cheering on the Via Spontana was loud. Schmidt called these events "Gilbert and Sullivan." Even the hundred-yard-long, dark red marble floor of the gallery leading to the Führer's office, which could be slippery and hazardous, making involuntary skiers of visitors in military boots, was cooperative on this day.

Unfortunately, the visit coincided with the exact moment when word arrived for the Führer that the friendly Yugoslav government had been toppled. This was a great setback for Germany, since Prince Regent Paul and Prime Minister Zvetkovitch were admirers.

While Hitler dealt with the new Yugoslavs ("Attack them!"), von Ribbentrop told Matsuoka, Ambassador Eugen Ott, who headed Germany's Tokyo embassy, and Hiroshi Oshima, the Japanese ambassador in Berlin, "I have to confess that the relationship between the Soviets and us is at present correct, but not particularly friendly."

Obviously, he wanted to prevent the ally Japan from steadying its relations with Russia. After all, Japan's ally Germany was having problems with the Soviets. Von Ribbentrop cited the "betrayal" of Cripps's recent visit to Moscow and hinted broadly that if the Russians showed any sign of hostility, they "would be smashed."[10] This sentence startled Matsuoka.

The next day it was Hitler's turn to preach: "Britain is beaten. When will she show enough intelligence to admit it?" He then switched to the "look south" motif. Russia seeks southern expansion, as does Germany and Italy. Why not Japan? How about Singapore? Matsuoka spoke carefully in English.* His answer was, to the Führer's evident disappointment, "No promises. Sorry!" Matsuoka explained that he had to overcome the resistance of the "British-educated and American-educated Japanese intellectuals in Tokyo."

Astonishingly, in several earlier meetings with von Ribbentrop, Matsuoka had warned that if Japan attacked Britain by way of Singapore, America was bound to come into the war, and von Ribbentrop kept calming him and insisting, "We have absolutely no interest in war with the United States."[11]

After leaving Berlin, Matsuoka paid a short visit to Rome and then returned once more to Berlin. In a final meeting, the Führer asked the Japanese foreign minister to deliver the following ominous message: "When you return to Japan, you must not tell your emperor that conflict between Germany and the Soviet Union is impossible."

To the dismay of Hitler and von Ribbentrop, on his way home to Japan Matsuoka stopped in Moscow. And there he concluded a mutual nonaggression pact with the Soviets, another diplomatic crash landing for von Ribbentrop's Axis policy. The Japanese end of the Axis was being steered independently.

What Hitler did not seem to know was that, starting in April 1939, on the Manchurian-Mongolian border, there had been a series of military confrontations when the aggressive Japanese Army commanders imagined the Soviet Russians to be the czarist weaklings of Port Arthur. To their shock, the Russians had administered the first of several beatings to Japanese troops on May 12, 1939, in Mongolia.

---

*He spoke no German and Schmidt no Japanese, so English was their diplomatic tongue.

The Japanese had retreated with heavy casualties. On July 2, a Japanese counterattack by infantry and air under General Kantogun was again repelled with heavy Japanese losses. Against orders, Kantogun launched a major attack, almost an offensive, on July 23. On August 20, the Russians under General Georgï Zhukov had nearly destroyed the Japanese 6th Army.

The embarrassed Japanese of course failed to report their defeat to the Germans. It colored all subsequent Japanese actions and probably explains their reluctance to attack Russia's eastern flank.

It also explains why Matsuoka stopped in Moscow to sign the Russian-Japanese neutrality pact of April 1941. Russian troops released by this pact made the difference at Stalingrad, Leningrad, and Moscow, and General Zhukov put his experience to full use all the way to Berlin.

A minor scene of interest was enacted in Moscow during Matsuoka's visit. It probably failed to reassure von Ribbentrop, although Josef Stalin had played it to calm Berlin. In an unusual gesture, Stalin came to the Moscow railroad station to bid farewell to Matsuoka. There he turned to von der Schulenburg, the old German ambassador, put his arm around his shoulder "in a demonstrative manner," and said, "We must stay friends. Now you must do everything to that end." He then said to Colonel Hans Krebs, an assistant military attaché, "We shall stay friends with your country no matter what." Both of Stalin's sentences were reported in breathless detail to Berlin, but von Ribbentrop must have known better than to believe them. Japan was lost to Germany as a threat against Russia, another hedge to a great gamble was gone. Japan's Russian treaty had diminished Germany's chances. Even a supreme optimist could hardly call Japan's action a rousing endorsement of its Teutonic allies.

So far, most of Adolf Hitler's war plans were roughly on schedule. Britain's coastal areas and airfields were still being pounded by the Luftwaffe, and London was being hit "in reprisal for RAF raids on German cities," reportedly with good results (although, inexplicably, the RAF was growing and so were German air losses). France was vaguely under control, although Pétain was obstreperous and Laval a slippery customer. The "Jew-cleansing" measures had not yet succeeded entirely, but new initiatives were being planned. German troops were stabilizing the Balkans. On May 31 Crete fell to a paratroop attack in which Master Sergeant Max Schmeling, the former heavyweight boxing champion, had taken part. (He was not an enthusiastic Nazi and his "heroic death" would have been fairly welcome, but the beetle-browed Max would not oblige. He survived and was still heroic.) Luftwaffe losses were substantial and should have served as a warning for all future parachute operations. A hundred and fifty troop-carrier JU-52 planes were lost, as were the many paratroopers aboard them.[12]

In Hitler's view, Rommel was performing brilliantly in North Africa. Mussolini had turned out to be a bag of hot air and his troops a failure, but then, the Führer had always suspected his black-shirted friend's conceited strutting. Japan? Well, that strange alliance was another one of von Ribbentrop's notions, but Hitler was certain he could handle Stalin without the help of the samurai. He had postponed the invasion of Great Britain. Göring would have to do better at battering the British; he would have to soften them up a lot more. At sea, Germany's U-boats had excellent hunting while trying to quarantine Britain, but so far stubborn Britain was surviving. Admittedly, America was a threat, but he understood from the Washington embassy that there was great isolationist opposition to entering the war, although the Americans were "lending" old destroyers to Britain.

Then came trouble from the most unexpected direction. On May 11, Rudolf Hess flew a fast and dangerous Messerschmitt-110 fighter plane in the direction of Britain on a private peacemaking mission. People who knew him were stunned. Could Hess fly this dicey plane? Indeed he could. He was a trained and skilled pilot. Why did he fly to Britain? Whom did he try to contact in Britain? He was trying to reach the Duke of Hamilton, who had no idea why such an "honor" was being bestowed on him by Hess. (Some people suggest a case of false identity: Hess was trying to reach Sir Ian Hamilton, who had been to Germany with British veterans' groups, rather than the Duke of Hamilton.) Had Hess reached his destination? As yet, no one knew.

Walter Hewel described the scene at the Berghof, as Göring, who had raced to the Führer's side by special train and fast car, rushed in to meet Hitler, a "white-faced" von Ribbentrop, Hewel, and Martin Bormann, who was Hess's chief of staff.[13] Hitler thrust Hess's letter under Göring's nose. It said, in effect, "Willing to risk my life to make peace . . . and end bloodshed." Hess had long been an intimate part of Hitler's personal and political life. They were jailed together in the twenties. Hess had even done the secretarial work on *Mein Kampf* and had become Hitler's deputy in the Nazi Party.

Von Ribbentrop must have had his own shocked thoughts, because Hess had provided him with his first office (the Büro Ribbentrop was technically part of Hess's organization), and Hess's flight to Britain demonstratively repudiated von Ribbentrop's "Britain is the enemy" thesis. Would Hess's arrival in Britain shatter the Tripartite Alliance? Mussolini would be delighted by Hitler's embarrassment, and the Japanese had already proved their lack of trust in German policy. What about the minor players, the Hungarians, the Romanians? And how would it look in France, Holland, Belgium, Denmark, and Norway? Worst of all, this would surely stiffen Churchill's resolve.

Hitler had Willy Messerschmitt brought to him. He yelled at the aircraft manufacturer, "You allowed him to practice at your airfield. How dare you?" Messerschmitt pointed out that Hess was an important man, and that he was not in a position to say no to the Führer's deputy. "But you knew Hess was insane!" yelled Hitler.

It turned out that Hess had practiced with guidance systems and navigation. Hitler hoped Hess would crash; Schmidt heard him say so.[14] But Hess did not crash. He parachuted into Scotland not far from the Duke of Hamilton's estate, was arrested, and never made the contacts he was hoping for, including the duke, who would not see him. The Goebbels machine immediately pumped out the "explanation" that Hess was insane. Von Ribbentrop rushed to Rome to explain to the Duce that Hess was *non compos*.

These were the events that began the drumroll to Barbarossa, the campaign that would lead Hitler into hell. More important, hundreds of thousands of German soldiers were consigned to their frozen death or to years of hopeless misery as prisoners of war in Russia.

First came another meeting on the Brenner Pass, this time in beautiful early June weather. Not a word was mentioned to the Duce about Hitler's plans for the impending attack on Russia. It was clear that he was purposely deceiving the Duce. A few days later, Marshal Ion Antonescu, the Romanian head of state, attended a ceremony in Munich. It was a mark of Hitler's respect and trust for the Romanian marshal that he laid before Antonescu the timetable for Barbarossa. Antonescu was delighted, particularly after he was promised Bessarabia, which von Ribbentrop had let slip to Russia in the 1939 negotiations.[15]

A final part of the rising drumroll was a bombastic ceremony. On a beautiful day in the Palace of the Doges in Venice, Croatia joined the Tripartite Alliance during a lavishly choreographed event. It was breathtaking theater in a superb setting, all arranged for the insignificant addition of a minor nation to a crumbling alliance. Then, at last, the crash of the cymbals.

Schmidt, an eyewitness, described the scene:

> It is just before four on the morning of Sunday, June 22, 1941, in the office of the foreign minister. He is expecting the Soviet ambassador, Dekanozov, who had been phoning the minister since early Saturday. Dekanozov had an urgent message from Moscow. He had called every two hours but was told the minister was away from the city. At two on Sunday morning, von Ribbentrop finally responded to the calls. Dekanozov was told von Ribbentrop wished to meet with him at once. An appointment was made for 4 A.M.
>
> Von Ribbentrop is nervous, walking up and down from one end of his large office to the other, like a caged animal, while saying over and over, "The Führer is absolutely right. We must attack Russia, or they will surely attack us!" Is he reassuring himself? Is he justifying the ruination of his crowning diplomatic achievement? Now he has to destroy it "because that is the Führer's wish."

Dekanozov was punctual to the minute. He brought his own interpreter, and he began by asking some questions Moscow wanted clarified, but von Ribbentrop stopped him: "That's not what I wish to discuss." He continued, "The hostile attitude of the Soviet government toward Germany and the severe threat we perceive toward the Reich by the massing of Russian troops on our eastern frontier have forced us to take military countermeasures." There was no mention of war or a declaration of war. Schmidt thought perhaps it would have sounded too "plutocratic" to declare war. Also, Hitler had given instructions to avoid the use of the word. Von Ribbentrop continued, "Since this morning such military countermeasures are being taken." The Yugoslav agreement with the new "rebel" government was then trotted out as one of the many sins of the Soviets. Von Ribbentrop said he regretted that he could add nothing to these statements. He had come to the conclusion that "my strenuous efforts for peace between our nations were futile." Finis! The gates were opened; the flood released. Dekanozov quickly got hold of himself. He "regretted exceedingly" the course of events. It was largely due to the "confrontational views" of the German government. "All that remains is for your chief of protocol to assist us with transportation for our embassy staff." He stood up, made a small bow, but did not extend his hand. Then he was gone.

Valentin Berezhkov, Dekanozov's interpreter for this meeting, told the story differently. He believed that von Ribbentrop had taken a few drinks to give himself courage for the unpleasant meeting; his face had red blotches and his hands shook, according to this version.

Dekanozov listened to von Ribbentrop's announcement and replied that Germany was guilty of criminal aggression and one day would deeply regret its action. He then strode to the entrance of the office without a word of parting. Ribbentrop rushed after Dekanozov and the interpreter, whispering urgently that he had tried to keep the Führer from making war on Russia. He had tried to dissuade Hitler from this madness . . . "Tell Moscow that I was against this attack." These were the last words Bereshkov said he heard from von Ribbentrop; Dekanozov was already on his way down the stairs.

Ever since the end of World War II certain military historians have advanced the revisionist theory that Hitler's attack on Soviet Russia was pre-emptive. They maintain that Russian troops, tanks, and aircraft were deployed for attack, not for defense, and that Russia had multiplied her western military strength in the six months previous to Barbarossa. They also offer in evidence the clearing of Russian defensive minefields in the Polish buffer zone and the disarming of explosive-charged bridges. The preamble for the supposed Russian plan to attack Germany probably began in 1939, when the Russians, under Marshal Zhukov, had their military victories in Mongolia against Japan. The November 1940 Molotov meetings in Berlin, at which Russia demanded control of Romania (and the oil Hitler needed), then caused Hitler to begin the plan for Barbarossa on December 18, 1940. Eleven days later Moscow was informed and decided to strike first. Supposedly, Hitler's attack anticipated theirs by two weeks. This theory was again expounded in articles by Walter Post and Joachim Weber in the political magazine *Criticon*, May–June 1991.

The revisionists also insist that Germany was ill prepared to attack the Soviets, since German war production had been scaled back after the western victories and partly reconverted to peacetime manufacturing. German tanks, the Mark I and II, were inferior to Russian T-34s, and Germany was short of shells and bullets.

It is possible that, following the contentious November 1940 Berlin meetings and the subsequent Barbarossa plan, the Russians hastily decided to forestall Hitler. However, every other indication leads one to conclude that Moscow believed the August 1939 Nonaggression Pact would hold. Hitler, when informed of Russian troop movements, used anything he deemed "offensive" (in the pejorative, not the military sense) to justify his own military acts. This was the course he had followed in Czechoslovakia, Poland, Denmark, Norway, Holland, Belgium, and France. It seems unlikely that he would have abandoned his successful strategy in the case of Barbarossa. Valentin Berezhkov, who translated for Stalin and Molotov as well as for other diplomats, reported in his memoirs that there was never a hint of aggressive planning on the part of Stalin. On April 28, 1941, Ambassador von der Schulenburg, in a meeting with Hitler, assured the Führer that there was no possibility of Russia's attacking Germany. Hitler peremptorily rejected the old statesman's assurances.[16]

Many miles to the west, a group of German occupation soldiers in France were ready to eat their comfortable Sunday dinner in their favorite small restaurant. They were waiting for their food when a Wehrmacht motorcycle messenger roared up on his BMW, and the man in the sidecar jumped out, rushed over, and yelled to his comrades in field gray, "Listen! The Soviet Union's been attacked since early this morning! There's a fifteen-hundred-kilometer front from the Baltic to the Black Sea. I just heard it on Radio Sieben." (Channel Seven was the BBC, and the soldiers were all radio monitors; otherwise it would have been illegal for them to listen to London.) The French restaurant owner turned on his own radio, which broadcast the *controllé* news. They heard the same report in French, the words now dressed up *à la* Goebbels. Little Hans, the meteorologist of the radio team, was first to speak. "Three and a half months is all they've got before winter sets in," he said.[17]

The official *Wehrmacht* bulletin of the day was terse.

Sunday, June 22, 1941
Since early this morning there has been combat action on the Soviet Russian frontier. An attempt [by Russian planes] during the evening to penetrate into eastern air space was repelled with heavy losses. German fighters shot down numerous Red aircraft.

The rest of the report dealt with the air war over Britain, France, and Germany, and some Navy action. Not until Sunday, June 29, a week after the initial attack, did the Oberkommando der Wehrmacht (Armed Forces Headquarters) give a lengthy report on the Russian campaign. It was an immense success. The final sentences told the euphoric facts: "The German people owe their courageous soldiers the very deepest thanks." The score was forty thousand prisoners of war, six hundred artillery pieces captured, 2233 armored vehicles captured or destroyed, masses of antiaircraft, antitank infantry weapons, 407 aircraft destroyed. Germany's pilots and equipment "tower over the enemy (*Die Überlegenheit is eine turmhohe*).[18]

From the view of a typical German Army division, the attack was equally exciting. This is how that same day came to the 19th Panzer

Front row, left to right: protocol chief "Tall Sandro" von Dörnberg, Prime Minister Neville Chamberlain, and Joachim von Ribbentrop during the 1938 Munich conferences. *Der Spiegel*

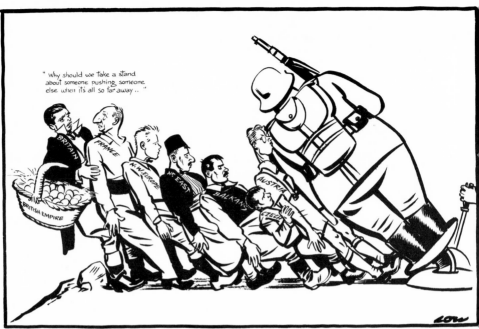

INCREASING PRESSURE.

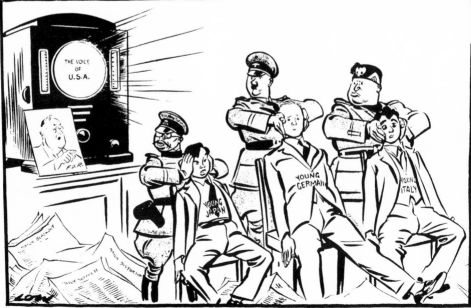

BLASPHEMY! NOT FIT FOR YOUNG EARS!

Opposite and below: David Low's cartoons in the *Evening Standard,* uncompromisingly anti-appeasement, often irritated the Chamberlain government. *Evening Standard/Solo*

Right: Hitler's self-caricature as a broke gambler.

NEMESIS RESTAURANT.

Returning triumphantly from Moscow aboard the Führer's airplane, August 25, 1939. *Der Spiegel*

Von Ribbentrop and Japanese Foreign Minister Yosuke Matsuoka, Berlin, 1940. *Der Spiegel*

Der 28. September

Der deutsch-russische Grenz- und Freundschaftsvertrag besiegelt. Die gemeinsame Front gegen die Kriegshetzer in Westeuropa gebildet. Ein sicheres Fundament für den Dauerfrieden in Osteuropa geschaffen: Die Dokumente vom 28. September werden unterzeichnet. Stehend von rechts: Stalin, Reichsaußenminister von Ribbentrop und der Generalstabschef der russischen Armee Schaposchnikoff, sitzend Außenminister Molotow.

The signing of the full Soviet-German nonaggression pact on September 28, 1939. Left to right: Russian Chief of Staff Shaposhnikov, von Ribbentrop, Molotov (seated), and Stalin. *Ullstein Bilderdienst*

Berlin, June 22, 1941. Von Ribbentrop announces to the German and
foreign press that Germany has invaded the Soviet Union. *Keystone*

Rudolf von Ribbentrop, first lieutenant
SS Leibstandarte, with Knight's Cross
and First Class Iron Cross, 1942.
National Archives

Annelies, Barthold, Adolf, Joachim, and Ursula, January 1941.
National Archives

Joachim von Ribbentrop, defendant at the War Crimes Trials, writing in his cell in Nürnberg, November 1945. *United States Army*

Division, usually garrisoned in Hannover, now on the northern end of Germany's Russian frontier.

At 3 A.M. on June 22, artillery prepared the way across the Niemen River, the border between East Prussia and the Soviets. German bombers began to pound the Russians at daylight. As soon as the fog lifted from the river valley, the brand-new 19th Panzer Division (it was originally infantry) crossed over the bridge into Russia. The time was exactly 9 A.M. The soldiers were far from their home in Hannover.

The division's senior Protestant chaplain, a husky man who wore the Iron Cross First Class and who had seen many battles through his round, steel-rimmed glasses, ate a hasty meal from his messkit and then climbed into one of the open, field-gray cars. A few hours later, he became the division's first fatality, when a bomb splinter sliced into him. Was it a bad omen? Not yet. The 19th Panzer Division was on its victorious drive east toward Moscow.

Hitler's life, and thereby the lives of those who orbited him, now shifted to his headquarters, the Wolfsschanze (Wolf's Lair), near Rastenburg in East Prussia.[19] He had the notion that, as commander-in-chief, he had to be near the troops, although it was more a matter of emotion than geography. While East Prussia was somewhat nearer to Russia, the enormous and extended Russian front could have been coordinated from Berlin, in the eastern sector of Germany.

Perhaps it was the Nibelungen atmosphere of East Prussia that Hitler relished. Wolfsschanze was in one of the deepest, darkest, most oppressive forests in Germany, a gloomy evocation of the woods in the Grimm Brothers' fairy tales. The atmosphere was haunted, foreboding, and cheerless. Concrete barracklike buildings, with the insides shelled in plain wood trim, were made as livable as possible, but electric lights burned even at midday. Eventually, windowless aboveground concrete air-raid bunkers augmented the network of headquarters, connected by concrete passageways. The insides of all these thick-walled bunkers were damp and resounded to the constant whirring of air-circulation pumps. Those who worked in Wolfsschanze were prone to attacks of melancholy and depression, although there was a cinema, where even taboo English and American films were shown, along with the usual Goebbels-style newsreels. Of course, Wolfsschanze also had the latest in communications equipment.

This is where Hitler now received his foreign guests and his associates. Foreign guests were impressed, but they were there only occasionally. Von Ribbentrop, and the others around Hitler who spent much time there, were depressed.

After a state visit by Mussolini to the Wolfsschanze on August 27, 1941, during which nothing was achieved except a flood of posed photographs and pompous communiqués, Schmidt reported a typical von Ribbentrop fight for the sake of his vanities.

A final communiqué on the Duce's visit was to be issued, dealing with the "heroic alliance" of the two Axis giants. The message that reached the departing Mussolini's southbound train said, "Dispatch canceled by order of the Reichs Foreign Minister," which sent Mussolini into a tantrum at von Ribbentrop's impertinence. He wanted the train stopped. He insisted on an immediate explanation. Then the original communiqué was reinstated.

This is what had taken place behind the scenes. The first version ended with "Also participating in the military and political discussions were Field Marshal Keitel and Reichs Foreign Minister von Ribbentrop." Joachim von Ribbentrop's efforts to remain in command of his precarious status during the time of the generals now found pathetic expression. Infuriated that he was named *after* Keitel, he demanded that the communiqué be held up. The matter was quickly submitted to the judgment of the Führer, who howled about von Ribbentrop's vanity but gave in. When von Ribbentrop was told that Hitler had approved the change, he said airily, "Oh, leave it as it is." The part of the message Mussolini saw was an internal memo about holding up the communiqué until the order of precedence had been settled.

Von Ribbentrop's focus of attention should have been directed toward Martin Bormann, a squat, porcine man who was gaining power as "head of Chancellery" for the Führer. Bormann, an early Nazi and party factotum, had burrowed his way up from local power to Hess's office and then, after Hess's flight to Scotland, had become Hitler's creature. He held the strings to confidential purses and knew many secrets. In time, he would be the driving force behind the adoption of euthanasia, the antichurch campaign, and most anti-Semitic measures.

Earlier, Bormann had been helpful to von Ribbentrop in persuading Hitler to allow the removal of Gauleiter Ernst Bohle from the Foreign Ministry. Bohle, chief of the Auslandsorganisation, the Foreign Agency of the Nazi Party, was a constant irritant to von Ribbentrop. Bormann soon became everybody's distasteful key to the Führer's door.

The winds of war had blown away many of Joachim von Ribbentrop's favorite dreams. No longer could he forge alliances of powerful nations and bring diplomatic pressure to bear on those who would oppose Germany. No longer could he taste the triumph of successful diplomacy or feel pride when the old powers kowtowed to the new player on the diplomatic field. Now success was counted in men killed, prisoners taken, tanks destroyed, planes shot down, ships sunk. Maps were marked with the symbols of military units, with arrows of advance or retreat, not shaded into new colors by the horse trading of diplomatic negotiators. He had built a worldwide organization to deal with Germany's diplomatic business, but he feared that it would be dismantled by his warlord master. How could he make himself needed? What functions could the Foreign Ministry's staff of thousands now perform to please Adolf Hitler in war? Von Ribbentrop decided on an answer that would eventually be fatal for him. His commitment, probably made with the shielded eyes of the unquestioning disciple, was to order the Foreign Ministry to help with the so-called Final Solution.

It was not a sudden walk into quicksand. The whole thing began much earlier. Reinhard Heydrich, the Gestapo and SD Chief, "received his orders" from Reichs Marshal Göring to "find a *Gesamtlösung* [total solution] for the question of European Jewry."

Actually, according to the historian David Irving, Heydrich had drafted the entire order on a faked letterhead of Göring's and got the harried Reichs Marshal to sign it without much attention to detail, because Göring was rushing to meet his wife at the station.

On November 29, 1941, Heydrich wrote to Martin Luther, the von Ribbentrop import from Dahlem, now a senior official in the Foreign Ministry, requesting his help in the matter and enclosing a copy of the Göring "order."[20]

Von Ribbentrop's first personal contact with this cruelty came through a department called Deutschland, which dealt with the Nazi Party aspects of his ministry. Von Ribbentrop had appointed Martin Luther, his Nazi Party "expert," to take charge of Department D (for Deutschland) with the rank of deputy state secretary. (Von Weizsäcker was state secretary or chief of staff.)

Luther, the clever, loud-mouthed Berliner, was ruthless and, like a lot of old party hands, almost anti-SS. He had always been loyal to the Proletarian SA, the brown shirts, and never got over the shock of the SS's execution of Röhm. Luther knew his way around the circle of "old fighters" close to the Führer. Most of them had been SA, and did not like Himmler or the SS.

The section of Department D that handled Jewish matters was DIII; its head was a former lawyer named Franz Rademacher. It was Rademacher who had once avidly furthered the Madagascar solution, until it dissipated in 1941. This was the first time that a branch of von

Ribbentrop's ministry was directly connected with SS actions involving the Jews. (Madagascar was only meant for "western" Jews. "Eastern," that is Polish and Russian Jews, were to be handled differently.)

Luther's next contact was through the Einsatzkommandos in the Baltics, Romania, and Russia. The following Einsatzkommando reports are from the Foreign Ministry archives, collected by Hans-Jürgen Döscher.

> Sept. 1941 — The finishing of 4000 Jews in Jussy [Romania].
> — Many snipers and functionaries, mainly Jews, were liquidated [Einsatzgruppe A, action near Riga, Latvia].
> — In the environs of Riga, 459 people were shot, among them were 237 mental patients from Riga and Migan. In all, in this territory 29,246 persons were liquidated.
> — The Jewish persons liquidated by one Sonderkommando increased to 75,000.
> — In the districts Roskiskis, Sarzai, Perzai, and Prienai, the figure of executed rose to 85,000. These districts are now cleansed of Jews.[21]

All of the SS–SD reports were passed on to the Foreign Ministry's Department Deutschland, Division DIII.

Dr. Georg Bruns, a lawyer for the ministry and a nephew once removed of von Weizsäcker, reported to Döscher in an interview on July 27, 1976, that Ribbentrop did not like to see the Einsatzgruppen reports passed through to the Foreign Ministry.[22] Was it that von Ribbentrop knew the horror and wanted to sweep it under the rug? Was he himself horrified? Was it that he feared being compromised? Was it all of these? But it did him no good to try to dodge the issue. Heydrich would not permit it. After the first five Einsatzgruppen reports were ignored by the Foreign Ministry, Heydrich sent a personal report, Number 6, dated November 25, 1941, on Einsatzgruppen activities and their situation in the USSR, with a request for acknowledgment, and Dr. Bruns was forced to furnish such acknowledgment by the minister.[23]

There followed other atrocious reports, "The liquidation (*Liquidirung*) of 3000 Jews in Witebsk; more than 33,000 Jews executed (*hingerichtet*) in Kiev; 3000 Jews shot in Shtomir; east of the Dnieper River nearly 5000 Jews shot." One report states, "All male Jews over 16 with the exception of physicians and the elders." State Secretary von Weizsäcker (it is assumed a sickened von Weizsäcker) saw report Number 6 before Luther had a chance to show it to von Ribbentrop. Von Weizsäcker's initials but no marginal comments were on the report. Usually such communications are initialed by each reader.

Though von Ribbentrop strenuously denied any knowledge of the murders — pointing to the official euphemisms "removal, resettlement, displacement" as proof that he never could have guessed they meant murders — how could he not have been aware of the horrors? The Einsatzgruppen reports were explicit enough.

It is entirely likely that for the first time in his career he withheld information from his wife. This is one matter in which she might not have been the "tougher of the two," as Hitler once said. By 1942, rumors of the murders were rife among senior Foreign Ministry officials, particularly because men like Martin Luther insisted that Einsatzkommando reports be widely circulated among those who were entitled to "classified" information.

The SD people charged with the task of killing considered themselves unsung heroes, patriotically doing the Reich's dirty work with iron resolve and a stomach for bloodshed.

Nothing in von Ribbentrop's background could have trained him for such bloody business. But like the man in the dinner suit who sees a derelict lying on a park bench, he hurried on to the dinner party. There was probably little he could have done to stop the SS murders; he was too involved, too committed, too dependent.

Axel von der Busche, who was to be one of the heroes of the officer resistance of 1943 and 1944, a man who volunteered to blow up the Führer by carrying a live grenade, tripping its mechanism, and embracing Hitler, told of the first time he saw an SS mass murder in the Ukraine. Von der Busche was an officer in an old regiment with nearby headquarters. "I suppose," he said, "the Christian thing would have been to take off my uniform and join the nude victims on their way to their execution. The SS would have arrested me, called me insane, committed me to a mental ward, and the executions would have continued the following day." This was the attitude of the SD. Once they had hardened themselves, most SD men and police behaved with the bored efficiency of the staff in a slaughterhouse. A few "weaklings" collapsed and were hospitalized.

This is how Germany returned to medieval laws:

Police order for Identification of Jews 1944 (August 1, 1941):
    Paragraph 1: (1) Jews who have completed their sixth year of life are not permitted to appear in public without displaying a Jew Star.
    (2) The Jew Star must be the size of the palm of the hand, a six-pointed, black star on yellow background with the black word *Jüde* (Jew). It is to be worn in open view on the left side of the chest, sewn on in a permanent manner.

Paragraph 2: Jews are prohibited from
(a) leaving their residential district without carrying written police permission;
(b) wearing orders, decorations, or other insignia [to prevent decorated World War I veterans from getting sympathetic treatment].[24]

These regulations did not apply to a few "mixed" (intermarried) categories or to those who had lost a son in the current war. (Men who were one-quarter Jewish could serve in the Wehrmacht, depending on the distinction and war service of their fathers.)

They were followed by another from the Reich's Finance Ministry, dated November 4, 1941. Any Jew who was not employed in enterprises vital to the German economy would be removed (*abzuschieben*) to the "eastern territories." Their money would be confiscated by the Reich. Each Jew was to retain a hundred marks and fifty kilograms (110 pounds) of personal luggage.

The return to the dark ages, the failure to acknowledge the rights of individuals, which had begun on January 30, 1933, was now in full progress while Germany's sons were bound for the immense, snow-covered steppes where Napoleon's Guards had once frozen to death.

More of these regulations were added with frequency by various branches of government. They could not have been ignored or overlooked by professional officials like those of the Foreign Ministry. In fact, if the rules seemed in any way suspect or especially harsh, the old hands made sure that they were distributed as widely as the "secrecy" classifications permitted, usually upward. These men may have suspected that one day they would have to prove that the guilt was shared by their chiefs.

The Russian campaign began with a vast rout of the Soviets. By July 9, 1941, German troops had taken 320,000 Russian prisoners; by October, the figure had risen to 1.2 million.

In North Africa, Rommel and his new Afrika Korps were still on their triumphant advance after their April defeat of the British at Bardia, Derna, and Halfaya inside Egypt. Not until December was Rommel to suffer a setback, but it was only temporary. By January 1942, he was back on the attack.

This was not the case in Russia. The Moscow government had moved to Kuibyshev, but the German attack ground to a halt on December 1, sixteen miles from the Kremlin.[25] By then, German losses in the campaign were 158,773 dead, 31,191 missing, 563,082 wounded. Aircraft lost numbered 2093. The Russians blocked the way with fresh troops released from their eastern areas by the Japanese nonaggression agreement. Germany's diplomatic loss, with this treaty, meant a loss of lives. But that was no longer in von Ribbentrop's hands. All he could do was listen to the reports of the military. On December 5 and 6, 1941, the Russians launched a massive winter offensive against German troops, who were ill equipped to handle such an attack in 50-degree-below-zero weather in their summer uniforms. Back in Germany people were asked to contribute their fur coats. The lack of winter combat gear was a scandal.[26] It was the first time the German foot soldier, the *Landser,* was to taste the bitter brew of Hitler's personal strategic command. Stalled on the rim of Moscow that December, 286 German tanks were lost, 305 artillery pieces and their tractors. Men retreated in near panic for a hundred miles in 50 degrees Celsius below zero. The myth of German invincibility was gone.[27]

On December 19, Marshal von Brauchitsch, the official commanding general in Russia, was discharged without so much as a handshake, and Hitler took personal tactical as well as strategic charge. Now, behind his back, Hitler was often called the *Gröfaz* (pronounced in English *Growfuts*). It sounds as slanderous in Berlinese as it does in English. *Gröfaz* is an acronym meaning "the greatest warlord of all time."

Within hours of the beginning of the Russian offensive, Japanese aircraft carriers launched their attack on Pearl Harbor, and the United States declared war on Axis partner Japan. The fat was in the fire. Now the tripartite treaty would oblige Hitler to declare war on the United States, the very thing von Ribbentrop had tried for so long to avoid. It was a diplomatic shambles.

The Führer's aggressive plans had wrecked von Ribbentrop's grand design. The Russians now had fresh troops because, safe from attack by Japan as a result of the Matsuoka-Molotov treaty of April 4, they could move up eastern forces. The United States, whom the Germans had wanted to keep out of the war, was attacked by Japan because the Japanese felt safe from Russia. How to explain all this to Italy? Or was it worth explaining anything to Italy? According to Ciano's diary, the Duce had already said he hoped that the Germans would "lose a lot of feathers" in Russia.[28] In his memoirs von Ribbentrop insisted that neither he nor Ambassador Oshima had an inkling of the impending carrier attack on the American fleet in Pearl Harbor. If so, Ambassador Oshima must have felt deeply betrayed by Tokyo, and his urge to commit *seppuko* (the thing foreigners called *harakiri*) must have been strong.[29]

Meanwhile, Heinrich Himmler's empire, the dark world of the SS, held sway. Vengeance was theirs. A large number of Foreign Ministry department heads held SS rank, ranging from major to general, although it was often the "honorary rank," given at the request of von Ribbentrop. The bestowal may have been only a gesture, but it provided Himmler with a tool. Even "honorary" SS were, after all, SS.

In Russia, the SS continued its rampage. At the beginning of the war, orders had been given to shoot without trial any Soviet commissars captured with the Russian Army. This so-called Commissar Order provoked resentment among German officers, who considered it against their code. But that was only the beginning. Rudolf Christoph von Gersdorff, an officer of traditional Prussian background, told a story about the staff of the Middle Army (Heeresgruppe Mitte), with headquarters a few miles from Smolensk.

> A Silesian friend, Nanne von Heydebrand, came into my room, chalk-pale. I thought he had been airsick on the flight to headquarters, so I offered him some brandy. He told me that the JU-52 transport that brought him back to the front from home leave had made a stop at Borisov. He heard pistol and machine gun fire near the airstrip. When they took off, they flew at low altitude over a dreadful execution scene. Thousands of people, probably Jews, had dug deep ditches and were then shot with machine guns and pistols. The next shift had to step on top of the fallen, dead or alive, and they were shot in their turn. Also, babies and naked women, begging for their children. Everyone died in a hail of bullets.

The SS men, it turns out, were Latvians. The matter was investigated and found to be true. Commander-in-chief General von Bock ordered the field commander of the Borisov area to report to him at once. The man shot himself on the way to headquarters.

This massacre and others like it inspired the nucleus of officers who planned to kill Adolf Hitler.[30] Many of them belonged to Potsdam's legendary 9th Infantry Regiment, which was descended from the Kaiser's Guards Regiments. Many officers of the 9th were the sons of the Kaiser's Guards officers. And many were to die after their attempt to kill the Führer on July 20, 1944, when Colonel Claus von Stauffenberg tried to blow up Hitler but did not succeed. By then, the attempts on Hitler's life in the eleven years between 1934 and 1945 numbered forty-two.

The acts of the Einsatzgruppen, scavenging after combat troops had passed, were only a primitive first attempt. Soon the SS prepared more efficient ways to eliminate such undesirables as Jews, homosexuals, Gypsies, Freemasons, Jesuits, Poles, Jehovah's Witnesses, the terminally ill, and the mentally disabled. (One new category was *Nacht und Nebel* [Night and Fog], prisoners who fitted none of the other groupings. They were arrested without warning for any true or fancied enmity to the Reich. For example, one of the original camps, Ravensbrück, was for women only.) The camps, which had begun as prisons for political opponents, became cruel labor camps. Many were turned into death camps. The mortality rate from overwork, starvation, and disease was immense, but the killing factories dwarfed these "natural" deaths.

Lest the Army be portrayed as totally averse to the Einsatzgruppen debauch, it should be noted that certain Army commanders, either opportunists or Nazi believers, approved SD actions. In an order to the 6th Army Group, Field Marshal Walter von Reichenau told his troops that "they were the standard bearers of an inexorably popular concept" and that they "must have full understanding for the necessity of this severe but justified atonement required from the Jewish subhumans."[31]

One Einsatzgruppe reported that Army Group Center had liquidated nineteen thousand "partisans and criminals," mostly Jews. There were so many requests from local commanders for liquidation by the Einsatzgruppen that an SS major named Lindow felt constrained to point out that "the Gestapo was not the Wehrmacht's hangman."[32] When the murders were dressed up in governmental definitions, Nazi cant, Hitler's views, Army orders, oaths of office, "honor of loyalty," even decent men were capable of seeing the victims as criminals, justifying the urgency of war to circumvent morality.

Most of these acts were primed in Berlin by officials dubbed "desk murderers." At the other end of the disaster was the expectation by the SS that they could appeal to their members on the basis of duty and honor. ("You must be hard. Your task is one of unparalleled hardness.") Ideologically, the murders were described as "cleansing, surgical" acts. "Judaism in the east is the source of Bolshevism and must therefore be wiped out in accordance with the Führer's wishes." The Einsatzgruppen believed they were entitled to the sympathy and thanks of all good Aryans. "The job is not a pretty one," complained SS General Harald Turner.[33] To support the legality of it all, this was the particular vocabulary for murder: "special action," "special treatment," "elimination," "cleansing," "resettlement," "relocated elsewhere."

Not all SS functioned the way Heinrich Himmler and Reinhard Heydrich wished. Several top SS leaders requested transfers from Einsatzgruppen duties. Among the best known were SS General Nebe, a former senior police officer, who beat a hasty retreat back to Berlin. (His deputy said, "Artur, if you can't go on, I'll take your place.") Another of Himmler's top SS officers, General Erich von dem Bach-Zelevski, was taken to the hospital with a nervous breakdown. Such reactions were multiplied in the ranks.

Himmler himself once insisted on trying to watch as two hundred Jews were shot in Minsk. SS General Karl Wolff, his deputy, barely kept him from collapsing. Himmler turned green when a piece of human brain flew into his face.[34] Because the shootings had sickened the SS chief, he insisted that a better system be found for the extermination of unneeded or undesirable human beings; the result was the gas van. Huge closed trucks were built, capable of holding dozens of victims. When the truck was stopped and the exhaust gases were switched by lever from the outside to the inside of the locked rear compartment, the occupants were killed, and the trucks were unloaded and washed out. The corpses were cremated or buried in mass graves.

The trucks then returned to the stockades, where more prisoners were loaded to be "transported elsewhere." On July 12, 1941, an SS officer named Schröter, in command of an Einsatzkommando in the Ukraine, reported, "The Jews are remarkably ill informed about our intentions toward them."[35] This new system of mass murder occasionally brought some need for technical modification.

These are excerpts from an official memorandum by the administrative section of the concentration camp:

Berlin 5 June 1942
no copies

Secret Reich Matter
  I. *Memorandum:*
  Concerns: Mechanical modifications on special vehicles currently in use or being manufactured:
  Since December 1941, 97,000 were processed in three vehicles in an exemplary manner without any problems concerning the equipment. However, the following modifications are suggested.
    1. To expedite entry of gas, two additional vents of approximately 10 cm × 1 cm are suggested, with valves to avoid excessive pressure.
    2. It is suggested that the freight area be reduced to lighten the load capacity. The problem is not in the strength of the undercarriage but in the truck's cross-country capability. This refers to the trucks built by Saurer. The shorter freight area might be thought to cause a problem in overloading the front axle. In fact, this does not apply,

because the freight tends to shift to the rear, trying to reach the rear doors.

3. The connecting hoses between exhaust and truck have been rusting through due to collected fluid. Their position should be moved.

4. Modifications (scuppers) are needed to facilitate the washing out of the truck's inside rear, cleansing it of fluids and other matter.

5. The observation peepholes can be eliminated, since they are never used. This should save problems of making them leakproof, and shorten production time.

6. Inside lights are to be better shielded from destruction. The lights are needed only for the first few minutes to avoid a rush toward the rear in the darkness when the doors are first closed.

7. A grid on rollers would be desirable to facilitate faster unloading. The company we asked to build it thought it impracticable. Can another supplier be found?

There are ten Saurer special vehicles now on order. May we have one prototype with all the above modifications?

> Head of Group *II* D
> [signed] SS Colonel Rauff

> Request for acknowledgment and decisions.

This was how 97,000 human beings went to their death in the backs of trucks built by the Saurer Company between December 1941 and June 1942. SS Colonel Rauff thought that there might be a more efficient way.[36]

In January 1942 Rommel gathered his forces and counterattacked the British. By June 30, he had pushed them past Bengasi and Tobruk to El Alamein, well on the way to Cairo. It was to be the zenith of Rommel's efforts in Africa.

During that summer of 1942, Hitler temporarily moved his headquarters east into the Ukraine near Winniza, and von Ribbentrop opened a separate headquarters nearby. This was Hitler's choice; he did not want von Ribbentrop under foot, "bothering him with all sorts of matters."[37] In East Prussia von Ribbentrop established headquarters a short distance from the Wolfsschanze at Castle Steinort, owned by the von Lehndorff family, on a lake named Schwentzeitsee. Another part of the minister's staff was at the other end of the lake in a hotel. To friends, von Ribbentrop explained that the reason for having separate headquarters was that he found being near the Führer at this time too "difficult and strenuous."

There was a constant coming and going of staff from Berlin to these outlying headquarters. Each night a train of luxury sleeping cars waited at the Schlesischen Railroad station in Berlin, ready to leave for Hitler's advanced field headquarters; it took over two laborious days to reach Winniza. On the second day the train stopped at 3 A.M. to discharge foreign diplomats who were visiting von Ribbentrop at his separate headquarters. After lunch he and his guests would fly to Winniza for a Führer monologue, then return by car, over bouncing, gutted roads, to his headquarters, and often go to a small station where the Winniza train stopped to pick up the visitors on its way back to Berlin. The visit by foreign diplomats, a trip of three days and four nights, often accompanied by ministry staff, was an exercise in futility, empty ceremony, and needless expense. Probably it was von Ribbentrop's way to "look busy" or, as Spitzy put it, to "reign."

During this time, to show complete devotion to his Führer, von Ribbentrop was becoming involved, through Martin Luther, in the Final Solution. The ministry's first official connection was made in a January 8, 1942, letter dictated in Prague, signed by Heydrich, addressed to "Dear Party Comrade Luther." It said that the conference originally scheduled for December 9, 1941, dealing with the solution of the Jewish question had to be postponed because of "well-known events" (the Russian winter offensive and Pearl Harbor). This conference, with an early meal to follow, was now set for noon on January 20, 1942, in Berlin, at Grossen Wannsee 56–58. The list of those originally invited to participate was unchanged. The letter was stamped as having been received by Department DIII on January 12, 1942, was marked Secret and identified as #181. Each ministry involved was represented by a senior official. With the five Gestapo and SD officers was their "Jewish specialist," SS Lieutenant Colonel Adolf Eichmann.

Wannsee is a sparkling, peaceful lake west of Berlin, surrounded by resort villas, woods, and a beach. Berliners sailed on Wannsee, motorboated on Wannsee, flirted and made love and played tennis and danced and got sunburned and drank champagne or beer. It was an unlikely venue for the planning of mass murder. The luxurious and secluded lakeside house chosen for the conference had earlier been requisitioned by Berlin's criminal police for their own use.

The crux of the ten-page agenda for the conference was this: We have attempted to remove Jews from Germany's life and lands. We tried to cajole, force, and help them to emigrate, and we managed to get rid of about 537,000 from Germany, Austria, and Czechoslovakia. The Jews were told to finance their own emigration. We even had them pay for their impoverished brethren. Besides, 9.5 million American dollars were put at our disposal by foreign Jews. Now the time has come to shove the remaining Jews — about eleven million — into the eastern territories. Page 6 of the agenda was this listing:

LAND		ZAHL [totals]
A. Altreich [Germany]		131.800
Ostmark [Austria]		43.700
Ostgebiete		420.000
Generalgouvernement [Poland]		2,284.000
Bialystok		400.000
Protektorat Böhmen und Mähren [Czecho.]		74.200
Estland [Estonia] — judenfrei [free of Jews]		0
Lettland [Latvia]		3.500
Litauen		34.000
Belgien		43.000
Dänemark		5.600
Frankreich/Besetztes Gebiet [occupied]		165.000
Unbesetztes Gebiet [Vichy]		700.000
Griechenland [Greece]		69.000
Niederlande [Netherlands]		160.800
Norwegen		1.300
B. Bulgarien		48.000
England		330.000
Finnland		2.300
Irland		4.000
Italien einschl. Sardinien		58.000
Albanien		.200
Kroatien		40.000
Portugal		3.000
Rumänien einschl. Bessarabien		342.000
Schweden		8.000
Schweiz [Switzerland]		18.000
Serbien		10.000
Slowakei		88.000
Spanien		6.000
Türkei		55.500
Ungarn [Hungary]		742.800
UdSSR [Soviet Russia]		5,000.000
Ukraine	2,944.684	
Weisrusland [White Russia] aus-schl. [excluding] Bialystok	446.484	
Zusammen [grand total]: über		11,000.000

For today's reader the following begs attention:

This was the beginning of 1942. The Jews of England, Ireland, Finland, Portugal, Sweden, Switzerland, Spain, and Turkey were listed, although these countries were by no means in German hands or under German control. It was simply taken for granted that they would be.

Estonia had already made itself "free of Jews" through some of the most thorough Einsatzgruppen action, zealously aided by native Estonian auxiliary police. The total to be "processed" once Germany ruled all of Europe was eleven million. On page 9 of the agenda, Luther, who was there to represent the Foreign Ministry, was quoted as suggesting that these actions should be delayed in the "difficult Nordic" states (Norway, Denmark) but that the Foreign Ministry anticipated no problems in the eastern countries.

Not mentioned in the agenda or during the conference was that the extermination camps at Auschwitz, Chelmno, Belzec, Sobibor, Maidanek, and Treblinka were already being constructed. Whatever cooperation Heydrich obtained from the participants at Wannsee would send men, women, and children straight into the work gangs, gas chambers, and ovens of these newly built outposts of hell.

Jews over sixty-five were exempt. They were to be sent to the "show" concentration camp at Theresienstadt in Austria, where they were joined by disabled Jewish war veterans, winners of the Iron Cross First Class, and prominent Jews whose disappearance into a death camp might have aroused queries from abroad. Occasionally, this former playground of an Austrian Empress was used to show the world that all of the camps were humane. The actual content and purpose of Theresienstadt, the "show" camp, was often completely overlooked even by those of the anti-Hitler opposition. How could they justify a policy whereby elderly citizens of Germany and Austria, and later of other nations, were taken by force or bullying from their homes, robbed of their possessions, rights, children, and friends, and locked away in crowded conditions in a place not of their choice? Their children and grandchildren were often murdered in other camps.

One of the most ironic and terrifying stories of the Final Solution took place around Minsk in White Russia. The general commissar of the area was an old-line anti-Semitic Nazi Party functionary, Gauleiter Wilhelm Kube. He fully subscribed to the theory that, in his own words, "this plague must be exterminated." Most probably his first objection to the murders by SS Einsatzkommandos was that they invaded "his" province and killed off "his" Jewish workers. Then

Kube changed. When he found out that among the German Jews who had been deported into his province were decorated veterans of the World War, his hatred for the SS suddenly found no limit. He interfered everywhere with the executions, warned Jews to escape, confronted SS commanders and men with threats and even with a drawn pistol.[38] His deputy, a man named Karl, reported to him about the "disgusting, indescribably brutal treatment given to the area's Jews by German police and Lithuanian auxiliary police."[39] Kube became even more disruptive.

His activities were answered by a memorandum from the area's SD commander, SS Lieutenant Colonel Eduard Strauch. Excerpts from his report, which he filed and also forwarded to Heydrich, said, "The Gauleiter wished to see me at once. He said that our behavior and actions were abhorrent to any German and not worthy of the Germany of Kant and Goethe." He went on, "My men have been accused of barbarism and sadism, though we were merely doing our duty. Even the removal of the gold teeth and fillings of Jews selected for special treatment was carried out in an orderly manner by medical specialists. It seemed incomprehensible to me that two Germans could have disagreements over a few Jews . . . [Kube] said that my men got their thrills from executions (*aufgeilen*), which I denied strenuously. I emphasized that I found it regrettable that, after doing sordid work, we are also to have offal poured on us. That finished our conversation."[40]

The following year Kube was murdered by anti-German partisans, blown up by a bomb set under his bed by his chambermaid. His death brought little unhappiness in the headquarters of the SD and Gestapo in the Prinz Albrecht Strasse in Berlin.

At about the same time, Heydrich, appointed deputy governor general of the former Czechoslovakia, was assassinated in Prague by two British-trained Czech secret agents, on May 27, 1942. He was succeeded as head of all German police by the tall, pockmarked, scarred Ernst Kaltenbrunner; though Kaltenbrunner had neither the talent for evil nor the ice-cold blood of his predecessor, his rule was marked by even more murders.

Although the secrecy about the death camps imposed by the SS was stringent, rumors surfaced everywhere. Among the letters to his wife from Count Helmuth James von Moltke, an official at Armed Forces Headquarters in Berlin and a leader of the resistance, is this one of October 10, 1942: "Yesterday's lunch was interesting because the man I ate with had just come from the 'Government' and gave an authentic report on the 'SS blast furnace.' Until now, I had not believed it, but he assured me that it was true: 6000 people a day are 'processed' in this furnace. He was in a prison camp [as a visitor] 6 km away, and the officers there reported it to him as absolute fact."[41] ("Government" was the contemporary German term for Poland, the *Generalgouvernement.*)

As a legal expert in Army Headquarters, Count von Moltke was certainly privy to many rumors. He was firmly anti-Nazi, at the center of the legendary Kreisau Protestant resistance circle (Kreisau was the name of his family's estate), and was executed in 1945 by the Nazis for his resistance activity. Yet even he had heard only vague rumors of the extermination camps.

Had von Ribbentrop heard them? It was most likely, in part because of the constant fighting among all the Nazi higher-ups. Sooner or later someone would have told of the evils of the SS. Certainly von Ribbentrop's plenipotentiary in the field, Martin Luther, must have been aware. Von Ribbentrop's only semi-ally in Hitler's immediate circle, however, was Heinrich Himmler, whose SS units built and administered the extermination camps. Did von Ribbentrop prefer not to believe his ears? Did he prefer to shut these ugly things out of his mind so that he believed he knew nothing about them?

Von Ribbentrop's memoirs contain this paragraph about his Führer: "Never, until April 22, 1945, when I saw him for the last time at the Reichs Chancellery, did he speak a single word about the killing of the Jews. To this day, I cannot believe he ordered the extermination of the Jews. So I must conclude that Himmler presented him with a finished deed [*vollendete Tatsachen*]."[42] An opposite view was offered by Walter Schellenberg, Himmler's chief of espionage. He reported that after Heydrich's death some British contacts had been established with Churchill's approval. Schellenberg asked Himmler whether he could follow up. Himmler turned down the idea because "I am sick of working against the Führer. You will have to accept that!" Schellenberg continued in his memoirs that for Himmler every Hitler word was law — a "religious taboo" — even the horror of the Jewish massacres. According to Schellenberg, "these were originally not Himmler's idea; rather, they were born in Hitler's mind."[43] Still, he reported that after a warm reception by Latvian children in Riga, a touched Himmler heard that the Latvian and Estonian auxiliary police were holding two hundred Jews for "sabotage, espionage, and price gouging."

"Shoot them," said Himmler.

Himmler did hedge some of his bets. That same summer of 1942 he obtained a twenty-six-page medical report stating that Hitler was suffering the effects of syphilis and would in time become paralyzed. One day Himmler asked Felix Kersten, his medical practitioner and masseur, whether the Führer, who was also a patient of Kersten's, was mentally ill. Kersten said Hitler belonged in a hospital for mental diseases, not in the Chancellery. Kersten was one of the men, like Kube, who discovered the need to save Germany by saving the Jews. He frequently made attempts to get life-saving information or to make Himmler change some harsh measure.

The most pathetic of these attempts was a letter directed to "the Führer of the Greater German Reich," from Dr. Wilhelm Hagen, a member of the Tuberculosis Commission of the German Occupational Government in Warsaw.[44] The letter questioned the wisdom and morality in the name of "tubercular treatment" of expelling 200,000 Poles and treating 70,000 others "like the Jews" by killing them. All this was to make room for German "defense farmers." In the thousand-word letter, he outlined the consequences of these actions from a military, diplomatic, political, and moral standpoint. He put his request for kindness and decency "trustingly into the hands of you, my Führer" and ended with *Heil Hitler!* The letter was dated December 7, 1942.

Dr. Hagen's letter was followed by a directive, issued by the head of the Reichs Health Organization, addressed to an aide of Heinrich Himmler's, marked Secret, dated March 3, 1943.

"Reference to your letter of 29.3.43, Dr. Hagen has been removed from any activities licensed by the Reichs Health Organization and has been rebuked sharply." It pointed out that Dr. Hagen had stated he was urged to write his letter at the suggestion of SA Brigadier Weber, an old comrade of the Führer's. Hagen was "an idealist who has made a fool of himself." It was suggested that he "continue to practice emergency medicine back in Germany to preserve his medical knowledge for the good of the community."

More than a year had passed since the collapse of France and the *sauve-qui-peut* rout of Britain's weaponless soldiers at Dunkirk. By 1942 Britain was supposed to have been a conquered nation; Russia was to have been a battered bear. Rommel was supposed to have reached Cairo, with the Suez Canal in the Wehrmacht's hands. Spain was to have been a firm ally, putting the Mediterranean under Hitler's control. Göring's Luftwaffe, after smashing Britain's military and emotional defenses, was to have administered a similar fate to Russia. Japan would own the Orient and Germany the Occident.

Instead, Britain was stubbornly unbeatable. Rommel, held at bay, was in danger of being chased back to Libya. In Russia, Germany was trying one last time to break through before winter. The United States was gaining in its battle against Japan, and a vast flow of American men and matériel was on its way to Britain. Supplies were also going to Russia, and the U-boats could not stop them. And Mussolini? The Duce was not even worthy of mention.

The only progress Hitler could measure visibly was in his fight against the Jews and the Poles, against the mentally ill and the incurable.

No wonder that a minor, probing attack on the French coast was publicized as a major battle. On August 19, 1942, a small force of Canadian and British commandos landed at Dieppe and did some damage before being killed or captured. It was a strange action, hard to explain in retrospect, since it had few chances of success. The rationale ranged from "morale" to "rehearsal," from "deception" to "plain miscalculation."

In North Africa Rommel failed to push through El Alamein to Cairo. On November 2, 1942, a new British general, Bernard Montgomery, took back El Alamein, and thereafter most of Rommel's North African campaign unraveled fast. He lost almost all the ground he had gained. The British took thirty thousand prisoners and Tobruk, which Rommel had seized earlier in the year. The Allied landings in Morocco, Operation Torch, put the Afrika Korps wholly on the defensive.

Hitler ordered all Vichy France occupied on November 11 to counter the new threat from North Africa. That was the end of collaborationist France under Pétain. Three days earlier Hitler had inquired whether the French were willing to fight on Germany's side against Britain and America, but he had received no assurances, even though he had promised the French an alliance "through thick and thin." Supposedly, on November 11 Pétain secretly instructed Admiral Jean Darlan in North Africa to make peace with the Allies and to fight once more against the Axis. That also failed, and Darlan was relieved on December 16 and then assassinated by a de Gaulle agent, Bonnierd la Chapelle, a student.

Now Abetz in Paris was even more helpless than before. All of France was run by the military, the Nazi Party, and their police. Von Ribbentrop's influence was minimal.

Rommel fell ill on September 22, 1942, and went on convalescent leave to Germany and Austria.[45] The remainder of the Afrika Korps, under Hans Jürgen von Arnim, had no future. Nevertheless Abetz sent a senior official, Rudolf Rahn, to represent the ministry at von Arnim's headquarters in Tunisia.

In November, after the occupation of Vichy France, Abetz was recalled by von Ribbentrop. It was a strange recall, because Abetz had never been accredited as ambassador to France. There was never a peace treaty between Germany and France.[46] Abetz knew he was in disfavor, although he did not understand why. He saw neither Hitler nor von Ribbentrop for a full year. He was consulted only once, on the formation of a French volunteer Waffen SS unit called Charlemagne. In his memoirs, Abetz assumed that he was considered "too francophile" and that his constant warnings about the loss of the French fleet and the loss of the French North African colonies were a thorn in the side of von Ribbentrop, particularly now that they had turned out to be correct. The scuttling of the French fleet at Toulon on November 27 had ensured that the French would not join the Axis.

However, this was the smallest of Adolf Hitler's many problems. His offensive launched toward Stalingrad in August had stalled. The entire German 6th Army, under the newly promoted Marshal Friedrich Paulus, was now encircled by the Soviets and anxiously waiting for the Führer's permission to break out. From his headquarters, Hitler gave Paulus his answer: No retreat. But there was no way the frozen German soldier, the *Landser,* short of ammunition and food, could hold out. Göring's promise to supply the troops by air was empty. Hitler should have sensed that Mars had turned his face from him. And Joachim von Ribbentrop?

He spent as much time as he could near his Führer, mostly in East Prussia. As 1942 went on, his hatred of those "rigid creatures" of the Foreign Ministry became more profound. Martin Luther, his "spy," his Wannsee deputy, now became his watchdog in the Wilhelmstrasse. At the ministry, Luther had to concern himself more with negative attitudes than with the danger of actual rebellion. No professional member of a senior German ministry could convince himself that the time for active revolt had come. The staff was held together by the decency and steadfastness of State Secretary Ernst von Weizsäcker, who was running the ministry for its usually absent minister.

The state secretary's dilemma was insurmountable. He hated his chief, von Ribbentrop, as well as Adolf Hitler, von Ribbentrop's chief. He could not stomach the foreign minister's arrogant dilettantism, lack of diplomatic skills, and his absence of courage in dealing with Hitler. Von Weizsäcker's immediate concern was for the men working in the ministry, most of whom he considered honorable. He also wanted to "preserve" the German diplomatic service for postwar Germany, though he obviously misjudged the extent of the world's bitterness toward that service. Like the British colonel in *The Bridge on the River Kwai*, he tried to save the fruit of his men's work, even if it served the Nazi enemy. In carrying out his bitter duties, he could not help signing papers and orders of atrocious content, often the outcome of Under Secretary Luther's collaboration with the SD. Luther's allegiance toward those who executed the Final Solution was maintained at the request of the insecure von Ribbentrop, to "help [him] preserve the Wilhelmstrasse." Originally, von Weizsäcker, like the Kordt brothers and other professionals whom von Ribbentrop had brought into the ministry, was tainted as a "Ribbentrop creature," but by 1942 he had gained the respect of the staff and had the confidence of anti-Hitler people in other ministries. Still, no matter how strenuously he tried to distance himself from von Ribbentrop and to block the party collaboration of Luther's Department Deutschland, he himself had to slog through the mud of the regime. His initials on deportation orders, which became virtual death orders, would haunt him to his last days.

Decency was not enough, but revolt was suicide. It is unlikely that von Weizsäcker was more afraid of death than any other patriot, but if he died, who would act as buffer for the "helpless" ministry officials? This, in all probability, was at the base of his misjudgment. It was also the direct result of the creed of German officialdom: Obey! If von Weizsäcker could have convinced himself that each and every official of the ministry was individually responsible for the fate of Germany, he could have climbed down from his precarious perch.

The blinkers worn by many members of Germany's diplomatic service were astonishing. For instance, Dr. Paul Schmidt, who had been an official and chief interpreter of the ministry for over twenty years, since early Weimar days, said about the bombing of his native Berlin: "I had listened to Goebbels's jubilant announcement in the fall of 1940 of the bombing of London with a heavy heart. Now, after the bombings of Berlin, I would be able once more to look my English friends in the eye."[47] He considered Berlin's suffering in the bombings a kind of atonement for the evils it had inflicted on Britain: "They could take, and we could take it." He failed to take account of the absolute revulsion German murders and atrocities had caused in the outside world, barbarities that could never be sanitized or erased by the bombardment of cities. After all, the original bombings of Warsaw, Rotterdam, and London had brought their own cruel reward, but he did not see that there could never be atonement for the millions killed by the Einsatzgruppen and their foreign helpers and the camps.

Joachim von Ribbentrop's place at the end of 1942 was precarious. His Führer was stumbling and demanded more blind loyalty than ever, but the Führer no longer required the advice of his expert on foreign policy. That need had long passed. To preserve his ministry in Berlin, von Ribbentrop had to depend on von Weizsäcker, whom he disliked but could trust, and on Martin Luther, whom he neither liked nor trusted. Von Ribbentrop's eyes were firmly closed against the future. Personally, he must have worried about his son Rudolf in the Waffen SS. Annelies and Joachim von Ribbentrop were devoted to their firstborn.

Following the Allied landings in North Africa, Hitler had called a meeting in Munich at the old "Chamberlain" hall with von Ribbentrop, Laval, and Ciano. The subject was the occupation of the Vichy government area to achieve "combined vigilance against attack." The actual proclamation spoke about the French Army and the German Wehrmacht cooperating to protect the French frontier and "to shield the African possessions from criminal attacks." The occupation of Corsica and Tunisia was also announced. Laval, fearful, tried to persuade Hitler to avoid the occupation of Vichy France. He failed and soon left the meeting. Ciano looked bored, and von Ribbentrop kept quiet.[48]

When Göring tried separately to persuade French General Alphonse Juin to help to hold Rommel's defensive line against the British, Juin said, "I cannot expect my officers to do that while there are still French prisoners of war in Germany." Late in December 1942, there was another conference in the gloomy Wolfsschanze in East Prussia. Göring again was present. Ciano brought a message from Mussolini: "Stop all offensive operations in Russia. Hold the line with fewer men and assign troops to North Africa." Hitler merely accused the Italian troops of being the weak link that had caused the disaster at Stalingrad, and Laval was assailed with a catalogue of French sins. There were no recorded comments either from Göring or from von Ribbentrop. Such silences became usual.

As part of the program to help the SD in its evacuations for the Final Solution, Dr. Werner Best, an SD general of proven brutality, was dispatched as governor general to stubborn little Denmark. Best became one of the most controversial figures of the war. He was among the original organizers, with Heydrich, of the Gestapo and SD and had then become part of the Foreign Ministry under von Ribbentrop. In Denmark, Best decided to turn a blind eye to the successful efforts of the Danish resistance to smuggle Denmark's Jews to safety in neutral Sweden. Because he was known for his brutality to members of the Resistance in France, it is difficult to understand his decision to allow the Danes to save their Jews. Once word got back to Berlin, he was severely criticized but was allowed to remain in office. As a result of the work and the courage of the Danish resistance, 7906 Danish Jews and part Jews, or people married to Jews, were saved. Four hundred and ninety-two were sent to Theresienstadt; 423 survived.

A hundred and thirteen Danes were executed under Best, though not in connection with the save-the-Jews action. (As in all such events, nothing is pure or clear. Some Danes even confessed to being anti-Semitic. A well-known Danish surgeon once told the author, "We saved the Jews because they were *our* Jews. No one could tell us what to do with *our* Jews. Disliking them was *our* business, not theirs.")

After Best ignored further orders to institute severe reprisals against mounting Danish resistance, he was summoned to Berlin by von Ribbentrop. Hitler, in a screaming fit, refused all reasonable explanations about the ineffectiveness of reprisal measures in stubborn Denmark. "I will not listen!" Hitler howled.[49] A few hours later von Ribbentrop told Best, "Do what you think is right and sensible, but the Führer's orders must be carried out."

Probably the document that most closely described the interlocking machinery of the Foreign Ministry as a newly adopted instrument of mass deportation (and thereby murder) is the following, issued before the Danish evacuation of the Danish Jews:

U. St.S.–D.–Nr. 6862   Berlin 24 Sept. 1942
(Under State Secretary — Dept. D. No. 6862)   SECRET
Memorandum

The Foreign Minister instructed me on the telephone today to expedite the evacuation of Jews from the various countries of Europe, because it is certain that Jews everywhere are maligning us and must be held responsible for acts of sabotage and assassination. After informing me about the current Jewish evacuations from Slovakia, Croatia, Romania, and the occupied territories, the minister ordered me to approach the Bulgarian, Hungarian, and Danish governments to inform them that they are to initiate the evacuations from their countries.

Regarding the Jewish question in Italy, the Foreign Minister has decided to reserve decision. This subject is to be discussed personally between the Führer and the Duce or between the minister and Count Ciano.

Remitted to the State Secretary [von Weizsäcker] with request for personal acknowledgment:
All written documents will be submitted to you for approval.
(signed) Luther
H322897   K213397
E310856   J.J.H.81.[50]

Everyone in this document got involved, from von Ribbentrop to von Weizsäcker to Luther. It also concerned Best in Copenhagen and his opposite numbers in Slovakia and Bulgaria. The document was a clear demonstration of von Ribbentrop's struggle to stay in every way possible within the circumference of his Führer's desires and plans.

13

1943–1944

Prussian Marshals Do Not Mutiny

ON JANUARY 13, 1943, a cursing, screaming Adolf Hitler heard the news of the imminent disaster at Stalingrad. On January 14, Churchill and Roosevelt met at Casablanca, and Roosevelt (without consulting Churchill) for the first time uttered the words "unconditional surrender." This term was greeted with great joy by Goebbels, since he thought he could use it to wring a final terrible effort from tired Germans to win the war.

On February 2, a stunned Hitler heard that Marshal Paulus (*"But I have only just promoted that coward!"*) had surrendered with his surviving ninety thousand men. (*"Why did he not shoot himself?"*). Paulus, under the Russians, founded the anti-Hitler organization called Free Germany and appealed to German troops everywhere to surrender.

In April it was Joachim von Ribbentrop's turn to taste treachery, this time at the hands of Under Secretary Luther.

Luther's original anti-SS stance had slowly eased during the time of his collaboration on the Final Solution with the SD following the Wannsee Conference. In August 1942 Luther had a confidential discussion with Himmler about von Ribbentrop's anti-British mania, which he claimed had forced Germany into a two-front war. Himmler instructed Walter Schellenberg, survivor of the unsuccessful Duke of Windsor caper, to investigate through his espionage network whether peace feelers could be sent to the west. Schellenberg told Luther that he was sure von Ribbentrop had a disastrous influence on the Führer, and asked Luther to provide documentation to speed the fall of the foreign minister.[1] Luther was delighted to comply. He and von Ribbentrop had been at each other's throats, in part because of the mutual dislike of their wives. Another matter of contention was that of von

Ribbentrop's expensive tastes. Luther, who had special access to party funds, had been able to supply the money for the von Ribbentrops' indulgence — in 1942 the wallpaper in the Dahlem villa was changed four times to please Annelies von Ribbentrop — but now the disbursements came to a stop. These were Luther's claims.

Although Himmler still liked von Ribbentrop, Heydrich and the SD had always hated him. One of the points of friction between Heydrich and von Ribbentrop was that the SD wanted to install its own secret agents in the ministry's embassies and ministries. Von Ribbentrop tried to stipulate that they be controlled by him, and a major contest about areas of competence and supervision soon developed. Eventually, through Luther, a deal was made that showed the SD's strength. SD agents were to become part of most of the missions, carried as members but not directly responsible to von Ribbentrop. For instance, they would use special green envelopes because their mail was to remain uncensored. Special radio transmitters were to be built for them, but not inside embassies. In certain emergency cases, the SD could use the broadcast facilities of the missions.

During this contest, Schellenberg reported to Professor de Crinis, a well-known SS medical adviser, that von Ribbentrop's face would slacken on one side whenever he got tired, and his eyelids would droop. Dr. de Crinis claimed that these dysfunctions were due to von Ribbentrop's early kidney problems and would get worse.[2]

According to Schellenberg's memoirs, Luther's attack on his own minister was meant to ingratiate him with Himmler; for years he had not been loved by the black-shirted fraternity. Luther probably sensed that von Ribbentrop was sliding while Himmler was growing in power. When Schellenberg first brought Luther's evidence of von Ribbentrop's extravagance and diplomatic incompetence to Himmler, the Reichsführer SS was tempted to take action, but his aide, SS General Wolff, the man von Ribbentrop had once flown to Scotland, came to the minister's defense. Wolff said, "You cannot allow SS General von Ribbentrop, one of our highest officials, to be wrecked by his miserable crook Luther." Himmler, who had been sitting on the fence, agreed, particularly after Wolff correctly pointed out that Hitler would never dismiss his "Bismarck" because of accusations brought by Luther, a nobody.

The next day a feared senior Gestapo official named Heinrich Müller questioned several quaking subordinates of Luther. A week later Luther was arrested, and von Ribbentrop was given the file of accusations Luther had compiled. He took them to Adolf Hitler, pointing out that Luther had committed treason by criticizing Adolf

Hitler's own foreign policy, and demanded that Luther be hanged for "defeatism." Hitler thought that excessive for an old party comrade, so he ordered that Luther be jailed in Sachsenhausen concentration camp. He became a "privileged" prisoner and was later freed by the Russians. Some say they shot him. Others report he died of a heart attack. The file of accusations against von Ribbentrop remained locked in Himmler's desk. He need not have worried; von Ribbentrop was now umbilically linked to the SS.

In Rome, for instance, he reprimanded a head of mission, Consul Eitel Moellhausen, for interfering with the SS. The consul wanted to warn the minister that eight thousand Jews were to be deported from Rome by the SD for liquidation in Mauthausen concentration camp. On October 10, 1943, the consul was told "to leave things in the hands of the SS and not to interfere." Great offense was taken by the ministry in Berlin that the consul had used the word "liquidation" in his cable.

On May 10 the North African campaign collapsed in Tunis. Von Arnim surrendered to Montgomery. It was the beginning of the avalanche.

It could not have failed to reach the ears of the von Ribbentrops that there was a small but growing anti-Hitler resistance movement. It was probably strongest among certain Army officers, most of them from titled families. Other resistance groups formed around the newly formed "confessing Christians," who refused to accept the official Nazi-tainted Protestant "Reich Church," which had its own Nazi bishop.

The most professional anti-Hitler cell grew around Admiral Canaris, the head of German Armed Forces Intelligence, and several of the senior officers around General Beck, who had wanted to take over the government just before the Munich Conference in 1938. Although there were rumors about these resistance cells, there had been no arrests.

More than ever, Germans, particularly those in the upper strata, with their international connections, looked over their shoulders in fear of the growing strength of the SD and the Gestapo. The SS, like a bull terrier that would rather drown than relinquish its hold on a swimming victim, committed its horrors until the very moment the Allies poured through the walls of their concentration camps and jails.

One case of open resistance became known in many parts of Germany: the White Rose, an innocent, defenseless, and deeply religious group of young Catholics, who chose the gentle flower as their symbol. The *White Rose* fliers, which they wrote and distributed at the University of Munich, condemned Nazi thought and antireligious bias. Their leaders were Hans Scholl, an army medic, his sister Sophie, a student at the university, and their mentor, a professor of music named Kurt Huber. Hans had been an enthusiastic Hitler Youth but became disenchanted after seeing the Einsatzkommandos in action against Jews and Poles. He and his sister and Huber were arrested, convicted of treason, and beheaded. The entire process, from arrest to execution, took four days.

The student resistance groups of 1942, of which there were several, all sang a great German folk song. They would take it up spontaneously whenever they were forced to listen to Goebbels's propaganda:

> *Die Gedanken sind Frei, wer kann sie erraten,*
> *sie Ziehen vorbei wie nächtliche Schatten.*
> *Kein Mensch kann sie wissen, kein Jäger erschiessen.*
> *Es bleibt dabei, die Gedanken sind Frei.*
>
> *Und sperrt man mich ein in finstere Kerker,*
> *das alles sind rein vergebliche Werke;*
> *denn meine Gedanken zerreissen die Schranken*
> *und Mauern entzwei, die Gedanken sind frei.*

> Thoughts are free, who can guess them,
> They pass like the shadows of night.
> No man can know them, no hunter can shoot them
> That's the way it is. Thoughts are free.
>
> And if you lock me in a dark vault,
> It will be a waste of effort.
> My thoughts will tear up gates and walls,
> Because thoughts are free.

In 1943 the bombings of Germany intensified. The RAF continued its night attacks, and now the American Eighth Air Force added saturation daylight attacks with its large new B-17 Flying Fortresses. The old building of the Foreign Ministry on the Wilhelmstrasse suffered severe damage, but the staff kept working, although the top floors were gone. The work was carried on with no heat that cold autumn and winter, and with pools of water on the thick carpets whenever it rained. Each chandelier became a fountain; windows were haphazardly nailed shut. Von Ribbentrop's own office had been "moved" by the bombers to the floor below its usual location.[3]

The minister had stayed as long as he could in East Prussia, lambasting his Berlin staff from a distance, exhorting them to greater efforts in the Führer's task of resettling people to suit his vision of the future. Meanwhile, Berlin was bombed day and night, and the ruined Kaiser Wilhelm Memorial Church stands to this day at the end of the Ku'damm, preserved in its grotesque 1943 agony.

Probably the heaviest loss of human life in 1943 through air attacks came in Hamburg, which was attacked twice during July by over twelve thousand British bombers. Fatalities were 30,480 people; 277,330 apartments were burned out. Twenty-four hospitals were destroyed. Two hundred and twenty schools and fifty-eight churches were razed. This was only a token of the terrible destruction yet to come.

The Luftwaffe was no longer able to keep its enemies at bay. The industrial Ruhr was smashed, its capital, Düsseldorf, flattened by two thousand tons of bombs, and two vast dams in the valley were breached, drowning thousands. Nürnberg, Hitler's mecca, was blasted in March, and a day later, the *Geburtsstadt der Bewegung,* the birthplace of the movement — Munich. Göring took to his bed and then to several of his homes, isolating himself from the truth that Germany was not able to keep up the air contest. Even the visit from young General Adolf Galland, when the fighter ace told him of the fantastic new Messerschmitt jet pursuit craft, the ME-262, had failed to rouse Göring from his daydreams of shopping and collecting *objets d'art.* Hitler barely spoke to him, and Göring did not seek contact with the Reich's leaders. His only moments of joy came when he was introduced to V-1, the self-propelled, jet-powered bomb later known as the buzz bomb in England. Revenge! V for *Vergeltung* (vengeance).

Von Ribbentrop's activities in 1943 were limited. In February, he had the dubious joy of traveling to Rome to explain the Stalingrad disaster to a cynical Duce and his less than sympathetic son-in-law, Ciano, who was about to lose his job (he was sent to the Vatican) and, less than a year later, his life.

Early on July 10, the Allies landed in Sicily, and the Duce himself was only fifteen days from being deposed. After a meeting with the King, he was arrested by the Carabinieri, ushered into a waiting ambulance, and taken into confinement at a Carabinieri barracks.

It became von Ribbentrop's task to meet with Badoglio's new regime at Tarvisio, a border town. Badoglio, Italy's most distinguished marshal, was commanded by the King to form a post-Mussolini government. Von Ribbentrop tried to save some semblance of Axis solidarity, but just to make sure that he would not be kidnaped, he brought along a bodyguard of pistol-wielding SS. Raffaele Guariglia, the new Italian foreign minister, swore solidarity, but General Vittorio

Ambrosio, the new Army chief of staff, tried to stem the flow of German troops now crossing the border to "protect" Italy. There followed two hours of lie-filled interchange. At the end, no Italian raised an arm in the old Fascist salute as von Ribbentrop's train pulled out. Schmidt, who had interpreted for von Ribbentrop, was amused to see the embarrassed grins on the non-saluting Italian officials, the same people he had worked with in their salute-filled Mussolini days. On September 8, Italy surrendered to the Allies, and Mussolini was put under arrest by his King, the man Hitler despised.[4]

In 1943, with everything nearing disaster, von Ribbentrop must have realized that the worst was yet to come, that the Allies would soon invade the heart of Europe from Britain and from Italy, that the Russians would drive west, and that Germany was doomed.

The German Army, which got mauled so fiercely in Russia, had not yet faced the mighty invasion force massing in Britain. The Luftwaffe was helpless to stop the bombers. The U-boats had failed to destroy the enormous American expeditionary force and its mountains of supplies. How could the truth have failed to impress von Ribbentrop? Was he still hoping for the Japanese to finish the job? They were being pushed back across the Pacific, and Tokyo was under heavy bombardment. Did he believe Hitler's talk of miracle weapons? What remained of the worldly businessman who had joined forces with Adolf Hitler?

On September 12 an unshaven Mussolini, tears streaming down his face, was rescued from confinement in the resort hotel Campo Imperatore high up on Gran Sasso Mountain. "I knew my friend Adolf Hitler would not abandon me!" He pulled a black overcoat over his blue suit and followed his rescuer, SS Colonel Otto Skorzeny, and the group of German parachutist commandos to a small plane.[5] With only centimeters to spare, the little overloaded Fieseler Storch groped its way down a rock-strewn meadow and barely got airborne with its load of three men: the pilot, behind him Benito Mussolini, and then the six-foot-three Skorzeny, Hitler's favorite tough guy and secret agent. They made it only because the pilot, one of the Luftwaffe's best, ran the plane off the side of the mountain and used the thousand-meter drop into the valley below to gain air speed. When he pulled out of the dive, the plane barely cleared the trees below. Mussolini, who fancied himself a good pilot, was white. Skorzeny grinned. He had pulled it off! They connected with a larger plane to Vienna.

In the Imperial Hotel, in the suite reserved for the Duce, Skorzeny was decorated with the Knight's Cross ("tin necktie") by an Army colonel who had been ordered by the Führer's personal phone call to take off his own Knight's Cross and hang it around Skorzeny's vast neck. Adolf Hitler still had a sense of drama, though the wasteful and dangerous act of saving Mussolini, his old patron and idol, was merely a sop to Hitler's vanity. It turned out to be poisonous for Mussolini's self-esteem.

Himmler was delighted. The rescue was an SS operation, and the "Black Knights" had received another enormous boost in prestige, though one asks oneself, "For what?" Surely the Reichsführer of the SS must have known that the Reich's days of glory were ending. Was there still hope?

There were to be a few more moments of elation, a few fleeting hours when Hitler's stubborn belief in his destiny would seem nearly justified, but not in 1943 during that September.

The Duce was flown to the Wolfsschanze, but he was reluctant to leave the plane to meet Adolf Hitler. His disgrace was too immense, and he was in tears when he finally shook hands with the Führer. He thought perhaps his dignity would now be restored, but he soon learned his new place in Hitler's scheme of things. He was quickly accused of being a failure. He was asked, "What is this Fascism that it melts like snow under the sun?"[6] Hitler wanted Mussolini to head a new Italian state and to announce that the monarchy was abolished. Ciano was to be executed. He was held in a Munich Nazi Party guest house, where Mussolini had just heard his son-in-law's confession before flying to the Wolfsschanze. Mussolini was aware that Ciano had betrayed him; on July 25, 1943, he had voted in a secret Fascist council to depose Mussolini. But to execute him? Aghast, he said to Hitler, "This is the father of my grandchildren!"

"Duce, you are too good," said Hitler. "You can never be a dictator."

On September 25, 1943, from a borrowed chalet in Bavaria, Mussolini tried, on a priority Führer-phone, to gather a cabinet of old Fascist collaborators, all scattered in exile and safety from Madrid to Bucharest and Bern, but each of them turned him down.

So he flew back to Italy. His chief new associate was Marshal Graziani, the African failure, who hated Badoglio, the new chief of state. Graziani also hated the Germans and he barely put up with Mussolini. Nevertheless, he accepted when he was offered the post of senior minister in Mussolini's new puppet government.

The Germans installed the patched-up Duce in a villa on Lake Garda near the town of Salo. On September 27 he had his first pathetic cabinet meeting. He was a puppet and was to die a few days before Hitler, the puppeteer. Shot, hanged, kicked, splashed by urinating women, the carcasses of Mussolini and his mistress, Clara Petacci, were hung upside down, *pour épater la canaille,* from the beams of a garage on April 28, 1945, near Como.

And von Ribbentrop? Had he believed that the ruined Duce and his false new regime could once more run Italy? Was he delighted to see the end of his old sparring mate, the satyr Count Ciano? The old playboy had been handed over to an Italian tribunal of the new "Republic of Salo," named after the little town on Lake Garda, and executed on January 11, 1944. In his memoirs, von Ribbentrop called Ciano vain and jealous, unreliable and tricky, and careless with the truth. He accused him of betraying his father-in-law. According to von Ribbentrop, Mussolini complained that Ciano had lied to him for years, and von Ribbentrop claimed that Ciano forged his own diaries, which were indeed used against von Ribbentrop during the War Crimes Trials. He specifically referred to an entry in one of the Ciano diaries, October 1, 1939, number XXII, following the Polish campaign. Italy was still reluctant to join the battle. Hitler had pointed out at length that Italy should participate to "satisfy her aspirations" in the Mediterranean. Now von Ribbentrop, according to Ciano, said, "I am of the opinion that in the present circumstances Germany must proceed forthwith to settle the situation by means of force."

Hitler: "Many people think like Ribbentrop. Particularly the Army."

It was Joachim von Ribbentrop's contention that this entry was faked long after its date to cast him as a warmonger.

The bombings of Berlin steadily continued. On a trip to report to Adolf Hitler about events in Turkey, Franz von Papen, then ambassador in Ankara, told how he sat in the cellar under his family's mansion, in Berlin's distinguished Unter den Linden district near the Hotel Esplanade, while bombs fell throughout the night.[7] The family's house burned above him, and the Wilhelmstrasse was in complete ruins. Everyone fled into the neighboring hotel for the night because the windows and doors in the house were gone. All of Berlin's railroad stations had been smashed, but an occasional train still ran on the few tracks left intact or quickly patched by railway engineers.

The irrepressible and beautiful young Russian Princess "Missy" Vassiltchikov, who lived in Berlin while working for the German Foreign Ministry, gave a vivid picture of life under the bombs. She noted on Tuesday, November 23, 1943, "Last night the greater part of central Berlin was destroyed." Daily there came the curious mixture of banality and danger, of life constantly on the brink of death. The next day she had to rush to a meeting through the pouring rain when the air-raid alarm went off at Danger 15, the highest level. "The streets were full of people standing around. I decided to walk home." On the way she stopped at a mailbox to post a long letter she had written to her sister. She had not lunched, and she was ravenous, so the old family cook started to heat some soup while Missy went upstairs to put on slacks and a sweater, her air-raid gear. The sirens wailed once more, and Missy, the cook, and Missy's old father huddled in the kitchen. It was their first taste of massive daylight carpet bombing with its immense crashes, heavy air pressure, huge noise, showers of glass. All three doors flew into the kitchen, torn off their hinges. The two women and the old man managed to prop the doors back into place. When an incendiary bomb fell into the house entrance, they tried to put it out. They turned on all the water taps in case of fire. In the middle of it all, the old cook suddenly served the soup. When Missy jumped up after one nasty crash, her father said, "Sit down. That way you're farther off when the ceiling collapses." They had Schnapps. The bombing continued until early evening. Then the phone rang. A friend, Count Bismarck, called to make sure they were all right.

These American daylight bombings went on for weeks. At night, the British bombers had their turn.

At one point, Missy told of running down a street of burning houses when a nearby wall began to collapse. She lay on the street, covering her head with her arms. When she got up, she spotted the dust-covered face of a Japanese diplomat whom she and her sister had often dodged because he fancied himself a Lothario; under the circumstances, having just shared near-death, she decided to say hello in English. He stared at her dusty face and asked in German, "Have we met?" She decided it was not the time for formal re-introductions.[8]

The von Ribbentrops spent part of late 1943 in Fuschl, because Joachim must have felt useless in East Prussia near the Führer. According to his memoirs, late in 1943 he had advised Hitler by memorandum to make peace with Stalin as quickly as possible. In reply he received a message through Ambassador Hewel, his liaison man at Hitler's headquarters, that "there is no compromise in the fight against Bolshevism. I cannot accept von Ribbentrop's 'business politics.' This war cannot be won by diplomatic means." This was the crux of von Ribbentrop's dilemma. His role had ended.

When the Allied bombing of Berlin intensified, von Ribbentrop returned to the capital. What drove him voluntarily to expose himself to the danger? James von Moltke, the anti-Hitler conspirator, wrote in his diary on November 28, 1943:

> All the military officers are alike. They think [only] of making their lives more comfortable and are indifferent to everything else. On the other hand Ribbentrop and Goebbels, for whom I have no love, concern themselves with everything: they visit their wounded and bombed-out, inspect the damaged sections of their offices, and see to it that their office functions again. Ribbi in particular refuses to return to East Prussia and remains firmly in Berlin.[9]

He probably preferred the danger and purpose of being near his ministry in bombed Berlin to the ignominious treatment Hitler had been handing him.

On December 5 von Ribbentrop had one of his few diplomatic duties of the month, following a severe raid on Berlin. Tough reprisals had been taken against anti-German Norwegian students in Oslo; there were widespread arrests. The Swedish government had protested to the German government. Even Hitler agreed that these measures were too sweeping, but von Ribbentrop was instructed to answer the Swedish protest "in the sharpest language."[10]

That day came the terrible raid on Leipzig, one of the most destructive of the war. It ruined the splendid Baroque city and made hundreds of thousands homeless. And still, no one in the party admitted the end was near. Instead, Joseph Goebbels kept talking of "British fears of reprisals" because of their "bad conscience."[11]

The following day in Berlin there was another confrontation between von Ribbentrop and the Swedish chargé about the Oslo affair. There was a heated exchange. Von Ribbentrop, probably less than convinced by his own words, was a good and faithful servant. To Goebbels, the whole Norwegian affair "stank," and the Führer was angry about the way it had been handled by Norway's Nazi government. Himmler was especially upset (an example of the poor judgment of the Reichsführer SS), because he had planned to recruit forty thousand to sixty thousand volunteers in Norway for SS Division Viking, which comprised the shreds of earlier volunteer SS regiments. These units were Nordland (Danes and Norwegians), Westland (Dutch and Flemish), Germania (Germans and Baltics), plus a battalion of Finnish volunteers. He was sure that the arrest of the Norwegian students would ruin the SS recruiting efforts.

On December 9, Goebbels's diary for 1943 described an apocalyptic fight between himself and Joachim von Ribbentrop. The conflict was about who was to conduct propaganda in Paris. Von Ribbentrop felt it was the Foreign Ministry's function, and tried to get the Army in Paris to back him up, but Hitler seemed to side with Goebbels. The Reich's propaganda minister wrote in his diary, "If Ribbentrop is as clever in his foreign policy as he is toward his colleagues in matters of internal politics, I can well understand why we don't achieve any notable success in our dealings with foreign nations."[12] Bombings, the Allied victories, and the threatened invasion all seemed to take second place with Hitler's staff.

A social note about that same time from Chips Channon in London: "Ciano has been shot . . . He was forty-one . . . He was shot on Mussolini's orders, and I find it rather shocking to shoot one's son-in-law."[13]

Beginning with 1944, von Ribbentrop created a "new" Foreign Ministry. Because of the Luther affair, he eliminated Department Deutschland, the liaison with the party. Its duties were taken over by two other departments directly under his control.[14]

Von Weizsäcker was fired from his post as state secretary and assigned to the Vatican as ambassador. His place as was taken by a nonentity, Baron Adolf Steengracht von Moyland, who had once worked for von Ribbentrop in the embassy in London. Steengracht was weak and inconsequential, but he had an extremely beautiful wife who dressed up many embassy parties. Now he became von Ribbentrop's "parrot," and the sometimes obstreperous von Weizsäcker was safely out of the way. Yet even the most complaisant of Hitler's creatures could at times prove he had a conscience. Steengracht once had added a zero to four hundred, the number of Hungarian Jews permitted to emigrate, thereby saving thirty-six hundred lives.[15]

Germany's efforts on the Russian front were shaking, ready to collapse. On January 28, 1944, Hitler ordered all his senior commanders to the Wolfsschanze. A stormy meeting followed in a large, converted barracks.[16] There, Hitler berated the generals as if they were schoolboys until his greatest commander, Marshal Erich von Manstein, interrupted him. Hitler had melodramatically spoken of "fighting on alone, surrounded by only a few of his generals who remain loyal." Now a furious von Manstein yelled, "You're right, my Führer! That's exactly the way it will happen!" as if to emphasize that the Führer would certainly be alone unless he stopped interfering. On March 30, 1944, one of Hitler's four-engined Condors landed near Lemberg, the southern headquarters of the Russian front, to bring Marshals von Manstein and Ewald von Kleist to the Berghof, where they were relieved of their commands. The mood on the plane was one of deep gloom.

They stayed at a hotel near the Berghof complex. In the dining room they had to witness a raucous, drunken group of senior SS officials who partied with some young Luftwaffe girls. "A birthday party," the marshals were told. It was in sad contrast to the freezing men on the Russian front. But the two marshals and their aides said nothing. They were in Berchtesgaden, strictly Nazi Party territory, where even marshals kept their mouths shut.

The next day at the Berghof, von Manstein was handed one final decoration. The Führer then read a *laudatio,* and that ended the career of Hitler's most valuable military tactician. The reason he gave was ludicrous: the time for "operational knowledge" was over. Now one needed "only to defend."

Why did von Manstein not rebel? "Because," as he had often explained, "Prussian marshals do not mutiny."[17]

How could Hitler still have believed? Even before the invasion from across the Channel his house of cards was ready to tumble. Nowhere could he have found a single hopeful sign. Perhaps he was banking on the V-1 buzz bombs and the V-2 high-altitude rocket missiles. Or perhaps it was the new Messerschmitt jet-engine planes, supposedly going into immediate production.

No matter how bad the news actually was, the Wehrmacht reports showed nothing but success.

January 1, 1944
At the Bridgehead Nikopol, strong combined attacks by Soviet fighters, artillery, and infantry were beaten back with heavy enemy losses.

At Saporitje and Krowgard, a strong enemy unit was split up.

Near Schitomir, 59 enemy tanks were destroyed.

Near Vitebsk enemy breakthrough attempts failed. Near Retschiza, German panzers closed a gap in the line. Fifty-eight enemy tanks and 226 artillery pieces were captured.

In southern Italy, enemy attacks collapsed.

British and U.S. bombers attacked Paris. There was heavy loss of French lives. Nineteen enemy bombers, mostly American four-engine planes, were downed.

The Luftwaffe and German Navy sank 35 merchant vessels in December [1943], total, 225,200 tons. Another 24 were heavily damaged by bombs and torpedoes.

Also: Eighteen destroyers, 1 torpedo boat, 2 gunboats, 2 cruisers, one midsized warship were sunk; one destroyer and five torpedo boats were heavily damaged.

The Luftwaffe and German Navy sank 6 Soviet subs, 4 torpedo

boats, 2 gunboats, 1 icebreaker, 15 landing craft. Others were heavily damaged.

Obviously, Hitler was an avid reader of his Wehrmacht's reports.

The Russians were gathering for the final offensive into Germany. Allied bombers were devastating Germany's cities. Anglo-American forces were in command of North Africa, Sicily, Crete, and the lower boot of Italy, and what was most ominous, even the tightest security could not hide the gathering of millions of troops in Britain, ready to invade the continent. The Axis alliance was gone, with Italy now on the Allied side, Hungary about to defect, Japan fighting her own, and desperate battles in the Pacific.

What, then, was Hitler's cause? How did he maintain his faith in the destiny he had chosen for Germany?

Meanwhile, the slaughter of thousands in the eastern camps continued with mounting savagery, and in Germany itself the SD and the Gestapo pounced on any sign of opposition. Many who were physically and mentally handicapped were disposed of under a regulation called Aktion 1413k2, code-named T4 because the location of the office administering this horror was on the Tiergarten Strasse Number 4.[18] Everything was molded into bureaucratic form, couched in bureaucratic jargon. Nazi Germany in 1944 was probably the only country that made its victims pay for their own beheading by dunning their surviving relatives.

For example, a government bill was sent to the family of a man arrested for the crime of *Wehrkraftzersetzung* (loosely translated as "subversion of the will to fight"). The accused, a lawyer, was overheard by someone on a tram and denounced to the police for this fatal statement: "When the Italians formed a new government after Mussolini's fall, the Führer should have stepped down, because we can no longer win and we'll be burned alive." He was condemned to death and executed. His arrest was on December 24, 1943. He was beheaded on May 8, 1944. The statement sent to his wife included the costs of punitive detention, execution, and bill-mailing. The total was 746 marks, 60 pfennigs.

Several anti-Nazi groups had existed, without formal organization, since before the beginning of the war. The purpose of most of them was to assassinate Hitler and to institute an anti-Nazi government that could now negotiate with the invaders from the east and west. Would the Allies have halted their attacks? Probably not. But Germany would have removed Hitler's gang before the Allies could do so.

Would there have been sympathy among Germans for the killing of Hitler and the removal of Göring, Goebbels, and Himmler? The conspirators did not concern themselves with this question. They were sure that, no matter who agreed or disagreed with them, they were right and their duty clear.

The conspirators, mostly officers and descendants of old titled families, had been planning the coup for years and had been forced to abort several earlier attempts. Hitler often changed his schedule at whim. In some ways he was still the artist *manqué* who hated rigid schedules.

These were typical days in Hitler's life.

| | 1943 | | 1944 | | 1945 | |
	Nov. 25	Dec. 25	Nov. 27	Dec. 25	Jan. 25	Feb. 28
Wake up	10:30	10:30	11:30	11:45	12:00	13:00
Situation	12:35	12:30	15:00	15:00	16:25	16:15
Lunch	14:15	15:30	14:15	14:00	14:00	14:30
Situation	22:00	22:00	—	0:15	0:50	1:15
Tea	1:10	24:00	0:50	2:00	2:10	2:30
Bed	2:45	2:00	5:00	4:00	4:00	5:15

Any man who kept these strange hours was hard to pin down.[19]

One attempt, a bomb placed on Hitler's plane, failed because the fuse was faulty. Retrieving it unexploded from the airplane and getting it out of sight of the SD was dangerous, but it was done with *élan* by one of the conspirators: "Where's that bottle of cognac I was promised? Ah, that must be the briefcase . . ." The plotters included two field marshals and several generals and also many young captains and lieutenants who were aides and adjutants. It finally centered on the magnetic person of Colonel Claus Schenk von Stauffenberg, a badly wounded and heroic man, a soldier-intellectual, an athlete and horseman, a southern German, and a Catholic. The task fell to him because he had access to Adolf Hitler, and the assassination had to be done with a bomb because von Stauffenberg, wounded during the Africa campaign, had but one hand and only three fingers on it. He could not hold a pistol. He was often in Hitler's presence because his distasteful job was to provide reserve units by scavenging what remained of Germany's manpower and of foreigners willing to volunteer.

There were also civilians among this group of conspirators: Carl Goerdeler, a former mayor of Leipzig, Count Helmuth James von Moltke, and Adam von Trott zu Solz, both government officials. There were clergymen and businessmen. Probably the key man in the action was Field Marshal Erwin Rommel, who had at last come to understand how low Hitler had brought Germany.

What sort of government did these men plan? The outline was ready. It was to be anti-Nazi and anti-Communist. It was to be democratic, though not primarily so. Goerdeler, who was to be chancellor, envisioned a semidemocracy, run by a semi-elite. Curiously, although he had protested the Nazis' anti-Semitism, he wanted to treat the post-Hitler Jews as honored strangers in Germany, without returning them to their German citizenship.

The entire Stauffenberg group distanced itself from an earlier and much larger resistance group the Gestapo had code-named the Rote Kapelle, or Red Orchestra, which dealt directly with Moscow. They were not Communists, but they found that the Soviets were their most accessible, potent, and trustworthy sponsors. The German members of the Rote Kapelle conducted some espionage for Moscow, wrote propaganda pamphlets, and were eventually joined by some German Army officers. By the time of the von Stauffenberg attempt, most members of the Rote Kapelle had been executed or jailed.

Von Ribbentrop was not high on the resistance movement's list of those to be eliminated. By this time, just a few months before the invasion, he no longer mattered enough.

Many of the Stauffenberg resistance people were well known to earlier members of von Ribbentrop's own staff. General Beck, one of the key officers, had collaborated with the Kordt brothers as early as the 1938 Munich crisis, and many of Canaris's Abwehr men, like General Oster, were known by the Kordts. Even Reinhard Spitzy, once von Ribbentrop's adjutant and then his secretary, had found a place working with General Oster. It is unlikely that von Ribbentrop could have remained completely in the dark. He must have known there was organized opposition to Adolf Hitler. There were too many obvious connections, both in his diplomatic and his social life.

However, had he been in possession of solid information, there is no doubt that he would have warned the Führer. By 1944 his life was so closely linked to his Führer's that losing him through an assassination would have been intolerable. Everything in Joachim and Annelies von Ribbentrop's life focused on Adolf Hitler. All other bonds had long been cut. The von Ribbentrops' prewar social connections, several with Jewish friends, had not endured. Their family ties had been ruptured. The Henkells stayed away from them. Their friendships abroad had faded in the war. Certainly there was no one inside the Nazi Party whom they could call friend. The one man on whom Joachim von Ribbentrop had relied, the only one von Ribbentrop called by the familiar *du,* Heinrich Himmler, was no longer a friend. All that remained were people like the weak-willed Steengracht, now state secretary. Even the Führer kept the von Ribbentrops at arm's length. Only their children were a genuine source of affection and pride. Rudolf had been awarded the Knight's Cross.

Hammer blows kept raining on Germany. On June 4 Rome fell to the Allies. On June 6 Rommel, who was in command of the Seventh Army on the Channel coast, was home in Germany, feeling reassured that there would be no invasion. It was too unlikely, considering that the Navy had predicted rough seas in the Channel and the meteorologists looked for poor flying weather. There was no reason Rommel would not have visited his home in Herrlingen before keeping a rendezvous with Adolf Hitler in Berchtesgaden. Rommel's only son, Manfred, was also in uniform, a private soldier in the Air Force, and Rommel longed to see him. Then, despite the adverse conditions, in the ugly, stormy dark, at 1:30 A.M. on June 6 came the invasion. The Wehrmacht's report, usually so laconic, began that day in 1944 with a trumpet call.

> Special Report! *Sondermeldung!* The long-expected attack by the British and North Americans against the French coast began last night. A few minutes after midnight, after a heavy bombardment, enemy airborne troops landed in the Seine estuary. Other troops were landed from the sea.[20]

One can only guess what it meant for heavily armed and equipment-laden American and British soldiers to dive out of their Douglas C-47 transport planes to face the stormy unknown, eight hundred feet below, in hedgerow-gridded Normandy. Others waded through rough surf. The report also told of the landings on the obstacle-strewn and mined beaches and of bitter fighting.

How could von Ribbentrop in Fuschl have guessed at the blunders that followed, precipitated by the Führer's personal habits and the fear he instilled in everyone near him, even in generals who had been decorated for bravery? When the invasion was still balanced between success and disaster, Hitler was asleep and could not be disturbed.

From Fuschl to the Berghof is only a short drive, but even if von Ribbentrop had known the true nature of the events, it is unlikely he would have awakened the Führer. The days when he would have braved Hitler's fury had long passed. He was to record in his memoirs that in 1941 he had once violently disagreed with Hitler, who had clutched his heart and feigned a coronary crisis. "Don't ever do that to me again, Ribbentrop; disagree with me so vehemently." Von Ribbentrop, guilt-ridden, never forgot it. In fact, the image lasted until the very end, when he told the Nürnberg prison psychiatrist that killing Hitler would have been "like killing my own father."

At 6 A.M. Rommel's chief of staff, General Hans Speidel, called Rommel at his home in Germany. The night had been wasted because General Gerd von Rundstedt thought the Normandy attack was only a feint. Since Allied fighter planes dominated the skies, Marshal Rommel, like all senior officers, had been forbidden by Hitler to fly. So he drove back as fast as he could, arriving in Normandy late in the afternoon after canceling his Berghof visit.

That day Hitler slept until 3 P.M. This meant that certain available panzer divisions, which might have quashed the invasion on the beaches, could not go into action. No one could commit them without Hitler's express permission. At 4:55 P.M. on June 6 Hitler issued an impossible order from the Berghof that "the beachhead must be cleaned up no later than tonight."[22] Of course it could not be done. The bridgeheads were held and consolidated.

William Shirer reported that General Speidel remembered Rommel later forced Hitler into a showdown in northern France near Soissons. They met on June 17 in a concrete bunker that had once been built as advance Führer headquarters for the victory in France. Rommel came straight to the point. "The battle is hopeless. Let us take the troops back and regroup beyond the naval guns." The western campaign was lost, as was that in the east. Make peace! Hitler's cold reply was "Just take care of your invasion front. I shall take care of the future of the war."

On June 20 the Russians launched their next offensive and von Rundstedt was fired after telling Keitel to "make peace, you fool!"

Disastrous news was to follow. Trying to crisscross his patched-up command, Rommel was gravely wounded on July 17 when his staff car was machine-gunned on a Normandy road by an Allied fighter plane. His skull was fractured in several places. He was never to recover completely, robbing the von Stauffenberg group of a great central figure, who, if healthy, might have salvaged that effort and achieved some semblance of success.

The attempt on Hitler's life code-named Valkyrie, after the Nordic goddesses who floated high above a battlefield to point at those who were to die, finally took place on July 20, 1944, at the Wolfsschanze in Rastenburg. The bomb, set to go off at a conference table, killed and hurt several senior generals, but Hitler was only superficially wounded. The combination of circumstance and sheer incompetence was overwhelming and has been endlessly discussed since that day.

Probably the key error was depending on Adolf Hitler's death as the central element and having no Army units at hand loyal to the plotters; these could have breached the many concentric rings of SS guards at the Wolfsschanze and taken charge. The entire machinery of the revolt faltered the moment it became clear that Hitler had survived. The SS kept him safe, and there was no alternative plan to take over his headquarters and arrest his close henchmen. Hitler at bay, like Mussolini, might have been as impotent as Hitler dead; probably more so.

Yet the average German was still slavishly devoted to him and had been taught to link the defense of Germany against disaster with a paradoxical adoration for their Führer, the man who brought them to the edge of doom. They clutched the person of Adolf Hitler as their shield against the vengeance of the advancing Soviets. He would still save them.

On July 21 the revolt was finished. By daybreak, von Stauffenberg and his immediate associates were dead. They were shot in the courtyard of Army headquarters in the Bendlerstrasse in Berlin. The firing squad's targets were illuminated by the headlights of Army cars. Above the crash of rifles came Stauffenberg's shout: "God save our holy Germany!" In his office, General Beck tried to kill himself but failed. He only wounded himself, and was shot there and then by a sergeant.

Today, that street is called Stauffenberg Strasse, and the men of the resistance are national heroes to all but a handful of ultraconservatives. As many as two hundred others were to die barbarically, strangled by ropes while being hoisted on meat hooks fastened to beams of the execution hall at Plötzensee prison. Camera crews sent by Goebbels to film the execution for the Führer were sickened and had to abandon their task. Today the brick-walled building is a national shrine.

About eleven thousand others were arrested by the Gestapo and SD as co-conspirators or simply because they were relatives. Vengeance and cruelty continued even as the Allies' guns could be heard nearby. Among those executed were twenty-one generals, thirty-three colonels, two ambassadors, seven senior diplomats, one minister of state, three secretaries of state. In 1944, 5764 were arrested; in 1945, another 5684.

At the Wolfsschanze on that fateful July 20, a shaky and stunned Hitler found his right arm temporarily out of action, one eardrum shattered, his legs singed. But he was alive. Some of his aides were badly wounded and near death. His valet helped him dress in a clean uniform to go to the small nearby terminal, where the puppet Mussolini was arriving by train. Hitler reached out with his left hand to shake the shocked Duce's right hand and conducted him on a tour of the devastated scene of the act, as if to prove that the fates had made him immortal. During tea at 5 P.M., Mussolini was witness to the scene of Admiral Dönitz, head of the Navy, attacking Göring for the Luftwaffe's failures. Then the fat Reichsmarschall blasted von Ribbentrop for his disastrous foreign policy and almost struck him with a raised marshal's baton. Göring screamed, "Ribbentrop, you lousy little champagne peddler!" Von Ribbentrop shouted back, "I am still the Reich's foreign minister and my name is *von* Ribbentrop."[23] Mussolini was embarrassed. Hitler was not listening. He was deep in his own thoughts, sucking lozenges, his ears stuffed with cotton wool. He paid no attention to his squabbling henchmen or to his Italian guest until someone mentioned Röhm and his treason. Then Hitler came furiously to life. He yelled for bloody revenge on the conspirators, their wives, relatives, and children. He used his very survival as proof, to himself, to his subordinates, to every last German in the armed forces or civilian life, that he was fated to lead Germany. The fact that he had survived proved that God, whose name he used only on momentous occasions, had chosen him for the task.

The German people believed him. They suffered more bombs and fought on. Hitler's survival also stiffened the resolve of the SS, men who had "steeled" themselves to do the business that "had to be done by those of courage" in the concentration camps and the killing camps.

Joachim von Ribbentrop also seemed reinforced by "judgment of God and the proof of His benevolence to Germany's Führer." Oddly, the man whom the conspirators had planned on as the future chancellor, Carl Friedrich Goerdeler, had been against assassination; he too called Hitler's survival "the judgment of God."

The question is often asked why the German resistance movement was so belated and why Germany's leading classes originally endorsed Hitler's anti-Semitism. Many titled and *haute bourgeois* Germans were anti-Semitic in the old-fashioned, conservative "social" way. In this respect, they did not differ from their British, French, or even American contemporaries. "One invited" only a few Jews. "One married" them only if one could explain that they were the wealthy daughters of titled Jewish banking families. Hitler's early anti-Semitism fell on sympathetic ears among many in Germany's upper classes who accepted anti-Semitism as a *specific* manifestation, not as a *symbolic* one. They could not or would not see that the attack on Jews was a signal of impending attacks on everyone who differed from the National Socialist standard — Catholics, Masons, artists, millionaires, eccentrics, cynics, homosexuals, derelicts, avant-gardists, recluses.

Pastor Niemöller is said to have confessed, "When they came to arrest the Jews, I said nothing. I was not Jewish. When they came to arrest the Catholics, I said nothing. I was not Catholic. When they came to arrest the Communists, I said nothing. I was not Communist. When they came to arrest me, I had nothing left to say."

The German "gap" seemed to be that missing link of protective reaction to be found in (often anti-Semitic) upper-class Britain, which nevertheless allowed a Jew to take his oath in Parliament wearing his hat and without reference to Jesus, which appointed a Jewish (by descent) prime minister and a Jewish viceroy of India. These appointments were too important to be discounted as mere tokens. The British seem to have a built-in alarm system that rings whenever there is a genuine threat to individual liberty. It had been part of British thinking since Runnymede. Americans, who certainly have their problems with racial prejudice, react with supernatural speed to any attack on personal liberties. For every hundred admitted offenses against citizenship and decency there are a thousand instant protests.

The French, as anti-Semitic if not more so than the Germans, also had a Jewish prime minister and, before him, Émile Zola and *J'accuse* and the redress of the brutal treatment of Captain Dreyfus, and before Zola, Voltaire and Rousseau.

Why had Germany's upper classes not developed this quick awareness of *wrong to one, wrong to all?* Once they did recognize the evil, their courage was immense, but belated.

The Hitler of old would never be again. From July 20, 1944, onward he was a sick man, unsure of his step, slower of speech and reaction, and more deeply in thrall to the treatments of Dr. Theo Morell, the man who had revived the tired, ill President Hacha of Czechoslovakia in 1938 in Berlin when Göring frantically called for a doctor. Morell, who began his career as a young ship's doctor, had set up practice in Berlin. An expert in the use of injected stimulants and sedatives, he soon developed a large circle of famous patients, much like the so-called Dr. Feelgoods of New York in the sixties. Hoffmann, who was Hitler's photographer, originally introduced Morell to Hitler in 1936, when the Führer, fearing he had stomach cancer, was suffering only psychosomatic cramps. He became one of Morell's most devoted patients. Karl Brandt, another Hitler doctor (sentenced to death in 1948 for euthanasia and other SS medical murders), dubbed Morell the "Reichs injection master."[24] There was hardly a day when Hitler did not have his rendezvous with Morell.

There is a theory that Hitler introduced Morell to Göring and von Ribbentrop. Göring was a morphine addict since his days in Sweden after the First World War, when he was battling the pain of a war wound.[25] Von Ribbentrop, whose cast-iron stomach withstood alcohol, probably because of his pre-Hitler business life, had never been addicted to drugs, although he was always a high-strung man. During the last year of the war, when his world was shaken by Hitler's cold reserve, it is possible that he asked Morell for help. It would explain some of the sleepwalking, apathy, and unawareness of the imminent dangers and his collapse at the beginning of his imprisonment at Nürnberg. Kersten did treat him for stomach cramps.

Adolf Hitler wanted to mount one final military thrust while he waited for the supposed flood of Messerschmitt jet planes and the devastation to be caused in London and elsewhere by Wernher von Braun's newest ballistic rocket missile, V2, first launched against London on September 8, 1944. There would be more than a thousand shot against the same target. Over two thousand were launched that year against Brussels and Antwerp from V2's Peenemunde oceanside pads. The V2 was the father of today's SCUD.

Hitler's surprise offensive was a blitz attack against the Americans in the Ardennes Forest (later called the Battle of the Bulge) in which a large panzer army, most of it robbed from the Russian front, aimed to punch through the Americans and rush to the Channel coast to outflank them. The attack was to be spearheaded by German soldiers in American uniforms, trained to play-act the part of GIs by Hitler's favorite secret agent and Mussolini liberator, SS Colonel Otto Skorzeny.

On a gray, cold, mist-shrouded day early in December 1944, they attacked the unsuspecting GIs at Stavelot in hilly southwest Belgium, and for a short while confused them with fake American MPs, who misdirected traffic and did other frightening but minor harm. But the U.S. 101st Airborne Division, under General A. C. McAuliffe, rushed to Bastogne to block the German troops. When the snow and foul weather lifted on Christmas Day, the U.S. Air Force did the rest, in combination with part of General George Patton's Third Army, which sped reinforcements into the Bulge.

In the final western assault, the Germans lost 120,000 dead, wounded, and missing, 1600 planes, 600 tanks and assault vehicles, and 6000 vehicles. The Americans lost 8000 killed, 48,000 wounded,

21,000 captured and missing, 733 tanks and tank destroyers. Even in its last gasps, mortally wounded, the German Army still had fierce clout.

That was Hitler's last military adventure. It was mounted against the advice of Günther Blumentritt, Walther Model, Hasso von Manteuffel, some of his best generals. Even SS General Sepp Dietrich, commander of the SS Leibstandarte Adolf Hitler, a man who began as one of Hitler's street toughs, was reluctant. Hitler ignored them all. "I need no advice from you, gentlemen," said a bent and shaking Hitler, his left arm twitching, one leg dragging. "I have commanded the Army for five years. I have read Clausewitz and Moltke." General von Manteuffel reported these words, according to William Shirer.

During the last days of January, some of Marshal Zhukov's troops reached the Oder River. The Russians were now a short peacetime car trip from Berlin, about fifty miles away.

To study the Wehrmacht reports for the time between Christmas 1944 and February 1, 1945, is to learn the art of creative writing. While history tells us that American and British troops advanced toward Germany, each day's *Wehrmacht Berichte* brought news of thousands of burned American tanks, tens of thousands of prisoners. Each attack by the Allies, east or west, was "beaten back in a bloody manner." Only the map shows that each "victory" was closer and closer to the heartland of Germany. No doubt Germany's soldiers and airmen were courageous, but the writers at the Oberkommando der Wehrmacht matched them in sheer audacity. One detects the usual "kill the messenger bearing bad news" syndrome of all dictatorships.

14

1945

Justice from the Bomb Bay
of a Boeing's Belly

ON NOVEMBER 20, 1944, Adolf Hitler left his dark, gloomy fortress in the forest, where fate had once spared his life. He returned from the Wolfsschanze to the rubble of his capital city and the scarred Chancellery.

On December 10 he moved on to another block of concrete bunkers, this time in the Friedberg area of Hesse. Those who had not seen him since July 20 were shocked by the man's deterioration.[1] Morell's injections? Parkinson's disease?

On January 16, with the Russians nearing the Oder River, Hitler returned from the safety of Hesse to his Chancellery in Berlin.[2] He was never again to leave it or the bunker beneath it except for a few brief sorties into the rubble and bomb craters of the ruined Chancellery gardens and the neighboring Foreign Ministry garden.

January 30, 1945, brought a harsh reminder of what might have been. It was the twelfth anniversary of Hitler's coming to power in 1933, and of the oath of office taken a few houses away, down the bombed Wilhelmstrasse in the old Presidential Palace.

The Wilhelmstrasse's neoclassic buildings were now skeletons. First there was Speer's masterpiece, Hitler's Chancellery, once *faux* Greco-Teuton. Next came von Ribbentrop's Foreign Ministry and, across the street, the Deutsche Bank. Diagonally across from it stood the Prusso-Imperial Presidential Palace, also von Ribbentrop's. Alongside the Presidential Palace stood the Ministry of the Interior, where Frick, the jurist of the regime, had devised the so-called Nürnberg racial laws, and then the British Embassy, where Sir Nevile Henderson had fought that losing battle with his own good manners. At the Unter den Linden corner was the Hotel Adlon, Berlin's finest, with its special air-raid cellar reserved for Nazi and foreign dignitaries. Herr Adlon, the owner, was still in residence, managing his battle-weary establishment. Unter den Linden, the wide boulevard, was named for its linden trees, which had long disappeared, either splintered by bombs or chopped down for the stoves of Berlin's shivering survivors. The great Tiergarten Park beyond the Brandenburg Gate looked like any forest after armies had fought for its possession, although the Russians were still at the Oder.

The Führer's bunker under the Chancellery was large, built on two levels, with many bedrooms, kitchens, bathrooms, conference rooms, dining rooms, and offices. About twenty of its rooms were in use. Underground passages connected the Chancellery bunker with two others: that of the Foreign Ministry next door and a large one under the Voss Strasse.

By now, Adolf Hitler was shaking and uncoordinated. He could read only from the pages his secretaries typed in special Führer script, an extra large typeface, and he seemed to have trouble standing and walking.[3] But this was deceiving. Whenever he subjected Army Chief of Staff General Heinz Guderian to his rage and anger, whenever he screamed his bitterness, he seemed in complete physical control of himself. No one knew whether his disabled appearance was play acting, or whether the Morell injections caused the violent swings in mood and physical coordination. Perhaps Professor de Crinis's diagnosis of Parkinson's was correct. It is astonishing that the people around Hitler still listened, feared, and believed. Maybe they felt trapped, beyond redemption. Had the Russians been physically and directly at the door, they might have been quickened into an act of self-preservation. Perhaps it was Martin Bormann's threatening presence that had held them together so long.

Among the many German divisions chased west by the Soviet Army was the 19th Panzer (Hannover), the unit which had set out that early morning in September 1939 on its road to glory, the one whose chaplain was killed on the first day. Now they knew: it was indeed a bad omen. Some of the division's few survivors, those who lasted through war and Russian prison camps, would not return to their homes in Germany for ten years.

On January 24 General Guderian told von Ribbentrop in private at the wrecked ministry offices that the war was lost and asked him to persuade Hitler to make peace. How could Guderian have known that von Ribbentrop had no influence on Hitler but welcomed this chance to regain Adolf Hitler's attention by repeating Guderian's statements?

Two hours later, during his daily situation conference, with Guderian in attendance, Hitler raged at "all those who talked defeat." "Come and tell me, but I forbid you to tell anyone else! It is high treason!"[4] This was the last meeting in Hitler's large office in the Chancellery. Thereafter, the meetings were held in the bunker. Also, from that day on, Kaltenbrunner, head of the SD, hovered in the background.

Everyone was still frightened and cowed by the palsied Adolf Hitler. The man was a wreck. He confessed to Speer on January 18 that his hand shook so badly, no one could read his writing — and he handed Speer a birthday present, an inscribed photograph. Speer checked the dedication, and Hitler was right. It was barely legible. Speer was shocked when Hitler then calmly issued orders to destroy most of the things that would enable the German people to rebuild their lives after the war. Hitler wanted scorched earth. "If Germany is a weak nation, it deserves to die! Only the inferior would survive . . ."[5]

Perhaps Hitler's Germany was collapsing, but its viciousness continued without pause. In the People's Court Building some of the men who had planned Hitler's death in July 1944 were still on trial. Their prosecutor was Roland Freisler, president of the court. A converted former Communist who became the Reich's Torquemada, Freisler had spent the day berating the accused Ewald von Kleist-Schmenzin, the same man who visited London in 1938 to try to convince Chamberlain's people to stem Hitler's tide. Von Kleist proved to be a tough man to frighten, so Freisler temporarily switched his attack to another prisoner, Fabian von Schlabrendorff, a lawyer and officer. Von Schlabrendorff, who despised Hitler, was the man who had placed the faulty bomb on his plane.

Just when Freisler was shouting, "You are a traitor!" the air-raid sirens sounded. The prisoners were shackled hand and foot and taken to the cellar; the prosecutor and his staff were rushing for the same shelter as the first American B-17 Flying Fortress bombers came overhead. Justice was dealt from twenty-seven thousand feet. Freisler, who had berated, belittled, insulted, humiliated, and condemned so many courageous men, had only seconds to live. A beam crushed his chest. He died still clutching von Schlabrendorff's folder. The victim was alive and the prosecutor dead. When the prisoners were returned to Gestapo headquarters on Prinz Albrecht Strasse, that building was also on fire.

Von Schlabrendorff was one of the few plotters who survived. Most lost their lives even though Freisler was dead. Hitler could not win a war against Germany's enemies, but he defeated many patriotic Germans.

At the end of January 1945, von Ribbentrop screwed up his courage to ask Hitler for permission to establish unofficial contact with the Russians. He even offered the services of Annelies, who would fly to Stockholm to make contact with Madame Alexandra Kollontay, the powerful Soviet ambassador to Sweden. Annelies would claim to be a divorcée to gain the Russian woman's sympathy and then would offer to make contact with the Führer. When Hitler rejected the scheme, von Ribbentrop offered to take his family to Moscow and to leave them there as hostages while peace was being negotiated. Hitler again shook his head. "Ribbentrop, don't give me any troubles like Hess!" he said.[6]

Von Ribbentrop should have remembered the time after Mussolini's final visit to the Wolfsschanze, when the Italian received his "instructions" as a puppet dictator. For some reason, Hitler told Mussolini he might make peace with Moscow. Later, an amazed von Ribbentrop tried to see Hitler to pursue this idea, but he was rebuffed for even mentioning it. Later, Hitler came to his quarters, seemingly contrite, and said, "If I made peace with them today, I'd fight them again tomorrow. I can't help myself" (*Ich kann halt nicht anders*).* For Hitler, the idea of another treaty with the Soviets was too repugnant to consider.

The world outside became more and more remote from the Führer, von Ribbentrop, and most of the others in their bunkers. Hitler would occasionally take his Alsatian dog, Blondi, for a walk in the shattered gardens, but he always came back grim-faced.[7] He took refuge in his dreams. Speer and he often studied the model of a redesign of his hometown of Linz that had been set up in a nearby room.[8] By now, the truth had penetrated. Hitler knew that the end was near, and his brain was beginning to create the scenes to come.

Although von Ribbentrop could now clearly see into the grim future, his ministry still functioned, and his Department II, successor to Luther's Department Deutschland, was more helpful to the SS than ever. It had full charge of "Jewish matters," and, until the final days, it helped to hurry the remaining Jews to their fiery death. The machinery of hatred and destruction continued to function until the very moment

---

*This seems contrary to the pre-emptive theory about Barbarossa.

when an Allied soldier, American, British, Russian, or French, stood at the gate of a concentration camp or the door of a Gestapo prison.

Department II of the Foreign Ministry, under Eberhard von Thadden and Horst Wagner, had condensed its immediate task into:

1. The delaying tactics or rejection of all neutral intervention regarding deported Jews.
2. The blocking of enemy reports as "horror propaganda."
3. Refusal to give information to chargés or to international organizations, like the Red Cross, about the fate of deported Jews.
4. The prevention of the emigration of several thousand Jewish children to Palestine.
5. Personal and propagandistic support for the deportation of Slovakian, Greek, Hungarian, Romanian, and stateless Jews into Auschwitz.[9]

After the German defeat, Horst Wagner outlined the duties and responsibilities of Department II for the American authorities without even mentioning its close association with the SS. When his outline was uncovered as a lie, Wagner fled to South America. He returned to Germany in 1952 under a false name as correspondent for an Argentine newspaper and was finally indicted by a court in Essen for complicity in the murder of 356,642 Jews. Legal maneuvers and illnesses postponed his trial. He died of natural causes in Germany on March 13, 1977, without having been prosecuted.

To prove how crushing was Himmler's continuing machinery of Hitler's revenge, on February 2 Goerdeler, the former mayor of Leipzig and resistance fighter, was executed at the same time as Himmler tried to make contact with Sweden. Goerdeler's younger brother was executed on March 1, 1945.

Even the trial of von Kleist-Schmenzin continued. Freisler had died on February 3 and was buried without ceremony. Hitler himself insisted that there be no semblance of state funeral. But von Kleist-Schmenzin was convicted and on April 9 was executed while Hitler and his entourage cowered in their bunker and their enemies were within artillery range.

Equally harsh retribution was handed out by kangaroo courts of hastily convened Army field police or roving SD and Waffen SS. Many soldiers or officers who were deemed deserters or civilians whose identification papers were suspect were hanged on the spot from trees or lampposts. According to Wehrmacht figures, the number of executions by formal courts-martial and firing squads, added to lynchings by roving squads, was 14,500.

On March 7 the Americans crossed the bridge at Remagen over the Rhine, and with them came the deluge of Allied troops into Germany.

After Hitler's orders to Speer to destroy everything, Speer decided to put an end to the man. He planned to pump poison gas into the bunker but was foiled by someone who had raised the level of the air intake well above shoulder height, probably to avoid smoke from the nearby government buildings.

On March 19, Eva Braun, Hitler's mistress, arrived in the bunker from her safe haven in Bavaria. She stayed with Hitler despite his halfhearted protestations.

Von Ribbentrop was living in his own bunker, close to his Führer. Annelies and the family were in Fuschl, but she had rented a small villa near Dachau, the notorious Munich suburb, in case she had to leave the castle. On March 25 Joachim decided to ask the Japanese ambassador, his old friend Oshima, to initiate some peace feelers in Stockholm through the Japanese Embassy. A Japanese military attaché flew from Stockholm to Berlin on March 28 but was sent back to Stockholm because von Ribbentrop had acted on his own. Hitler listened to his "idea" but turned it down *kategorisch* (categorically). He actually told von Ribbentrop, "I am absolutely convinced I will win final victory."[10] Could von Ribbentrop have believed him? In any case, he did ask the Japanese to cancel his request for peace talks.

This was von Ribbentrop's second Stockholm contact within the month. Earlier, he had had an inconclusive visit from Count Folke Bernadotte, cousin of the King of Sweden, who came to negotiate for the release of millions of Jews in return for certain political offers to Germany.* Bernadotte's dealings began with Himmler, who was hiding out at a clinic at Hohenlychen near Berlin for treatment of "stomach disorders." Again the mission was aborted, since Hitler was not involved, but von Ribbentrop met with Bernadotte. The disgusted Swedish count later described von Ribbentrop's one-hour monologue as filled with arrogant banalities.

On March 28, the high-strung, truthful General Guderian was fired, and his place was taken by General Hans Krebs, a devoted Nazi and a friend of Bormann's. The only thing left for Krebs to do was

---

*Bernadotte, later the UN mediator in Palestine, was assassinated in 1948 by Jewish extremists.

listen to Adolf Hitler's daydreams about units that no longer existed. He would witness Hitler's last testament to the German people. Guderian's eventual survival was ironic, because he was a member of the military tribunal formed after the July 20 assassination attempt. He had channeled many victims toward Freisler's tender mercies.

During this time came the great raids on Dresden, which decimated the Rococo city and killed tens of thousands. Hitler proposed to his circle in the bunker that "harsher measures" be taken against Allied troops. According to the historian David Irving, two nerve gases, Tarin and Sabun, were ready for use, but Göring, von Ribbentrop, and Admiral Dönitz were bitterly opposed to their use.[11] Only Goebbels approved, but in the end they were not used.

This was not the time for claustrophobics. All who lived in the bunker, or who had to go there for Hitler's eternal meetings, spoke about the dank air, the monstrous hum of air compressors and generators, the unvarying artificiality of electric lights, and the concrete-cushioned shocks of the hammer blows on the city overhead. Von Ribbentrop mostly stayed in his own nearby bunker, isolated from his wife, his children, his Führer. The others, the men who had always been his enemies, were now near the Führer, although Göring, the man of empty promises, was in deep trouble with his chief.

Goebbels came into the bunker on the night of April 12, crowing with delight. Roosevelt was dead! For a moment Hitler thought this was the long-promised sign from Providence, but on the sixteenth, the Russians slammed their way across the Oder River, and there was little now between them and Berlin. Providence had lied. Everyone had lied, even the SS. Just before his birthday Hitler gave Guderian a last distasteful task: order the Leibstandarte Adolf Hitler to remove its sleeve band with his name. Guderian refused. He said only Himmler could do so. Sepp Dietrich, old Nazi fighter, personally went to the bunker to complain about the undeserved insult. Hitler canceled the order.[12]

Hitler's fifty-sixth and last birthday came on April 20. That morning he went to the desolate Chancellery garden to decorate a group of young boys for their fighting courage; they had attacked tanks and lobbied mortar shells at Soviet troops. The last known photo and film of Hitler were taken at that time.

Later, back in the bunker, in the crowded situation room, Hitler took his seat at the small map table. Göring was wearing a new, olive-drab, American-style uniform.[13] He and everyone around the table said that Berchtesgaden should become the new headquarters, but Hitler refused. "How can I ask troops to fight for Berlin if I withdraw to safety? I shall leave it to fate." His words were prophetic. Zhukov had crossed the Oder.

Göring said he would leave, but Hitler barely paid attention.[14] There and then he split command of Germany into north and south. Admiral Dönitz was to command the north from Plön, twenty kilometers southeast of Kiel, and Göring, the south from Berchtesgaden, near the Berghof. Göring left at once for his nearby home, Karinhall, where he collected a vast load of art and other belongings on the way south via his private train. He then ordered Karinhall destroyed.

Dönitz left for the north to take up his command.

Speer was one of Hitler's last visitors in the bunker, and Bormann asked him to persuade Hitler to go south; instead, once alone with Hitler, Speer said, "It seems to me better, if it must be, that you end your life here in the capital rather than in your weekend house."[15]

Those who saw Hitler in the bunker during those last days spoke of his spotted uniform, his slovenly appearance, his apathy. Only once was he roused from it. A telegram arrived for von Ribbentrop from Göring in Berchtesgaden:

> *To Reichs Minister von Ribbentrop.*
> I have asked the Führer to provide me with instruction by 10 P.M., 23 April. If by this time it is apparent that the Führer has been deprived of his freedom of action to conduct the affairs of the Reich, his decree of 20 June 1941 becomes effective, according to which I am heir to all his offices as his deputy. By 12 midnight, 23 April 1945, if you receive no other order from the Führer or from me, you are to come to me at once by air.
>
> Göring. Reichsmarschall

Bormann yelled, "Treason!" An apoplectic Hitler at once stripped Göring of all rights of succession. He was to resign "for reasons of health." The original fury was followed by a huge outburst of anger and self-pity. Speer, who witnessed it all, was amazed when Hitler howled about Göring's corruption and neglect of the Luftwaffe. Then the storm passed. Hitler collapsed. "Let Göring negotiate the surrender. It's over anyway."

Nevertheless, Göring resigned by telegram, "due to coronary illness." Bormann told Hitler that von Ribbentrop was waiting for an audience. Hitler was irritable; "I've already said several times I don't want to see him." Bormann persisted. He said, "Ribbentrop said he won't budge. He'll wait there like a faithful dog until you call him."[16]

When Hitler allowed Bormann to admit von Ribbentrop, they spoke alone. They discussed some Czech engineers who wanted permission to surrender to the Americans instead of falling into Russian hands. Speer had told Hitler of their plight and how painful it would be to lose them to the Russians. As von Ribbentrop left, he saw Speer in the hallway and said, "About those Czechs, that's really a matter for the Foreign Ministry. But all right, if you mention that it's with the approval of the foreign minister, I'll approve it." Ever the man to guard his empire. Shortly afterward von Ribbentrop left the bunker and Berlin — as did Dr. Morell.

Von Ribbentrop never again saw Hitler, who married Eva Braun. The newlyweds committed suicide on April 30, after Hitler poisoned Blondi, his dog. The house of cards kept collapsing. Dönitz became Germany's short-term head of state on May 1, and Berlin surrendered to the Russians on May 2. Bormann was killed trying to escape the city. General Krebs shot himself. Goebbels and wife committed suicide in the bunker, after poisoning their children. Looking at photographs of the prisoners in the dock at the Nürnberg War Crimes Trials, one never fails to be amazed by how many of the leading figures of the Nazi time were found and put on trial. Of the men at the peak of the Hitler time, only Goebbels and Himmler killed themselves before the trials, Goebbels in loyalty, Himmler in treason.

Sebastian Haffner, the great German journalist, pointed out that the German people were besotted with *the man* Hitler, not with his political theories. This was true also of the men and women who were his closest associates. His death cut them adrift and, with the exception of a few internationalists like Hjalmar Schacht, they stayed adrift. Many of the old guard (party number under 100,000) and "old fighters" (under 300,000) had spent the major part of their adult lives attached to, devoted to, working for, propagating the ideas of, saying prayers for — and often to — Adolf Hitler. Now they had only themselves, and, more often than not, they found one another insufficient. Hitler's men, those who survived, were in shock. On May 11, 1945, the author witnessed Hermann Göring's first press conference after his capture in the garden of the villa of OSS General William Quinn in Augsburg. Perched on a gilded armchair, Göring looked and behaved like the fat little boy who had lost his daddy at the zoo. He was sweating, shaking, nervous, dressed up in light blue for the sad costume party.

Later, removed from drugs and distanced from the time of Hitler's death, he seemed to gather himself into a semblance of the cohesive and intelligent fighter pilot he had once been. Göring was always one-third big mouth, one-third gallant, one-third coward. Others, like Hess, never regained their equilibrium. In the case of von Ribbentrop, the period of post-Hitler shock was lengthy. He became, in turn, a boulevardier in Hamburg, a frazzled and frayed wreck as a prisoner in Nürnberg, and, at the very end, a man of some courage and bearing.

After Berlin, his first destination was north, toward Hamburg and Kiel to be near Dönitz's headquarters. Those weeks in Hamburg he tried to live a strange return to the international world of business and the boulevards. Was he looking for old friends from his business days?

> As a businessman I was interested in politics but not anxious to take an active part. But when I saw that Germany was aiming for the abyss during 1931 and 1932, I tried hard to help with the formation of an alliance between the conservative (*Bürgerlich*) parties and the National Socialists.[17]

Annelies von Ribbentrop, in her notes to his memoirs, wrote, "He joined the Nazi Party after his first meeting with Adolf Hitler."[18]

The enormity of his decision to join Hitler can be gauged only when in context. Joachim von Ribbentrop was wealthy and successful, on the threshold of social acceptance by the snobbier people of the capital. No doubt he was desperately eager to show an impeccably conservative face and to conduct his life in a most conventional manner. But the Nazi Party was seen by most upper-class Berliners as a radical group of dangerous and violent men who brawled and pushed their way into national prominence. Their figurehead and leader was a former Austrian, a nobody. Some people of "good" family joined the Nazi Party, but most were black sheep. To make common cause with this boisterous and rowdy mob from the beer cellars of Munich was not the best way to reassure Berlin society and its industrialists. Yet Joachim von Ribbentrop joined the Nazi Party and jeopardized his standing as a successful man of commerce in order to take his place alongside these revolutionaries. He explained: "Even on my first meeting him, Adolf Hitler made such a strong impression on me that I was convinced only his party could save Germany from Communism."

Thirteen years had passed since that first meeting on the Obersalzberg, when von Ribbentrop was a handsome, well-groomed, self-assured thirty-eight-year-old entrepreneur. Now he was a worn-out fifty-two, deserted by everyone but his wife and children. Von Ribbentrop gave a hint about how he left Berlin after that final meeting in the bunker: "I often thought it would have been better if they had sent back the Storch to Nauen, and I could have taken part in the final battle for Berlin."[19]

(Hitler must have ordered him to be flown out of Berlin by a
Fieseler Storch, the little aircraft that resembled the British Moth or
the American Piper Cub. One had taken Mussolini out of Italy. Several
formed the final air link from the city, because they could land on the
few short remaining pieces of road near the Brandenburg Gate. They
flew low and slowly and were difficult targets for fighter aircraft.)

Grand Admiral Dönitz had returned to his Navy headquarters at
Plön, where word of Hitler's death reached him via a telegram from
Bormann, who informed him that Hitler wanted him to take charge.
He became Hitler's heir, the head of state, and moved to Flensburg,
the little coastal town on the Danish border, to form a makeshift
government. He made his headquarters on the ship *Patria*. On May 1,
1945, he issued a declaration to the German people, filled with Nazi
jargon, proclaiming "deep respect and sorrow for the dead Führer and
for his life's mission to protect the world from the storm flood of
Bolshevism."

He followed it with a similar appeal to the armed forces, explaining that he must continue his fight against the English and Americans
"as long as they hinder me in the execution of the battle against the
Bolshevists." He informed the people and the armed forces that "the
oath of loyalty which you gave to the Führer is now due from each
one of you to me, as the Führer's appointed successor."

It took weeks for Dönitz to begin to distance himself from Hitler's
thoughts and language.[20]

Von Ribbentrop, waiting not far away, was contacted by Dönitz's
adjutant, Ludde, who wanted to locate Konstantin von Neurath for
Dönitz through von Ribbentrop. (Dönitz was not known for his tact.)
Actually, von Neurath was in the Alps, so Dönitz had to make another
choice for foreign minister. Von Ribbentrop went to Dönitz to offer
his services, and the admiral informed him that he had almost chosen
Count Schwerin von Krosig, the former finance minister. To get rid of
von Ribbentrop, and purely as a gesture, he asked for other suggestions. Von Ribbentrop telephoned the following day, offering one
name: Von Ribbentrop.[21] When it was not accepted by Dönitz, he
returned to Hamburg.

On May 3, Kiel and Flensburg were declared open cities. Then,
according to a mournful addendum of the *Wehrmacht* report:

> Berlin fell on 4 May [two days after the fact] . . .
> In a singular act of heroic fighting, troops of regular and reserve units
> resisted to their last breath in accordance with their oath to the flag.

To the very end, the Wehrmacht's writers relied on Hitlerian bombast.[22]

Shattered, scarred Hamburg was trying to return to life. As if to mock its legendary neo-British style ("When it rains in London, everyone in Hamburg opens umbrellas"; "Hamburg is the only British city Germany ever held") on May 4 Hamburg was occupied by British troops.

Von Ribbentrop had rented a flat on the fifth floor of one of the few remaining apartment houses. He was in a near-somnambulant flashback stage, trying to reach old friends and to start some form of social life. He was described as "making the rounds of the city, dressed in a double-breasted blue suit and homburg hat, trying to revive old acquaintances."

Early in the morning of June 14 he was arrested by British troops. He was still in bed.[23] The son of an old acquaintance had tipped off the British authorities about where to find this "big fish." Now did he remember a 1944 conversation with Fritz Hesse, once the London bureau chief of the German wire service DNB, and a quasi-publicist for the embassy?

Hesse had said that something must be done to save Germany from total destruction. "It is quite clear," he said to von Ribbentrop, "that even then you might not be able to save your life. You know what the Allies plan to do to the leading National Socialists." Von Ribbentrop stared at him. "Do you mean" — he faltered — "that they intend to hang us all?"

"Why not?" said Hesse.

"What have I done? Do you really believe Lord Simon's statement in the House of Lords?" Lord Simon, usually a mild man, had talked of hanging all German leaders. Von Ribbentrop continued, "Do you think that's really true? But why? After all, I only did my duty like any patriot, and I can assure you I did what I could to soften the Führer's harsher decisions."[24]

Hesse had brought up the subject to punish a man who had frequently been impatient and unkind to him, and it must have raised cold fear in von Ribbentrop. Could he guess the full extent of the crimes in which he had participated? He had often complained about those who "pampered the enemy" and who failed to "take a hard stand when it is needed." But did he understand the consequence of his ministry's cooperation with the SS in "displacing, relocating, resettling, cleansing," and all those other euphemisms? Could he conceive of murder and extermination by those "courageous men and women" of the SS who "had to steel themselves to do the Reich's foul work to save the German people from mongrelization and moral decay?"

There is a curious passage in a 1943 book about von Ribbentrop by the former ministry official Dr. Paul Schwarz, an exile living in New York. The book was completed long before the Nürnberg War Crimes Trials and their consequences, and it was uncanny in its forecast. This is the final paragraph of the final chapter.

> My sleep is usually undisturbed. But in the days when I finished this manuscript [1942–1943], the old German Foreign Office appeared in my dreams. I was walking along beside the old Chancellery, and finally I reached the entrance to Number 76, the entrance which is called the *Ministertreppe*, the staircase reserved for the minister and his visitors of diplomatic rank. Old Schmidt, the doorman with the white beard, greeted me. He was friendly, as he had always been. He pointed to the tall lamppost which flanked the entrance on its left, and there I saw a body hanging, Ribbentrop's body, dressed in the uniform he had introduced for the Foreign Service. I woke up, shuddering. But thinking it over, I must confess that I knew this lamppost would do![25]

The arrested von Ribbentrop was taken to Luxemburg, where a large number of the Reich's surviving Nazi leaders were interned at the Palace Hotel in Bad Mondorf, a spa on the French border. It must have been cold comfort to see that men he had despised were now his fellow prisoners. Göring, Frank, von Papen, Daluege, Darre, Frick, Funk, Marshals Jodl and Keitel, Kesselring, Speer, Ley, Rosenberg, Streicher, and even Admiral Dönitz, who "could not use him as foreign minister." For years he had looked down on nearly all of them as drifters, opportunists, dreamers, or, in the case of Streicher and Ley, vulgarians. They had always heartily reciprocated. Only von Papen came from von Ribbentrop's old Berlin circle, and they had often fought.

The old luxury hotel was stripped of most comforts. It was a quasi-prison under the command of a U.S. Cavalry colonel named Burton C. Andrus, a heavyset, mustachioed, bespectacled, spit-and-polish American career officer and an imitation George Patton. Some prisoners were held at Neuheim in the Taunus Mountains at Kransberg, a castle that had once been renovated for Göring by Speer, but the Palace Hotel at Mondorf, nicknamed the Ashcan, held most of the senior Nazis. Around August 16, 1945, the Allies began to transfer them to Nürnberg for arraignment before the International Military Tribunal for what came to be known as the War Crimes Trials. The actual prosecutors were provided by each of the victorious Allied powers, as were members of the panel of judges. The trials were held in the city's restored and patched Palace of Justice, which had large, attached prison wings. The Nürnberg cells were sparse, cold, and uncomfortable, but the food was adequate. Many in defeated Germany were starving, but not those accused of war crimes. The prison guards were young American soldiers, filled with Hollywood ideas about these evil Nazi bosses, and sometimes they became petty tyrants. In the middle of the night they made as much noise as they could, and they used contemporary cartoon descriptions for the prisoners. ("Send up Fat Stuff" meant Göring was needed.) They were good-natured but disrespectful, and the Nazi prisoners, all men of standing in their own dubious world, were often more upset by the disrespect than they would have been by stern treatment. There were classic German complaints about treatment "unsuitable to a field marshal or to a senior minister." The oil of American military informality and the water of German military and bureaucratic pomposity failed to mix.

Most of the prisoners were accustomed to comfort if not luxury. They were not young men, and even the soldiers among them had led the cosseted lives of generals, with military servants, aides, and adjutants. For Joachim von Ribbentrop, who had continued to live as the internationalist *homme du monde,* with custom-made clothes and haberdashery in the care of good valets, the change must have been acute. The cell walls were covered with stained, peeling whitewash. There was one small, barred window about five feet from the floor. A cot covered with a brown U.S. Army blanket stood against one wall, flanked by a small wooden table. It was too weak to carry the weight of a potential suicide. Against the other, shorter wall stood a rickety wooden chair, cushioned with another folded blanket. This chair was also purposely flimsy. Göring usually sat on his cot. One wall contained a small alcove, like a narrow fireplace, that housed a toilet. A window and peephole in the heavy wooden door guaranteed that each prisoner could be under twenty-four-hour surveillance. Most prisoners kept their washing gear and personal books and papers on the small table or on the narrow ledge over the toilet alcove. It was a spare and probably foul-smelling life, yet von Ribbentrop wrote few complaints in his memoirs. By contrast, Speer, the only one of the prisoners who acknowledged his criminal guilt by association with the actions of the Nazi regime, complained of discomfort and occasional maltreatment. Yet he had been a young architect, with few of the luxuries of life, when Hitler first reached out for him.

Perhaps von Ribbentrop's acceptance of prison conditions can be credited to absolute, complete, and uncomprehending shock. Nürnberg photographs and eyewitnesses depict the boulevardier gone to seed, with stringy, rumpled gray hair, crushed clothes, and an air of complete disorganization. He spent his Nürnberg prison term in cell number 7, between the cells of Keitel and Jodl, on the lower level of the prison wing.

As a defendant, he was the exact opposite of Speer. Speer accepted his guilt and had written to his wife about "the truth about the whole madness."[26] Von Ribbentrop, from the beginning to the end of the trial, never cast a single moment's doubt on his allegiance to Adolf Hitler. He had believed in the man. He had followed him and carried out his wishes. He did not now question them. He could not conceive of the horrors he was learning whenever films or eyewitnesses told of the camps or the Einsatzgruppen. He was shaken by some of the footage.

He never disavowed Hitler and would not accept any personal guilt as a result of his great act of faithfulness. He admitted all signatures on all incriminating documents. He had followed his Führer's orders. He would not acknowledge that the attack on Poland was an act of aggression. He had accepted Hitler's view of a spiteful country brutalizing German minorities. Nor did he acknowledge aggression against Denmark or Norway. Those were pre-emptive attacks to forestall Churchill. His plea? "In the sense of the indictment, not guilty."

Of which categories of crimes were they all to be accused?

1. Crimes against peace
2. War crimes
3. Crimes against humanity

Or the launching of premeditated military aggression, the maltreatment of prisoners of war, and acts of brutality against conquered people, as well as Jews, Masons, Gypsies, the medically incurable, and others.

None of these charges was acknowledged by von Ribbentrop. In fact, he stated that he knew of only two concentration camps, Oranienburg and Dachau. Dönitz concurred; he too knew the names of only two camps. Sir David Maxwell-Fyfe, the British prosecutor, was baffled and outraged.

Von Ribbentrop was the only defendant to send the Russian prosecutors into a similar fury. By asking Ambassador Gaus, the ministry's legal head who had accompanied him to Moscow in 1939, to testify in detail about the friendly meetings with Stalin, he saw to it that the entire course of events relating to those days of Nazi-Bolshevist collaboration was told openly. Even the "secret protocols" relating to the Baltics were read into the record. It caused no end of embarrassment to the western judges on the bench.[27] Yet when von Ribbentrop returned to his seat on the defendants' bench between Hess and Keitel after this testimony, he received no praise or acknowledgment from his benchmates. The disturbed-looking and -sounding Hess was barely present, and Keitel still hated his cell neighbor, the "champagne salesman."

Meals were served in the Palace of Justice's dining hall, and prisoners were seated in groups of four to avoid the influence of Göring and his open attempts to "forge cohesion." Göring had made grandiose promises to several of the accused that he would take their guilt upon himself. But after a few gestures, he ended up distancing himself from culpability by implicating others.

Almost a year was spent shuttling between the prison cells and the large courtroom, which looked like a ship's nave, with a rising set of benches on one side for the judges and another rising set on the other for the accused and their attorneys. Toward the stern stood the prosecutors, and toward the bow was the witness stand. In the belly of the ship, astern of the courtroom, were rows of seats for the world's press. Proceedings began each morning at nine and were recessed at noon for lunch. Court resumed between 2 P.M. and 5 P.M. in the afternoon. Most prisoners then met with their attorneys or occasional visitors and took care of their personal chores, such as the barber (German, supervised), the dentist (extractions only — no treatment), and the shower (once a week).[28] They could get their civilian or uniform suits pressed. These they only wore in the courtroom and to meals. The rest of the time they wore prison fatigue uniforms. Clergymen and psychiatrists conducted frequent rounds of visits, the clergy to help the prisoners, the psychiatrists to help themselves. There were even Rorschach test "experts."

Annelies von Ribbentrop and several of the other wives obtained permission to visit the accused, although they did not see the trials. The women met with their husbands in small glass-partitioned, side-by-side booths in the inhibiting presence of American guards. Toward the end, after his father had been sentenced, Waffen SS Captain Rudolf von Ribbentrop, a prisoner of war, was temporarily released to accompany his mother on her last visit with her husband.

Did Joachim von Ribbentrop ever plan to commit suicide? According to Colonel Andrus and his men, the day the trials began, some pills, wrapped in tissue paper, were found inside one of von Ribbentrop's garters.[29] These could, however, have been old Morell pills to calm his nerves. They were never analyzed, and nowhere in his memoirs did von Ribbentrop write of taking his own life.

The men in the dock were natural targets for journalists and psychologists. Everyone wanted to "know the inside," to understand these men who had administered a regime of such bestiality and brutality. They were to be disappointed: these men were like any others. Adolf Hitler, the true genius of evil, the Satan who had sparked all the horror and stood back to watch while others administered it, lay dead in the garden above the bunker, doused with gasoline and set on fire. His most vicious associates were also dead, Heydrich assassinated, and Himmler a suicide, like the man who helped him to spread his poison, Goebbels.

Also in the Nürnberg dock sat the last head of the Gestapo, Kaltenbrunner, a man whose vulpine looks were deceiving. He was only a pale replica of Heydrich. Kaltenbrunner was ill during most of the trials, a wreck in a wheelchair. No one was too sorry for him. Streicher, the former schoolteacher who became the Nazis' chief vulgarian and Jew-baiter, had once invented the very style of stereotyping the Jew. When arrested, bearded and with a black hat, he looked like one of his own anti-Semitic stereotypes. Hitler had discarded him long before, and the men in the dock looked down on and ignored him. His type of Nazi bully had been out of Nazi fashion since the early days of the regime.

It may be significant that of the twenty-one major war criminals who were available for IQ testing, Kaltenbrunner and Streicher took the bottom two spots. These were the scores:

1. Schacht — 143	12. Speer — 128
2. Seyss-Inquart — 141	13. Jodl — 127
3. Göring — 138	14. Rosenberg — 127
4. Dönitz — 138	15. Von Neurath — 125
5. Von Papen — 134	16. Funk — 124
6. Raeder — 134	17. Frick — 124
7. Frank — 130	18. Hess (estim.) — 120
8. Fritsche — 130	19. Sauckel — 118
9. Von Schirach — 130	20. Kaltenbrunner — 113
10. Von Ribbentrop — 129	21. Streicher — 106
11. Keitel — 129	

Dr. Gustave M. Gilbert, a psychiatrist assigned to the trials, along with Dr. Douglas Kelley, published his memoirs in 1947, a year after the executions. He had interviewed Göring in his cell on November 11, 1945, and quoted Göring as complaining about von Ribbentrop's "tactlessness in England." He then trotted out the usual two examples: the newly appointed ambassador's anti-Soviet speech upon arrival at the train station, and the Nazi salute to King George VI. "I said to Hitler," related Göring, to his own vast amusement, "how would you like it if the Russian ambassador greeted you with 'Long live the Communist revolution!'"[30] He had told the identical story to Dr. Kelley and probably to others. Göring also said Hitler had never traveled and "therefore thought von Ribbentrop had connections with English aristocrats." At the signing of the Axis pact, von Ribbentrop had wanted Göring to stand behind him for the photographs. Göring said he told von Ribbentrop that "*he* could stand behind *me*! I was the number two man in the Reich! I had not read the treaty. Who knows? I did not really want to be there."

Apparently nothing the "number two man in the Reich" said could unseat von Ribbentrop as German foreign minister. Long before his Luftwaffe failed to hold off the Allied bombers, Göring had overestimated his own power. No doubt he now tried to make up for the last few years of disdain from Hitler by displaying his newly detoxified virtuosity at Nürnberg.

On December 8 and 9, 1945, when Dr. Gilbert interviewed von Ribbentrop in his cell, the subject turned to anti-Semitism. The doctor said that the former minister had been accused of certain anti-Jewish statements. Von Ribbentrop protested, "I could not have said those anti-Semitic things! Impossible! *Ausgeschlossen!* I always thought the anti-Semitic policy was madness. But I was a loyal follower. Hitler had a very magnetic personality. I still cannot shake it off, six months after his death. He overwhelmed Chamberlain and Daladier at Munich. Himmler and Goebbels intensified Hitler's anti-Semitism. I once asked about Maidanek [an extermination camp], and he told me to mind my own business."

So he had heard about a camp other than the two he mentioned!

One morning a film about Hitler was shown in court, a composite of old newsreels. Later, at lunch, von Ribbentrop was overcome and wept. "Can't you see the strength of his personality? How he swept people off their feet? It [the film] was *erschütternd* (shattering, devastating), as if a dead father had returned to life."[31] He added that if Hitler were to walk into his cell and "would say, 'Do this!' even now I would do it."[32]

Then followed this exchange with Dr. Gilbert.

GILBERT: Was Hitler crazy? At the end of his life?
VON RIBBENTROP: No. You can't say that.
GILBERT: Neurotics flare up when contradicted.
VON RIBBENTROP: Well, after I argued with Hitler in 1940, I never again had a calm discussion.[33]

Von Ribbentrop insisted that Hitler did not become rigid and fixated until the end of the war. After his escape of July 20, 1944, one of Hitler's eyes seemed cloudy, and his face and hands were pale. Was it lack of sleep? Or Morell's injections? Von Ribbentrop suggested these but had no sure answers.[34]

The only time von Ribbentrop amused the court — involuntarily — was during cross-examination about the famous Berlin meeting with Czech President Hacha, during that snow-swept night early in 1939. Von Ribbentrop insisted that Hacha was never threatened. Sir David Maxwell-Fyfe then asked, "How can you threaten a man beyond bombing his capital and invading his country?" Von Ribbentrop answered, "War, for instance."

The courtroom rang with laughter.

On April 2, 1946, to the hypothetical courtroom question "Would you have helped to assassinate Hitler if you had known the full content of the extermination camps?" Von Ribbentrop answered, "I could never had killed him. I could never repudiate him now or renounce him. I don't know why."[35]

Dr. Gilbert brought up the famous personal argument with Hitler when the Führer nearly "had a coronary attack." Von Ribbentrop said it was about the Jewish question, and that it took more courage to face Hitler on the Jewish question than to face an atom bomb. On May 4 he said to Dr. Gilbert, "I told Hitler he was lining up yet another power against us, added to England, France, and Russia; [there] now [were] the Jews. As for world Jewry starting the war, that is nonsense!"

He was still puzzled that Britain would fight over "reasonable" demands for the return of Danzig from Poland and a right-of-way through the Corridor in exchange for certain concessions.[36]

He also wrote, quite paradoxically, that he was "so sorry I never told Adolf Hitler what the British Empire meant. They say I gave him bad advice, that the British are weak and degenerate. The opposite is true! I always emphasized in my talks with Hitler the mighty power of their empire and the heroic attitude of their ruling circles."[37] Perhaps, since his memoirs were written in his jail cell, they reflect revisions of some of his earlier views, or perhaps he believed these things but could never convince his Führer of them.

Eventually von Ribbentrop was indicted and convicted on four main counts, which emerged from the millions of words, in the tens of thousands of pages.

1. His January 2, 1938, memorandum to Hitler.*
2. His participation in the Sudeten crisis.
3. His part in the attack on Poland.
4. His orders to the Foreign Ministry's full staff everywhere to help with the deportations that were part of the Final Solution. Also, his participation in crimes against the people of the occupied countries and Vichy France.

On October 1, 1946, these brought the sentence of death by hanging. The entire trial of the twenty-three men and the absent Martin Bormann had lasted ten months. (Ley committed suicide before being indicted.) There were twelve sentences of death, three of lifetime imprisonment. Also, sentences of ten to twenty years for four defendants; three of them, von Papen, Schacht, and Fritsche, were acquitted. Krupp was too ill to stand trial, and Bormann was sentenced in absentia. Von Papen, who had guided Hitler's beginnings, and Schacht, who had made it possible for him to succeed economically, both seemed unlikely culprits to escape scot free, but they did. Fritsche, Berlin radio's chief announcer, was only the empty, strident pompous voice of Germany on the world's radio sets. He was Goebbels's mechanical spokesman, who dispensed bombast without having written it.

There were many rumors about which place would be chosen for the execution. It turned out to be the gymnasium of the Palace of Justice. A gallows and trap doors were built onto a platform mounted by an eerily symbolic thirteen steps.

The executioner was almost type-cast by Hollywood, a burly Texas master sergeant named John C. Wood, who wore his overseas cap with the jaunty "twin peaks" favored by American garrison and rear-line administrative troops. In the U.S. Army they were called "latrine lawyers." Sergeant Wood proclaimed that he had never lost any sleep carrying out his gruesome specialty. It had to be done by a military executioner, because it was a military tribunal that had con-

*The proud, final A5522 of his London embassy days, describing England as the archenemy who had to be fought.

demned the prisoners. The journalists attending the trials had devised a form of pool to bet on the odds of who would be hanged, and their list of death sentences was headed by Göring, von Ribbentrop, and Kaltenbrunner.

On the morning their sentences were to be pronounced, the prisoners assembled in a large room in the basement of the Palace of Justice. Most of these men had spent their lives together in the stream of the National Socialist revolution, its victories, and final defeat, and with few exceptions they were never to see one another again. Von Ribbentrop was handcuffed to an American MP, who wore the usual white helmet, Sam Browne belt, and leggings. They went to a small lift he had never seen before, ascended two floors, and walked a few steps. A door opened, and now they stood on a small platform in the courtroom, facing the judges. After von Ribbentrop was freed of his handcuffs, a headset was handed to him and he fumbled it into place over his ears.

Then he heard the mechanical impersonal voice of an interpreter delivering the harshest words of von Ribbentrop's life: "You are to be executed by hanging."

He held himself together. He and his guard turned toward the small lift and went back to his cell through strange new passages. It was done. It was over.

Most people who saw him after the sentencing noticed how he had aged. His cheeks sagged, his unkempt hair was lifeless, like a wig, and his eyes rimmed in red like those of the sleepless. And yet he held together. The next days would find him writing notes, memoirs, and last letters. His mind functioned well. He was quite clear now. Earlier, Göring had said to Colonel John H. Amen, the chief interrogator, that "Ribbentrop was cracking up."[38] He need not have worried. Von Ribbentrop stayed intact, surprisingly so for such a brittle man.

Quite calmly, he wrote a protest against the proceedings that had brought him to this no-exit end. This was his rebuttal.

1. The jury could not be impartial. It consisted only of victors.
2. The court was based on a statute written *after* the alleged crimes. Therefore, it was not legal.
3. He had disputed and disproved that he had ever "conspired" to make war.
4. If he was accused of waging "offensive war," what of the USSR? (He meant Poland and its partition according to the treaty.)

5. Many documents he wanted to submit regarding foreign policy were not admitted.

6. About the atrocities: those who committed them were dead. Most of those who survived had been kept in the dark. Also, the Russians committed equal atrocities.

7. Every convicted German in the trials will stand in the way of German reconciliation with the west.[39]

He also presented the following:

As a believer in the Geneva Convention, I brought about the unshackling of western POWs and prevented the branding of Russian POWs. I also prevented the shooting of 10,000 POWs, particularly airmen, after the Dresden bombings, although Hitler wished to cancel the Geneva Convention in protest against these terror bombings. I tried to change anti-Jewish laws when no one in the party had the mental strength to approach Hitler [on this subject]. I found it obvious for humanitarian reasons. I also tried through the whole war to reopen peace talks . . . I never heard Hitler speak of world domination, but Hitler was convinced that the defense against eastern Bolshevism depended on Germany alone.

How can anyone blame Germany for her government when it was the Versailles Treaty that produced such a government? We were willing to compromise. Look at the Fleet Agreement and Alsace-Lorraine [which Germany decided not to claim]. But England would not go along [with our efforts]. She saw the "balance of power" disturbed. There was no peace to be made with Russia. Hitler said there can be no compromise with Bolshevism. A contented Germany is the best guarantee for peace in Europe. I hope the victorious powers have learned this lesson.[40]

These memoranda were edited and published by Annelies following her husband's death. They are a classic résumé of self-justification, since few ever acknowledge having done evil things. In a letter to Annelies, written on October 5, five days after he was sentenced to death, he said: "If Hitler were alive, his testimony would clear me. I did not wish to air my many strong disagreements with Hitler, or the German people would say, What kind of a man is this who now opposes Hitler for his own selfish reasons in front of a jury of foreigners?

"History will show that Hitler awakened Europe to the danger of Bolshevism."

These are fairly calm and cohesive statements for the man Göring thought was cracking up.

On October 6 he described himself as "ground up by the millstones of history."

The last letters released by his wife were written by a father and husband. To Rudolf von Ribbentrop, he wrote on October 14:

> I shall walk the last steps sure that I was a patriot and did everything I could. I always did what I thought was right, although Adolf Hitler would not accept much advice about foreign policy. My thoughts and my workdays and nights were only for the good of Germany. The truth will out one day.
>
> It is very hard to part from you, but it must be, and we must not complain. Stick together through good and bad, and know that I shall always be among you and will surround you with all my love.
>
> I embrace you, my dear son . . .

Then, the night before his execution on October 15, he wrote to his wife:

> . . . I tried to help Adolf Hitler to build a strong flowering Germany. But the Führer and his people failed. Millions died. The Reich was destroyed and our people lie prone. Is it not right — not because of the Nürnberg verdict by foreign judges — but because of some higher judgment, that I too should fall?
>
> I am calm and shall face what comes with head high, which I owe to the history of my family and to my own as German foreign minister.
>
> You, my beloved wife, must now give your courageous heart and all the love you once had for me to the children. I know I can depend on you completely. You must know this is my final comfort.
>
> I shall go on my way with pride and belief in eternal life.
>
> Once more I take your beloved face in my hands and look deep into your eyes with all the love one human being can give to another.
>
> Farewell . . . I shall see you again in another world. God help you.[41]

At 1 A.M. on October 16, 1946, Joachim von Ribbentrop, handcuffed between two American soldiers, took his last walk into the converted gymnasium where he was to die. He was accompanied by an Evangelical chaplain named Gerecke, assigned to those condemned who were Protestants. Von Ribbentrop showed all the wear and tear of the last year of defeat and trial. At the bottom of the stairs, his hands were tied behind his back with a black cord. He was asked to state his name. He walked upright when he was led up the thirteen symbolic steps of the scaffold, where a black hood was pulled over his head. Sergeant Wood then pulled the loop of the hanging rope around his neck. His legs were tied at the ankles. Because of Göring's suicide, discovered minutes before he was to be led to the place of execution, von Ribbentrop was the first condemned man to be hanged.*

After the trap door was sprung, it took ten minutes for life to leave him. Those who were experts said the hanging was bungled.[42]

Joachim von Ribbentrop's last words, both in his memoirs and as recorded shortly before his death, were:

> God protect Germany.
> God have mercy on my soul.
> My last wish is that Germany can stay united and that east and west will reach agreement about this.

The bodies of the executed men were laid out on cots and marked with name tags. They were photographed both dressed and naked and placed in wooden coffins. The ropes used for their hangings were put in the caskets with the bodies.

Arrangements for immediate cremation had been made earlier, and the ashes were scattered by U.S. Army personnel.

• • •

In 1950 André François-Poncet, once Hitler's respected adversary during the prewar days in Berlin, received a letter from a man named Kannenberg who identified himself as the Führer's former major domo and butler. He was applying for a position in the François-Poncet household.

"Your Excellency will recall that the Führer's household always functioned smoothly."[43]

Who would argue that a well-run household is an eternal goal?

---

*The details of Göring's suicide have never been established. He killed himself with the standard Nazi-leader cyanide pill provided by the SS doctors. How he managed to conceal it despite many physical searches, or whether it was smuggled to him, is unknown.

BIBLIOGRAPHY • NOTES

BIBLIOGRAPHY

Abetz, Otto. *Das Offene Problem*. Cologne: Greven & Bechtold, 1951.

Agee, Joel. *Twelve Years: An American Boyhood in East Germany*. New York: Farrar, Straus & Giroux, 1981.

Allen, Peter. *The Windsor Secret*. New York: Stein & Day, 1984.

Anger, Per. *With Raoul Wallenberg in Budapest*. New York: The Holocaust Library, 1981.

Angolia, J. R., and A. Schlicht. *Uniforms and Traditions of the German Army*, vol. 2. San Jose, CA: Bender, 1984.

Archives of the Auswärtige Amt, Bonn.

Arenhövel, Alfoms. *ARENA der Leidenschaften, 1910–1973*. Berlin: Willmuth Arenhövel, 1990.

Aster, Sidney, ed. *British Foreign Policy, 1918–1945: A Guide to Research and Research Material*. Wilmington, DE: Scholarly Resources, 1984.

AUFBAU: Dokumente einer Kultur im Exil. Will Schaber, ed. New York: Overlook Press, 1972.

Bach, Jurath Arne. *Franz von Papen in Der Weimarer Republik*. Düsseldorf: Droste, 1977.

Bailey, George. *Germans: The Biography of an Obsession*. New York: World Publishing, 1972.

Baker, Leonard. *Days of Sorrow and Pain: Leo Baeck and the Berlin Jews*. New York: Macmillan, 1978.

Barnett, Correlli, ed. *Hitler's Generals*. New York: Weidenfeld & Nicolson, 1989.

Bender, Roger J., and Richard D. Law. *Uniforms, Organization and History of the Afrika Corps*. Mountain View, CA: R. J. Bender, 1973.

Bender, Roger J., and H. P. Taylor. *Waffen SS*, vol. 2. Mountain View, CA: R. J. Bender, 1971.

Bendt, Vera. *Wegweiser durch das jüdische Berlin: Geschichte und Gegenwart*. Berlin: Nicolai, 1987.

Bentley, James. *Martin Niemöller, 1892–1984*. New York: Free Press, 1984.

Berber, Friedrich. *Zwischen Macht und Gewissen*. Munich: C. H. Beck, 1986.

Berkley, George E. *Vienna and Its Jews: The Tragedy of Success*. Cambridge, MA: Abt Books, 1988.

Berliner Illustrirte Zeitung: Zeitbild, Chronic, 1892–1945. Christian Ferber, ed. Berlin: Ullstein, 1985.

Berliner Stadbilder Aus Zwei Jahrhunderten. Berlin: Ago Galerie, 1987.

Berthold, Eva, and Norbert Matern. *München im Bombenkrieg*. Düsseldorf: Droste, 1983.

Berthold, Will. *Die 42 Attentate auf Adolf Hitler*. Munich: Goldman, 1981.

Bielenberg, Christabel. *The Past Is Myself*. London: Corgi, 1984.

Bloch, Michael. *The Duke of Windsor's War: From Europe to the Bahamas, 1939–1945*. New York: Coward McCann, 1983.

———. *Operation Willi*. New York: Weidenfeld & Nicolson, 1984.

Bock, Helmut, ed. *Sturz ins Dritte Reich*. Leipzig: Urania, 1983.

Bohlen, Charles E. *Witness to History, 1929–1969*. New York: Norton, 1973.

Bower, Tom. *The Pledge Betrayed: America and Britain and the Denazification of Postwar Germany*. Garden City, NY: Doubleday, 1982.

———. *Klaus Barbie: The Butcher of Lyons*. New York: Pantheon, 1984.

Bracher, Karl Dietrich. *The German Dictatorship: The Origins, Structure and Effects of National Socialism*, trans., Jean Steinberg. New York: Holt, Rinehart & Winston, 1970.

Breitman, Richard. *The Architect of Genocide: Himmler and the Final Solution*. New York: Knopf, 1991.

Brown, Anthony Cave. *The Last Hero: Wild Bill Donovan*. New York: Times Books, 1982

Burdick, Charles, Hans-Adolf Jacobson, and Winfried Kudszus, eds. *Contemporary Germany: Politics and Culture*. Boulder, CO: Westview, 1984.

Busse, Horst, and Udo Krause. *Lebenslänglich Für NS-Verbrecher: Der Fall Schmidt*. Berlin: Pfaffenweiler, Centaurus, 1989.

Buxa, Werner. *Der Kampf am Wolchow und um Leningrad, 1941–1944: Ein Dokumentation in Bildern*. Dorheim: Podzun, 1969.

Campbell-Johnson, Alan. *Viscount Halifax*. New York: Ives Washburn, 1941.

Cartarius, Dr. Ulrich. *The German Resistance Movement, 1933–1945*. Stuttgart Exhibition, 1988.

Channon, Sir Henry. *Chips: The Diaries of Sir Henry Channon*. London: Weidenfeld & Nicolson, 1967.

Churchill, Winston S. *The Second World War*. Vol. 5: *Closing the Ring*. Boston: Houghton Mifflin, 1951.

Ciano, Conte Galeazzo. *The Ciano Diaries, 1939–1943*, Hugh Gibson, ed. New York: Doubleday, 1946.

Coats, Peter. *Of Generals and Gardens: The Autobiography of Peter Coats*. London: Weidenfeld & Nicolson, 1976.

Collier, Richard. *Duce: A Biography of Benito Mussolini.* New York: Viking, 1971.

Craig, Gordon. A. *The Germans.* New York: Putnam, 1982.

Davis, B. L., and P. Turner. *German Uniforms of the Third Reich.* New York: Arco, 1980.

Deacon, Richard. *A History of the British Secret Service.* London: Grenada, 1985.

Deakin, F. W. *The Brutal Friendship: Mussolini, Hitler and the Fall of Italian Fascism.* New York: Harper & Row, 1962.

Deighton, Len. *Blitzkrieg: From the Rise of Hitler to the Fall of Dunkirk.* New York: Knopf, 1980.

De Jonge, Alex. *Stalin and the Shaping of the Soviet Union.* New York: Morrow, 1986.

D'Este, Carlo. *Decision in Normandy.* New York: Dutton, 1983.

Dirksen, H. von. *Moscow, Tokyo, London.* London: Hutchinson & Co., 1952.

Dodd, Martha. *Through Embassy Eyes.* New York: Harcourt Brace, 1939.

Döscher, H. J. *Das A.A. im Dritten Reich.* Berlin: Siedler, 1987.

Douglas, Roy, ed. *1939: A Retrospect Forty Years Later.* London: Macmillan, 1983.

Dumbach, Annette E., and Jud Newborn. *Shattering the German Night: The Story of the White Rose.* Boston: Little, Brown, 1986.

Dunker, Ulrich. *Juden in Preussen: Ein Kapitel Deutscher Geschichte.* Dortmund: Harenberg, 1981.

Eckhardt, Wolf von, and Sander L. Gilman. *Bertolt Brecht's Berlin: A Scrapbook of the Twenties.* New York: Anchor Books, 1975.

Eliach, Yaffa, and Brana Gurewitsch, eds. *The Liberators: Eyewitness Accounts of the Liberation of Concentration Camps. Liberation Day,* vol. 1. New York: Center for Holocaust Studies, 1981.

Emery, Edwin. *The Story of America as Reported by Its Newspapers, 1690–1965.* New York: Simon & Schuster, 1965.

Engelmann, Bernt. *Germany Without Jews,* trans., D. J. Beer. New York: Bantam, 1984.

———. *In Hitler's Germany: Everyday Life in the Third Reich,* trans., Krishna Winston. New York: Schocken, 1986.

Essame, Hubert. *Normandy Bridgehead.* New York: Ballantine, 1970.

Everett, Susanne. *Lost Berlin.* London: Bison, 1979.

Fest, Joachim C. *Hitler,* trans., Richard and Clara Winston. New York: Vintage, 1975.

———. *Das Gesicht Des Dritten Reiches.* Munich: R. Pieper, 1988.

Fleischauer, Inge. *Diplomatischer Widerstand.* Berlin: Ullstein, 1991.

Ford, Corey. *Donovan of the OSS.* Boston: Little, Brown, 1970.

François-Poncet, André. *The Fateful Years: Memoirs of A French Ambassador in Berlin, 1931–1938,* trans., Jacques LeClercq. New York: Harcourt Brace, 1948.

Fraschka, Günter. *Mit Schwertern und Diamanten*. Munich: Universitas, 1988.

Friedrich, Otto. *Before the Deluge: A Portrait of Berlin in the 1920s*. New York: Harper & Row, 1972.

Fromm, Bella. *Blood and Banquets*. New York: Birchlane Press, 1990.

Galante, Pierre, and Eugene Silianoff. *Voices from the Bunker: The True Account of Hitler's Last Days*, trans., Jan Dalley. New York: Putnam, 1989.

German Foreign Office. *Nazi Soviet Relations, 1939–1941*. Washington, D.C.: Department of State, 1948.

German Resistance Movement, 1933–1945. Stuttgart: Catalog, Institut für Auslandsbeziehungen, 1988.

Gerwin, Robert, ed. *Wie Die Zukunft Wurzeln Schlug. Aus Der Forschung Der Bundersrepublik Deutschland*. Berlin: Springer, 1989.

Gilbert, G. M. *Nuremberg Diary*. New York: Farrar, Straus, 1947.

Gillman, Peter, and Leni Gillman. *Collar the Lot*. London: Quartet, 1980.

Gisevius, H. B. *Bis zum bittern Ende*. Zurich: Fretz & Wasmuth, 1946.

Gladwyn, Hubert M.G.J. *The Memoirs of Lord Gladwyn*. New York: Weybright & Talley, 1972.

Glen, Douglas. *Von Ribbentrop Is Still Dangerous*. London: Rich & Cowan, 1941.

Glendinning, Victoria. *Vita: The Life of Vita Sackville-West*. New York: Knopf, 1983.

Glueck, Sheldon. *War Criminals: Their Prosecution and Punishment*. New York: Knopf, 1976.

Goebbels, Joseph. *The Goebbels Diaries*, trans., Louis Lochner. New York: Popular Library, 1948.

Goldmann, Nahum. *Mein Leben als deutscher Jude*. Munich: Langen-Muller, 1980.

Gordon, Leonard A. *Brothers Against the Raj*. New York: Columbia University Press, 1990.

Griffiths, Richard. *Fellow Travellers of the Right: British Enthusiasts for Nazi Germany, 1933–1939*. London: Constable, 1980.

Gross, Leonard. *The Last Jews in Berlin*. New York: Simon & Schuster, 1982.

Grubel, F. *Catalog of the Archival Collections: Leo Baeck Institute*. Tubingen: Mohr, 1988.

Grunfeld, Frederic V. *The Hitler File: A Social History of Germany and the Nazis, 1918–1945*. New York: Random House, 1974.

Gun, Nerin E. *Eva Braun: Hitler's Mistress*. New York: Meredith, 1968.

Haffner, Sebastian. *Anmerkungen zu Hitler*. Frankfurt: Fischer, 1987.

———. *Von Bismarck zu Hitler: Ein Rückblick*. Munich: Knaus, 1989.

Hanfstaengel, Ernst. *Zwischen Weissem und Braunem Haus*. Munich: R. Pieper, 1970.

Hansen, Thorkild. *Der Hamsun Prozess.* Hamburg: Knaus, 1979.

Harris, Robert. *Selling Hitler.* New York: Pantheon, 1986.

Hassell, Fey von. *Hostage of the Third Reich: The Story of My Imprisonment and Rescue from the SS,* David Forbes-Watt, ed. New York: Scribner, 1989.

Hassell, Ulrich von. *Die Hassell-Tagebücher 1938–1944: Deutscher Widerstand 1937–1945.* Berlin: Siedler, 1988.

Hastings, Max. *Das Reich: The March of the 2nd SS Panzer Division through France.* New York: Holt, Rinehart & Winston, 1981.

———. *Victory in Europe: D-Day to V-E Day in Full Color,* photog., George Stevens. Boston: Little, Brown, 1985.

Haupt, Werner, and J.K.W. Bingham. *Der Afrika Feldzug, 1940–1943.* Friedberg: Podzun, 1968.

Heiden, Konrad. *Hitler: A Biography.* London: Constable, 1936.

Heilburt, Anthony. *Exiled in Paradise.* New York: Viking, 1983.

Henderson, Nevile. *Failure of a Mission: Berlin 1937–1939.* New York: Putnam, 1940.

Henry, Frances. *Victims & Neighbors: A Small Town in Nazi Germany Remembered.* South Hadley, MA: Bergin & Garvey, 1984.

Herwarth, Hans von. *Zwischen Hitler und Stalin.* Frankfurt: Ullstein, 1982.

Herzstein, Robert Edwin. *The Nazis.* Alexandria, VA: Time-Life Books, 1980.

Hess, Wolf R. *Rudolf Hess Briefe, 1908–1933.* Munich: Langen-Muller, 1987.

Hesse, F. *Das Vorspiel zum Kriege.* Leoni am Starnberger: Druffel, 1979.

Higham, Charles. *Trading with the Enemy: An Exposé of the Nazi-American Money Plot, 1933–1949.* New York: Delacorte Press, 1983.

———. *American Swastika.* Garden City, NY: Doubleday, 1985.

Hildebrandt, Fred. . . . *ich soll dich grüssen von Berlin, 1922–1932.* Munich: Ehrenwirth, 1966.

Hillesum, Etty. *An Interrupted Life: The Diaries of Etty Hillesum, 1941–1943,* trans., Arn O. Pomerans. New York: Pantheon, 1983.

Hinze, Rolf. *Die 19, Panzer Division, 1939–1945.* Friedberg: Podzun-Pallas, 1979.

Hitchens, Marilynn Giroux. *Germany, Russia, and the Balkans: Prelude to the Nazi-Soviet Non-Aggression Pact.* New York: Columbia University Press, 1983.

Hitler, Adolf. *Mein Kampf.* Munich: Franz Eher, 1927.

Hofer, Walter. *Der Nationalsozialismus. Dokumente, 1933–1945.* Frankfurt: Fischer, 1988.

Höhne, Heinz. *The Order of the Death's Head: The Story of Hitler's SS,* trans., Richard Barry. London: Pan, 1972.

———. *Die Machtergreifung: Deutschlands Weg in Die Hitler-Diktatur.* Hamburg: Spiegel-Buch, 1983.

———. *Canaris: Patriot im Zwielicht*. Munich: Bertelsmann, 1984.

Horstmann, Lali. *Nothing for Tears*. London: William Clowes & Sons Ltd., 1948.

Hubmann, Franz. *Das deutsche Familienalbum: Die Welt von Gestern in alten Photographien*. Vienna: Molden, 1972.

International Military Tribunal, vols. XII and XIII. Nuremberg, 1949.

Infield, Glenn B. *Hitler's Secret Life*. London: Hamlyn, 1979.

———. *Skorzeny: Hitler's Commando*. New York: St. Martin's, 1981.

Irving, David. *The Trail of the Fox*. New York: Dutton, 1977.

———. *Göring*. New York: Morrow, 1980.

Jacobson, H. A. *Nazionalsozialistische Aussenpolitik*. Frankfurt: Metzner, 1968.

Kahn, Leo. *Nuremberg Trials*. New York: Ballantine, 1972.

Keegan, John. *Six Armies in Normandy: From D-Day to the Liberation of Paris, June 6–August 25, 1944*. New York: Viking, 1982.

Kehr, Helen, and Janet Langmaid, eds. *The Nazi Era, 1919–1945*. London: Mansel, 1982.

Keneally, Thomas. *Schindler's List*. New York: Simon & Schuster, 1982.

Kiaulehn, Walther. *Berlin*. Munich: Biederstein, 1958.

Kirkpatrick, Ivone. *The Inner Circle*. New York: Macmillan, 1958.

———. *Mussolini: A Study in Power*. New York: Hawthorn, 1964.

Knötel, Richard, Herbert Knötel, and Herbert Sieg. *Uniforms of the World*. New York: Scribner, 1980, revised ed.

Koch, Hannsjoachim W. *Volfsgerichtshof Politische Justiz in 3 Reich*. Munich: Universitas, 1988.

Koch, Peter-Ferdinand, ed. *Die Dresdener Bank und der Reichsführer-SS*. Hamburg: Facta-Oblita, 1987.

Koerfer, D. "Ernst von Weizsäcker im Dritten Reich," *Schatten der Vergangenheit*. Frankfurt: Propyläen, 1990.

Konsalik, Heinz A. *Stalingrad: Bilder vom Untergang der 6 Armee*. Bayreuth: Goldmann, 1979.

Kordt, Erich. *Nicht aus den Akten . . .* Stuttgart: Deutsche Union, 1950.

Kruger, Horst. *A Crack in the Wall: Growing Up Under Hitler*, trans. Ruth Hein. New York: Fromm International, 1982.

Lang, Jochen von. *The Secretary: Martin Bormann — The Man Who Manipulated Hitler*, trans., Christa Armstrong and Peter White. New York: Random House, 1979.

———. *Der Adjutant: Karl Wolff — Der Mann Zwischen Hitler und Himmler*. Munich: Berbig, 1985.

Lange, Annemarie. *Berlin in der Weimarer Republik*. Berlin: Dietz, 1987.

Laqueur, Walter. *Weimar: A Cultural History, 1918–1933*. New York: Putnam, 1974.

——— and Richard Breitman. *Breaking the Silence*. London: Bodley Head, 1986.

Leber, Annedore, Willy Brandt, and Karl Dietrich Bracher. *Das Gewissen*

Steht auf: Lebensbilder aus dem deutschen Widerstand, 1933–1945. Mainz: von Hase & Koehler, 1984.

Leo Baeck Institute. *Yearbook,* vols. 29, 1984; 31, 1986; 33, 1988; 34, 1989; 35, 1990. London: Secker & Warburg.

Lester, Elenore. *Wallenburg: The Man in the Iron Web.* Englewood Cliffs, NJ: Prentice-Hall, 1982.

Lêvai, Jenö. *Raoul Wallenburg,* trans., F. Vajda. University of Melbourne, Australia, 1989.

Levenstein, Aaron. *Escape to Freedom: The Story of the International Rescue Committee.* Westport, CT: Greenwood Press, 1983.

Linge, Heinz. *Bis zum Untergang,* W. Maser, ed. Munich: Herbig, 1980.

Lorant, Stefan. *Sieg Heil! An Illustrated History of Germany from Bismarck to Hitler.* New York: Norton, 1974.

Lucas, James S. *Last Days of the Third Reich: The Collapse of Nazi Germany, May 1945.* New York: Morrow, 1986.

Lyons, Graham, ed. *The Russian Version of World War II.* Hamden, CT: Archon Books, 1976.

MacDonald, Callum A. *The Killing of SS Obergruppenführer Reinhard Heydrich.* New York: Free Press, 1989.

Macksey, M. C. *Afrika Korps.* New York: Ballantine, 1972.

Manchester, William. *Krupp: Chronik Einer Familie.* Munich: Wilhelm Heyne, 1978.

———. *The Last Lion: Winston Spencer Churchill. Alone, 1932–1940,* vol. II. Boston: Little, Brown, 1988.

Marrus, Michael R., and Robert O. Paxton. *Vichy France and the Jews.* New York: Basic Books, 1981.

Maser, Werner. *Nuremburg: A Nation on Trial,* trans., Richard Barry. New York: Scribner, 1979.

———. *Adolf Hitler: Das Ende der Führer Legende,* Düsseldorf: Econ, 1980.

Mechow, Max. *Die Ost- und Westpreussen in Berlin.* Berlin: Haude & Spenersche, 1975.

Metcalfe, Philip. *1933.* Sag Harbor, NY: Permanent Press, 1988.

Michaelis, Meir. *Mussolini and the Jews: German, Italian Relations and the Jewish Question in Italy, 1922–1945.* Oxford: Clarendon Press, 1978.

Michalka, Wolfgang. *Ribbentrop und die deutsche Weltpolitik 1933–1940.* Munich: Wilhelm Fink, 1980.

Moltke, Helmut James von. *Briefe an Freya 1939–1945.* Munich: Beck, 1988.

Mosley, Diana Mitford. *A Life of Contrasts.* New York: Time Books, 1977.

Neave, Airey. *Nuremburg.* London: Hodder & Stoughton, 1978.

Nelson, Walter Henry. *The Berliners: Their Saga and Their City.* New York: David McKay, 1969.

Norris, John. *Strangers Entertained.* Vancouver, Canada: Centennial Committee, 1971.

Organisationsbuch der N.S.D.A.P. Munich: Franz Eher, 1943.

Padfield, Peter. *Dönitz: The Last Führer.* New York: Harper & Row, 1984.

Papen, Franz von. *Der Wahrheit eine Gasse.* Munich: Paul List, 1952.

Paucker, Arnold, Sylvia Gilchrist, and Barbara Suchy. *Die Juden im National-sozialistischen Deutschland 1933–1943.* Tübingen: Mohr, 1986.

PEM. *Heimweh nach dem Kurfürstendamm.* Berlin: Lothar Blanvalet, 1962.

Persico, Joseph. *Piercing the Reich.* New York: Viking, 1979.

———. *The Spiderweb.* New York: Crown, 1979.

Peters, A. R. *Anthony Eden at the Foreign Office, 1931–1938.* New York: St. Martin's, 1986.

Picker, Henry, and Heinrich Hoffmann. *Hitler Close-up,* trans., Nicholas Fry. New York: Macmillan, 1973.

Piekalkiewicz, Janusz. *Spione Agenten Soldaten.* Munich: Herbig, 1988.

Poliakov, Leon. *Geschichte des Antisemitismus: von der Antike bis zu den Kreuzzügen,* vol. 1. Worms: Heintz, 1977.

Pollack, Wolfgang, ed. and trans. *German Identity: Forty Years After Zero.* Sankt Augustin, Comdok: Friedrich Naumann Foundation, 1987.

Pomrehn, Arno, Hans Sanger, and Dr. Hans Joachim Schaeffer. *Der weg der 79 Infanterie Division 1939–1945.* Dorheim: Podzun, 1971.

Pryce-Jones, David. *Paris in the Third Reich: A History of the German Occupation, 1940–1944.* New York: Holt, Rinehart & Winston, 1981.

Reichel, Sabine. *What Did You Do in the War, Daddy? Growing Up German.* New York: Hill & Wang, 1989.

Reider, Frederic. *The Order of the SS: How Did It Happen?* Tucson, AZ: AZTEX Corp., 1981.

Ribbentrop, Annelies von. *Die Kriegsschuld des Widerstandes.* Leoni am Starnberger: Druffel, 1975.

Ribbentrop, Joachim von. *Zwischen London und Moskau.* Annelies von Ribbentrop, ed. Leoni am Starnberger: Druffel, 1953.

Richarz, Monika, ed. *Jüdisches Leben in Deutschland.* Stuttgart: Deutsche Verlags-Anstalt, 1982.

Riess, Curt. *Goebbels.* Munich: Universitas, 1989.

Ritter, Gerhard. *Carl Goerdeler und die deutsche Widerstandsbewegung.* Stuttgart: Deutsche Verlags-Anstalt, 1954.

Roters, Eberhart. *Berlin, 1910–1933.* New York: Rizzoli, 1982.

Russell, Francis. *The Secret War.* Alexandria, VA: Time-Life Books, 1981.

Sasse, Heinz Gunther. *100 Jahre Botschaft in London.* Bonn: Auswärtiges Amt, 1963.

Sayer, Ian, and Douglas Botting. *Nazi Gold.* London: Congdon & Weed, 1984.

Schaumburg-Lippe, F. C. *Dr. Goebbels.* Kiel: Arndt, 1990.

Schellenberg, Walter. *Memoiren.* Cologne: Verlag für Politik und Wirtschaft, 1956.

Schmidt, Dr. Paul. *Statist auf Diplomatischer Bühne, 1923–1945.* Bonn: Athenaeum, 1951.

Schmitz, Gunther. *Die 16 Panzer Division.* Friedberg: Podzun-Pallas, 1979.

Schwarz, Dr. Paul. *This Man Ribbentrop.* New York: Julian Messner, 1943.

Schwerin von Krosigk, Count Lutz. *Es geschah in Deutschland.* Tübingen: Rainer Wunderlich, 1951.

Sellenthin, H. G. *Geschichte der Juden in Berlin und des Gebäudes Fasanenstrasse 79/80.* Berlin: Jewish Community of Berlin, 1959.

Shirer, William L. *The Rise and Fall of the Third Reich.* New York: Simon & Schuster, 1959.

Siewert, Curt. *Schuldig?: die Generale unter Hitler.* Bad Nauheim: Podzun, 1968.

Smith, Truman. *Berlin Alert: The Memoirs and Reports of Truman Smith.* Robert Hessen, ed. Stanford, CA: Hoover Center, 1984.

Sonnleithner, Franz von. *Als Diplomat im "Führerhauptquartier."* Munich: Langen-Muller, 1989.

Speer, Albert. *Inside the Third Reich,* trans., Richard and Clara Winston. New York: Macmillan, 1970.

———. *Spandauer Tagebücher.* Frankfurt: Propyläen, 1975.

———. *Infiltration,* trans., Joachim Neugroschel. New York: Macmillan, 1981.

Spitzy, Reinhard. *So Haben wir das Reich Verspielt, Bekenntisse eines Illegalen.* Munich: Langen-Muller, 1988.

Squadron Signal Publications, 2004, 3001, 3002, 3004, 6101. Carrolton, TX: 1972, 1973, 1980.

Staden, Wendelgard von. *Darkness Over the Valley,* trans., Mollie Comerford Peters. New Haven: Ticknor & Fields, 1984.

Stahlberg, Alexander. *Die verdammte Pflicht: Erinnerungen 1932 bis 1945.* Berlin: Ullstein, 1987.

Stoiber, Rudolf, and Boris Celovsky. *Stephanie von Hohenlohe.* Munich: Herbig, 1988.

Studnitz, Hans-Georg von. *Menschen aus Meiner Welt.* Berlin: Ullstein, 1985.

Swearingen, Ben E. *The Mystery of Hermann Goering's Suicide.* New York: Harcourt Brace Jovanovich, 1985.

Tetens, Tete Harens. *The New Germany and the Old Nazis.* New York: Random House, 1961.

Titzenthaler, Waldemar. *Berlin: Photographien von Titzenthaler.* Berlin: Nicolaische, 1987.

Tokayer, Marvin and Mary Swartz. *The Fugu Plan.* New York: Paddington Press, 1979.

Toland, John. *The Last 100 Days.* New York: Random House, 1966.

———. *Adolf Hitler.* New York: Doubleday, 1976.

———. *Hitler: The Pictorial Documentary of His Life.* New York: Doubleday, 1978.

Tutas, Herbert C. *N.S. Propaganda und deutsches Exil, 1933–1939.* Meisenheim: Anton Hain, 1973.

The Twentieth Century, Television Series. Arts & Entertainment Network, February 1990.

Urdang, Laurence, ed. *The Timetables of American History*. New York: Simon & Schuster, 1981.

Vansittart, Sir Robert Gilbert. *The Mist Procession*. London: Hutchinson, 1958.

Vassiltchikov, Marie (Missie). *The Berlin Diaries, 1940–1945*. London: Chatto & Windus, 1985.

"Volkswagen," in *Automobile Quarterly*, vol. 18, no. 4, pp. 340–361, Princeton, NJ, 1980.

Vormann, Nikolaus von. *So Begann Der Zweite Weltkrieg*. Leoni am Starnberger: Druffel, 1978.

Warlimont, Walter. *Im Hauptquartier der deutschen Wehrmacht, 1939 bis 1945*. Augsburg: Weltbild, 1990.

Watson, Francis. *Dawson of Penn: A Biography*. London: Chatto & Windus, 1950.

Watt, Donald Cameron. *How War Came: The Immediate Origins of the Second World War, 1938–1939*. New York: Pantheon, 1989.

Wehrmacht Berichte, 1939–1945. Cologne, 1989.

Weizsäcker, Ernst von. *Die Weizsäcker Papiere, 1933–1950*. Berlin: Propyläen, 1974.

Werbell, Frederick E. and Thurston Clarke. *Lost Hero: The Mystery of Raoul Wallenburg*. New York: McGraw-Hill, 1982.

Werlich, Robert. *Orders and Decorations of All Nations*. Washington, DC: Quaker Press, 1974.

Westphal, Uwe. *Berliner Konfektion und Mode 1836–1939 die Zerstörung einer Tradition*. Berlin: Hentrich, 1986.

Whiting, Charles and Friedrich Gehendges. *Jener September: Europa beim Kriegsausbruch 1939*. Düsseldorf: Droste, 1979.

Willett, John. *The Weimar Years: A Culture Cut Short*. New York: Abbeville Press, 1984.

World Guide. New York: Rand-McNally, 1953.

Wortmann, Michael. *Baldur von Schirach: Hitlers Jugendführer*. Cologne: Bohlau, 1982.

Wykes, Alan. *Goebbels*. New York: Ballantine, 1973.

Zentner, Christian, and Friedemann Bedürftig. *Das Grosse Lexikon des Dritten Reiches*. Munich: Südwest, 1985.

Ziemke, Earl F. *Battle for Berlin: End of the Third Reich*. New York: Ballantine, 1968.

Zoller, Albert. *Hitler Privat*. Düsseldorf, 1949.

NOTES

2. Wesel to London, 1893–1910

1. Dr. Paul Schwarz, *This Man Ribbentrop* (New York: Julian Messner, 1943), p. 39.
2. Ibid., p. 40.
3. Joachim von Ribbentrop, *Zwischen London und Moskau*, ed., A. von Ribbentrop (Leoni am Starnberger: Druffel, 1953), p. 20.
4. Ibid., p. 11.
5. Ibid., p. 12.
6. Ernst Hanfstaengel, *Zwischen Weissem und Braunem Haus* (Munich: R. Pieper, 1970), p. 320.
7. J. von Ribbentrop, p. 13.
8. Author's interview with Dr. Franz Werner Michel, Mainz, Germany, September 21, 1990.
9. Author's interview with Jacques Français, New York, October 1, 1990.
10. J. von Ribbentrop, p. 13.
11. Reinhard Spitzy, *So Haben Wir das Reich Verspielt Bekenntisse eines Illegalen* (Munich: Langen-Müller, 1988), p. 92, and H. J. Döscher, *Das AA im Dritten Reich* (Berlin: Siedler, 1987), p. 146, n. 7.
12. Schwarz, p. 41.
13. Ibid., pp. 33–34.
14. Spitzy, p. 92, and Döscher, p. 147, n. 7.
15. J. von Ribbentrop, p. 12.
16. Ibid., p. 14.
17. Idem.
18. Ibid., pp. 14–17.
19. Ibid., p. 16.
20. Idem.
21. Sir Henry Channon, *Chips: The Diaries of Sir Henry Channon* (London: Weidenfeld & Nicolson, 1967), p. 36.
22. Schwarz, pp. 42ff.
23. John Norris, *Strangers Entertained* (Vancouver: Centennial Committee, 1971), pp. 101ff.

3. Canada, 1910–1914

1. J. von Ribbentrop, p. 19.
2. Schwarz, p. 44.
3. Idem.
4. J. von Ribbentrop, p. 19.
5. Schwarz, p. 43.
6. Norris, p. 102.
7. J. von Ribbentrop, pp. 20ff.
8. Schwarz, p. 48.
9. Ibid., p. 40.
10. J. von Ribbentrop, p. 24.

11. Idem.
12. Christian Zentner and Friedemann Bedürftig, *Das Grosse Lexikon des Dritten Reiches* (Munich: Sudwest, 1985), p. 246.
13. J. von Ribbentrop, p. 23.
14. Idem.
15. André François-Poncet, *The Fateful Years* (New York: Harcourt Brace, 1948), pp. 60ff.

4. War

1. Richard Knötel, et al., *Uniforms of the World* (New York: Scribner, 1980), p. 131.
2. Ibid., p. 150.
3. Joachim Fest, *Hitler* (New York: Vintage, 1975), pp. 68–69.
4. Schwarz, p. 51, and Wolfgang Michalka, *Ribbentrop und die Deutsche Weltpolitik, 1933–1940* (Munich: Wilhelm Fink, 1980), p. 25, n. 9.
5. Douglas Glen, *Von Ribbentrop Is Still Dangerous* (London: Rich & Cowan, 1941).
6. Schwarz, p. 52.
7. J. von Ribbentrop, p. 29.
8. Ibid., p. 28.
9. Schwarz, pp. 52ff.
10. Zentner, p. 602.

5. Berlin, 1919

1. J. von Ribbentrop, p. 30.
2. Idem.
3. Schwarz, p. 11.
4. Ibid., pp. 10ff.
5. Ibid., pp. 55–66.
6. Ibid., pp. 68ff.
7. Daniel Koerfer, "Ernst von Weizsäcker im 3. Reich," in *Die Schatten Der Vergangenheit* (Frankfurt: Propyläen, 1990), p. 382; citation from *Die Weizsäcker Papiere, 1933–1950* (Berlin: Propyläen, 1974), p. 71.

6. Berlin

1. J. von Ribbentrop, p. 31.
2. Idem.
3. Hanfstaengel, p. 320.
4. Michel interview; Spitzy, p. 87.
5. Spitzy, p. 81.
6. Michel interview; Schwarz, pp. 16, 57.
7. Schwarz, p. 13.
8. Ibid., p. 12.
9. Michel interview.
10. Schwarz, p. 16.
11. Ibid., p. 12.
12. PEM, *Heimweh nach dem Kurfürstendamm* (Berlin: Lothar Blanvalet, 1962), p. 150.
13. Ibid., p. 157.
14. Schwarz, p. 66.
15. J. von Ribbentrop, p. 33.
16. Schwarz, p. 58.
17. Ibid., pp. 60–61.
18. Ibid., p. 63.
19. Ibid., pp. 63–64.
20. Ibid., p. 66.
21. Michel interview.
22. Lali Horstmann, *Nothing for Tears* (London: William Clowes & Sons, 1948), p. x.
23. Marie (Missie) Vassiltchikov, *The Berlin Diaries, 1940–1945* (London: Chatto & Windus, 1985), p. 25.
24. Spitzy, p. 93.
25. Schwarz, pp. 66–67.
26. Zentner and Bedürftig, p. 413.
27. François-Poncet, p. 20.

7. Hitler to 1934

1. François-Poncet, p. 23.
2. J. von Ribbentrop, p. 36.
3. Ibid., p. 36.
4. Döscher, p. 148.
5. Ivone Kirkpatrick, *The Inner Circle* (New York: Macmillan, 1958), p. 72.
6. François-Poncet, p. 55.
7. Schwarz, p. 73.
8. Ibid., 102.
9. Ibid., p. 77.
10. Ibid., p. 78.
11. Nevile Henderson, *Failure of a Mission: Berlin 1937–1939* (New York: Putnam, 1940), pp. 42ff.
12. François-Poncet, p. 289.
13. Heinz Höhne, *Die Machtergreifung* (Hamburg: Spiegel-Buch, 1983), p. 242.
14. Ibid., pp. 244–246.
15. Alexander Stahlberg, *Die verdammte Pflicht: Erinnerungen 1932 bis 1945* (Berlin: Ullstein, 1987), p. 28.
16. Höhne, pp. 248ff.
17. Konrad Heiden, *Hitler: A Biography* (London: Constable, 1936), p. 279.
18. Höhne (1983), pp. 254–255.
19. Ibid., pp. 256–257.
20. Stahlberg, p. 32.
21. Ibid., p. 34.
22. Schwarz, p. 67.
23. Leo Baeck Institute, *Yearbook*, vol. 29 (London: Secker & Warburg, 1984), p. 29.
24. Ibid., vol. 31, pp. 31ff.
25. AUFBAU, March 1989.
26. Kirkpatrick, p. 53.
27. AUFBAU, March 1989.
28. François-Poncet, note p. 56.
29. Stahlberg, p. 39.
30. Ibid., p. 44.
31. François-Poncet, p. 65.
32. Ibid., p. 79.
33. J. von Ribbentrop, pp. 44ff.
34. Richard Griffiths, *Fellow Travellers of the Right* (London: Constable, 1980), p. 112.

8. Büro to Embassy, 1934–1936

1. Kirkpatrick (1959), p. 52.
2. Erich Kordt, *Nicht aus den Akten* (Stuttgart: Union Deutsche, 1950), p. 51.
3. Schwarz, p. 95.
4. H. A. Jacobson, *Nationalsozialistische Aussenpolitik* (Frankfurt: Metzner, 1968), p. 253.
5. Michalka, p. 78, n. 46.
6. Jacobson, p. 253.
7. Ibid., pp. 254ff.
8. Schwarz, p. 99.
9. Kordt, pp. 62–63.
10. Jacobson, p. 265, no. 6.
11. Kordt, p. 70.
12. Ibid., pp. 76–77.
13. Heinz Höhne, *The Order of the Death's Head* (London: Pan, 1972), p. 94.
14. Ibid., p. 85.
15. Ibid., p. 88.
16. Ibid., p. 114.
17. Ibid., p. 117.
18. Ibid., p. 66.
19. John Toland, *Adolf Hitler* (New York: Doubleday, 1976), p. 263.
20. Kirkpatrick (1959), p. 56.
21. Franz von Papen, *Der Wahrheit eine Gasse* (Munich: List, 1952), p. 379ff.
22. Ivone Kirkpatrick, *Mussolini: A Study in Power* (New York: Hawthorn, 1964), p. 294.
23. Ibid., p. 296.

24. Idem.
25. Jacobson, p. 793.
26. François-Poncet, p. 156.
27. Kordt, p. 82.
28. Ibid., p. 84.
29. Griffiths, p. 117.
30. Ibid., p. 124.
31. Ibid., p. 14.
32. Ibid., p. 40.
33. Ibid., pp. 54ff.
34. Ibid., p. 55.
35. Ibid., pp. 65ff.
36. Ibid., pp. 69–70.
37. Interview with Franz Werner Michel, Mainz, 1990.
38. Schwarz, pp. 130ff.
39. Dr. Paul Schmidt, *Statist auf Diplomatischer Bühne, 1923–1945* (Bonn: Athenaeum, 1951), p. 315.
40. Griffiths, pp. 160, 182.
41. Ibid., p. 134.
42. *Organisationsbuch der NSDAP* (Munich: Franz Eher, 1943), p. 566.
43. Ibid., p. 568.
44. Döscher, pp. 278ff.
45. Kordt, p. 122.
46. Kirkpatrick (1959), p. 72.
47. Michalka, p. 114.
48. Schmidt, p. 327.
49. J. von Ribbentrop, pp. 141ff.
50. Truman Smith, *Berlin Alert* (Palo Alto: Hoover Center, 1984), pp. 87ff.
51. Ibid., p. 89.
52. Ibid., p. 134.
53. Ibid., p. 163.
54. Charles Higham, *American Swastika* (New York: Doubleday, 1985), p. 14.
55. Channon, p. 108.
56. Sir Robert Vansittart, *The Mist Procession* (London: Hutchinson, 1958), p. 445.
57. J. von Ribbentrop, p. 90.
58. Schwarz, p. 189.
59. Kordt, p. 151.
60. Schmidt, p. 332.
61. Schwarz, p. 193.
62. Jacobson, p. 824.
63. J. von Ribbentrop, p. 94.
64. Channon, pp. 106ff.
65. Griffiths, pp. 221–222.
66. J. von Ribbentrop, pp. 96ff.
67. Ibid., pp. 98ff.
68. Dodd, p. 245.
69. James Bentley, *Martin Niemöller, 1892–1984* (New York: Free Press, 1984), p. 89.
70. Schwarz, pp. 36–37.
71. Ibid., 216.
72. Michalka, p. 155.
73. Griffiths, pp. 225ff.
74. Ibid., p. 228.

9. Embassy, 1936, 1937, 1938

1. Kordt, p. 154.
2. Schwarz, p. 34.
3. Ibid., p. 35.
4. Interview with Spitzy.
5. Kordt, p. 154.
6. Schwarz, p. 217.
7. Interview with Spitzy.
8. Kordt, p. 160.
9. Spitzy, p. 87.
10. Kordt, p. 156.
11. Spitzy, p. 98.
12. Schwarz, p. 70.
13. Spitzy, p. 111.
14. Schwarz, pp. 194ff.
15. Ibid., p. 208.
16. Spitzy, p. 102.
17. Heinz Günther Sasse, *100 Jahre Botschaft in London* (Bonn: Foreign Office, 1963), pp. 74ff.
18. Spitzy, p. 88.
19. Michalka, p. 157, n. 36.
20. Schwarz, p. 216.

21. Griffiths, p. 254.
22. Schmidt, p. 458.
23. Interview with Spitzy.
24. Spitzy, p. 153.
25. Manchester (1988), pp. 256ff.
26. Spitzy, p. 164.
27. Ibid., pp. 124ff.
28. Foreign Ministry Archive, Bonn.
29. Spitzy, pp. 167ff.
30. Henderson, pp. 66ff.
31. François-Poncet, p. 212.
32. Richard Collier, *Duce!* (New York: Viking, 1971), p. 134.
33. Spitzy, p. 173.
34. Ibid., pp. 173ff.
35. Ibid., p. 176.
36. Collier, p. 149.
37. Ibid., p. 147.
38. Spitzy, p. 177.
39. Griffiths, pp. 272ff.
40. Michael Bloch, *Operation Willi* (New York: Weidenfeld, 1984), pp. 36ff.
41. Griffiths, pp. 273ff.
42. Bloch (1984), p. 37.
43. Spitzy, p. 178.
44. François-Poncet, p. 255.
45. Spitzy, pp. 185ff.
46. Ibid., p. 188.
47. Channon, p. 141.
48. Spitzy, p. 186.

10. Embassy — Ministry — Munich — Kristallnacht, 1938–1939

1. Foreign Ministry Archives, Bonn, March 9, 1938.
2. Zentner, p. 488.
3. Döscher, p. 158, n. 3.
4. Fest (1975), pp. 542ff.
5. Zentner, p. 195.
6. François-Poncet, pp. 29ff.
7. Henderson, p. 120.
8. George E. Berkley, *Vienna and Its Jews* (Cambridge, MA: Abt Books, 1988), p. 315.
9. Spitzy, p. 229.
10. Kordt, p. 194.
11. Idem.
12. Berkley, p. 323.
13. Ibid., p. 259.
14. Griffiths, p. 292.
15. Ibid., pp. 295ff.
16. Channon, p. 151.
17. François-Poncet, p. 255.
18. Henderson, p. 128.
19. Berkley, p. 259.
20. Schwarz, pp. 237ff.
21. J. von Ribbentrop, pp. 125ff.
22. Spitzy, p. 260.
23. Griffiths, note p. 360.
24. Meir Michaelis, *Mussolini and the Jews* (Oxford: Clarendon Press, 1978), p. 147.
25. Walter Schellenberg, *Memoiren* (Cologne: Verlag für Politik und Wirtschaft, 1956), pp. 56ff.
26. Spitzy, p. 261.
27. Kirkpatrick (1964), pp. 366ff.
28. Idem.
29. Ibid., p. 367.
30. Michaelis, p. 148.
31. Collier, p. 139.
32. Schmidt, p. 388.
33. Idem.
34. Kordt, p. 225.
35. Schmidt, pp. 389ff.
36. Henderson, pp. 238ff.
37. Kordt, pp. 226ff.
38. Ulrich Dunker, *Juden in Preussen* (Dortmund: Harenberg, 1981), p. 352.
39. Stahlberg, p. 115.
40. Rudolf Stoiber and Boris Celovsky, *Stephanie von Hohenlohe* (Munich: Herbig, 1988), pp. 167ff.
41. Kordt, pp. 315ff.

42. Griffiths, pp. 301ff.

43. Heinz Höhne, *Canaris* (Munich: Bertelsmann, 1984), p. 329.

44. Schmidt, p. 394.

45. Ernst von Weizsäcker, *Die Weizsäcker Papiere, 1933–1950* (Berlin: Propyläen, 1974), p. 136, August 19, 1938.

46. A. Whitman, *Come to Judgment* (New York: Viking, 1980), p. 126ff, and *Webster's Biographical Dictionary*, 1983.

47. Griffiths, pp. 307ff.

48. Schmidt, p. 394.

49. Idem.

50. Ibid., pp. 397ff.

51. Kordt, p. 261.

52. Henderson, p. 155.

53. Ibid., p. 158.

54. Schmidt, p. 408.

55. Ibid., p. 411.

56. Henderson, p. 168.

57. Schmidt, p. 413.

58. Kordt, pp. 273ff.

59. Ibid., pp. 275ff.

60. Spitzy, p. 320.

61. J. von Ribbentrop, p. 145 and note.

62. Spitzy, p. 324.

63. Ibid., p. 322.

64. Heinz Linge, *Bis zum Untergang* (Munich: Herbig, 1980), p. 151.

65. A. Zoller, *Hitler Privat* (Düsseldorf, 1949), p. 219.

66. Schmidt, p. 422.

67. Channon, p. 177.

68. Leonard Baker, *Days of Sorrow and Pain* (New York: Macmillan, 1978), pp. 231ff.

69. Ibid., p. 226.

70. Higham, p. 1ff.

71. Schwarz, pp. 180ff.

72. Döscher, pp. 186ff.

73. Interview with Karl Max von Schaesberg, Munich, 1990.

74. J. von Ribbentrop, p. 160.

75. Ibid., p. 150.

76. Manchester (1988), p. 303.

77. Ibid., p. 396.

78. J. von Ribbentrop, p. 152.

79. Ibid., pp. 162ff.

80. Ibid., p. 163.

81. Manchester (1988), p. 408.

82. Ibid., p. 409.

83. Will Berthold, *Die 42 Attentate auf Adolf Hitler* (Munich: Goldmann, 1981), pp. 122ff.

84. Schmidt, p. 437.

85. Roy Douglas, ed., *1939: A Retrospect Forty Years Later* (London: Macmillan, 1983), "The Soviet View," Margot Light, p. 74ff.

86. Ibid., pp. 74–86.

87. Manchester (1988), pp. 418ff.

88. Ibid., p. 421.

89. Donald Cameron Watt, *How War Came* (New York: Pantheon, 1989), p. 393.

90. Hans von Herwarth, *Zwischen Hitler und Stalin* (Frankfurt: Ullstein, 1982), pp. 162ff.

91. Charles Whiting and Friedrich Gehendges, *Jener September: Europa beim Kriegsausbruch* (Düsseldorf: Droste, 1939), p. 9.

92. Herwarth, pp. 185ff.

93. J. von Ribbentrop, pp. 177–184.

94. Schmidt, pp. 445ff.

95. Hofer, pp. 234ff.

96. *Der Spiegel*, no. 47, 1966.

97. Kordt, p. 447.

98. Watt, p. 462.

99. Hofer, p. 236.

100. Herwarth, p. 188.

101. Henderson, p. 270.

102. Whiting, p. 13.
103. Ibid., p. 15.
104. Ibid., p. 22.
105. Idem.
106. Schmidt, pp. 458ff.
107. Whiting, pp. 44ff.
108. Henderson, pp. 298–299.

11. War, 1940

1. J. von Ribbentrop, p. 203.
2. Höhne (1972), pp. 273ff.
3. Ibid., p. 261.
4. Schmidt, pp. 466ff.
5. Ibid., p. 469.
6. Kirkpatrick (1964), pp. 441ff.
7. Schmidt, p. 474.
8. Kirkpatrick (1964), p. 448.
9. Ibid., p. 451.
10. Count Galeazzo Ciano, *The Ciano Diaries, 1939–1943* (New York: Doubleday, 1946), p. 294.
11. Jochen von Lang, *Der Adjutant: Karl Wolff* (Munich: Herbig, 1985), pp. 140ff.
12. Schmidt, pp. 482ff.
13. Ibid., p. 483.
14. Ibid., pp. 484ff.
15. Kordt, pp. 387ff.
16. Schmidt, pp. 484ff.
17. Kirkpatrick (1964), p. 467.
18. Ibid., p. 469.
19. David Pryce-Jones, *Paris in the Third Reich* (New York: Holt, Rinehart & Winston, 1981), pp. 12ff.
20. Ibid., p. 38.
21. Ibid., p. 25.
22. Ibid., pp. 26ff.
23. Ibid., p. 39.
24. Ibid., p. 26.
25. Otto Abetz, *Das Offene Problem* (Cologne: Greven & Bechtold, 1951), p. 300.
26. Pryce-Jones, p. 90.
27. Michael R. Marrus and Robert O. Paxton, *Vichy France and the Jews* (New York: Basic Books, 1981), pp. 10ff.
28. Interview with René Dreyfus, New York City, 1990.
29. Michael Bloch, *The Duke of Windsor's War* (New York: Coward McCann, 1983), pp. 76ff.
30. Ibid., p. 76.
31. Ibid., pp. 89ff.
32. Bloch (1984), p. 96.
33. Schellenberg, pp. 108ff.
34. Ibid., p. 116ff.
35. Ibid., p. 118.
36. Schmidt, p. 496.
37. Ibid., p. 498.
38. Ibid., p. 504.
39. David Irving, *The Trail of the Fox* (New York: Dutton, 1977), p. 63.

12. 1941–1942

1. J. von Ribbentrop, pp. 217ff.
2. Anthony Cave Brown, *The Last Hero: Wild Bill Donovan* (New York: Times Books, 1982).
3. Ibid., p. 224.
4. Ibid., p. 237.
5. Ibid., p. 238.
6. Roger J. Bender and Richard D. Law, *Uniforms, Organization, and History of the Afrika Korps* (Mountain View, CA: R. J. Bender, 1973), p. 20.
7. *Wehrmacht Berichte*, February 26, 1941, p. 431.
8. Irving (1977), p. 69.
9. *Wehrmacht Berichte*, April 6, 1941, p. 467.
10. Schmidt, p. 531.
11. Ibid., pp. 537ff.

12. David Irving, *Göring* (New York: Morrow, 1989), p. 326.

13. Ibid., p. 323.

14. Schmidt, p. 538.

15. Ibid., p. 539.

16. Inge Fleischauer, *Diplomatischer Widerstand* (Berlin: Ullstein, 1991), pp. 308ff.

17. Bernt Engelmann, *In Hitler's Germany* (New York: Schocken, 1986), p. 240.

18. *Wehrmacht Berichte*, June 29, 1941, p. 596.

19. Schmidt, pp. 544ff.

20. Döscher, p. 221.

21. Ibid., pp. 246–247.

22. Ibid., p. 247.

23. Idem.

24. Hofer, p. 297.

25. Zentner, p. 508.

26. Schmidt, p. 551.

27. Will Berthold, p. 176.

28. Ciano, p. 373.

29. J. von Ribbentrop, p. 326.

30. Will Berthold, pp. 178ff.

31. Höhne (1972), p. 85.

32. Ibid., p. 339.

33. Ibid., p. 335.

34. Lang (1985), p. 172.

35. Höhne (1972), p. 330.

36. Lang (1985), pp. 390–394.

37. Schmidt, p. 553.

38. Höhne (1972), pp. 340ff.

39. Ibid., p. 341.

40. Hofer, pp. 277ff.

41. Helmut James von Moltke, *Briefe an Freya, 1939–1945* (Munich: Beck, 1988), p. 252.

42. J. von Ribbentrop, p. 276.

43. Schellenberg, pp. 295ff.

44. Lang (1985), pp. 403ff.

45. Correlli Barnett, ed., *Hitler's Generals* (New York: Grove Weidenfeld, 1989).

46. Abetz, pp. 258ff.

47. Schmidt, pp. 558ff.

48. Ibid., p. 564ff.

49. Höhne (1972), p. 460.

50. Döscher, p. 251.

13. 1943–1944

1. Döscher, pp. 256ff.

2. Schellenberg, p. 211.

3. Schmidt, p. 559.

4. Ibid., p. 569.

5. Glenn Infield, *Skorzeny* (New York: St. Martin's, 1979), pp. 40ff.

6. Collier, pp. 270ff.

7. Franz von Papen, *Der Wahrheit eine Gasse* (Munich: Paul List, 1952), p. 577.

8. Vassiltchikov, pp. 103–105.

9. von Moltke, p. 368.

10. Joseph Goebbels, *The Goebbels Diaries* (New York: Popular Library, 1948), December 5, 1943, p. 613.

11. Idem.

12. Ibid., December 9, 1943, p. 618.

13. Channon, p. 384.

14. Döscher, p. 261.

15. Koerfer, p. 396.

16. Stahlberg, pp. 356ff.

17. Ibid., p. 372.

18. Zentner, p. 21.

19. Werner Maser, *Adolf Hitler* (Düsseldorf: Econ, 1980), p. 139.

20. *Wehrmacht Berichte*, June 6, 1944.

21. Maser (1980), p. 142.

22. William L. Shirer, *The Rise and Fall of the Third Reich* (New York: Simon & Schuster, 1959), p. 1038.

23. Ibid., p. 1056.
24. Maser (1980), p. 140.
25. Irving (1989), pp. 82–83.

14. 1945

1. Jochen von Lang, *The Secretary: Martin Bormann* (New York: Random House, 1979), p. 295.
2. Fest (1975), p. 724.
3. Toland (1976), pp. 727ff.
4. Albert Speer, *Inside the Third Reich* (New York: Macmillan, 1970), p. 423.
5. Ibid., p. 440.
6. J. von Ribbentrop, pp. 266ff.
7. Pierre Galante and Eugene Silianoff, *Voices from the Bunker* (New York: Putnam, 1989), p. 138.
8. Walter Laqueur and Richard Breitman, *Breaking the Silence* (London: Bodley Head, 1986), p. 139.
9. Döscher, p. 294.
10. John Toland, *The Last 100 Days* (New York: Random House, 1966), pp. 306–307.
11. Irving (1989), p. 454.
12. Roger J. Bender and H. P. Taylor, *Waffen SS*, vol. 2 (Mountain View, CA: R. J. Bender, 1971), p. 71, and Gunter Fraschka, *Mit Schwertern und Diamanten* (Munich: Universitas, 1988), p. 188.
13. Speer (1970), p. 474.
14. Ibid., p. 475.
15. Ibid., p. 479.
16. Ibid., pp. 483ff.
17. J. von Ribbentrop, p. 35.
18. Ibid., p. 37.

19. Ibid., p. 298.
20. Peter Padfield, *Dönitz: The Last Führer* (New York: Harper & Row, 1984), pp. 411ff.
21. Count Lutz Schwerin von Krosigk, *Es geschah in Deutschland*, p. 239, and Karl Dönitz, *10 Jahre und 20 Tage*, p. 446.
22. *Wehrmacht Berichte*, vol. 3, May 4, 1945.
23. Werner Maser, *Nuremberg: A Nation on Trial* (New York: Scribner, 1979), p. 50.
24. F. Hesse, *Das Vorspiel zum Kriege* (Leoni am Starnberger: Druffel, 1979), pp. 296ff.
25. Schwarz, p. 298.
26. Speer (1970), p. 517n.
27. Maser (1979), pp. 126ff.
28. Ibid., pp. 63–67.
29. Ben E. Swearingen, *The Mystery of Hermann Goering's Suicide* (New York: Harcourt Brace Jovanovich, 1985), p. 42.
30. G. M. Gilbert, *Nuremberg Diary* (New York: Farrar, Straus, 1947), p. 31.
31. Ibid., p. 66.
32. Ibid., p. 68.
33. Ibid., p. 108.
34. Ibid., p. 130.
35. Ibid., p. 236.
36. Ibid., p. 438.
37. J. von Ribbentrop, p. 17.
38. Irving (1989), p. 484.
39. J. von Ribbentrop, pp. 294–295.
40. Ibid., p. 297.
41. Ibid., pp. 303–306.
42. Swearingen, p. 55, and Maser (1979), p. 253n.
43. Kirkpatrick (1959), p. 99.

INDEX